KEY TO ENDPAPER ILLUSTRATION

1	Scafell	20	Lobstone Band
2	Scafell Pike	21	Stonethwaite
3	Pillar	22	Derwent Water
4	Looking Stead	23	Langstrath
5	Kirk Fell	24	Pavey Ark
6	Great Gable	25	Stickle Tarn
7	Red Pike	26	Crinkle Crags
8	High Stile	27	Bowfell
9	Green Gable	28	Rossett Gill
10	Allen Crag	29	The Band
11	Brandreth	30	Mickleden
12	Crummock Water	31	Wetherlam
13	Stake Pass	32	Wrynose Pass
14	Whiteless Pike	33	High Tilberthwaite
15	Grasmoor	34	Blea Tarn
16	Robinson	35	Side Pike
17	Crag Hill	36	Little Langdale Tarn
18	Pike of Stickle	37	Path to Tarn Hows
19	Dale Head		

The Lake District

THE REGIONS OF BRITAIN
Previous and forthcoming titles in the series include:

The Pennine Dales   Arthur Raistrick
The Upper Thames   J. R. L. Anderson
Cornwall   W. G. Hoskins
The Peak District   Roy Millward
           and Adrian Robinson
Pembrokeshire   John Barrett
*Northumberland and the
   Scottish Border*   John Talbot White

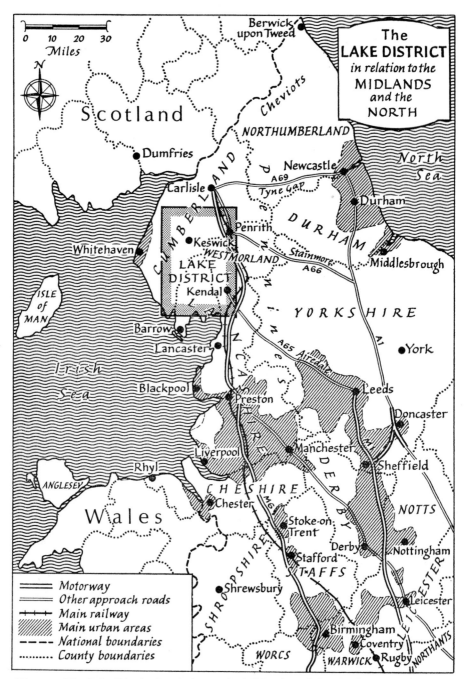

Map 1 *The Lake District in relation to the Midlands and the North.*

ROY MILLWARD
and ADRIAN ROBINSON

The
Lake
District

EYRE & SPOTTISWOODE · LONDON

To Gwyneth and Helen

First published 1970
© *1970 Roy Millward and Adrian Robinson*
Printed in Great Britain for
Eyre & Spottiswoode (Publishers) Ltd
11 New Fetter Lane, London EC4
by Cox & Wyman Ltd
London and Fakenham
S.B.N. 413 27840 9

The Lake District

Contents

Illustrations

The Lake District

Acknowledgements

The authors wish to thank the following who have helped during the preparation of the book: Roger Richards who prepared plates from the authors' photographs and his wife Suzanne who typed the manuscript; Miss R. Macalpine of the Lake District Festival Society; C. R. Patrick of the Mary Wakefield Westmorland Festival; R. McNeill of the Century Theatre; J. C. Pike of the Rosehill Theatre; the staff of the Abbot Hall Art Gallery, Kendal and C. J. Hanson-Smith of the National Trust Office in Ambleside. We were fortunate in having Christopher Stafford, with his own deep love of the Lake District, to see the book through the press and John Bright-Holmes who has been a source of encouragement throughout. Finally we owe a special debt of gratitude to Professor W. G. Hoskins who first suggested that we should write this book.

Acknowledgements and thanks for permission to reproduce photographs are due to Aerofilms Ltd for plates 8, 9, 21, 23b, 25, 26b, 27, and 37; to C. H. Wood (Bradford) Ltd for plates 15, 17, 33, and 38b and the endpaper; and to Fox Photos Ltd for plates 19a, 19b, 24a, 24b, and 36a.

Introduction

Scarcely any region of Britain has attracted greater publicity to itself over the past century and a half than the English Lake District. Even the elementary statistics of landscape placed the region in front with the highest mountain and the biggest lake in England. The variety of its scenery, prospects of lake and mountain and the often dramatic and ever-changing patterns of its skies that attracted the first tourists at the end of the eighteenth century have not relaxed their grip over the hundreds of thousands who come to the Lakes each year in the twentieth century.

Wordsworth, in his *Guide to the Lakes*, was the first to measure up the personality of the Lake District. In his account of the elements of the landscape – mountains, lakes, tarns and valleys – he laid great emphasis on the importance of scale. The inaccessibility of Alpine peaks he considered a drawback and he compared Loch Lomond unfavourably with the lakes of his native country on account of its greater size: 'Who ever travelled along the banks of Loch Lomond without feeling that a speedier termination of the long vista of blank water would be acceptable.' The rightness of scale in the Lake District makes itself felt in the view from any of the summits of the higher mountains. Always the limits of the region are clearly visible. Away to the east lies the long skyline of the Pennines; to the west and south is the encircling blue haze of the Irish Sea, and northwards, across the Solway Firth, the outlines of Criffel and the mountains of Galloway reveal a world that has always been alien to Cumbria. The Lake District has the qualities of an island; it is contained and comprehensible.

The miniature scale of the Lake District and its location in relation to the great conurbations of northern England now present the region with some of its

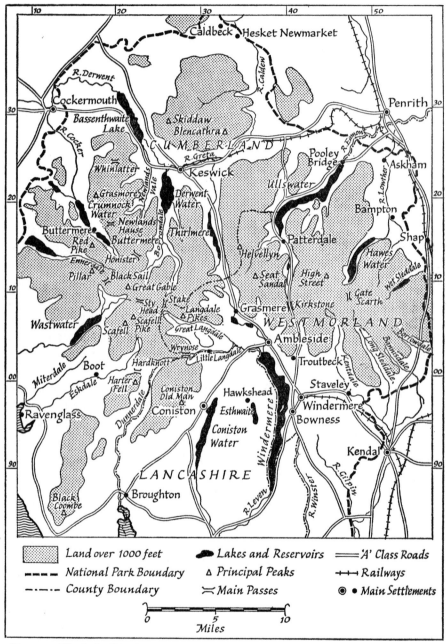

Map 2   *The Lake District.*

greatest problems. Wordsworth was used to walking across the heart of the Lake District in a single day; now for coach tours that hurry their clients from London to Skye and back in a week the Lakes represent little more than an hour's diversion on the road from Loch Lomond to Leeds. Within sixty miles of the high wilderness that stretches from the head of Langdale to the summit of Scafell lie the largest concentrations of population in northern England – Tyneside, rapidly expanding Tees-side, the conurbation of the West Riding and the urban masses of Manchester and Liverpool. The further extension of motorways in the 1970s and the anticipated habit of increased daily mileages on the part of the pleasure motorist will bring the scenery of the Lake District within reach of the day-tripper from Birmingham and the northern fringes of London.

The highest parts of the Lake District are gathered around an axis that extends eastward from the Scafell massif to the flattened summit ridge of Helvellyn. From this watershed a semicircle of northward-pointing valleys ranges through Wasdale, Ennerdale and Buttermere in the west to the northern and north-easterly valleys that contain Derwentwater and Ullswater. Southward from this upland divide, that for several miles of its course forms the boundary between Cumberland and Westmorland, valleys drain southwards towards the Irish Sea and Morecambe Bay – the Duddon, the troughs containing Coniston and Windermere, and the Kent and its tributaries. Where the valleys leave the mountains for the fringing lowlands a number of regional centres have grown up, small market towns that form excellent starting-off points for the detailed exploration of the region (Chapter 12). Cockermouth gives access to Butter-mere and the remoter western fells, Keswick serves Borrowdale and the Thirl-mere corridor, Penrith opens up the eastern valleys of Ullswater and Hawes-water. In the south Kendal stands as a regional capital for the unspoilt country of the eastern fells. Ambleside acts as a market centre and hub of communications for the vales of Troutbeck and Grasmere as well as the Langdale valleys. In the less-frequented south-west, Coniston focuses the life of its own valley and lake-shore, while Broughton is a sleepy little town near the mouth of the unspoilt Duddon.

The eastern part of the Lake District lies astride the great traffic arteries between England and Scotland. The main western route of British Railways from London to Glasgow crosses Shap Fell and, following almost the same line, the northern section of the axial motorway from London to Carlisle is rapidly approaching completion. The chief trunk road of the Lake District through Kendal, Ambleside and across the Dunmail Raise to Keswick is scarcely less important as a traffic artery between northern and southern Britain. Within range of these busy roads the region faces its greatest problems of traffic congestion and also many of the unpleasant aspects of the tourist industry from vandalism in small towns to the incessant drone of motor-boats on Windermere. But it has been so for a century and a half; Wordsworth's feelings about the Windermere Railway were the first expression of the effects of the outside world on the life and landscape of the Lake District. The western fells and valleys, westward of a line drawn along the Ambleside–Keswick road, are much more remote and inaccessible. A recent traffic survey has shown that of the day and half-day trippers entering the Lake District about sixty per cent spend their time in the district of Ambleside and Windermere and less than ten per cent reach the lonelier western valleys. At present the great contrast between the busy eastern parts of the region and the less frequented west is likely to be reinforced by the growth of the motorways and the closing of railways. Only the building of a Morecambe Bay barrage and a fast motor road into the Furness peninsula seems likely to change this important fact in the human geography of the region.

Within itself the Lake District displays traits that are found nowhere else in the British Isles. The ice-scarred shaggy landscapes of the Borrowdale Volcanic rocks contribute to the individuality of the region in the same way that the granite of Dartmoor or the Torridonian sandstones of the North-West Highlands form part of the personalities of Devon and northern Scotland. The farmhouses of Cumberland and Westmorland, whitewashed and deep-shaded by sycamores against bare fellsides, are as distinctive a feature of landscape as the gaunt grey limestone buildings of the High Peak. History has added to the individuality of the Lake District a thick overlay of Scandinavian place-names. The 'gills' and 'tarns', 'thwaites' and 'garths' in their very abundance distinguish the region from almost every other part of the British Isles.

In the following pages we try to explain the many different elements that make up the personality of the Lake District – rocks as they influence the shapes of the landscape and the colours and tones of buildings, the Ice Age as it has created a variety of landforms, and Man himself as an agent in the evolution of the region from the first forest clearances of almost five thousand years ago to the extensive plantings that now mantle hundreds of acres of hillside and valley floor in High Furness and Ennerdale.

The landscape of the Lake District, as Wordsworth already realized when he wrote his *Guide to the Lakes*, is one of the most valuable items of our national property. Ever since the impassioned verbal battle over the building of the Windermere railway and the successful struggle at the end of the nineteenth century to prevent the extension of the line to Ambleside, there has been a sense of threat from the outside. The conservationist and the conservative have often become confused in the affairs of the Lake District. At one extreme, the conservative would wish to keep the region unchanged by influences from the outside, a regional museum where the idealized view of the 'statesman' and his way of life would be perpetuated. This Wordsworthian attitude to the life and economy of the region was untenable even in his own day. Society changes and already in the years about 1800 the world of the statesman was crumbling. The conservatives have concerned themselves with many aspects of change in the landscape and economy of the Lake District from reservoirs and pipe-lines and the laying of electric cables to the straightening and widening of roads and the colour of pillar boxes. Among those who have concentrated on the past we owe much to the National Trust whose properties now represent almost every facet of the Lakeland scene – from farmhouses and woods to famous views and mountain summits.

Today the science of nature conservation proposes different attitudes towards the Lake District and its problems. Communications, above all through the motor-car, have placed the region in close contact with England's large centres of population. Over the Easter holiday period as many as a quarter of a million cars invade the roads of the Lakes. Recent signs of a new attitude towards the resources of the Lake District may be glimpsed in the laying out of 'nature trails' – marked routes that expound the features of the landscape for the town-dweller. Even more important as a symptom of this new trend is the opening of the National Park Centre on the Brockhole estate between Windermere and Ambleside. It stands on the busiest approach to the region and its grounds that run down to the lake present one of the classic views of the Coniston Fells and the Langdale Pikes. It has already been said that once the centre becomes known 'its biggest problem will be coping with visitors'. The centre has a permanent exhibition that displays for the newcomer the chief themes of the region through maps, animated displays, projected photographs and tape-recordings. The hardy Victorian fell-walkers, guided only by the infallible Baddeley, who opposed the distinctive marking of mountain footpaths with sign-posts and splashes of paint would probably have felt a similar antipathy towards the new methods of education in the countryside. But are our modern techniques of enlightenment so remote from that exposition of the Lakes as a region that Wordsworth wrote more than a century and a half ago?

At the beginning of this century a pioneer British geographer, Hugh Robert Mill, proposed the writing of an exposition of the features of each one-inch Ordnance Survey map as a means of deepening and spreading the knowledge of the regional geography of this country. Alas that such a scheme hardly got past

I

The physical background – geology and scenery

At a time when the Lake District was beginning to attract visitors in ever-increasing numbers in the early years of the nineteenth century, it was perhaps both fortuitous and appropriate that a local guide, Jonathan Otley, should publish the first scientific account of its geology in 1820. From his house at Brow Top in Keswick, where he carried on a small business as a watchmaker, he would occasionally take time off to wander across the fells or by the lake edge noting the various types of rocks and the way in which they influenced the scenery. This familiarity with the district and his fund of local knowledge soon led to a reputation as a guide and scientific authority. Both George Airy, the Astronomer Royal, and Adam Sedgwick, the Professor of Geology at Cambridge, sought his views and advice. Sedgwick, in particular, born not far away at Dent on the Lakeland fringe, became a close friend of Otley and on various occasions paid tribute to his pioneer work on the geology of the area. Shortly before Otley's death in 1855 Sedgwick wrote of him as 'the teacher on all we know of the country'. He had good reason to be grateful for, although his relationship was that of able professional to gifted amateur, he was able to build upon the foundations of geological knowledge so painstakingly worked out by the Keswick guide.

Jonathan Otley was fifty-five before he published the results of his geological observations. As a true amateur he chose the pages of the local *Lonsdale Magazine* to expound his views in a short paper with the title 'Remarks on the succession of rocks in the District of the Lakes'. In this account he set out, in his own clear informative style, the basic tripartite division of the slaty rocks of the central core area. In the north, forming Skiddaw, Saddleback and Grasmoor, he recognized a variable group to which he gave the name clay slate (now termed the

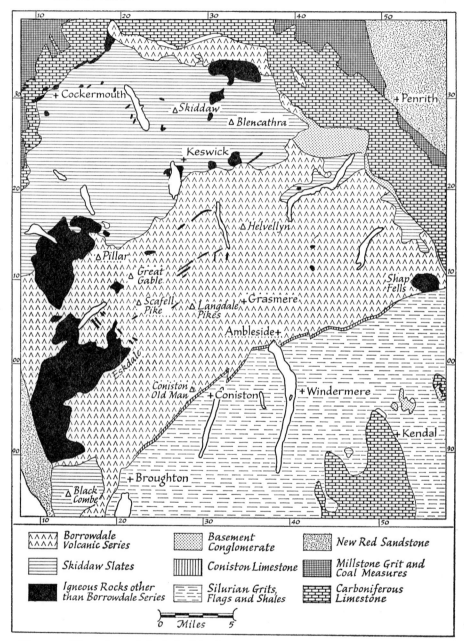

Map 3 *The geology of the Lake District.*

Skiddaw Slates). Not only did he suggest that these were the lowest beds and therefore the earliest rocks of the whole Lake District, his knowledge of the area was such that he noted that a similar outcrop formed the mountain of Black Coombe, in the extreme south-west (Map 3). His middle group of rocks, the Greenstone, in his own words 'comprehends the mountains of Eskdale, Wasdale, Ennerdale, Borrowdale, Langdale, Grasmere, Patterdale, Martindale, Mardale and some adjacent plains, including the two highest mountains of the district, Scafell and Helvellyn, as well as the Old Man of Coniston'. Today this group, lying athwart the highest central part of the Lake District as Otley noted, is referred to as the Borrowdale Volcanic Series, to take account of their very variable nature. The third division, the most variable of all, consists of beds of limestone, shale, slate and flags,* and was grouped by Otley as the Greywacke formation. In its distribution it is restricted to the southern Lake District where it forms the lower plateau country bordering on Morecambe Bay. At its base is the thin but persistent bed of Coniston Limestone, which Otley traced across country for forty miles from Broughton (2187)† north-eastwards across the head of Windermere and thence through the upper ends of the vales of Troutbeck, Kentmere and Long Sleddale (4805). It is a tribute to his observant eye and willingness to explore the remote corners of the south-eastern fell country, that enabled him to map the outcrop of this thin though important bed which divided his Greywacke formation from the underlying volcanic rocks.

Much of the content of this preliminary essay in the *Lonsdale Magazine* was later incorporated by Otley in his guide book for tourists, first published in 1823. This ran to no fewer than eight editions, the last in 1849. In the intervening period Sedgwick was carefully adding the details within the framework provided by Otley. Some of the results were published in a series of papers which he prepared for the newly founded Geological Society of London between 1831 and 1855. Perhaps better known is the account which was written by Sedgwick for Wordsworth's *Complete Guide to the Lakes* published in 1842. This took the form of three letters describing the various rock types present and the way in which they influenced the scenery. This latter aspect had been foremost in Otley's mind when he wrote of the Borrowdale Volcanic Series that 'all our fine towering crags belong to it and most of the cascades among the lakes fall over it. There are indeed some lofty precipices in the first division (the Skiddaw Slates),

* Sandstones which split easily into slabs along bedding planes, from the old Norse *floga* – a slab.
† National Grid reference as used on Ordnance Survey maps.

but owing to the shivery and crumbling nature of the rock, they present none of the bold colossal features which are exhibited in this.'

Otley's appreciation of the different landscapes associated with the Skiddaw Slates and Borrowdale Volcanic rocks has been a recurring theme in all subsequent writings on the scenery of the Lake District. It figured prominently in the first official *Geological Memoir* covering the northern part of the area prepared by Clifton Ward after he had spent more than a decade in the field. The same aspect is dealt with at length in Marr's classic *Geology of the Lake District* which, although now over fifty years old, is still the only all-embracing account covering the entire area. Even to the unpractised eye, the contrasting landscapes associated with the two rock types can be clearly seen, especially when in close juxtaposition. In the lower part of Borrowdale, for example, where the boundary runs diagonally from below Walla Crag (2721) to Grange (2517) and then up on to the slopes of Narrow Moor (2317), the relatively smooth outlines associated with weathered Skiddaw Slates on the Cat Bells ridge (2419) stand out in marked contrast to the precipitous slopes of Walla Crag and Falcon Crag (2720) on the opposite side of the valley. This is simply a reflection of the difference in character between the basic rock types, for whereas the Skiddaw Slates have a fairly uniform composition, mainly shales with occasional grit bands, the Borrowdale Volcanics comprise a succession of toughened lava beds interspersed with softer tuffs.* In places however, these tuffs have been altered by igneous activity and then they, too, stand out as sheer rock walls. Where there is a succession of hard and soft beds, the whole hillside takes on the appearance of a gigantic staircase where the treads coincide with the more resistant beds. The Skiddaw Slates, in contrast, are much more uniform and tend to weather evenly to give uniform slopes with shaly debris completely masking the underlying solid rock. On these more gentle slopes there is often a complete grassy sward. Seen from afar, like the famous view of Skiddaw looking northwards from Ashness Bridge (270197), the landscape takes on a subdued appearance even though the actual height of Skiddaw itself (3,053 ft) approaches that of the highest peaks within the whole Lake District.

Broad generalizations can be misleading, however, for there are areas within the Skiddaw Slates outcrop where rugged scenery is characteristic. In the western fells, bordering on Crummock Water (1519) and Buttermere (1715), the presence of hard grit bands and massive flags gives rise to craggy upper slopes with sweeping screes fanning out below. A walk up Gasgale Gill from a point

---

* Fine-grained rocks formed of volcanic ash.

near the lower end of Crummock Water (1520) enters an area where rock type, valleyside weathering and stream erosion have combined to produce a landscape as forbidding in its grandeur as any associated with the Borrowdale Volcanic Series. The valley itself is V-shaped in cross profile with the present relatively small stream threading its way round any rocky buttresses in its path or cascading down over the harder beds in its upper section (Plate 2a). Bare crags on the north side of the valley grade almost imperceptibly into a scree of angular rock fragments often considerably dissected by stream courses which cover the hillside after heavy rain. On reaching the col of Coledale Hause (189210) the landscape changes completely. We are now in the midst of a broad open valley with a small stream passing through a succession of boggy hollows. Above lie the smooth grassy slopes leading on to the flat top of Grasmoor (1720). After the toil up the narrow defile of the Gasgale Beck, the open scenery of the plateau all around is one of commanding views in every direction. From the cairn at the western end of Grasmoor the view to the east takes in the unfrequented country running across towards Newlands Valley and Keswick with isolated knolls like Grisedale Pike (1922) rising above the general level. To the south Whiteless Pike (1819) in the foreground is similar, but beyond the land falls away rapidly to the over-deepened trough which contains Buttermere and Crummock Water. Beyond, Skiddaw Slates give way to other rocks and the majestic ridge running from High Crag (1814) to Starling Dodd (1415), with its great armchair-shaped hollows, betrays a change of rock type. On a fine day the view southwards is completed by the fragmented country which ultimately rises to Great Gable (2110) and Scafell Pikes (2107) (Plate 27).

To the casual visitor, fell walker or rock climber it is this scenery associated with the Borrowdale Volcanic rocks which typifies the Lake District. Starting from the south-west fringe where volcanic rocks encircle Black Coombe (1486), the outcrop extends as a broad strip in a north-easterly direction to include most of the fells, high plateaux and high mountain peaks of the central Lake District. In the Coniston Fells many of the mountain tops are above 2,500 ft and include Coniston Old Man (2797), Dow Crag (2697), Swirl Howe (2700) and the broad saddleback ridge of Wetherlam (2801) (Plate 15). Here the varied assemblage of volcanic beds is responsible for a landscape of contrasts. The undissected plateau tops such as that of Brim Fell leading up to Coniston Old Man tends to be gently rounded with a few bare rock outcrops projecting through a superficial cover of broken rock fragments which the short tufty grasses have only partially colonized. The Old Man itself represents a rocky tor dominating the end of the ridge. From its top the view eastwards lies across Coniston Water to the bevelled plateau surface of the Furness Fells, composed of Silurian flags, shales and grits. To the west and within a stone's throw, across the deeply-set darkened hollow which encloses Goat's Water, lie the great rock buttresses of Dow Crag (2697). Although slightly lower than the Coniston Old Man, the sheer face of the crag rising out of its own screes is one of the finest in the whole Lake District (Plate 18a). The rock wall is broken in places by great gullies or rakes which have been etched out along narrow zones of shattered rock. The volcanic rocks, with their regular joint planes, are particularly prone to shattering in this way, and where weathering and stream erosion have exploited the weakness the massive rock is broken up into great slices. The main gash on Dow Crag is only a few feet wide, but looking down from the top it forms an almost vertical 'chimney' descending to the dark placid surface of Goat's Water. Some of these gashes are formed where dykes of intruded rock weather more easily than the surrounding volcanic beds. The wide cleft of Mickledore (210069) which separates the twin peaks Scafell and Scafell Pike is associated with a dyke of less resistant rock passing through it. On Dow Crag the effect of the development of clefts has been to give it the appearance of a number of tor-like rock masses rising abruptly out of the general level surface of the narrow ridge crest. Around lie a mass of broken angular boulders reminiscent of the clitter* slopes which encompass the Dartmoor granite tors.

Impressive though the precipice of Dow Crag is, it is in the Scafell area (2006) that the Borrowdale Volcanic Series gives rise to the most rugged and wildest scenery (Plate 37). Had the eighteenth-century etchers been able to penetrate this innermost recess they surely would have chosen the sheer rock buttress of Great End (2208) (Plate 38a) or Lord's Rake (2006) rather than the Jaws of Borrowdale or the Bowder Stone (2516), their more usual subjects. Not only is this the highest part of the Lake District but it is also the great knot at the centre of a series of radiating valleys. Seen from many of the surrounding low peaks both Scafell and Scafell Pikes stand out unmistakably. This is country far away from the roads where the fell walker can thread his way through the upper valley sections, up the rock-strewn slopes to his goal of the twin summits separated by the col of Mickledore. The volcanic rocks of the Scafell region form part of a great syncline† or downwarp in the strata. In character they consist of a variable suite, ranging from the coarsest breccia‡ of broken rock fragments down to the finest volcanic dust. Many of the rock types present are flinty in character and

* A spread of angular boulders resulting from frost shattering.
† A downfold of rock strata.
‡ A rock composed of angular fragments set in a cemented matrix.

these resist erosion. This is particularly true of the thick ash bands which have been altered and hardened by heat. Some of the ash bands have escaped this alteration and it is in these beds that the workable slates are found. In the past they have been extensively quarried in a broad band which runs from Walna Scar (2596), through the slope below Coniston Old Man (2797) past Tilberthwaite (3000), and the Elterwater area (3204), and then across to the valleys of south-east Lake District like Kentmere and Long Sleddale. Only a few of these areas still produce workable slates at the present time (see Chapter 9).

The same influence of altered rocks on the topography is well seen in the valley of Great Langdale and its bordering fells (Plate 38b). Here the Borrowdale Volcanic beds consist of alternating beds of tuffs and lava flows. Where the former have been hardened by heat they tend to stand out as precipitous crags forming minor breaks on the valley side or more spectacular scarps like those along the southern face of the Langdale Pikes (2707). In contrast the lava beds both above and below the altered tuffs are associated with more gentle slopes. Many of the hard rocks are easily shattered and it was on the scree slopes below Langdale Pikes that Neolithic man found that he could shape the rock fragments in much the same way as flints from the chalk. His axe 'factory' flourished and its products distributed far and wide (pages 103–5).

Great Langdale is unique among the Lakeland valleys in that it has a distinctive twisting form rather than that of a straight trough like Borrowdale or Ennerdale (Map 4). At its upper end in Mickleden (2606), the valley is running southeast until it is joined by Oxendale near Stool End Farm (277057). From this point the direction of the valley changes to run east-north-east for about a mile before it resumes its original south-east alignment once again as far as Skelwith Bridge (3403). In its segmented plan Great Langdale exhibits the effects of structural control, viz. folding and faulting of the rock beds. The Borrowdale Volcanic Series have been folded into a broad elongated dome whose main axis is west-south-west to east-south-east. Both Oxendale and the main section of the Langdale Valley between Stool End and the New Dungeon Ghyll Hotel (2906) result from erosion along the anticlinal axis.* In contrast, the other segments of the valley like Mickleden and that downstream from Chapel Stile (3205) have been excavated along a zone of shattered rock coinciding with a series of joint planes. Even away from the main valley floor on the low col which leads over to Blea Tarn (2904), the weaker rock has given rise to a distinct topographic feature. On the hillside above the Bleatarn House (295048) there is a narrow wooded

---

* The main direction assumed by an upfold of rock strata.

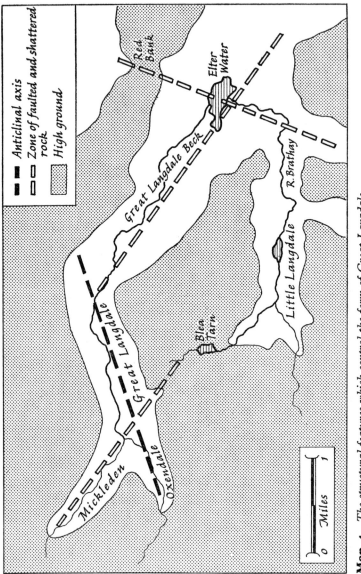

Map 4 *The structural features which control the form of Great Langdale.*

gully running diagonally across the main slope which coincides with the same zone of weakened rocks. Much of the country hereabouts and in the Great Langdale valley has been fashioned by ice (Chapter 2), but in areas such as this there is no doubt that its erosional tendency has been greatly helped by the pre-existing structural control.

Not all the scenery associated with the volcanic rocks is as spectacular as that found around Scafell or the head of Great Langdale with the long ridge of Bowfell. Around Ambleside and Grasmere, the countryside is both lower and tamer, and with wider valleys there is not quite the same enclosed atmosphere (Plate 19b). It is true that individual beds still give rise to impressive buttresses like that of Nab Scar (3506) which towers over Rydal Water. On top the fells have a very broken appearance of humps and hollows forming what is usually termed mammilated* topography. Bare rock outcrops have been shorn by ice passing over them and in between are damp boggy hollows often with small tarns fringed with reeds and cotton grass. This mammilated topography is characteristic of the thousand-foot plateau of Loughrigg Fell (3405) and many of the broad ridge tops like that running down from Heron Pike (3608) towards Rydal Water. Much farther west, in the aptly described area of the Haystacks (1913), this broken topography with its alternation of rocky knolls and scooped-out hollows is developed to perfection (Plate 19b). Many of the upland tarns here are quite large and because of their depth have escaped infilling. Elsewhere the hollows have become morasses of sodden peat.

Unlike the Scafell range, the Helvellyn mass, at first sight, does not appear to have the same spectacular features, especially if the approach is made by the old packhorse trail which leads from Grasmere to Grisedale Hause (3411) and thence by Dollywaggon Pike. These relatively smooth western slopes overlooking Thirlmere are deceptively dull, but once the summit ridge is reached at Dollywaggon Pike the scalloped landscape running down towards Ullswater comes into view and more than compensates for what has gone before (Plate 23b). The volcanic rocks, largely as a result of glacial erosion, are once again responsible for craggy precipices, steep scree spreads, narrow spine-like ridges and rocky glacis where the slope coincides with bedding planes. As elsewhere the Borrowdale Volcanic Series consists of an alternation of different rock types. To the north and north-west of Helvellyn bedded tuffs, up to two thousand feet thick, are dominant. Within them the lava flows are usually thin, but at the Stang (3517) basalts occupy much of the plateau top. They are very dark in colour

---

* A land surface with numerous smoothed rock projections.

31

and often weather to give a spongy surface texture. To the south of Browncove Crags (331158) the lavas give way once again to thick beds of tuff and it is from them that Helvellyn, Dollywaggon Pike, Seat Sandal and Fairfield have all been fashioned. The landscape developed on the tuffs is far from uniform, however, for weathering has added its own variation to the basic theme. On Swirral Edge (343155), the knife-like ridge thrusting out north-east from Helvellyn's dull summit, the rock disintegrates into small slabs. In contrast, on the neighbouring Striding Edge (347150), the cleavage in the beds runs almost parallel to the narrow crest and as a result the ridge is very broken and crenulate. From time to time great blocks are prised away and slide downslope to add to the jumbled mass of debris which line the sides of Nethermost Cove to the south. A final contrasting element in the landscape of the Helvellyn massif is provided by the extensive lava flows which occur north of the col of the Sticks Pass (3418). They give rise to Stybarrow Dodd (3418), Watson's Dodd (3319) and Great Dodd (3420), all of which exceed 2500 ft. In the field the lavas are light in colour, and where bare rock outcrops project above the general plateau surface they often have a rough columnar appearance.

Many of the valleys which run down to the shores of Ullswater from the Helvellyn summit plateau have been carved out along lines of faulting. Grisedale Beck (3715) and the Glenridding valley (3717) are in this category while the high-level col of Sticks Pass also coincides with a belt of shattered rock caused by faulting. Where this has been extensive, the slopes tend to be strewn with screes instead of craggy rock outcrops. Associated with the faulting are many mineral veins and in the past this area was one of the more important mining areas of the Lake District. At Sticks Pass veins of copper were formerly worked, while at Greenside (3617) in the Glenridding valley the lead mines only closed about ten years ago (Chapter 9). Apart from the gaunt slag heaps remaining from past mining, this landscape of the eastern part of the Borrowdale Volcanic outcrop is lush in appearance. Around the shores of Ullswater the creation of estates in the eighteenth and nineteenth centuries led to exotic trees being introduced, and now that these are mature they add considerable diversity. Forming a backcloth are the bracken-covered slopes running up to the fell tops. Bare rock still abounds and some of the scree slopes are still active. Those above Greenbank Farm (397146) carry little or no vegetation because they are so unstable. Where the harder volcanic beds dip at a steep angle to the hillslope they stand out as a succession of rock ribs. Belts of shattered rock are common and they are followed by diagonal valleys behind Greenbank Farm. This is a replica in miniature of the landscape typical of much of the volcanic rock outcrop.

In addition to its main outcrop lying athwart the central and highest part of the Lake District, the Borrowdale Volcanic beds also occur along the northern fringe beyond Skiddaw. Their distinctive character and the way they have influenced the scenery can be seen when one is passing through the strip of country between Cockermouth (1230) and Caldbeck (3239). The hill above Bothel Crags (1837) with the Roman fort of Caermote on its eastern flank, and the isolated conical hill of Binsey (2235) with its bare rocky slopes, are but two of the distinctive topographic features associated with the harder rock in this foot-hill zone. Farther east the volcanic beds also form the northern rim of the Caldbeck Fells, and beyond the eastern edge of the Skiddaw mass they make their final appearance on Eycott Hill (3829), overlooking the marshy trough of the Mungrisdale Valley. The lavas here have a very distinctive appearance, with large elongated crystals of felspar running throughout the rock. Other softer beds are present so that the western slope of the hill has a markedly terraced appearance. On top there is a jumble of bare rock ribs with intervening marshy hollows, a reminder that at this north-east extremity of its outcrop the Borrow-dale Volcanic Series does not bow out without making its own distinctive con-tribution to the landscape.

The country of the southern fringes of the Lake District, the part first seen by visitors making their way from the motorway near Kendal towards the innermost valleys and fells, has a more subdued appearance. Apart from the flanks of the high plateaux of the Eastern Fells around Staveley (4798) the land is nearly all below a thousand feet. Much of the area known as High Furness, between Coniston Water and Windermere, is typical of a countryside developed on a succession of different rock types, mainly of Silurian age. To Jonathan Otley this was greywacke country, so named from the prevalence of gritty material in the rocks. Individual beds with distinctive characteristics have been given local names, like the Stockdale Shales from the hamlet – now a single farm lying in a tributary valley of Long Sleddale (4905). Similarly the Bannisdale Slates refers to the valley in the Eastern Fells where they are typically developed, while the Brathay Flags are associated with the estate at the head of Lake Windermere (3603) (Map 5).

At the base of the whole series is the Coniston Limestone, seldom more than two hundred feet thick and consequently forming a very narrow outcrop. In spite of its name there are only impure limestone beds, and calcareous mudstone would be a more descriptive title. In areas where lime is scarce, small quarries were opened up in the past and the rock burned for agricultural purposes. At Stockdale Farm (4905) in Long Sleddale an old lime kiln stands in the farmyard

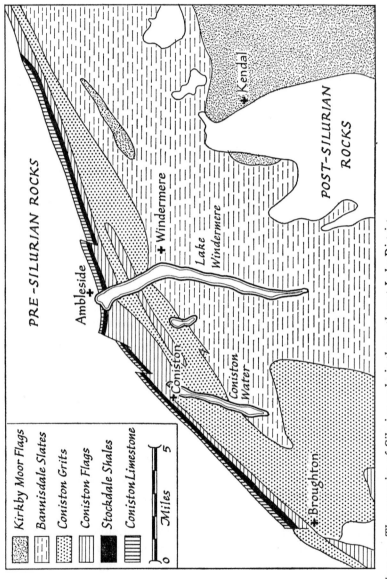

Map 5 *The succession of Silurian rocks in the south-east Lake District.*

Kirkby Moor Flags
Bannisdale Slates
Coniston Grits
Coniston Flags
Stockdale Shales
Coniston Limestone

Miles

0   5

PRE-SILURIAN ROCKS

POST-SILURIAN ROCKS

Kendal

Windermere

Lake Windermere

Ambleside

Coniston

Coniston Water

Broughton

within a few yards of the outcrop on the other side of the stream (Plate 34b). Although the actual outcrop is narrow, the persistence of the Coniston Limestone makes it a good marker bed separating the older Borrowdale Volcanic rocks from the newer Silurian strata above. Because of the limited thickness of the bed, the effect on the landscape is minimal. Towards the head of the Kentmere valley near Kentmere Hall (4504) the outcrop coincides with the col of the Garburn Pass which leads across into Troutbeck. Similarly parts of the pass which runs across to Long Sleddale from Stile End (467048) also coincide with the limestone. Both cols owe their present form to ice erosion, but undoubtedly the weaker strata here compared with the hard volcanic rocks to the north helped erosion.

Above the Coniston Limestone beds, the Stockdale Shales are also relatively soft and easily eroded so that a major topographic break occurs at the junction of the Borrowdale Volcanic Series and the Silurian rocks. Valleys like Kentmere (4504) and Long Sleddale (4903), which run through both types of rock, show contrasting scenery in their different sections. Whereas their lower parts have a soft landscape with relatively smooth green slopes and only occasional bare rock outcrops, the upper portions are a wilderness of crags, rocky buttresses and massive screes (Plate 36b). The geological boundary is equally distinct on the west side of Coniston Water, near Coniston itself (3097). Towering above the town are the slopes culminating in the Old Man, all formed of volcanic beds. Closer at hand, by the side of Yewdale Beck, long ribs of lava run down the hillside and rocky buttresses like Long Crag (298982) leave no doubt of the presence of the Borrowdale Volcanic Series. The vale of Yewdale Beck and the softer outlines of the country to the east come as an abrupt change once the Silurian strata is reached. The same discontinuity in landscape types is apparent to the south-west of Coniston along the approximate line of the pre-historic Walna Scar Road by the side of Mealy Beck.

To the south and east of this boundary, the Silurian country stretches away in a series of plateaux at different heights (Plate 21). A prominent surface occurs at about 800 ft and shows up well to the east of Coniston Water. Elsewhere, at a lower level, a more broken and hummocky topography has developed. Where hard grit bands occur they often give rise to a series of rocky knolls, many of which have been smoothed by the passage of ice. In between are small walled fields interspersed with rough pasture in the more ill-drained hollows. This is the type of landscape which is well seen on either side of the main road between Staveley (4698) and Windermere (4198) and also in the area around Underbarrow (4692), where even the contours of the Ordnance Survey map bring out the

35

broken character of the countryside. In the Underbarrow area it is the Kirkby Moor Flags, the uppermost beds of the Silurian succession, which are largely responsible. These same beds also outcrop to the east of Kendal where they form Hay Fell, crowned by the crags of Benson Knott (5494). Another bed of widespread occurrence is the Bannisdale Slates which forms much of the area around Windermere. This formation is over five thousand feet thick and is characterized by alternating bands of sandy mudstone and hard grit, giving it a stepped appearance which is readily recognizable in the field. Good views are lacking in the area largely because many parts are now covered with conifer plantations. On the steep edges of the hills deciduous woodland is more common as along the eastern shores of Coniston Water. This is one of the unspoilt parts of the Lake District, and in spring, when the shafts of sunlight penetrate the trees and when gaps allow occasional glimpses of Coniston Old Man across the lake, the drive through the woods is unsurpassed.

The geological setting of the central part of the Lake District is completed by igneous rocks which have been intruded into the various sedimentary formations. Many of the outcrops are quite small and even the well-known Shap granite occupies only a few square miles at the surface. It is an easily recognizable rock with its pink colour and elongated crystals of felspar. Huge quarries have been opened up on Shap Fells by the side of the A6 road (5608) as the rock is in great demand for railway ballast, heavy constructional work and, more recently, as a road metal. A much larger outcrop of granite occurs on the south-west fringe of the Lake District around Eskdale (1500) and the approaches to Wastwater (1404). Covering about thirty-five square miles, the outcrop is sufficiently large to make a direct impact on the scenery and character of the area. In appearance it is not unlike the Shap granite, but the felspar crystals are not so large. At one time it, too, was extensively quarried and used as a building stone. By many it was looked upon as the most attractive of the granites in the British Isles. Nowadays quarrying for this purpose has ceased and it is only in the older buildings and dry stone walls that its former widespread use can be appreciated. The lower two-thirds of Eskdale below Wha House (2000) and the whole of the adjacent Miterdale (1501) occur within the granite outcrop. It also forms the foothill zone between Muncaster Fell (1198) and Bootle (1088). This whole area is attractive, unspoilt country preserved largely through its relative isolation compared with other parts of the Lake District. The granite is not usually associated with spectacular scenery, and although rock crags do occur as, for example, about Spout House (1500) in lower Eskdale, they cannot compare with those of the Borrowdale Volcanic country. Running through the granite are vertical dykes of a harder and coarser-grained rock. That on the slopes below Whin Rigg (1503) is about fifty yards wide and can easily be picked out because of its rugged surface, which contrasts so markedly with the smooth grass-covered slopes of the granite.

Close to the Eskdale granite outcrop is another igneous mass which extends from the lower end of Wastwater across Ennerdale and then to Buttermere. It measures about ten miles from north to south and has a maximum width of almost five miles. The main rock type present, termed a granophyre,* floors both the valleys and occurs on the ridge tops. Between the Ennerdale and Buttermere valleys it is responsible for smooth rounded slopes like those of Red Pike (1515), which stand out in great contrast to the rugged crags of High Stile (1714), formed of Borrowdale Volcanic rocks. Glaciation, too, has seized upon the differences in rock type and by selective erosion has accentuated the landscape contrasts.

The third main group of igneous rocks occurs in the Skiddaw massif well to the north of the other main centres. The rock is again a granite with white felspar crystals to distinguish it from the Eskdale and Shap granites. A recent attempt to determine its age, by what is known as the potassium-argon dating method, has shown that it is about 400 million years old. In spite of its great age only a small part of its original roof capping prior to emplacement has been removed, so that exposures at the surface are limited. The largest outcrop is in the valleys of the upper Caldew and Blackhazel Beck (3130), but even here only about a square mile is exposed. Its small extent makes it of no consequence in fashioning distinctive scenery. It is rather the slates and grits altered by contact with the intruded granite which make the most impressive features of the area. Around Bowscale Tarn (3331), for example, the Bannerdale Crags tower above the corrie lake. From their precipitous slopes one can look northward to Carrock Fell crowned by the still distinct stone ramparts of the Iron Age Fort (3433). The Fell is composed of a complex sequence of igneous rocks which are all hard and resistant to erosion. As a result they give rise to the rocky crags which look out over the marshy valley of Mosedale.

The varied sequence of older rocks which makes up the heart of the Lake District gives way to a series of younger and for the most part softer rocks on their margins. The Carboniferous and New Red Sandstone rocks form an incomplete encircling rim breached only by the penetrating estuaries of Morecambe Bay in the south. Where harder beds occur, like the compact and massive Carboniferous Limestone, they give rise to a series of infacing escarpments. Faulting has isolated

* A type of granite with intergrown crystals of quartz and felspar.

37

the limestone into tabular blocks and in the country south-west of Kendal they rise abruptly from the marshes and estuarine meadows of the Gilpin (4786) and Winster (4286). Scarps like Whitbarrow (4486) and Underbarrow (4891) are impressive landscape elements, with the harder beds standing out as scars and the whole of the lower slope covered with rubble screes. On top, bare limestone pavements with deep grooves or grykes occur in a few places like Farrer's Allotment (4586) on Whitbarrow, but they are not nearly so extensive here as on Hutton Roof to the south-east. To the west of Kendal the road which leads across the tops of Underbarrow passes through a partially enclosed hollow just below Bradleyfield House (4992) which resembles, on a small scale, the basin feature known as a polje,* of common occurrence in many limestone areas on the continent. After heavy rain water often collects in the bottom and, for a time, a lake is formed which floods across the road.

Beyond Shap there is another extensive area of limestone largely taken up by Lowther Park (5222). This park, the creation of the Earls of Lonsdale, has given the area an artificial appearance, but no amount of landscaping by the eighteenth-century practitioners could alter the bold white scars which dominate the south-western face near Knipe Moor (5219). Across the Eamont valley the limestone scenery is very subdued, largely because the solid rock is masked by thick deposits of glacial drift. Quarries like those near Newbiggin (4630) mark the continuation of the limestone outcrop in a north-westerly direction into Inglewood Forest. Rocky knolls of limestone occasionally poke through the drift in Greystoke Park (4032) and the house is itself built of limestone obtained from quarries on the estate. It makes quite a good freestone for building, but its principal use is for dry stone walling. At Hutton Roof (3734) there is an impressive edge to the limestone with a drop of over 200 ft to the flat floor of the Mungrisdale trench. The river Caldew winds its way across the marshy valley, but beyond Hatcliffe Bridge (3636) the river cuts through the limestone in a small, though impressive, gorge. After a period of prolonged dry weather, when the river flow is low, much of the water disappears down swallow holes leaving only large pools in the river bed.

The most spectacular limestone gorge in the area is undoubtedly that which occurs just west of Caldbeck (3239). Here, in the area known as The Howk, a relatively small tributary of the Caldew forms what the nineteenth-century guide books describe as 'a picturesque cascade in a narrow glen fringed with firs'. When Whellan wrote his topographical history of Cumberland in 1860 he

---

* An enclosed basin in limestone country. The term comes from the karst area of Yugoslavia, where this type of feature is well developed.

described a natural arch cut in the limestone. This has now collapsed but the gorge still retains some gigantic circular swallow holes one of which, the 'Fairies Kettle', has the appearance of boiling water when the river is in spate. The whole gorge of the Howk is a most impressive piece of limestone architecture, but, judging by the overgrown mossy paths, few who come to Caldbeck in search of John Peel venture up the valley (Plate 7a).

In one part of the Lake District, north of Ullswater, the Carboniferous rocks form a conglomerate, with pebbles set in sandy matrix. The individual pebbles are derived from the Skiddaw Slate, Borrowdale Volcanic Rocks, Coniston Limestone, Silurian grit and even Shap granite. As some of the rock types occur some distance away, it is assumed that they were brought to their present site by powerful floods in the distant geological past. The conglomerate beds are 800–900 ft thick, and as they are resistant to erosion they form the isolated hills of Great Mell (3925) and Little Mell (4224). Both rise out of a plateau surface at about 900 ft and dominate the country to the south of the main Penrith–Keswick road (A594).

Beyond the limestone and conglomerate outcrops lies the richer landscape developed on the New Red Sandstone rocks. The latter formation is of variable composition with harder sandstone beds standing out as broad-topped hills while the softer shales form the lowlands and river valleys. This type of scenery is typical of the Vale of Eden, part of which lies within the Lake District One-inch Tourist Map around Penrith. Close to the town lies a belt of fell country at a height of about 800 ft running from Lazonby Fell (5139) in the north to Whinfell (5627) in the south. It is formed of the Penrith Sandstone, an easily recognizable rock with its coarse but rounded sand grains. When the individual grains are sufficiently cemented, the resulting rock is tough and compact and forms prominent topographic features like Penrith Beacon, which rises to 937 ft (5231). It also makes a good building stone and was much in demand when Penrith expanded rapidly during the nineteenth century. Lazonby Fell, in particular, has good freestone near the surface and the whole of the fell top is now pitted with former shallow workings. Another much sought stone for building was the St Bees Sandstone with its distinctive chocolate-brown colour. It, too, found favour in Penrith and was extensively quarried in the area to the east of the River Eden.

The varied sequence of rock types found in the Lake District has had a marked influence on the scenery, a constantly recurring theme in any discussion of the geological basis. In few parts of Britain is there such an awareness of the true foundations of the natural landscape. Even the casual visitor using the crowded roads in high summer must be acutely conscious of the great rock buttresses which seem to lie across his path in many of the enclosed Lakeland valleys. Much of the landscape of today, however, is not natural in the strictest sense but results from man wrestling with his environment over the past centuries. But even here the influence of the geological basis is apparent, whether it is portrayed in the humble fellside cottage, the stately home set in its own extensive parkland or in the simple stone walls which climb the steep hillsides. An accessible rock supply close at hand was a necessity both for the builders of the Iron Age camp crowning many a hill top and for their Anglican and Norse successors carving out their farms in more lowland situations. This did not usually present any problems, for often there was more than enough from simply clearing the boulders from the fields. At Wasdale Head (1808) the superabundance can be seen in the piles of stones left in the corners of the fields after large numbers had been used for building the dry stone walls (Plate 26a). Similarly at Boot in Eskdale (1701) the walls of granite boulders are often five feet thick to absorb all the stone from field clearance. Many of the cairns in areas like Subberthwaite (2587) represent prehistoric man's solution to the same problem of what to do with the unwanted stones.

In the central part of the Lake District much of the local stone is not a very suitable building material except for rough work. The volcanic rocks are usually too hard and difficult to dress, so that farm buildings are often a jumble of pieces of different shapes and sizes. Originally no mortar was used and considerable skill had to be exercised to piece together the variable shapes. Both the outer and inner faces were built of larger stones, with smaller fragments forming a rubble infill. The greenstone of the Borrowdale Volcanic Series was favoured for this type of wall and many of the buildings in places like Coniston and Ambleside made considerable use of it. Even some of the modern bungalows follow this traditional building technique where they have to conform to the planning requirements within the National Park. Many of the older buildings, in both the towns and rural areas, have suffered from a rough-cast finish in concrete over the original stone, presumably to keep out the rain. The practice became widespread in the nineteenth century and now it is only in the more isolated corners of the Lake District, as in Long Sleddale (4903), that many of the original farm buildings have remained unaltered. Great, roughly-shaped blocks of greenstone form the cornices or lintels over the doors, with the rest of the wall a jumble of rocks carefully fitted together. Another favoured building stone, especially in the south around Windermere, is the flagstone from the local Silurian beds. Although hard, it splits relatively easily and has been much used in the past. Its grey or

40

1. *Borrowdale – Rosthwaite straddles the flat valley floor on its rocky knolls.*

2a. *Scree covered slopes in the Skiddaw slates fall steeply to Gasgale Ghyll.*

2b. *Stone polygons on Grasmoor.*

3a. *Remains of a hut-circle at Threl-keld's deserted Dark Age settlement; looking to Blencathra.*

3b. *Castlerigg stone circle.*

4a. *Stonethwaite – a Norse hamlet in Borrowdale.*

4b. *Watendlath – setting for the Herries novels.*

brown hue gives the whole building a rather sombre appearance, especially under dull rain-laden skies.

Where igneous rocks like granite are available for building, the picture changes considerably. The Eskdale granite, with its even-sized crystals, is especially pleasing and was extensively used in the past. The same is true of the Threlkeld granite, a bluish-grey rock with pink patches, which was formerly in demand in the Keswick district. The Roman Catholic Church in Keswick completed a few years ago was built of this stone but it seems likely to be the last, as the quarries at Threlkeld (3224) have now gone over entirely to making road metal. Perhaps surprisingly the Shap granite, in spite of its great demand for heavy constructional work, makes little impact on the Lakeland landscape as a building material. Hardly a building in Shap itself uses the hard rock, preference being given to the more easily shaped limestone found only a few miles away.

The limestone in fact is a very favoured building material in many parts of the outer Lake District. The whole character of a town like Kendal stems from the use of the local light grey rock quarried only a short distance away on the hillside. The fact that the limestone can be easily shaped and arranged in courses often with an ashlar facing gives a clean-cut appearance to the building whether it be in the town centre or in the old mills by the side of the River Kent. On a smaller scale, limestone has been used in the planned villages of the Lowther estate as at Newtown (5224) and Lowther itself (5323) (Plate 14b). Nearby Askham, with its individual cottages and farms set well back from the road with a broad greensward in front, is equally pleasing. Where iron staining has affected the limestone or calciferous sandstone beds, a delicately coloured grey rock results. This was formerly quarried near Dacre (4626) and used in the Georgian front of the house at Dalemain (4726) by the banks of the River Eamont. In its beauty the rock is rivalled only by light purple varieties of the Penrith Sandstone, once extensively quarried in the Eden Valley a few miles away to the east.

On a grander scale the geology has had one final profound effect on the present landscape of the Lake District. After the rocks were formed they were subjected to intense pressure caused by earth movements. Occasionally the rocks were folded but more often they were subject to faulting and associated shattering, with the result that linear belts of weakened strata were formed. In time these belts were exploited by the various forces of erosion so that today many of the well-known valleys and passes of the Lake District have been carved out along these lines of structural weakness, as, for example, parts of the Great Langdale Valley, already noted (page 29). The fault zones vary in direction but many of the major dislocations have a distinct north-south trend. The result is that, although the drainage pattern is broadly radial in plan, the more dominant elements are north-south. One major zone of shattered rocks runs from the head of Coniston Water across the col of Holme Fell (3201) and then continues into the lower end of Little Langdale, across the col of Red Bank to Grasmere (3307). Its northward continuation from here is along the line of Dunmail Raise (3211), by Thirlmere into the valley of Naddle Beck and possibly extending right into the Skiddaw massif by the Glenderaterra Valley (2926). For much of its length erosion has succeeded in removing the weakened rock and thus created either valleys or low cols across the fells. The zone forms the one major break in the east-west watershed of the Lake District. On a much reduced scale the gorge of the River Duddon near Seathwaite (2296) follows another of these shatter belts. The same relationship is apparent in the valleys of Troutbeck, Kentmere and Long Sleddale which run deeply into the South-Eastern Fells. Although they do not break through the high country to the north they nevertheless form distinctive topographic elements in this little-known corner of the Lake District. The presence of belts of shattered rock and their relationship to the drainage pattern must not be taken to imply that all the Lake District valleys owe their alignment and form to this process of development. Clearly in many instances the more potent force of ice erosion has played a dominant role. But, even then, many of these faulted belts determined the lines along which the valley glaciers moved. The weakened rock also allowed the glaciers to bite deeply into the valley floor and thus create the hollows which later formed the lakes. These are, after all, the most distinctive features of the whole landscape and certainly the one element which has given the area its regional designation.

2

The physical background – the glacial interlude

'What sort of chisels, and in what workman's hands, were used to produce the large piece of precious chasing or embossed work, which we call Cumberland and Westmorland.' To this question posed by Ruskin, the earlier writings of Jonathan Otley did not contain an adequate answer. In spite of his intimate knowledge of the Lake District, he was clearly puzzled by the presence of what he called 'bowlder stones' far removed from their source area. In later editions of his descriptive guide he wrote, 'The granite blocks from Shap Fells are scattered over a great part of Westmorland. Bowlders from the sienite of Buttermere and Ennerdale are found on the west coast of Cumberland; but not in the Vale of Keswick and Windermere.' The origin of these boulders, or erratics as they are now called, was left unexplained by Otley, who was content to tell his readers that they 'are far more interesting to the geologist, yielding sufficient scope for conjecture as to the place of their origin and the mode of their removal'.

Two decades were to pass before their true significance was realized. Following studies of the glaciers and mountain scenery of the Alps, the glacial theory was evolved. In December 1850 the Reverend Professor Buckland, in an address to the Geological Society of London, drew attention to the abounding evidence in the Lake District for the former existence of glaciers. Not only did the ice scatter boulders of distinctive rocks, like Shap granite, far and wide – an explanation that would have satisfied Jonathan Otley – but it also dumped great assemblages of rocks and gravels on the margins of the area. In this connection Buckland mentioned the group of moraines by the roadside near Eden Hall, four miles east of Penrith (5632). The hummocky drift deposits left behind by the

43

ice, with hillocks and marshy hollows arranged haphazardly above the banks of the River Eamont, form what amounts to classical ground, where field evidence was first used in support of the glacial theory. Another area mentioned by Buckland was in the vicinity of Kendal where he noted that 'many hundreds of acres of the valley are covered with large and lofty insulated piles of gravel; and smaller moraines, or their detritus, nearly fill the valley from Kendal to Morecambe Bay'.

Since Buckland's day much more has been learnt about the Ice Age as it affected Britain and the efficacy of ice in fashioning landscape features. It is now known that there was a series of glacial episodes with intervening warmer phases, the whole lasting about a million years. At its maximum, ice perhaps covered the whole of the Lake District in the form of a huge ice dome with its centre in the Scafell region. At other times, however, the ice was mainly restricted to the highest part with long glacial tongues extending down the valleys. Towards the end of the Ice Age, when snow and ice had all but disappeared, only the deep armchair-shaped hollows or corries would contain small glaciers. This was the situation about 10,000 years ago when a sudden deterioration occurred in the climate. Once again the corrie glaciers grew and spilled out of their basins and into the adjacent valley heads. This happened at a number of places – at the foot of the Stake Pass (2607), at the head of Great Langdale and elsewhere. Although it only lasted about 500 years, the fact that a mini-glaciation could happen at all and so recently – a mere fraction in the geological time scale – is a reminder that we may still be in the Ice Age, a warmer interlude before cold conditions return once again.

With the events of the Pleistocene glaciation having taken place so recently, it is not surprising that the Lakeland landscape bears eloquent testimony of the powerful effects of ice erosion and deposition. While the major rock types determined a basic pattern, as we saw in the last chapter, many of the details of the scenery owe their origin to the work of ice. Here indeed was the tool and workman which Ruskin was hinting at. So little time has elapsed since the ice finally melted that most of the glacial features look as fresh as though they had just been uncovered from their blanket of snow. Indeed on some of the higher peaks and fells, the work of frost shattering and movement of debris downhill – a general process which we term periglaciation – is still going on each winter. This usually passes unnoticed as part of the whole cycle of landscape evolution, though occasionally in a severe winter or after heavy rainfall the effects are catastrophic and claim attention.

Perhaps the most typical of landforms which can claim to have been largely fashioned by ice is the U-shaped valley or glacial trough. With its straight sides and ice-shorn crags dropping steeply to the valley bottom, the form is familiar enough not to require much elaboration. Favourite valleys like Great Langdale, Borrowdale and Troutbeck all possess these basic features and have a common enclosed appearance, especially towards their heads where the fell slopes crowd in on every side. Each valley, however, has its own distinctive feature imparting a variety which is part of the charm of the Lake District landscape. Few greater contrasts exist than, say, between the rich greenery of Long Sleddale (4909) and the gaunt grey and often scree-covered slopes which surround Wastwater (1405). Again, the twisting form of Great Langdale is very different from Borrowdale, where straight contours are broken by the great rock constriction known as the Jaws (2516).

Variety within a single valley is also a feature of the area, as is apparent in traversing the upper section of the River Cocker. Starting as Gatesgarthdale Beck at the head of Honister Pass (2213), the youthful stream winds its way over boulder beds and around great rocky buttresses within a short distance of its source. The valley here has a typical V-shaped cross profile, for extensive scree clothing the lower slopes has modified the original U-section of the glaciated valley. At Gatesgarth (194150) the valley opens out and the beck now flows with greater serenity across flats which were once covered by the waters of an extended Lake Buttermere. At the present lake edge the river is gradually building out a promontory with debris brought down when it is in spate. From the head of Buttermere downstream for about five miles, the valley is more open although much of its flow is taken up with the lakes of Buttermere and Crummock Water. At Hause Point (1618) the rocky buttress comes right down to the edge of the lake and the valley is more constricted. Lower down it opens out again although the rocky end of Grasmoor (1620) and the crags of Mellbreak (1419) must have resisted any glacier as it moved down the valley, and were partly shorn away in the process. At the lower end of Crummock Water the valley bifurcates and the River Cocker chooses the eastern branch as it pursues its relentless course to join the Derwent at Cockermouth. The valley now is wide and open, forming the pleasant Vale of Lorton so loved by Wordsworth for its unspoilt beauty. In this lower section the former valley glacier began to dump some of the debris it had gathered by its erosion farther upstream. Near Armaside (1527) there is a small moraine, now capped with trees, marking a point where the glacier temporarily halted and began to melt. Although a mere ten miles from the head of the Honister Pass, the rich green acres of the Vale of Lorton represent the very antithesis to the bare boulder slopes of the source region.

To the early traveller Borrowdale was perhaps the most forbidding and awe-inspiring of the glacial valleys of the Lake District. From Keswick it was only a short distance southwards along the shores of Derwentwater to reach the great rock barrier known as the Jaws of Borrowdale (2516). Most travellers were content to view it from afar and not venture through it into the upper part of the valley. In many ways the barrier is a remarkable constriction in a valley which has felt the full power of a glacier. How it has managed to survive in its present form is something of a puzzle. Prior to the ice tearing at its slopes and plucking away its rocks, it must have been an even more impressive feature. The volcanic rocks hereabouts have been altered and hardened by heat and therefore made more effective in resisting erosion. In passing through the Jaws, the River Derwent has cut a fine wooded gorge. On its west bank the land rises steeply to the commanding knoll of Castle Crag (249159). The top of the crag was one of the viewpoints or stations recommended by Thomas West, whose *Guide to the Lakes* first appeared in 1778 and by 1812 had gone through ten editions. West was writing at a time when the first tourists were arriving in search of both the picturesque and awe-inspiring, or as one commentator put it 'beauty, horror and immensity united'. West's description of the view from the top of Castle Crag, though not quite in this vein, was nevertheless sufficiently tinted to whet the appetite.

> From the top of Castlecrag in Borrowdale, there is a most astonishing view of the lake and vale of Keswick, spread out to the north in the most picturesque manner . . . a beautiful mixture of villages, houses, cots and farms, standing round the skirts of Skiddaw, which rises in the grandest manner from a verdant base and closes this prospect in the noblest stile of nature's true sublime. From the summit of the rock the views are so singularly great and pleasing that they ought never to be omitted . . . This truly secreted spot is completely surrounded by the most horrid, romantic mountains that are in this region of wonders; and whoever omits this *coup d'oeil* hath probably seen nothing equal to it.

Beyond the crag there is a drop into a short valley before the land rises once again towards Lobstone Band. This high-level side valley was probably etched out by a stream running along the upper edge of the glacier when the whole valley was filled by ice up to a height of about 800 ft. Ice-marginal channels of this type are not uncommon in glaciated areas like the Lake District. Another, possibly formed at the same time as the Castle Crag channel, lies on the back of High Doat (247145) and again it has been cut at a height of about 800 ft. Below stretches the flat floor characteristic of the middle section of Borrowdale (Plate 1). A shallow lake must have existed here for some time after the ice melted and even today, after heavy rain, this low part of the valley tends to flood in the vicinity of Rosthwaite (2514). The existence of a temporary lake here was due to the rocky barrier of the Jaws of Borrowdale at its lower end, but, as the river steadily cut down through the hard rocks to form the present gorge, so the lake was ultimately drained. It is difficult to estimate the original height of the lake surface but it could well have been fifty feet deep, in which case it must once have extended back to Borrowdale hamlet (257140). Like the present Derwentwater it would have had its rocky islets and shallow sills especially around Rosthwaite. This hamlet, a focal point in Borrowdale, is in fact built by the side of a rocky knoll known as The How (257147). A little distance away towards the river there is a fine roche moutonée. This is a projecting rock whose upper surface has been smoothed by the passage of ice. On its downstream side the gentle back gives way to a steep roughened face where the ice has deviously plucked away any loose rock fragments. Also at Rosthwaite is the first of a series of morainic ridges where the glacier snout must have temporarily rested for a while, dumping an arcuate ring of stones and other debris. The most continuous of the low morainic ridges runs from the meander loop of the Stonethwaite Beck by the roadside south of Rosthwaite in an arc across to the Derwent bank opposite Longthwaite (256144), thence southward to near Borrowdale Church (Map 6). Opposite Longthwaite the River Derwent has cut into the moraine and exposed its constituent boulders, gravels and clays. Further moraines indicating subsequent halts during the general retreat of the valley glacier southwards into the mountain fastness occur around Great End (2208). Perhaps the most impressive of the morainic ridges lies at the entrance to the Seathwaite valley, with Thornythwaite Farm sitting imposingly on its crest (2413). The raised site of the farm is necessary because the valley floor upstream is liable to flood, and this in spite of control of the course of the beck.

This valley, the Grains Gill branch of Borrowdale, is one of many which originate in the mountain knot dominated by Scafell and Great Gable. On the leeward side of these high peaks snow accumulation must have been considerable at certain times during the Ice Age. Glaciers in valleys like Grains Gill were thus assured of a plentiful supply of new ice to compensate for the loss due to melting at their snouts. Not surprisingly this area witnessed the full effects of the mini-glaciation of about 8800 B.C. Upstream from Seathwaite to beyond Stockley Bridge (2311) there is an extensive area of hummocky drift with fresh-looking mounds lining the valley side above the tumbling beck. The footpath from

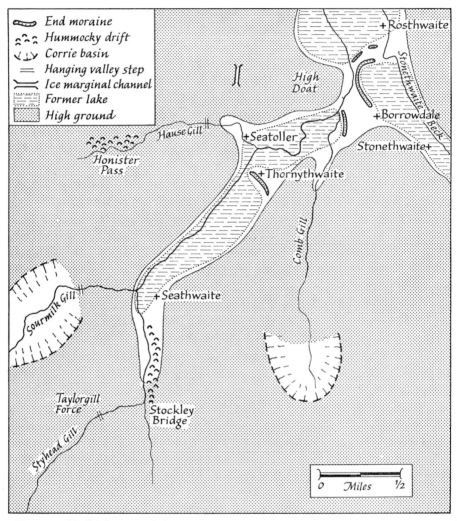

Map 6 *Glacial features of the upper part of Borrowdale.*

Seathwaite goes right through the centre of this glacial dumping ground, climbing one knoll after another. Thus although the glacier probably only existed for about 500 years it has left its unmistakable mark on the terrain. At Stockley Bridge there is another feature which is associated with the glaciation of the area, although in this case of much greater age than the hummocky drift. After crossing the bridge the path climbs steadily up to the lip of the side valley drained by

Styhead Gill (2210). This hanging valley lies some 500 feet above the main Grains Gill and the stream descends in a series of waterfalls – Taylorgill Force. Hanging valleys of this type, a result of the greater deepening of the main valley floor by the glacier compared with that of its tributary ice streams, occur widely in the Lake District. Some, like that of Sourmilk Gill above Seathwaite (2312), are the outer lips of combes lying high up on the valley side. The climb to the Honister Pass from the floor of Borrowdale is also up a hanging valley. Once on top the valley near the Pass is wide and open and there are the same conical mounds of hummocky drift as are found at Stockley Bridge. The upper part of Borrowdale, with its converging valley systems, has a wealth of glacial topography, which the early traveller would never have suspected. The limit of his penetration was usually the Bowder Stone (2516), a great up-ended mass of rock weighing perhaps 2,000 tons. Even the journey from Keswick to see this wonder at the entrance to Borrowdale was not to be undertaken lightly, if the eighteenth-century guide-book accounts were to be believed. Thomas Gray, who made a tour of the Lakes in 1769, in an exaggerated piece of descriptive writing, compared the journey into lower Borrowdale with that in the Alpine passes, 'where the guides tell you to move with speed, and say nothing, lest the agitation of the air should loosen the snows above, and bring down a mass that would overwhelm a caravan.' In spite of Gray's warning it is clear that many risked the 'perils' and visited the Bowder Stone, speculating on how it could have arrived in its precarious situation.

On the east, Borrowdale is bordered by the plateau country which rises to about 2,000 ft along its watershed crest. Although parts of the top are extremely flat and boggy, the land soon falls away to the next major valley, that containing Thirlmere. With the raising of the level of this natural lake by Manchester Water Corporation in 1906, the whole valley was transformed in appearance. In place of the valley slopes which tailed off gradually towards the water's edge there was now a steep pitch into the lake. At its upper end the lake was lengthened and now lay close to the col of Dunmail Raise (3211) leading across to Grasmere. This col coincides with a belt of shattered rock, a weakness which ice undoubtedly exploited. Masses of hummocky drift were also dumped so that the area by the roadside is not unlike that of the Honister Pass in appearance. At the lower end of Thirlmere, the valley splits into two, one branch forming the Vale of St John's and the other the valley of the Naddle Beck (2922). Ice in the Thirlmere section of the valley probably split into two but it seems that the glacier in St John's Vale was the more powerful of the two. When it finally melted, the river draining the lake chose this route rather than the Naddle valley.

Of all the glaciated valleys of the Lake District, Ullswater is perhaps the least typical. It also has the reputation of providing fell and lake scenery for the connoisseur. One of its most distinctive features, that of the twisting outline of the lake itself, is perhaps best appreciated from a good all-round viewpoint like Place Fell (4016). With the possible exception of Windermere, it is perhaps the most landscaped of the lakes. Its relatively flat shore, at least in part, was favoured for big estates like Glencoyne (3818), and Gowbarrow (4321). Exotic trees were introduced, and as they matured they gave the lakeside an artificial appearance, much appreciated by the romantics and their nineteenth-century tourist successors. And yet, in spite of all the landscaping, the Ullswater valley still bears the clear imprint of glacial shaping. With ice-brushed fell slopes, the shorn rock buttresses like those of Silver Crag (3918) and Kailpot Crag (4320), an over-deepened lake bed with a depth exceeding 250 ft in places, it is clear that a considerable glacier formerly occupied the valley. Once away from the artificially landscaped shores of Ullswater itself and into the remote and little known side valleys like Boredale (4217) and Bannerdale (4316), the effectiveness of glacial fashioning is even more apparent. The slopes of these two valleys are steep and extensive coverings of scree and drift occur towards the base. Some of this material is still in active movement downslope and there is also evidence of considerable gullying. On the east side of Martindale below Gowk Hill (4416) a recent gully has broken right through the stone wall marking the limit of the enclosed land of the valley floor. In nearby Boredale, the abrupt trough-end is almost a text-book example of a glaciated valley feature. Ice must have lingered long in such north-facing situations and when it finally melted it left behind its characteristic spread of hummocky drift well seen from Dalehead Farm (4316) looking across towards the projecting spur of the Nab. In the main Ullswater valley a small moraine occurs on the eastern side of the lake opposite the delta of Castlehows Point (4522). At its maximum the Ullswater glacier must have filled the valley floor up to a height of about 900 ft. Along the ice margin meltwater channels were cut similar to those of Borrowdale (page 46). A fine series occurs in the area between Priests Crag (4222), near Watermillock Church, past Bennethead Farm and across the col near the earthwork of Maiden Castle (4524).

Haweswater has taken on such an artificial appearance since the creation of the reservoir that it is difficult to realize that this was once a typical U-shaped valley with an overdeepened lake (Plate 10b). The building of a dam at its lower end and the raising of the water level by about fifty feet completely transformed the natural setting. As with Thirlmere, it is the steep valley sides plunging without a break into the waters of the reservoir which stick out like a sore thumb to

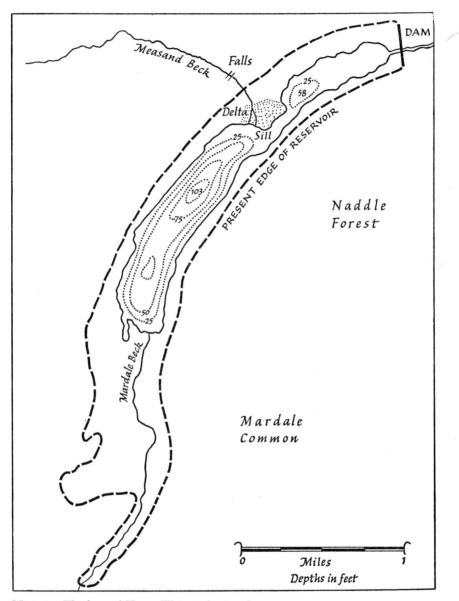

Map 7   *The form of Hawes Water prior to submergence.*

proclaim the artificiality of the whole scene. The valley is literally waist-deep in water, resembling a half-filled bath rather than anything nature could have devised. In its original state, the gentle curve of Mardale, as the valley was called, was not very different from other valleys on the eastern edge of the Lake District (Map 7). The feeding headwater valleys coming down from High Street (4411) and Harter Fell (4609) are still largely unaffected and the present marshy head to the reservoir is probably not very different in appearance from that of the original Haweswater though, of course, much higher up the valley. But many other features have gone, apart from the hamlet of Mardale and one or two farms. In its original state, the fine hanging valley of Measand Beck (4715) ended in a great torrent spread of gravel and boulders which projected well out into the lake. So large was the torrent fan that it effectively severed the lake almost in two. Now all this is submerged and there is no hint of it at the surface. Straight contours of the water edge have replaced the irregularities of surprise which nature seemingly always seeks to contrive. Only a mile or so away across the fells, the valley of Wet Sleddale (5411) has suffered the same fate, again in order to satisfy the almost insatiable demands of the urban conurbation for water.

The valleys of the south-eastern fell country are amongst the finest of the Lake District and again glaciation has played its part in moulding their form. Perhaps they lack some of the grandeur and splendid ruggedness of Borrowdale or Great Langdale but their unspoiled character more than makes amends. Apart from Troutbeck, immediately north of Windermere, they are all blind and thus saved from the effects of through traffic. Their narrow roads, little more than a track in the case of Bannisdale (5103) and not even that in Crookdale (5306), tend to discourage penetration so that to some extent this is a relatively unknown corner of the Lake District. Things might have been different if the main west coast railway line to Scotland had been driven through Long Sleddale. Long Sleddale is one of the more attractive of these eastern valleys, with the wild ruggedness at its head gradually giving way to softer contours near the southern entrance. The contrasting valley section is largely a reflection of the change in rock type and the way in which it has reacted to various external influences like glaciation. In its upper part above Sadgill (4805), it is the Borrowdale Volcanic series which outcrop, while downstream the Silurian slates, grits and flags take over. The glacier which once flowed down the valley has left its mark in both sections, though to different effect. Almost immediately above Sadgill hamlet there is a terminal moraine cut through by the River Sprint. The morainic debris is piled against a rock bar projecting into the valley from both sides at this point. Upstream the river flows across a wide, open flat and to prevent flooding has had to be artificially straightened. The valley flat marks the site of a temporary glacial lake, and its richer alluvial soils carry crops. Beyond lies the unreclaimed part of the valley, and it still retains its marshy character. Towards the valley head the floor rises steadily, as a rock step, coinciding with hard lava beds, is reached. Near the old Wrengill slate quarries (4708) the col leading across into the Haweswater valley begins. To the east there is a similar break in the valley wall leading across to the head of Mosedale (4808). Both cols must have been lowered by ice passing through them as diffluent tongues from the main glacier pushed out in various directions.

Below Sadgill in the softer country associated with the Silurian strata the valley is more open though still possessing steep sides (Plate 36b). In its journey towards the sea the River Sprint passes through a succession of basins and intervening rock barriers. From a point near where the Stockdale branch enters (4905), as far as Wad's Howe Farm (495032), the flat floor suggests a former lake basin (Map 8). The farm lies on a side moraine which later crosses the valley and restricts the former lake flat. Between here and Ubarrow chapel (5002) there is another basin. The chapel and nearby school lie on a moraine extending across the valley floor. Downstream from here and around Ubarrow Hall the open character of the lower part of Long Sleddale is well displayed. This is rich, well-farmed country with hayfields on the valley floor giving way to deciduous woods on the slopes. This, too, was once the site of a temporary lake following the retreat of the ice. At Bridge End Farm (5101), however, the valley becomes restricted once again and between here and Nether House (514004) the River Sprint flows through a small gorge. The farms in this section lie on a distinct bench, which represents an old valley floor level well above the present river. Glacial erratics, mainly flags, litter some of the fields, especially behind Nether House Farm, and must have been much more extensive before systematic clearance took place for farming. Yet another former lake basin lies below the farm, but within a quarter of a mile the river has begun to cut deeply into it and enter a steepened section of its course. Below Garnett Bridge (5299) a true gorge is developed before the river finally breaks out of its restricted valley to enter the glacial lowland country which extends to Kendal and beyond.

The succession of small basins with intervening breaks coinciding with rock bars or morainic ridges is a feature of many valleys which once witnessed the passage of ice. Another similar ungraded valley is that of nearby Kentmere. Here a much bigger lake once existed in the vicinity of Kentmere Hall (4502) in which diatomaceous* deposits gradually accumulated and led in time to its infilling. A

---

* Deposits formed of minute vegetable organisms with external casing of silica.

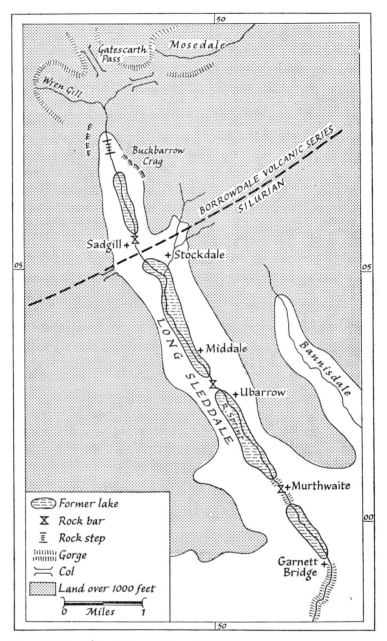

Map 8 *Landscape features of Long Sleddale.*

major break in the long profile of the valley occurs north of Kentmere Church (4504) where a pronounced rock bar, its edge plucked and accentuated by moving ice, is developed at the junction of the soft and well-cleaved Browgill Slates with the harder volcanic rocks. Against this bar, the glacier rested during its retreat stage and laid down a great boulder moraine just north of the church. Upstream a further rock step occurs near Kentmere Reservoir (4407), although the building of the dam has masked much of this glacially-derived feature.

Compared with the outlying valleys like Kentmere and Long Sleddale, Great Langdale experienced a much fuller and more intense glaciation over a long period. Lying in the lee of the highest peaks like Scafell and Great Gable, the valley head never lacked the heavy snowfall to nurture active glaciers. The area also felt the full force of outwardly moving ice streams when the whole central region was blanketed by a more or less continuous ice dome. Even after the Ice Age had 'officially' ended, its upland corries once more saw the growth of small glaciers for a short time about 8800 B.C. As at the head of Borrowdale and elsewhere, these grew and ultimately spilled over and moved slowly down into the trough end of Great Langdale at Mickleden (2606) to a height of only 400 ft. There the glacier laid down the same agglomeration of hummocky drift, with hillocks and intervening marshy hollows occurring over a wide area (Plate 18b). This was but the final dying phase of glacial activity in the valley. Earlier a more intense glacier action had already transformed what was originally a small V-shaped valley eroded by normal river action into the U-shaped trough we know today. With its steep rocky sides, scree slopes, abrupt combe end and marshy floor broken only by rock bars, it fulfils all the requirements of a typical glaciated valley. Micro-features like roche moutonées, great boulder trains left behind after the ice melted and striations* on the exposed rock surfaces, all occur as further evidence of intense local ice activity.

Many of the major features seen by those visiting Great Langdale date from a time when a great glacier occupied the whole valley during the Last (Weichsel) glaciation. There is evidence to suggest that at its maximum stage of development the upper surface of the glacier lay at a height of about 1,400 ft. At this time the snout lay well beyond the mouth of Great Langdale. While advancing in the direction of Ambleside and the head of Windermere it was constantly fed by ice accumulating in its source region around Bowfell (2406). In this active state the sole of the glacier gouged out hollows in the valley floor; these later became the sites of lakes like Elterwater (3304). The present lake is very much

---

* Grooves scraped by ice as it passed over bare rock surfaces.

the shrunken remnant of a larger original feature. Infilling has taken place and its irregular reedy margins show that the process is still going on and in time no doubt the whole lake will disappear. This has already been the fate of a similar lake which once occupied the valley floor upstream from Chapel Stile (3205). The glacier, for all its great erosive powers when at the height of its activity, never quite succeeded in removing the harder rock bars which lay across its path as at Chapel Stile and Skelwith Bridge (3403). Both rock bars coincide with beds of a toughened volcanic ash. The ice, by plucking at the well-cleaved slates and jointed lava beds on either side of the rock bars, tended to accentuate the features rather than remove them. With such prominent obstacles in its path the river has been forced to cut deep gorges through the rock bars. That at Skelwith Bridge is well known and much visited. Certainly after heavy rain the waterfalls make impressive viewing when seen from the footpath which wends its way up through the wooded glade of the gorge.

The adjacent valley of Little Langdale also contained an active glacier and gave rise to similar features of over-deepened rock hollows and rock bars. At its lower end it coalesced with the Great Langdale ice. Near Ambleside (3704), this double ice stream was joined by a glacier moving southwards from the Helvellyn range and also one from the Troutbeck valley (4000). Together these combined ice streams pushed southward across the lower Silurian country and etched out the great elongated hollow now forming Lake Windermere. At the southern end of the lake near Newby Bridge (3786) the glacier snout must have rested for a time. Here was laid down a complex sequence of end-moraines now severed by the outflow of the River Leven from Windermere. By comparison with the glaciated valleys of Great Langdale or Borrowdale, the scenery hereabouts is tame, a fact often commented upon by the early tourists in search of the awe-inspiring and the desolate. While Borrowdale Fells commanded respect for here 'nature reigns in primeval horror' the Windermere Fells were condemned as 'having nothing either picturesque or fantastic in their shape. Their rudeness softens into insignificance when they are seen o'er the wide channel of the lake.' Such was the comment of Mrs Radcliffe in her account of a journey made in the summer of 1794. Little did she appreciate that by the time the ice reached the marginal country it was a largely spent force incapable of achieving the same affects as in the heartland around Scafell and Bowfell. It also had to work on a very different rock type which succumbed to its smoothing effects much more readily than the tough volcanic beds of the central Lake District.

To many visitors it is the country around Windermere and Ambleside which provides their first glimpse of Lake District scenery. In time familiarity and perhaps the desire to escape from thousands who crowd into this area tempts many to explore the south-western valleys like the Duddon, Eskdale, Wasdale and perhaps Ennerdale. Through isolation they have been preserved from any form of commercialization and consequently have retained a rare unspoiled appearance. Valleys like Eskdale have, of course, witnessed the effect of man no less than Great Langdale, but with less recent development the basic natural and largely glaciated form shows even more clearly through the man-made trappings (Plate 28b). From Throstle Garth (2203) in upper Eskdale almost right down to the sandy estuary at Ravenglass (0896) the typical U-shaped cross profile of a glaciated valley is clearly discernible. On the valley floor, open sections as around Brotherilkeld (2102) intermingle with more broken terrain, as near Boot (1701), where the river has had to cut down through a succession of bare rock outcrops lying athwart its path. Also around Brotherilkeld, terrace features are well developed on the open valley floor. These represent former lake beds now gradually being cut into by the river. The main terrace lies about 30–40 feet above the present river bed, and cut into it is a very distinct old river channel about 400 yards upstream from Brotherilkeld Farm. Above this terrace is another which is older and more dissected in appearance. This gradually merges with the boulder scree which spews out into the valley from the lower slopes of Yew Crags (2202).

At the lower end of Eskdale the evidence for the existence of a former lake is even more convincing. Here, in the vicinity of Eskdale Green (1400), water was trapped between a valley glacier in Eskdale itself and a great ice sheet over the Irish Sea which impinged on the coastal lowlands of Cumberland (Map 9). The ice margin oscillated from time to time and caused the lake level to move up and down in sympathy. The main escape route for the lake waters was to the south, and on the fell side near Devoke Water (1597) there are high level channels used by the escaping waters at an early stage. As successively lower areas were uncovered so new escape routes were opened. At each end of the granite ridge of Muncaster Fell (1298) there are notches cut in the ridge top that once functioned as lake overflow channels from another lake, Lake Miterdale, to the north. Perhaps the most striking is that near Chapel Hill (1097) where the flat floor has been artificially dammed to form the present lake. Other channels exist at Branken Wall (0997) and north of Ross's Camp (1298). Each channel only acted as an outflow for a short period, but, with a great volume of water in the lake behind, the incision it made in the granite rock was both swift and effective. The channel at Chapel Hill functioned when the lake level stood at a height of about 500 ft OD, but as the lower Ross's Camp outlet became available so the lake level dropped to 425 ft. Still later, as the Irish Sea ice barrier retreated from the

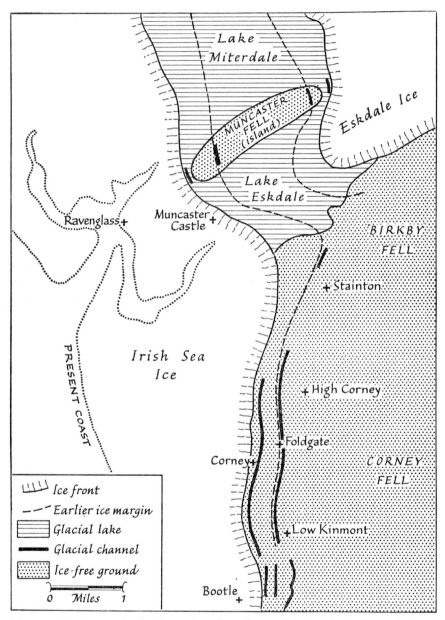

Map 9 *The ice marginal and overflow channels associated with the former lakes of Eskdale and Miterdale.*

western end of Muncaster Fell, the Branken Wall overflow was able to function at 270 ft, and so the lake level dropped yet again. On the south side of Muncaster Fell, Lake Eskdale existed at certain times. Overflow water from Lake Miterdale then flowed into it carrying great quantities of debris which was deposited as a lake delta. When the lake finally disappeared the delta remained as a distinct terrace on the hillside. At Muncaster Castle (1096) the terrace feature has been incorporated into the landscaping of the estate.

Unlike Eskdale, the other western valleys of Wasdale and Ennerdale still contain sizeable lakes. At one stage during the Ice Age they were considerably bigger. As elsewhere the lake basins were gouged out by glaciers cutting deeply into the original valley floor. Both glaciers were well fed by snows which accumulated around the higher mountains like Scafell and Great Gable. At the lower end of Wasdale erosion gave way to deposition so that between Yewtree (1105) and Easthwaite (1303) a great morainic dump was piled up against a rock barrier. Although this is an untidy landscape, difficult to farm with its chaotic assemblage of rocky howes, boulder spreads, hummocky mounds and marshy hollows, it has a fascination because of its brusque starkness. The basic features of nearby Ennerdale are very similar to those of Wasdale, with an over-deepened lake basin and the usual spread of ice-and water-deposited debris at its lower end. Its inaccessibility through the lack of a good road and the extensive plantings of conifers have made it the least known and least visited of the Lakeland valleys. The present lake is but a mere remnant of one which formerly existed during the Ice Age when water was caught between the Irish Sea ice along the coast and the higher ground inland. Near Ghyll Farm (0817) deltaic deposits exist which imply that at one time the lake had a height of about 800 ft OD and covered a much greater area.

It is the concentration of lakes, set within a series of radiating valleys, which more than anything else has stamped an almost unique imprint on the landscape of this corner of England. To the eighteenth-century topographic writers, it was simply 'The Lakes'. Lacking any scientific evidence to support or disprove their views, estimates of the depth of the various lakes varied between wide limits. A lake like Derwentwater, with its island, was not considered very deep. Pennant, the eighteenth-century traveller, in extolling the virtues of Keswick as a tourist centre, urged the visitor to 'Take boat on the water which makes the place so justly celebrated. The form is irregular, extending from north to south, above three miles and a half, the breadth one and a half. The greatest depth is twenty feet in a channel running from end to end, probably formed by the river Derwent which passes through and gives its name to the lake.' As it later turned out,

59

Pennant's estimate of depth was badly out but it was in keeping with the view that the lake was relatively shallow. Wastwater, on the other hand, was looked upon almost as a bottomless pit. With its dark screes plunging steeply into the south side of the lake and casting an overall gloom, it was clearly very different from Derwentwater or even Windermere. The early guide books seldom included it because of its inaccessibility even for the most penetrating tourist. Jonathan Otley in the later edition of his *Descriptive Guide* remarked that 'it has recently been sounded to a depth of forty-five fathoms; but we have been told of a particular shot, when a line of double the length did not reach the bottom; which must at any rate be several fathoms below the level of the sea. It is probably owing to its great depth, in proportion to the extent of surface, that it has never been known to freeze.' Local hearsay suggesting a depth of ninety fathoms or more has proved a gross exaggeration and the originally sounded depth of forty-five fathoms is much nearer the truth. Otley's suggestion that the deepest part of the lake might be below sea level has however been confirmed by later soundings.

Our knowledge of the depths and form of the lake basins dates from the end of last century when Hugh Robert Mill and some associates began a systematic survey. Working from a rowing boat and sounding with a lead line, Mill made a number of traverses of each lake. From the depths he obtained, contour lines were inserted and it is these which are shown on the current Ordnance Survey Tourist map. Although James Clarke had published a folio volume of *A Survey of the Lakes of Cumberland, Westmorland and Lancashire* as early as 1787, and Peter Crosthwaite, self-styled 'Admiral of the Keswick Regattas and Hydrographer to the Nobility and Gentry', made a series of rough maps of some of the lakes between 1792 and 1810, Mill's detailed surveys from 1893 onwards gave the first true picture of the lake basins. He was at pains to point out that their form varied considerably. Derwentwater, for example, had a very uneven bed of glacial debris. A central ridge which came to the surface in Derwent Isle and St Herbert's Island might be a partially submerged esker* for it is composed of flat stones. In contrast, the deeper hollows are floored with dark-brown mud which completely masks the stony bottom. In the shallow water towards the southern end of the lake there is often a mass of muddy peat consisting of roots and stems of water plants felted together. Occasionally this rises from the bottom to the surface and forms what has long been known as the 'Floating Island of Derwentwater'. It appears particularly after dry summers between June and September in a position about 300 yards north of the mouth of Watendlath Beck

* A sinuous ridge of sand and gravel formed by running water under an ice sheet or glacier.

60

(2619). The origin of the island has intrigued many and from time to time fanciful and varied explanations have been put forward. The most likely explanation, however, is that the decaying vegetation liberates a gas which gives buoyancy to the vegetation lying on the lake bed and brings it to the surface for a time.

Bassenthwaite Lake has the simple form of a deep elongated hollow with a mean depth of 70 ft, about the same as for Derwentwater. Its shape suggests that it was scooped out by a glacier as a distinct hollow quite separate from that containing Derwentwater. Along its eastern shore at Bowness (2229) and Broadness (2229) the ice left behind hillocks of boulder clay which run out into the shallow waters of the lake. At one time Bassenthwaite and Derwentwater formed one large lake but subsequent deposition of alluvium brought down by the River Greta on to the rock bar separating the two basins led to their separation. The difference in level between the two lakes is only 21 ft so that the river joining them is rather sluggish except after heavy rains in Borrowdale. When these occur the level of the lakes can rise by as much as $9\frac{1}{2}$ ft. One result of the changing level is that the lake is fringed by a fairly wide storm beach which can be washed by sizeable waves when a strong wind is blowing.

The paired lakes of Derwentwater and Bassenthwaite are repeated on a smaller scale at Buttermere and Crummock Water (Plate 27). Here again the original single lake has been split into two by deposition of sediment on the intervening rock sill. Both lakes are deep, Buttermere descending to 94 ft near its head and Crummock Water having a maximum depth of 144 ft at a point approximately halfway along its length. Their main distinctive feature is not their great depth, for this is exceeded in Wastwater and Windermere, but their abrupt trough ends rising out of a flat floor. Some of the side slopes exceed 45 degrees, but once the bottom is reached gradients fade off imperceptibly to only 1:300. In Crummock Water, off Hause Point (1618) the slope becomes almost precipitous. The trough-like form of the rock basins which hold the waters of Buttermere and Crummock Water is adequate testimony of the erosive power of valley glaciers. When the Ice Age was at its height, so that even perhaps the highest peaks were submerged beneath a great enveloping ice dome, powerful radiating streams of ice were generated. Some believe that the radial symmetry of the pattern of lakes, which Wordsworth in 1820 likened to the spokes of a wheel, has resulted from these outward-flowing glaciers. If this view is correct, such was the power of ice that it completely altered the original river valley system which was made up of mainly north-south elements. Not everyone subscribes to this view that the radial pattern of valleys and their lakes has been forged within the last million years of the Ice Age. Opinion, however, is unanimous that ice is a very potent force in over-deepening existing valleys. Wastwater, for example, has a maximum depth of 258 ft between Long Crag (1506) and Illgill Head (1604), which means that its bed is well below sea level in places (Plate 25). The gouging out of the valley floor was often greatest where the valley was restricted in width. The formation of any rock basin – which ultimately becomes the site of a lake – implies that the main energy of the glacier is expended in over-deepening its bed and not widening the valley. For this reason the lakes are all long and narrow and usually straight.

Of the major lakes only Ullswater, with its double dog-legged plan, shows a real departure from the typical finger shape. Standing on the pier at Pooley Bridge (4624), for example, only the lower third of the lake is visible, the view ending abruptly at Hallin Fell (4319). Once around this corner there then follows a long straight stretch which runs as far as Silver Point (3918). Here a further change of direction takes place so that the upper end of the lake is running almost north-south. In trying to understand why Ullswater should have this distinctive plan, it is perhaps significant that each stretch of the lake has its own separate rock hollow, as can be seen from the bathymetric contours on the One-inch Ordnance Survey Tourist map. Where the lake changes direction there is a prominent rock sill. That between the slopes of Hallin Fell and Skelly Neb (4320) is just over 75 ft deep compared with 125 ft on either side. The other bar between Silver Point (3918) and Glencoyne is even more impressive, and in the wooded islet of House Holm it even comes to the surface. It is possible that the sills in the lake bed coincide with cols which existed in pre-glacial time. The ice coming down the upper part of the Ullswater valley over-rode the cols and lowered them considerably. Certainly there is plenty of evidence of intense ice activity on the islets within the lake. All are of solid rock and show marked striations caused by ice as it passed over them. Their northern edge tends to be more broken as though the rock here has been plucked away by passing ice. In form they are not unlike the roche moutonées which occur around Rosthwaite in Borrowdale (page 47). When the glaciation was at its height, tributary ice streams entered the main Ullswater valley from many directions. Valleys like Grisedale (3715), fed from the snows which accumulated in the lee of the Helvellyn range, must have made a substantial contribution to the main Ullswater glacier and helped in both over-deepening the valley floor and lowering obstacles like cols. The process of change in the landscape, however, goes on relentlessly, and since the ice finished its work other agencies have taken over. The swift-flowing becks have brought down considerable quantities of debris which they dumped on reaching the placid waters of the lake. As a result deltas have been

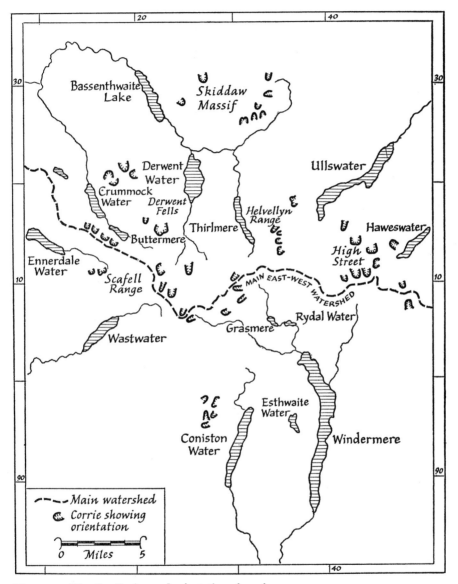

Map 10   *The distribution and orientation of corries.*

thrust out in a number of places like Aira Point (4019) and Glenridding (3816). At the latter the spoil from the former Greenside lead mines made a substantial contribution to the material brought down by the Glenridding Beck. When the mining activity was at its height during the latter half of the nineteenth century, the lake delta was growing at the rate of more than ten feet a year.

The southern lakes of Windermere and Coniston, set in what the eighteenth-century topographers referred to as 'the humble hills', are typical finger lakes. Windermere, for example, is almost ten miles in length but seldom more than half a mile wide. Partly because of their restricted width, glacial erosion concentrated on down-cutting with the result that the lakes are surprisingly deep, Coniston going down to 184 ft and Windermere to 219 ft. Their great length also allows the wind to pile up the waters, especially at the northern end. At Coniston the lake level can vary by as much as six feet, and five-feet waves are generated when the wind is blowing strongly from the south or south-west. Ponding up of water at the northern end of the lake due to strong winds is also apparent on Windermere. The lake level also responds to the flood water brought down by the River Brathay. Debris brought down by the river has led to the building of a small lake delta near the site of the Roman fort of Galava (3703), but due to the relatively deep water hereabouts it is only being extended slowly into the lake. Deposition in the past has led to the creation of extensive lake flats at the head of Windermere, but certainly during the past two thousand years their formation has been a very slow process. The remains of a stone jetty built by the Romans to serve their fort is still near the present low water line, but owing to the compaction of the soft lake sediments it is now largely submerged. The sediment of the lake bed consists mainly of fine mud in the deeper basins and multi-coloured clays in the shallow parts. Some of these clays have a distinctive layered appearance (varves★), each layer representing an annual accumulation of sediment. From these varve layers and the nature of the lake deposits, Dr Pennington has worked out a post-glacial time scale for the Windermere area and thrown considerable light on the events which followed the retreat of the ice (see page 76).

The mountain tops and upland slopes, no less than the glaciated valleys and lake basins, show clear evidence of being moulded and modified by ice action in the past. One of the surest indications that ice once over-rode even the highest parts is the presence of erratics, that is, rock fragments carried some distance from their source outcrop. Where these have a distinctive appearance and

★ Distinct banded layers of silt and sand representing different seasonal depositions in the still waters of a lake.

5. *The Surprise View – Derwentwater.*

6a. *Grange-in-Borrowdale – a manor on Furness Abbey's estate.*

6b. *Taylorgill Force and the glacial step at the northern end of the Sty Head Pass from Stockley Bridge.*

7a. *The Howk near Caldbeck – a gorge in the Carboniferous Limestone.*

7b. *Caldbeck woollen mill.*

8. Cockermouth – the medieval core lies between the castle and parish church and the seventeenth century quarter of Main Street occupies the bottom right foreground.

therefore are easily identifiable in hand specimens, they can be of great value in tracing former ice movements. Not all the rocks which litter mountain tops like Great Gable and Scafell are 'foreign' erratics. Many have been formed *in situ* by intense frost shattering when the peaks stood out above the blanket of snow and ice on the lower slopes. This special type of process – termed periglaciation – has left its mark in the great boulder fields and elongated strips of shattered rock on mountain tops like Saddleback (3227) and Grasmoor (1720). Although periglaciation reached its climax during the Ice Age and shortly after, it can still occur today. Towards the edge of the flat summit of Grasmoor, for example, at a height of about 2500 feet, winter frosts not only shatter the slates but also sort out the resulting fragments into a linear pattern resembling the furrows of a ploughed field. The coarser stones tend to lie on the ridge tops while the smaller fines accumulate in the intervening hollows. The sorting of the stones in this way is a complex process involving heaving of rock fragments of the surface layer when it is subject to alternate freezing and thawing. There is also a mass movement of debris downhill under gravity and this contributes to the linear appearance of the surface. At the present time, the effects of periglaciation are best seen after a severe winter of intense night frosts. By the summer the surface may have lost its distinctive patterning. A similar 'micro' form is the stone polygon which consists of a rough circle of broken angular stones often projecting through a thin turf or moss covering. These, too, are formed by frost action and can be seen at a number of places on the plateau summit of Grasmoor and the ridge to the north of Blencathra (3228) (Plate 2b).

Perhaps the most telling effect of the role of ice in fashioning the upland scenery can be seen in the creation of the corrie basins which bite deeply into the sides of the ridges (Map 10). Whereas the pre-glacial setting was one of rounded slopes gently curving upwards to merge with flat plateau tops, corrie development has led to a rough scalloped appearance. Not every part of the upland surface has been affected to the same degree and on many ridge sides there is a marked contrast between opposing slopes. The Helvellyn ridge, for example, presents its smooth face towards Thirlmere on the west, and this contrasts markedly with the indented, deeply cut angular topography which runs down to the shores of Ullswater. Valleys like those of Grisedale and Glenridding start in corrie basins, often with scooped out lake hollows – for example, Red Tarn (3415) and Grisedale Tarn (3412). They are backed by a steep headwall, and on their sides precipitous slopes reach up to the narrow divide or arête ridge. Two of the best known features of the Lake District landscape, Striding Edge and Swirral Edge, are arêtes formed by corries biting deeply into what was once almost a

E

continuous smooth eastern face of Helvellyn. Seen from the mountain top, the narrow spines are impressive enough, but if the scree which has accumulated on their sides were to be stripped away, the resulting solid rock slopes would be almost precipitous.

Many of the corries, though by no means the majority, contain small lakes held up either by rock sills or a boulder moraine. Impressive morainic ridges occur across the entrances to Blea Water (4410) above Mardale, Bowscale Tarn (3331) on the Skiddaw massif and Gillercomb (2212) at the head of Borrowdale. Most moraines resemble great heaps of boulders piled one on top of the other as they were left behind when the corrie glacier had lost its impetus and was only too willing to dump its load of debris. Crossing boulder moraines can be a tiring experience, as anyone who has negotiated the rock jumble across the entrance to the corrie containing Levers Water above Coniston (2799) knows. Most of the corrie tarns occupy quite shallow rock hollows, but in the case of Blea Water (4410) at the head of Mardale the surprising depth of 207 ft was found. The back-wall is usually very steep even when compared with the slopes of the side walls. Dow Crag (2697), formed of a hard andesite rock, is precipitous in its upper part and for that reason the vertical buttress is favoured by rock climbers (Plate 18). Although the detailed form of corries varies considerably depending on the rock type, orientation, the presence of secondary features like moraines and screes, there is a surprising uniform relationship between two of its major dimensions – the height of the backwall and the length of the 'seat'. Measurement made from the many corries scattered throughout the Lake District show that the ratio of backwall to seat varies within the narrow limits of 1:2·8 to 1:3·2. Rock type seems to play little part in determining the distribution or size of the corrie basins. The fine group which overlook the Buttermere valley from the south-west brings this out very clearly. Ling Comb (1515) is cut entirely in a hard igneous granophyre – a type of granite with large crystals. The adjacent corrie enclosing Bleaberry is hollowed out of both granophyre and slates, but in spite of this dual rock composition its form is not very different. In a wider context corries show no preference for any of the major rock types, as they occur both in the Skiddaw Slates, as around Blencathra (3227) and Black Combe (1385), as well as in the Borrowdale Volcanic Series at Coniston Old Man (2797), Langdale Fells (2807) and Helvellyn.

One striking feature of corrie basins is the way in which the majority have a north or north-east aspect (Diag. 1). There are obvious exceptions like those which serrate the southern slopes of Blencathra, but taken as a whole a north-east orientation is dominant. It is this preferential development which gives many of the ridges their asymmetrical appearance. No greater contrast of landforms exists than on the opposing sides of Helvellyn or the inter-valley ridge separating Ennerdale and Buttermere. On the one side are smooth even slopes broken occasionally by rock crags and low precipices while on the other glacial erosion has bitten deeply and successfully to create what has been called 'biscuit topography'. With rock type not exerting any great influence, other explanations have to be sought to account for the preferential north-east aspect. As early as 1917 Enquist noted that the corries tended to lie on the lee side of a mountain range, that is in relation to the dominant snow-bearing wind. More recently Manley has shown that in this situation the wind which blows over the ridge top – the

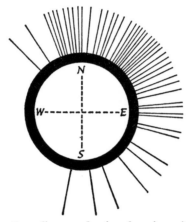

Diagram I *Rose diagram showing the orientation of corries.*

helm wind – considerably aids snow accumulation on the upper part of the lee slope through the development of a back eddy. The presence of the eddy can often be detected on the waters of a tarn where wavelets move towards the back-wall of the corrie basin. During the Ice Age thick snow would be likely to accumulate in any hollow on the lee slope, and through the addition of successive layers be ultimately transformed into ice. In time this ice would gouge out a deeper hollow and ultimately a true corrie basin. Having reached this stage, the rapid build up of snow and ice would bring about increased erosion of the floor of the hollow. Due to the effect of the helm wind, the greatest amount of snow would accumulate on the upper part of the corrie glacier just below the bare upper part of the backwall. Differential loading on the upper surface of the corrie glacier would tend to cause the ice to move in a rotatory manner. With continuous additions at the head and constant depletion at the snout through melting, the rotatory movement could be instrumental in scooping out the floor of the corrie (Diag. 2). Other processes like frost shattering of the bare rocks of the upper part of the backwall and the grinding action of rock debris within the glacier would also contribute to the enlargement of the corrie basin. It follows that if the prevailing snow-bearing wind was from the south-west then the north-east facing lee slopes would become the most suitable sites for corrie development. This north-east aspect also happens to be one of minimum isolation so that snow and ice would persist longer here. When the snow had long since disappeared from the upland peaks and plateau tops, some of the deep shadowy hollows would retain their active glaciers. Even today snow patches last until late May or early June in situations like the steep north-facing buttress of Great End (2208).

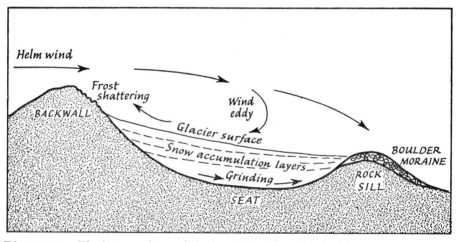

Diagram 2   *The features of a corrie basin and possible mode of origin.*

Wordsworth, in his poem *Fidelity*, mentioned the persistence of snow under the lee of Helvellyn which he had noticed on a walk across to Patterdale in early June.

The ice which was so prominent in fashioning the landscape of the central high part of the Lake District also left its mark in the peripheral lowland, though to different effect. Here various ice streams jostled for occupation of the low ground. In addition to the local glaciers fanning out from the mountainous core, a great wall of ice moved in from the Irish Sea and impinged on the western coasts. Passing over the softer rocks of the lowlands, the ice was able to incorporate great quantities of sands, clays and rocks which it subsequently deposited on melting. In contrast to the highland area, the glacial landforms of the margins

68

are nearly all associated with deposition rather than erosion. The countryside around Kendal (5192), often hurriedly passed over by the tourist seeking the mountains, is typical of this kind of landscape genesis. Although the upstanding limestone blocks like Underbarrow (4891) or the roughly hewn Silurian grit forming The Helm (5389) stand out as major topographic features, the lowlands below about 500 ft bear the unmistakable stamp of ice moulding its own ground moraine. Elongated whale-backed hillocks or drumlins, often one-third of a mile long and rising perhaps a hundred feet or more, dominate the rolling landscape.

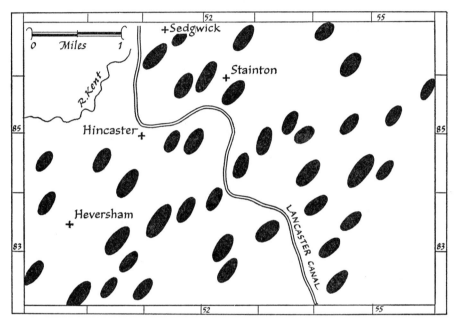

Map 11 *The drumlin swarm in the country to the south of Kendal.*

Seen from a high vantage point the patterning created by closely packed drumlins calls to mind eggs arranged in a basket, an expression often used to describe this type of landscape. Around Stainton (5285) the drumlins are elongated in a north-north-east to south-south-west direction, indicating the direction of ice movement (Map 11). Another area where a 'basket of eggs' topography developed is in the Eden Valley and the adjacent Inglewood Forest near Penrith (5130). The major ice movement here was to the north-west and into the Solway Plain. Not all ground moraine was shaped into drumlins and large areas within Inglewood Forest have a rather flat and featureless boulder clay surface, much of it ill-drained and marshy though it is over 700 ft high. The boulder clay is sufficiently thick here to mask nearly all the underlying solid rocks and it is only occasionally that the limestone breaks the surface.

The movement of the various ice streams in the lowlands can be traced by the distribution of any distinctive rock fragments or erratics within the drift deposits. The Shap granite is a well-known indicator because it is so easily recognizable. What is remarkable is that the Shap granite outcrop near Shap Wells (5508) covers less than two square miles and yet rock fragments broken from it by the ice were distributed over a large area, often more than a hundred miles from the source region. Another distinctive erratic is the Eycott Lava from Eycott Hill (3829). The rock is dark green in colour with light crystals of felspar up to two inches long within it and therefore very distinctive in appearance. As it is found in the drift deposits of the West Cumberland Lowland, ice must have passed right round the northern edge of the Skiddaw massif in an anti-clockwise direction. In the Solway Plain the local Lake District ice came into contact with the Scottish ice and together they moved west and south-west. Near Gilcrux (1138) and Plumbland (1439) the orientation of the drumlins shows that the dominant movement was in this direction. The Scottish ice brought its own peculiar suite of erratics like the granite of Criffel, that distinctive mountain which rises majestically across the shallow waters of the Solway Firth.

The 'foreign' ice which wrapped itself around the Lake District at various times was to effect landscape changes of another type. In the West Cumberland lowland ice moved in from the Irish Sea before coming to rest on the lower hill-slopes like those of Corney Fell (1391) and Birkby Fell (1396). Between the ice edge and the rising ice-free ground of the fell, marginal channels were cut by running water. That near Corney (1191) is typical with its flat floor, abrupt sides and twisting outline. In its northern section it is a dry valley but near Corney Hall it contains a small stream. The ice margin oscillated from time to time and so several channels could be cut on the same hillside slope at different levels. An upper channel at a height of about 400 ft has formed near Middle Kinmont Farm (1190), again parallel to the hillside slope. To appreciate the full effects of the glaciation in this peripheral area it is necessary to leave the by-road near Corney and tramp across the fields seeking out these discordant channels left behind by the ice margin perhaps some 20,000 years ago. The same Irish Sea ice also left behind a thick mass of boulder clay at lower levels. The cliffs around Annaside (0986) and Gutterby (1084) are formed entirely of glacial deposits, which are more than 200 ft thick at Gutterby Spa. The soft clay is susceptible both to wave attack and sub-aerial weathering and readily slumps down on to the storm beach below. Under the shadow of Black Combe, these clay cliffs are retreating steadily and thus narrowing even more the compressed coastal strip, here less than a mile wide.

One final effect of the glacial interlude remains to be considered. As the ice masses grew and then waned, there was a complementary movement of sea level. When not frozen during the glacial episodes, it tended to be low but as the ice melted so sea level rose, often to reach levels much higher than that of the present day. The effects of this up and down movement of the sea is best seen in the river valleys and estuaries which run into Morecambe Bay. During phases of high sea level, including that of the immediate post-glacial period, these valleys were flooded and the estuaries greatly extended. That of the Kent, for example, ran inland certainly as far as Helsington Moss (4689) while that of the Leven ran right back to the gorge at Haverthwaite (3483). During the earlier interglacial rises of sea level, the coastline reached the limestone cliffs of Underbarrow at White Scar (4585), but, in the post glacial phase, sea level was only about twenty feet above the present. The coastline at this time – marked by the twenty-foot contour – therefore lay a little distance away from the limestone edge. The main A590 road crosses and re-crosses this low 'post-glacial' coastline as it makes its way along the indented shore of Morecambe Bay. After the sea began to retreat about 3800 B.C. the present estuarine marshland came into being. For the most part this low-lying area has been converted into pasture by embanking and draining to prevent flooding. In places raised bogs lie on top of the estuarine alluvium and these are believed to have been formed when the post-glacial sea level reached its maximum height about 3800 B.C. This is a landscape where man has taken over from nature, where an ordered pattern of drainage ditches and straight raised embankments has replaced the original primeval state. Though perhaps dreary from within, it nevertheless has a quiet charm when seen from above, as on the top of the limestone scarp in front of Helsington Church (489889). Here the marshland of the Gilpin valley, broken only by limestone knolls like High Heads and Gilpin Bank (4687) which were once islets in the estuary, stretches away towards the dark wooded back slopes of Whitbarrow. This fenland landscape seems out of keeping with the true Lakeland scene and it is difficult to remember that only fifteen miles away to the north-west lies the highest mountain in England, Scafell Pike. Contrasts of this order are a measure of the diversity and richness found within the Lake District and do much to explain why the area has proved such a continuing attraction over the past two centuries.

3

Vegetation and related aspects

Apart from creating distinctive landforms, the Ice Age had another major contribution to make to the Lake District landscape. The enveloping sheet of ice swept away all the previous vegetation and, on melting, left in its wake a bare stony surface ripe for colonization by plants, shrubs and trees. Thus began a long and complicated history of vegetation succession. It is easy to regard much of what we see on the upland fells or the steep-sided glacial valleys as the natural end-product of ten thousand years of evolution, but this is to ignore one major influence in the present vegetation pattern, namely man himself. It is true that he may never have tilled the hostile and hungry soils of the highest parts, nor enclosed the uplands in the same orderly way as in the lowland valleys. Nevertheless, the upland fells did not escape his attention. The need for wood over the centuries and grazing grounds for his animals on the upland moors both altered the balance of nature and had a marked effect on the vegetation which we see today. Even in the innermost recesses of the Lake District, now seldom penetrated except by the enthusiast, the open vistas which he enjoys are those of a man-made landscape. Natural processes have, of course, played some part, for in a mountainous environment such as the Lake District factors like altitude, exposure to strong winds, heavy precipitation and the inevitable leached soils are all of considerable importance. Without man's help – going right back to prehistoric time – the landscape which the fell walker sees from the summit of Great Gable or the long ridge of Bowfell would be very different in its original natural setting. Almost certainly there would be woodlands, dominated by the upland oak perhaps up to a height approaching 2,000 ft, with alder carr in the damp undrained valley bottoms. That so little high level 'relict' woodland survives today is a measure of the way in which man has changed the upland environment and substituted his own. Even in the wooded southern part of the Lake District, as along the shores of Windermere or in High Furness, the forest cover is man-made, either to serve his needs for timber or simply to satisfy his aesthetic sense by the introduction of exotic trees to screen the lakeside mansions.

For some 5,000 years after the retreat of the ice, the vegetation succession was entirely natural. Much has been learnt about the initial colonization and the types of tree and shrub present by the technique known as pollen analysis. The pollen spores are produced in great numbers and widely scattered by the wind. The vast majority shrivel up but occasionally some fall in areas where they are preserved. A favourite habitat is a developing peat bog where the damp anaerobic conditions preserve the casing of the pollen spore and allow identification from its distinctive shape. By taking a peat sample with a coring tube, it is possible to extract the pollen, identify it, and then, by counting the distinctive individual grains, estimate the percentage of any one type. This can be done for different layers of the peat and in this way an evolutionary picture of the changing vegetation begins to emerge. In the Lake District several sites have been investigated using pollen analysis. Dr Winifred Pennington, for example, has studied the pollen found in the deposits from the bed of a number of upland tarns, while Dr Donald Walker has made similar observations from the damp hollows between the morainic mounds at the head of Great Langdale (page 55).

The pioneer vegetation which began to spread across the bare ground recently vacated by the ice was dominated by grasses and shrubs like juniper and the dwarf willow. A few scattered birch and pine trees succeeded in gaining a foothold but for the most part treeless conditions prevailed. In both the upland and lowland situations this period of pioneer vegetation came to an abrupt end and was succeeded by the spread of true birch woodlands. Later the hazel became dominant and it is the pollen from this tree which makes a striking contribution from about 7000 B.C. onwards. The expansion of the hazel, however, was later checked somewhat by the arrival of the oak and elm. The latter preferred the damp loamy soil found in pockets in the uneven cover of glacial drift. The oak, in contrast, spread more slowly but gradually made great inroads into areas once dominated by the hazel and birch. The pine, which had been an early colonizer of the lower ground, was now confined to the upper fells. By about 5000 B.C. an almost complete forest cover had established itself throughout the Lake District up to a height of almost 2,000 ft. It is perhaps difficult to visualize this former setting to the now open fells, especially on the evidence of preserved pollen grains in peat deposits. In places, however, the actual stumps of trees have

73

to make a limited impression on the forest cover dominated by hardwood trees like the oak and elm. Experiments carried out in Denmark, however, show that the stone axe was a very effective tool and a team of men working together could quickly clear a large area by felling the trees. In addition it seems likely that, even before forest clearance began systematically, the elm foliage was collected as animal fodder. This defoliation of the elm would in turn allow more light to reach the ground and thus encourage the growth of grasses, herbs and weeds. This is exactly what is found in the pollen record where a dramatic increase in the pollen of grasses, the dock and plantain, accompanies the marked drop in the elm contribution. There was no cultivation of cereals in these early forest clearings and Neolithic man was content to rely on his cattle and pigs for his food supply. If the clearing became overgrazed, it might be subsequently abandoned and for a time bracken would take over. Regeneration of the former woodland would begin with the hazel and birch and in time the high forest of oak might re-establish itself if allowed to develop unmolested.

Forest clearance by man continued sporadically throughout the rest of the pre-historic period. In the lowland areas surrounding the Lake District there is evidence that further extensive clearings took place from about 2000 B.C. on-wards. Round about 1750 B.C. cereal production began to play an important role in farming and this undoubtedly led to further destruction of woodland on the better soils. In the higher parts of the Lake District, however, crop farming was on a very limited scale and Bronze Age man continued to live in much the same way as his Neolithic forebears. The gradual clearance of woodland brought other changes to the area. Bare patches would become increasingly subject to soil erosion and leaching, thus diminishing their original fertility. From about 800 B.C. the climate became increasingly wet and blanket bog began to spread, especially in the lower areas cleared of woodland. Around upland tarns like Devoke Water (1596), the bog spread more slowly but there is no sign of woodland re-establishing itself. All the evidence here points to the almost complete destruction of the woodland in pre-historic time. In lowland valleys like Esthwaite Water (3696) pre-historic forest clearance was on a more limited scale and it seems that in these situations it was the Norse farmers of the ninth and tenth centuries who effectively finished a process begun almost 4,000 years before on the upland fells.

The vegetation history of the Lake District during the past ten thousand years, based largely on the evidence of pollen analysis, is thus one of gradual recovery from the ravages of the Ice Age for the first half of the period. During the past 5,000 years, however, man has played an increasingly active role in determining the vegetation likely to be found in the area. In this later phase, the changes in climate which have undoubtedly occurred have had only a minimal effect compared with those brought about by human interference. Even the marked changes in soil fertility represent the side effects of forest clearance rather than leaching away of natural soil bases through increased rainfall. This is clearly shown by a study of the sediments of Lake Windermere undertaken by Dr Pennington. The deepest layers record the events of the Ice Age when seasonal meltwaters brought down sediment and spread it out on the lake floor in distinctive layers or varves. Even the mini-glaciation of 8800–8300 B.C. is recorded faithfully in the lake sediments. Above the layered deposits come 12–15 feet of brownish mud which has accumulated during the past ten thousand years since the ice finally left the Lake District. These muds contain sparse remains of plants and resistant silica shells of diatoms which lived in the waters of the lake. There are also variations in the organic content of the sediments at different depths. Muds which were laid down immediately after the retreat of the ice – the bottommost layers investigated – are characterized by a high organic content, suggesting that, as the vegetation was developing, the rivers were bringing in considerable quantities of debris from a still partially bare surface. Once the oak-elm forest had established itself, from about 7000 B.C. onwards, the organic context fell and then remained fairly constant during the next 4,000 years. The period of forest clearance is marked by an increase in organic matter, possibly due to the leaching of the soils taking place on the partially bare slopes. In time the total absence of woodland cover on the fells led to a complete impoverishment of the soils whose organic bases were never replaced by leaf litter. In consequence the layers of mud representing the most recent accumulation over the past thousand years have a reduced organic content, as the now leached soils were contributing little in the way of nutrient salts. Thus man has not only brought about a direct change in the vegetation by his destruction of the former woodlands but has also triggered off a steady deterioration in the fertility of the soils, making it more difficult for re-generation to take place unaided. Much of the present poor grassland of the upland fells, for example, is the end-product of thousands of years of pastoral mismanagement.

The present pattern of vegetation in the Lake District is, in a broad sense, very clear cut and is largely a reflection of altitude. On the highest peaks and adjacent mountain slopes, a heath and grassland association predominates. Below, in the sub-montane zone, grassland of varying quality is found and now extends well beyond what was its original lower limit. In the wetter western fells, which meet the full force of the rain-bearing westerly winds, the present grassland-tree boundary is as low as 600–800 ft. Over in the east, however, the same vegetation boundary is much higher and trees will grow quite well above a thousand feet, as, for example, in the Forestry Commission plantations clothing the slopes of Skiddaw (2427). Natural woods, too, will survive at heights well above the thousand-foot contour in the drier north and eastern sections of the Lake District. High-level oakwoods occur on the flanks of valleys as in Keskadale (2019), Birkrigg (2220), Naddle Forest (5014) and elsewhere (Map 12). Of these interesting survivals, Keskadale is most accessible as it lies halfway up the hill-side above the road leading from the Newlands valley across to Buttermere. The wood covers about fourteen acres, and, although not enclosed, its boundaries are quite distinct. It occupies a broad strip on the hillside between 1,000 and 1,500 ft. The wood is almost entirely formed of sessile oak with the occasional hawthorn and sycamore. On the slopes below bracken has invaded and almost entirely covered what was once a hillside pasture. Towards Ill Gill stunted bushes of juniper are found with occasional hawthorn, mountain ash and holly. The oak trees of the main wood look healthy and actively growing, though towards the upper margin of the wood their trunks become more stunted. Some on the lower slopes reach thirty feet in height and considering their exposed situation are remarkably erect. Their tops show the effect of wind pruning, which has led to an almost horizontal canopy. Thus the tallest trees occur in the deeper hollows. The individual trunks of the oak trees are quite small and arranged in groups. They appear to arise from a common root source, although the stool of the tree is largely buried by mosses and other vegetative growth. From these buried stools young shoots grow up in much the same way as in coppice woodland. The whole apearance of the Keskadale wood is that of a very old coppice, and there is some evidence that in the early part of the nineteenth century the oak here was cut periodically to obtain bark for tanning. Occasionally the trees produce acorns, although in the fine summer of 1968, when the lowland oaks carried a heavy crop, none was seen in Keskadale wood. It seems therefore that the wood is maintained by new shoots arising from the old partially buried stools. The latter may be part of the original trees prior to the coppicing of past centuries and it is just possible that the Keskadale oaks form a relict woodland which has somehow managed to escape total destruction by man.

Like the Keskadale wood, Birkrigg lies on a steep hillside with a south-facing aspect overlooking Rigg Beck (2120). It is a smaller wood with a height range of between 1,200 ft and 1,400 ft. The oak is again the dominant tree with the occa-sional rowan interspersed. The trees are sufficiently well spaced to allow a varied ground flora to survive. Bracken, bilberry and heather are the chief plants, with

77

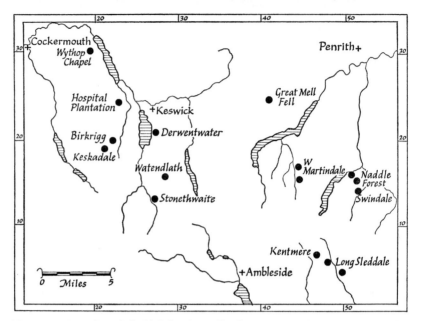

Map 12 *Location of the high-level woodlands, some of which are possibly relict.*

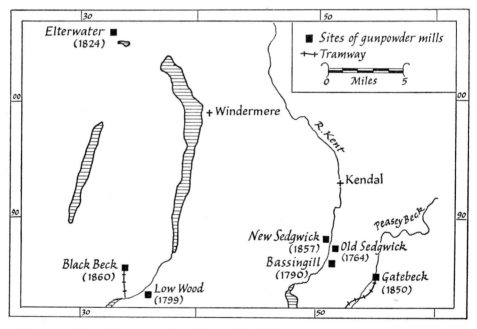

Map 13 *Sites of the gunpowder mills near Kendal.*

the bracken favouring the more open areas while the bilberry seems more tolerant of the shade cast by the oaks. Like Keskadale the almost pure oakwood of Birkrigg can be regarded as the remnant of what was once a natural woodland perhaps subject to coppicing or effected by the burning of the nearby heather. Some doubt on this suggestion has been cast by the fact that when William Gilpin made his famous tour of the area in 1772 and wrote a detailed account, he did not mention the high level oakwoods of either Keskadale or Birkrigg. Keskadale he described as 'a deep mountain recess, environed on every side except at the entrance by smooth, sloping hills which are adorned neither with wood, nor rock nor broken ground'. It is possible that when Gilpin made his visit the oakwood had been recently coppiced and was therefore not immediately obvious from some distance. When the wood is bare it does tend to fade into the sombre hues of the heather-clad hillslope above.

Another group of high-level woodlands occurs in the eastern Lake District around the lower end of Hawes Water forming Naddle Forest (4914). There are also two patches on the eastern side of Martindale, one of the valleys running down to Ullswater (4317). Naddle Forest is predominantly an oak-ash-birch association developed mainly on block scree formed of Borrowdale Volcanic rock. At the lowest levels, oak is the dominant tree, but above 1,000 ft it is gradually replaced by the birch, and there is much hawthorn scrub at the highest levels. The woodland is sufficiently open for bracken, bilberry and blackberry to grow in the light shade cast by the trees. On the other side of the valley below the ridge of the Harper Hills (5014) there is another patch of woodland and with its north-west facing aspect the ground is much wetter. At the lowest levels alder is now the dominant tree with birch, holly, ash and rowan making up the forest cover. The woods in Martindale occur in one of the less frequented valleys of the Lake District drained by the Ramsgill Beck. Two elongated patches line the eastern slope but they are mere remnants of a once more extensive forest cover (Plate 11a). The roe deer still roam the hillsides although the shelter afforded by the trees is now very limited. The upper wood at a height of about 1,000 ft is very damp and consequently dominated by the alder with straggling trees of holly, rowan and elm scattered throughout. The lower wood below Gowk Hill (4416) has been felled in the past and is made up largely of scrub which is at present re-generating the forest cover. Apart from the birch, all the common trees which might be expected to grow in such a situation are found in the wood. The soil cover of these eastern fells is much deeper than elsewhere owing to the thick deposits of head which mask the solid rocks below. Under natural conditions therefore it could support a dense forest. Clearance, however, began in pre-historic time and has left the area in its present rather impoverished state, with large areas of common land whose grazing rights are shared by the valley farms and villages like Bampton (5218).

These high-level relict woodlands cover such small areas that they contribute very little to the general wooded appearance of parts of the Lake District. Certainly the tree-covered landscape is the first striking visual impression of the landscape which greets the visitor approaching from the south. The shores of the southern lakes like Windermere and Coniston Water and the intervening fell carry extensive woodlands. For the most part this has all been planted in the past centuries in an attempt to restore the original forest cover after the depredations of the Norse colonizers and their monastic successors. In the eighteenth century the planting of trees was widespread in order to ensure a continuous supply of timber for the iron and local forest industries. Later, there were extensive plantings by landowners who were anxious to add to the picturesque appearance of their lakeside estates. The latter culminated in the introduction of foreign exotic trees which somehow have managed to flourish in their new habitat and are now accepted as a natural part of the Lake District scene. The small villa estates around Ambleside were in the forefront of a fashion which earned the commendation of Wordsworth. Trees natural to the area like the oak were also planted. Their beauty in spring, with the multi-coloured appearance of their leaf burst, has often provided a subject for the landscape painter or his modern successor recording the scene on colour film. The oaks which cover the western slopes of Windermere, as seen from Bowness Ferry, have delighted many with their fresh spring hues or deeper autumnal tints.

The great plantation movement began very early in the Lake District and certainly was well under way in the first half of the sixteenth century. The reason for the early start is not difficult to seek. Elizabethan mining activities, principally of copper, in both the Keswick and Coniston areas, created an almost insatiable demand for timber (Chapter 9). Together with the demands of the iron industry, based largely in the southern part of the Lake District and utilizing the wood resources of the Furness Fells, whole areas of remaining woodland were systematically cleared. The wood, principally the oak, ash and birch, was used for building purposes, for pit props, firewood and making charcoal. For the latter the ash was in particular demand in the manufacture of gunpowder, and perhaps it was no accident that the gunpowder mills were sited near the limestone areas where the ash flourished (Map 13). The demands of industry were so considerable that to possess a woodland was looked upon as a great fortune. In Elizabeth's reign there are records of the purchase of woodlands surrounding

9. *Penrith – with its collection of small market places.*

10a. *The Eastern Fells around Hawes Water.*

10b. *The head of Hawes Water drowned by the making of the reservoir.*

11a. *Relict woodland on the flanks of Martindale.*

11b. *Former open field across the Lowther valley at Whale.*

12a. *Low Hartsop –*
spinning gallery.

12b. *The abandoned workings*
of Greenside Mine.

Derwentwater from local landowners like the Ratcliffs and the Earl of Northumberland. One at Barrow (2620) consisted of 150 oaks, 300 ashes and 800 birches, and was therefore much prized for its valuable timber. Later in 1715 when the Greenwich Hospital Trustees were given the estates of the Earl of Derwentwater around Keswick they contained 6,000 oak, 5,000 ash and almost 3,000 other trees fit for cutting. As this area was once the centre of the flourishing Elizabethan smelting industry, it follows by implication that much of the Derwentwater woodland had been planted during the seventeenth century. Actual records of tree planting are few, although Richard Gilpin in the late seventeenth century stated that 'he was of the opinion that planting was the least expensive and one of the most productive modes of improvement.' In this he was echoing the much earlier views of Arthur Standish who in 1613 had published the first English book on forestry entitled *New Directions of Experience for the increasing of Timber and Firewood.* Vicar's Isle (now Derwent Isle) in Derwentwater (2622) contained a grove of sycamores recently cut down when Bushley was writing about the area in 1776, and planting here must have taken place early in the eighteenth century. About the same time the Ashness Hills (2718) above Derwentwater had been cleared of thorns and underwood, ploughed and planted with corn for two years before tree seedlings were introduced. Some of this wood still survives at a height of almost a thousand feet. Nearby, pines were planted and today these mature trees add greatly to the beauty of the 'Surprise View' overlooking Derwentwater known to everyone who walks up the Watendlath valley (Plate 5).

The great parkland estates, so characteristic of the Midlands and south of England, are not part of the Lake District scene. Where they do exist in the central mountainous area, they are usually small like those of Troutbeck (4205) and Glencoyne (3818). In spite of their small size they have many of the characteristic features of their larger counterparts. A sprinkling of trees amidst the green pastures, the occasional clump which might harbour pheasants or even an imposing avenue leading up to the house, are all found to some degree. Tree planting on these parkland estates was done mainly for its amenity and scenic values rather than for the economic return from its timber. Local trees like the oak and ash predominated although on many estates the sycamore, introduced into England from Central Europe after about 1550, was also greatly favoured because of its rapid growth and ability to withstand strong winds. The popularity of the sycamore was at its height during the eighteenth century, and great acreages were planted. Many of these were to become the ancestors of trees now found in the Lake District woods and along the lanes, for their winged seeds are ideal for rapid dissemination by the wind. Although the sycamore does not colonize bare ground, it readily infiltrates into existing woodlands.

For all the planting associated with the small parkland estates, it is the coppice woodlands of the southern Lake District which make the greatest impact on the scenery of the whole region. Here is one of the most wooded parts of Britain and all is virtually planted, with the original trees going back to medieval times (Plate 16a). It was then that heavy demands for timber arose through the establishment of bloomery hearths to smelt the local supplies of iron ore. So important was the charcoal obtained from the High Furness woods that the bloomery sites were located near the timber source rather than near the iron mine (Map 14). As a result numerous small bloomery smithies sprang up near the shores of Windermere and Coniston Water. It was here that the monks of Furness Abbey had their medieval bloomeries, bringing their iron from Low Furness on pack-horses or by boat along the lake. The site at Cunsey Wood (3793), half a mile up the beck from the shores of Windermere, is typical of many in the region. The smithy lay on the banks of the swift-flowing stream which provided the water power. Around lay the woods where the charcoal was prepared in hollow hearths or pitsteads. The iron probably came up the lake and was then carried for a short distance up the valley to the bloomery site. Right down to 1709 all the local iron was made 'in the bloomery way' as recorded by Stout in his *Autobiography*. Cunsey, however, had a longer period of activity than most, for when this rather primitive and wasteful medieval method of making iron came to an end a furnace was built on the site in 1711. Some of the remains of this, including the water leat, are still to be found amidst the heaps of slag. Working was always on a relatively small scale and this applied also to the supporting charcoal industry. This was based on small clearings in the woodland where the charcoal burner would live with his family in a hovel made of stones and roofed with turves while the burning took place (Diag. 4). For this a low circular wall or simply a hollow cut in the hillside was made and in it the wood was piled up to form a beehive mound and then covered with straw and finally a layer of earth. Inside, the wood was allowed to burn away slowly for about a week before the charcoal hearth was raked out. Although charcoal burning ceased just before the Second World War – the last site was working in 1938 near Town End Farm at Ealinghearth (3485) – the hearths or pitsteads are still occasionally seen in the woods. Good examples occur in the Graythwaite Estate Wood at Devil's Gallop (3694) and in Ridding Wood which forms part of Grizedale Forest (3394). At the latter site pitsteads are included in the Nature Trail laid out by the Forestry Commission. Years of wood-burning has led to a soil rich in potash, and so the

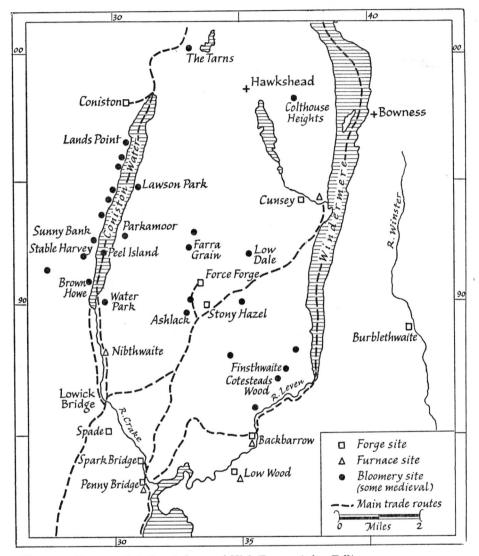

Map 14 *Features of the iron industry of High Furness (after Fell).*

pitstead area often stands out by its richer and more varied ground flora. The principal trees used in charcoal making were the hazel and ash, and the former is still very common in these Furness woodlands.

The heavy demands of the iron industry led to an almost complete exhaustion of local timber in many areas, and so a policy of forest conservation and management came into being. New woods were planted and existing timber supplies safeguarded by the practice of coppicing. This method of woodland management aimed at making the maximum use of the growing timber and thus ensuring a

turf roof

dry stone wall

hazel twig door

Diagram 4   *Charcoal burner's hut.*

lasting economic return. It involved cutting down the tree almost to ground level and then allowing new thin shoots to sprout from the base. These were then cut down at intervals of about fifteen years and the whole cycle was begun again. Only broad-leaved trees like the oak, ash, birch, hazel and alder could be treated in this way and in various parts of the Lake District pure coppices of one or other of these trees can be found. A good oak coppice occurs near Seathwaite (2296) in the Duddon valley, which doubtless supplied the furnace near Duddon Bridge (1988). Hazel coppice is more common in the Furness Fells, especially in the area between Coniston Water and Windermere. As the hazel is not really a 'natural' tree to the area, its presence implies that it was specially introduced for the purpose of coppicing. In the development of coppice woodland it was essential to enclose it to prevent grazing animals nibbling and destroying the young growing shoots. If enclosure was not possible, pollarding was often practised. Although this was not common in the Lake District, pollarded ashes do occur in the Watendlath valley (2716). It seems likely that these had their tops lopped to provide winter food for cattle who ate the bark and left the wood for fuel. Another variant of ordinary coppice was to allow certain trees like the oak and ash to grow to full stature. This kind of woodland, known as coppice-with-standards, was especially valuable as it supplied both a quick supply of timber for the charcoal industry as well as a source of larger timber for constructional purposes.

The coppice woods of the southern Lake District reached their greatest development during the eighteenth and nineteenth centuries when the iron furnaces were in full blast. The largest and most enterprising of these was founded in 1711 at Backbarrow (3584) in face of competition from ironmasters who had moved into the area from Cheshire and had established their own smelting furnace at Cunsey (3793) on the site of the much older bloomery. Other furnaces connected with the charcoal–iron industry flourished in the eighteenth century at places like Force Forge (3390), Burblethwaite (4189), Low Wood (3483), Spark Bridge (3084), Penny Bridge (3083), Duddon Bridge (1988) and Nibthwaite (Map 15). Apart from Backbarrow, where the ironworks has only closed down in recent years – now a rusting monument worthy of preserving as an example of industrial archaeology – little is to be seen at most of the smaller sites save heaps of slag or the water leat used to supply power (Plate 16c). At Nibthwaite there is a plan of the works as they existed in 1746 and it is possible to seek out the buildings which date from this time (Map 15). A large high barn, which might have functioned as a storehouse, lies near the road almost a mile from the southern end of Coniston Water (295882). Down by the Crake is the site of the forge, and, although the present mill is a later rebuilding, the old forge oven still survives. All these furnaces made heavy demands on the local coppice woods and by their presence encouraged large-scale plantings of trees like the hazel and oak. Demand often outstripped supply, and when Thomas Pennant visited the area in 1772 he reported that 'wood for the iron furnaces was sometimes wanting in those parts, so that charcoal was imported from Mull and other of the Hebrides.' He noted, however, on a journey from Ulverston to Coniston that there were 'thick coppices, or brush woods of various sorts of trees, many of them planted expressly for the use of the furnaces and bloomeries. They consist

85

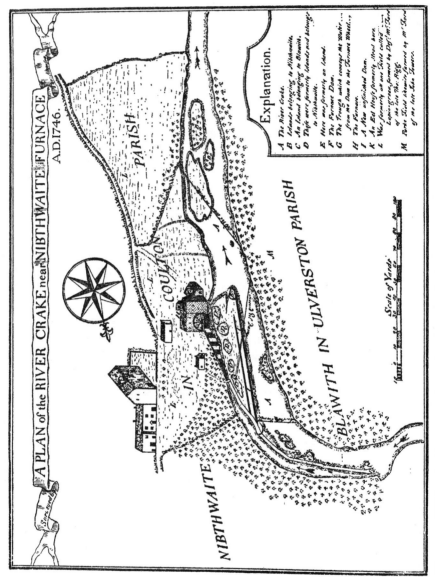

Map 15 *Nibthwaite Furnace, as it appeared in the mid eighteenth century.*

chiefly of birch and hazel; not many years ago shiploads of nuts have been exported from hence. The woods are great ornaments to the county, for they creep high up on the hills. The owners cut them down in equal portions, in the rotation of sixteen years and find them very lucrative.' It was this possibility of a good return from capital invested in woodland that caused John Curwen, the Cumberland agriculturist, to begin planting larch on Claife Heights (3797) above Windermere in 1794. This did not meet with the approval of Wordsworth, who could see no beauty in this introduced conifer.

The resources of the coppice woodlands had another use in the industrial economy of the area. Charcoal made from ash had long been recognized as the most suitable for gunpowder manufacture. Gunpowder mills were established on many of the streams where they could take advantage of water power and a nearby source of suitable charcoal (Map 13). The industry began in 1764 when a local Quaker, John Wakefield of Kendal, built the first gunpowder mill in the north of England. Previously it had only been manufactured in the south at places like Faversham and Waltham. Wakefield's first works were built on the east bank of the River Kent near Sedgwick (509875) where he could take advantage of a ten-foot drop of water to provide the necessary power. After working for some years, the power was found to be inadequate for his needs and he therefore built a further mill, half-mile downstream at Bassingill, in 1790. Here the massive foundations of the pits which housed the water wheels still remain. Great use was made of ash charcoal from High Furness and this prompted other similar gunpowder works at Low Wood (3483) in 1799, Elterwater in Langdale (3204) in 1824, Gatebeck (5485) in 1850 and Blackbeck (3385) in 1860. The main production was used for blasting in the mines of the Coniston and Keswick areas, although some was exported farther afield to places like Derbyshire. It was the invention of new explosives like dynamite for blasting purposes rather than inadequate charcoal supplies from nearby woods, that brought the industry to an end shortly after the First World War. By then most of the works were owned by I.C.I., who decided to concentrate the production of charcoal gunpowder at their factory at Ardeer in Scotland. Thus yet another of the local industries based in part on woodland resources came to an end after 150 years of continuous working.

One forest industry, the making of bobbins, has remained to the present time even though its days now seem numbered. Two bobbin mills are at present working in Furness, one at Spark Bridge (3084) and the other at Low Stott Park (3788) (Plate 16b). When the industry was at its height in the nineteenth century, small works were scattered throughout the woods of High Furness. Even sixty years ago it is said that some twenty-five bobbin mills were in production. Staveley (4698) was the main centre with five mills drawing their power from the rivers Kent and Gowan, but now only one survives. Competition from Norway and more recently the introduction of plastic has resulted in a gradual contraction of the industry. Up to now the bobbin mill at Stott Park has managed to continue working, though it now employs only eight men. Formerly great quantities of the local birch were stored in sheds alongside the mill but today they are virtually empty as good mature timber is now scarce. The mill has to use green wood and then dry it in kilns before being sawn into blocks from which the bobbins are shaped. How long it can survive under these conditions is problematical and yet while it is still working it gives a true glimpse of the past when many similar mills were turning out their products from the Furness woodlands.

If the planting of broad-leaved trees to form coppice woodland is looked upon as the main contribution to the developing landscape of the seventeenth to nineteenth centuries, then the Forestry Commission plantations – largely of conifers – must represent their twentieth-century equivalent. Prior to the formation of the Forestry Commission in 1919, softwood plantations had already been established in parts of the Lake District. The Marshall family, in particular, had been very active in the nineteenth century with their plantations at places as scattered as Chapel House (3986) at the south end of Windermere and the Hospital Plantation (2123) on the south side of the Whinlatter Pass. In the closing years of the same century, when the Manchester Corporation transformed Thirlmere into a reservoir, the surrounding area was heavily planted with spruce. This, they claimed, was a necessary part of the scheme in order to reduce siltation in the reservoir. The dark foliage and general forbidding atmosphere of the plantations were not to many people's liking and opponents of the Sitka spruce were as condemning as Wordsworth had been about the use of larch a hundred years earlier. The Forestry Commission, from the outset, was faced with similar vociferous opponents to their schemes of planting. Their policy and attitude in the early years did little to lessen the anxiety of those who feared that the whole of the Lake District would be turned into one vast coniferous forest. The woods the Commission established in areas like the Hospital Plantation, where the trees had all been recently cut down, did not prove objectionable in that they represented a continuing use of the land. When, however, they began to plant Ennerdale, largely with trees of a single species in strict uniformity, and then virtually excluded the public from the valley, opposition grew considerably. In 1935, however, an unofficial agreement was made between the Commission and various amenity societies to exclude planting in the central mountainous core of the

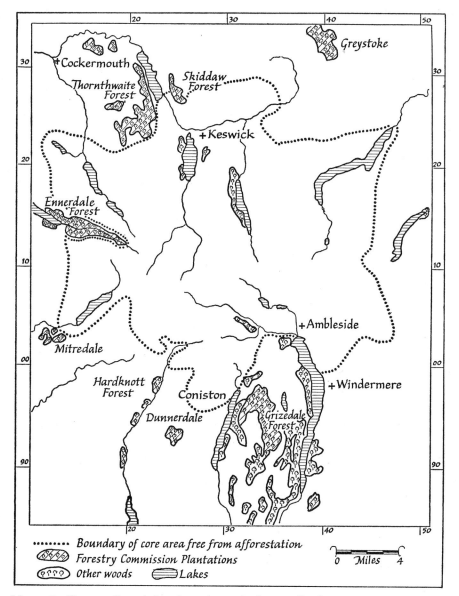

Map 16 *Forestry Commission plantation and other woodlands.*

Lake District (Map 16). Possibly more important was the fact that from that time the Forestry Commission adopted a less rigid policy with regard to types of tree planted and the exclusion of the public from their forests. There were, of course, considerable difficulties for the forester in achieving these desiderata. Much of the land they were able to acquire for planting was of poor quality, often degraded sheep walks. In such situations, with impoverished acid soils and heavy precipitation, only the spruce was likely to succeed. Access for the public would inevitably increase the danger of fire and so it became all the more necessary to have a regular geometric pattern of planting with wide fire breaks in between the blocks of trees.

Fortunately much has been learnt about the practice of silviculture during the past thirty years and this has helped to bring about a further change of attitude on the part of the Forestry Commission. When the 1935 afforestation agreement was re-affirmed in 1954 it showed much greater sensitivity to the amenity requirements of this unique region. In future plantings use was to be made of species to achieve as natural an effect as possible. Natural contours of the ground were to be followed as far as possible and notable viewpoints left unplanted. Roadside verges were to be encouraged and stream banks left free of trees. Many of these views were expressed in a report prepared in 1944 when it was decided to establish a Natural Forest Park at the head of Dunnerdale (known as the Hardknott Forest). Unfortunately many of the ideas to combine use and amenity were never really put into practice because of the continuing public hostility to afforestation, and the Hardknott Park was closed in 1959. In many respects this defeat for the Forestry Commission is to be regretted, especially as a new policy had much to commend it. New types of tree were capable of meeting the forester's needs and at the same time not infringing too much on the amenity value of the Lakeland. The Japanese larch, for example, which was introduced into this country in 1861, has great potentialities in this direction. It is very tolerant of the maritime conditions found in the Lake District and with its bluish-grey foliage and bright russet colour of its young twigs it is quite attractive. Compared with its European counterpart, so despised by Wordsworth, it casts a denser shade so that the plantations are darker and the ground flora less widespread. A possible alternative in the future is the hardwood 'rauli' beech which comes from South America. It is a very fast-growing tree comparable in this respect with the Sitka spruce. When more seed becomes available from the nursery plantation of Grizedale Forest, it is likely to make up an ever-increasing proportion of the trees planted each year by the Commission.

In spite of the fact that the Hardknott Forest Park no longer exists in name, a visit to the upper part of the Dunnerdale Valley (2195) clearly shows how a for-ward-looking policy of afforestation can be made acceptable even to those who associate the Lake District with open vistas of the upland fell. Planting began here in 1934, and although it was realized at the outset that only about 2,000 acres out of a total of 7,000 could be classed as plantable this did not discourage experimentation. This relatively low proportion of usable land is due to the fact that the former Forest Park included large areas of high fell where the soil is too thin and where there is virtually no shelter for trees to grow successfully. The upper limit of planting was therefore about 1,200 ft, and in many cases 1,000 ft was more usual. Even below these heights there is much bare rock and unstable scree which could not be planted. In some cases this was turned to advantage and on the western slopes of Dunnerdale around Hinning House (2399) the protrud-ing rock buttresses in a sea of green conifers is scenically very acceptable. Cer-tainly hereabouts the policy of afforestation has added to the beauty of one of the most lovely and unspoiled of the Lakeland valleys. Although the number of different species that could be planted was small because of the limitations im-posed by climate, aspect and soil, there is a pleasing admixture in many places. Both types of spruce, Norway and Sitka, are grown, the former on the better soils and in areas less likely to suffer from spring frosts. They are readily dis-tinguishable from each other because the needles of the Norway spruce are dark green and blunt while those of the Sitka have sharp points and are blue-green on top and silvery on their lower side. Next in importance to the spruces are the European and Japanese varieties of larch. Both shed their leaves in autumn and in spring burst into a new soft green foliage. With this seasonal rhythm and accompanying change of colour in their foliage, the larch has become much more acceptable as a plantation tree. Amenity planting of trees like the beech, which retains its russet leaves throughout the winter, and the red oak, have been attempted where the deeper soils give hope of success, often, as a roadside screen to the conifer plantations.

The development of Grizedale Forest (3394), which the Forestry Commission acquired in 1934, shows the new dual approach to afforestation and amenity perhaps better than any other area in the Lake District. Admittedly this part of High Furness lent itself to more adventurous treatment for, although it con-tained the usual run-down sheepwalks, there was also some old coppice wood-land and seven farms on improved agricultural land. Grizedale Hall, with its ornamental grounds, and Satterthwaite village were also included in the purchase so that there was great variety in the landscape even at the outset. This the Forestry Commission has tried to maintain through its policy of multiple land use. The first plantings began in 1937 and are still in progress. Rhododendron had been planted as an ornamental shrub in the area surrounding the hall but this had largely run wild and was smothering other vegetation. One of the first tasks of the Forestry Commission, therefore, was to clear part of this thicket before young seedlings from the nursery bed could be planted. As much of the coppice in the neighbourhood had been left unattended since the beginning of the century, it was untidy and overgrown. By allowing some of the bigger trees to develop, some of the coppice is in the process of being converted into high forest. In this way it is hoped to re-establish the original oak forest of Grizedale, putting the clock back a thousand years to the time before the Norse came to this 'valley of pigs' and cleared much of the natural woodland. On the surrounding fells the original degraded sheep pastures, dominated by bracken, heather and rushes, were planted with trees which could withstand the extreme conditions of the windswept uplands. On the slopes of Carron Peak (3294) rising to over a thousand feet, planting of Sitka spruce above and Japanese larch and Douglas fir below began in 1952. The use of larch has enabled grazing grounds for deer to be maintained and they have increased in numbers in recent years. The deer can, however, do considerable damage to young trees and therefore their numbers have to be limited by periodic shoots. Their venison and skins bring in a certain amount of revenue and at the Grizedale Centre a local cottage industry making leather articles has been developed. The Forestry Commission, through its Grizedale Estate, has gone to considerable pains to put itself on show to the visitor by establishing an information centre and shop, a forest nature trail, a wild life centre with a viewing tower and a research nursery. On average about 12,000 visitors a year come to see forestry conservation, in its accepted modern sense, in action.

In spite of an ever-increasing awareness on the part of the Forestry Commission of the need to take amenity values into account, the planting of vast acreages of softwoods – a policy largely dictated by the economics of forestry – has undoubtedly brought about a mass uniformity to many parts of the Lake District. The blanketing effects of managed woodland, the blocking out of viewpoints and the fencing off of large areas – mainly to keep out sheep and deer – have led to considerable resentment on the part of the fell walker, who wishes to enjoy an unbroken panorama. Fortunately the compromise reached in 1935 to the peripheral areas has helped considerably. Thus the central core with its highest peaks and upper sections of the radiating valleys will not see the mass planting which took place in Ennerdale. The central areas will thus be allowed to develop more naturally and it is to these parts that we must look increasingly for the minor differences in vegetation which lend so much character and unique-ness to the Lake District. It is here that one finds less common trees and shrubs like the holly, yew and juniper.

The holly is one of our few evergreen broadleaves and often forms sizeable trees when growing in oakwoods. Only its lower leaves are spiny to give protec-tion against browsing animals. Holly foliage, rather surprisingly, is quite pala-table and in High Furness it was formerly used as winter fodder for sheep. Thomas West in his *Antiquities of Furness*, published in 1805, describes how it was used in this way in the Middle Ages, and even when he wrote the practice had not completely died out. Clumps of holly were left after woodland clearance for use by sheep and it was claimed that animals fed in this way gave mutton of remarkably fine flavour. The holly had another practical use, for its white, even-grained wood was suitable for carving, turnery and inlay work. Its twigs were also gathered for firewood as they burned well.

The yew, a native conifer, is widely scattered throughout the Lake District although no longer as common now as place names like Yewdale (3098), Yew Pike (2092), Yew Bank (2690) and Yew Crags (2202) seem to imply. Perhaps the best known group of yews which has survived to the present day lies in the upper part of Borrowdale on the valley slopes opposite the hamlet of Seathwaite (2312). The yew is a common enough element in many of the mixed woods. In the Silurian foothill country to the south it often forms clumps crowning the rocky knolls where the soils are not so acid as in the surrounding areas. The tree shows a distinct preference for alkaline conditions and therefore commonly occurs in the 'flushes' of enriched soil. In the mixed woods of oak and ash, the dark green foliage of the isolated yew clumps often shows up better from a distance than within the wood itself. The tree casts a very deep shade so that ground flora is absent. It will, however, grow in shady conditions and will even thrive beneath the beech. Perhaps its most common setting is in the vicinity of many Lakeland farms. It is nearly always found within a walled enclosure as the foliage, bark and berries contain a poisonous alkaloid, taxine. If livestock browse the growing foliage when it is green they apparently come to no harm; rather it is the brown withered clippings of yew hedges that have proved fatal if eaten. The bright pink berries, too, can be swallowed by birds without harm and it is largely by these means that the yew spreads. In existing woods the yew regenerates freely and young seedlings are common. Many of the yews which are found in churchyards give the appearance of great age, but while it is believed that some can live for a thousand years many sizeable trees are probably not more than 200 years old. One difficulty in determining the age of a tree by the usual method of containery annual growth rings is that, in really old trees, the heart has rotted away leaving only a hollow casing. In younger trees this red heart wood is exceptionally durable and was formerly used to great advantage in gate posts and cleft fence stakes.

The native coniferous shrub, juniper, is also common in many parts of the Lake District and is often associated with degenerate woodland. Rather gorse-like in general appearance it is easily distinguishable by its blue-green needles, its blue-black berries and its resinous fragrance. Its survival in those areas where the original woodland has been cleared for sheep pasture is probably due to its unpalatable foliage. In some valleys, however, parts of the juniper thicket were once enclosed and encouraged to grow to give an early spring bite for sheep before the pastures were ready. Its most characteristic situation today is on the flushed soils of the valley sides. In Great Langdale juniper thickets occur at heights of 800 ft to 1,000 ft on the north-facing slopes of Lingmoor Fell above Oak Lowe Farm (3005). A more extensive spread, giving rise to an area of scrubland, occurs in the valley of Bleamoss Beck running down from the tarn into Little Langdale valley (2903). Other areas where it grows in a very stunted, almost prostrate, form are on the valley sides below the Coniston Fells, as around the old mine sites of Church Beck (2898) or below the slate quarries of Broughton Moor (2594). The juniper has few commercial uses, although its fine-grained odorous wood has been made into bowls or shaped for tool handles by the forest craftsmen.

Although the Lake District as a whole has a well-wooded appearance, certainly compared with other mountainous areas like Snowdonia, it is the grassland fells of the plateau tops which dominate the vegetation pattern. On the better soils and at lower elevations the most characteristic grassland species are the sheep's fescue and bents, generally termed Festuca-Agrostis pastures after their Latin names. These grasses will grow on the somewhat acid brown-earth soils but they do require good drainage and therefore are characteristic of steeper slopes. Pastures dominated by Festuca-Agrostis are the mainstay of the grazing animals of the fells. Over-grazing in the past has had serious consequences for the sheep seeking out the more palatable grasses. It has served to encourage the spread of mat-grass (*Nardus*) which is seldom, if ever, eaten. One of the surest signs of extensive grazing is the abundance of mat-grass together with the long slender green slaths of the moor rush (*Juncus*). This is particularly true of the wetter uplands above a thousand feet where the precipitation may exceed 100 inches and gives rise to thoroughly leached infertile soils. The long west-facing slope of the Coniston Fells below Walna Scar (2596) forms a typical habitat dominated by the stiff and brittle leaves of mat-grass. On the edge of peaty hollows, its dominance may be challenged by Blue Moor grass (*Molinia*), although this plant is not really common in the Lake District compared with the Pennines or Southern Uplands of Scotland. Where the boggy hollows contain standing water, as in the area of the Haystacks (1913), cotton grass, sphagnum moss and the moor rush are common elements of the vegetation and contribute to the formation of peat. At present deep peats are confined to a few of the flatter hill tops like those around Hawes Water. In the drier parts heather is common in similar situations although it only forms extensive moors on the Skiddaw Slate outcrop of the northern Lake District. Occasionally bilberry is associated with it as on the slopes

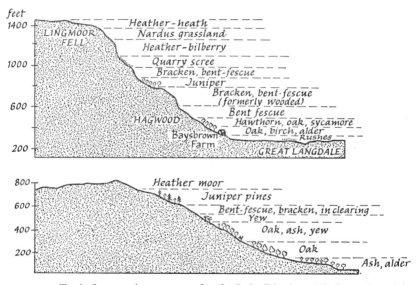

Diagram 5 *Typical vegetation transects for the Lake District: (a) Great Langdale (after Dewdney); (b) Silurian foothills (after Pearsall).*

of Great Langdale or the ridge of the Catbells (2419) between Newlands Valley and Borrowdale.

In the highest areas the sparse grassland is in competition with heath dominated by the woollyhair moss (*Rhacomitrium*). This plant seems ideally suited to colonizing the stony wastes found on many of the flatter mountain tops like Grasmoor (1720). The cover is usually incomplete and large patches of fine rocky debris may remain. On the summit plateau of Helvellyn (3315) there is some sparse sub-alpine grassland with a dwarf form of bilberry and the mountain sedge (*Carex*). This gives way in the more rocky places to the least willow (*Salix*

95

herbacea) while on the block screes of mountains like Scafell and Great Gable, the parsley fern, mountain fern and alpine lady's mantle often secure a precarious existence in the hollows between the rocky boulders. True alpine species of plant are rare even in the higher parts of the Lake District and where they do occur, as for example the Alpine Campion (*Lychnis alpina*) on Hobcarton Crags (1923) they have a very limited distribution. The alpine campion was formerly found on Coniston Old Man but the whereabouts of any plants now is kept a closely guarded secret in order to preserve them.

The details of the vegetation pattern in any one area are extremely complex and often difficult to unravel. On many of the steep-sided hillsides there is a pronounced zonation related to altitude. A study of the slopes of Place Fell (4016) overlooking Ullswater by Purrott and Harris in 1963 bears this out. The bold rock face of volcanic beds which outcrop in the upper part of the transect was under constant attack by weathering agents and has in the past contributed considerable quantities of debris which litter the slopes below. Soil cover is therefore thin at the top but attains a great depth towards the foot of the slope. This change from bare rock to a fairly deep soil is reflected in a corresponding progression from simple to more advanced plant communities. On the bare rock lichens formed bright green encrustations with fungi in places. Lower down where a soil cover existed mat-grass and bell heather had gained a foothold. Both had to withstand dry conditions at certain times because, with the rather large particle size, drainage was very rapid. Mat-grass can withstand dry conditions because its inrolled leaves reduce the rate of transpiration. Further down the hillside, as the soil cover becomes thicker, other plants like the wavy-hair grass and various ferns are found. They are in competition with bracken, the curse of many upland pastures because of its ability to choke out other forms of vegetation. Below the bracken zone, juniper takes over with individual shrubs reaching ten feet in height and en mass forming a dense thicket. A further bracken zone occurs below the juniper thicket but it is not so dense and other plants like the heath bedstraw and tormentil can gain a footing. The heath bedstraw, in particular, shows considerable tolerance of various habitats. Towards the lake shore grasses replace the bracken, and where the ground is very wet, sedges, rushes and ferns become dominant. Insectivorous plants like Sundew and Butterwort, with their special adaptation to derive mineral salts lacking in the soil, grow in the rocky crevices.

A similar zonal graduation of vegetation occurs on many of the lakeland valley sides, like that of Great Langdale above Baysbrown Farm (3104) (Diag. 5). On the plateau top, at a height of about 1,400 ft, Dewdney, Taylor and Wardhaugh showed that heather heath is dominant, hence the name Lingmoor. Where

13a. *Dacre Castle – an early-fourteenth-century pele tower.*

13b. *Lyulf's Tower, Ullswater – an eighteenth century folly.*

13c. *Miners' cottages, Glenridding.*

14a. *Askham –
an Anglian green
village.*

14b. *The estate
village of Newtown.*

14c. *The hollow
shell of Lowther
Castle.*

the heather is absent, perhaps due to past burning, mat-grass takes over, especially where the slopes are gentle and the soil waterlogged. At about 1,200 ft the plateau top gives way to the steep valley sides. Here a heather-bilberry association has developed, while below 1,000 ft grasses take over. As on Place Fell there is a dense juniper thicket at a height of 800–900 ft, and this is probably on the site of a former woodland, for tree stumps are occasionally encountered. In the disafforested area below the juniper thicket, bracken has invaded the pastures of bent-fescue grasses. Here in Langdale, as elsewhere in the Lake District, the bracken appears to have spread rapidly during the past sixty years, partly through a neglect of the pastures and partly through less intense grazing of the intake zone. Cattle, by trampling, even eating, the young green fronds seem to limit its spread, but sheep have little effect. Once established it is difficult to eradicate because it spreads through its underground stems or rhizomes. Only complete uprooting or continuous cutting of the fronds to exhaust the food supply of the plant seem effective in limiting its penetration into what was once good pasture land. With labour scarce and expensive, this often cannot be done and many of the former enclosures on the valley side have been virtually abandoned. While bracken is the curse of the local farmer there is no doubt that its russet autumn colouring on the fell side, especially in low evening light after a freshening shower of rain, has a certain attraction. To the botanist, however, it is yet another sign of man's inability to control vegetation changes he set in motion five thousand years ago when he began to clear away the woodland which once clothed the valley sides and lower fell tops.

4

The Lake District in prehistory

The great divisions of archaeological time seem to be extremely artificial as one surveys the history of man in the Lake District, not least when one considers the transition from prehistory to history. History begins when documents and written records provide the chief source of evidence; prehistory rests upon the finds of the archaeologist. In southern England prehistoric times end with the Roman Conquest. In the north this time-frontier is much more obscure, and never more than in the Lake District. Until the eleventh century A.D. there is an underlying unity in the history of the region, a unity that derives from the paucity of documentary evidence.

The last great phase of settlement in the British Isles took place in the tenth century A.D. with the Viking migrations. The economic life and society of the Lake District was profoundly influenced by this wave of settlement, but our knowledge of the period can hardly be drawn from documentary sources. It depends, above all, upon the interpretation of the hundreds of Scandinavian place names that have been given to topographical features, farms, fields, and hamlets among the mountains of the north-west. Place names provide a key to the unravelling of settlement history that stands between the hints thrown up by the distribution patterns of artefacts and the full documentary record of a series of events. Like the patterns on maps made by the finds of Neolithic stone axes or the stone rings and circles of the Bronze Age, the patterns of distinctive place-name elements must be understood against the bold features of the landscape. Then a geographical continuity is revealed in the fells and valleys of the Lake District that underlies the main epochs of prehistory from the settlement of the first Neolithic farmers in the fourth millennium B.C., through the period of upland

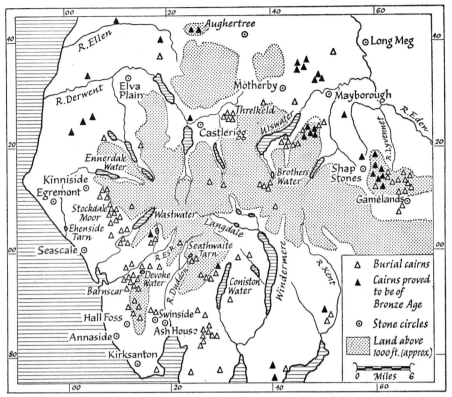

Map 17 *Prehistoric features, with their marked peripheral location.*

agriculture in the late Bronze Age, and through the Roman occupation to the shaping of the kingdom of Cumbria at the close of the Dark Ages.

The main tracts of prehistoric settlement lay in the lowlands that encircle the mountain core on every hand (Map 17). To the south and west, the Furness peninsula and the coastal plain of west Cumberland formed primary areas of occupation. Not only did they contain attractive flat-topped limestone hills but an extensive skin of cultivable boulder clays. A similar role was played by the limestone escarpments clustered around the head of Morecambe Bay. From Kendal to the mouth of the Solway Firth the peninsulas and valleys of the Lake District look out to the Irish Sea and Atlantic Europe. Neolithic farmers settled here from distant Iberia and almost three thousand years later the Romans established a port, *Glannaventa*, at Ravenglass (0896) on the mouth of the Esk. The lowland that encircles the mountain core to the east lacks any contact with the sea except where the Eden empties into the grey mudflats and sandbanks at the

99

head of Solway Firth. The links with the world beyond the Lake District lie across the long barrier of the northern Pennines. The Irthing–Tyne gap, threaded by the fortifications and settlements of the Roman Wall, and the pass of Stainmore have always provided the main corridors of access to the lowlands of eastern England. The Vale of Eden, like Furness and the West Cumberland plain, was an important zone of prehistoric settlement; and towards the west fingers of lowland stretch deep into the fells of the Lake District. The outcrops of the Carboniferous Limestone whose tilted table-topped hills attracted prehistoric settlement along the northern shore of Morecambe Bay recur even more extensively on the north-eastern fringe of the Lake District. Across Shap Fells the high limestone country of Westmorland forms an important focus of prehistoric settlement equal to that of the long lowland corridor of the Eden. The eastern flanks of the Lake District looked across the Pennines in prehistory. For instance, a wave of settlement in late Neolithic times, recognized by its distinctive Beaker pottery, reached this region from north-east Yorkshire. The Romans drove one of their chief trunk roads, much of it still heavy with traffic between England and Scotland, through the Stainmore Gap into the wide, spreading lowland of the middle Eden. At a later date, in the ninth century, the flood of Danish settlers that left such a deep mark on the human geography of Durham and the North Riding spilled through the Pennine gaps into the eastern fringe of the Lake District, impressing on the landscape its distinctive place-names and attractive village plans centred on wide rectangular greens (Plate 14a).

The Lake District and its encircling lowlands form one of the smallest and most compact regions of Britain. Scarcely twenty miles separate Ennerdale and the foot of Ullswater and yet at no stage in their histories can one discern many common features. The Ullswater region has always been joined to the Eden Valley. Ennerdale opens to the Cumberland plain and the Irish Sea, its link with the east closed by the crouching summits of Great Gable and Kirk Fell.

The mountain core of the Lake District, stretching from the High Street range in the east to the bleak unvisited outliers of Copeland Forest around Ennerdale, has been exploited and settled from its ring of surrounding lowlands and narrow plains concealed in valleys. Half a century ago, it was romantically believed on the evidence of the vast number of Scandinavian place-names that the mountainous heart of Lakeland remained an empty wilderness shunned by man until the incursion of the Vikings in the tenth century. In truth, man's long occupation of the mountains is evident at many places. Stone axes were quarried and roughly shaped high up on the screes that spread from the base of the Langdale Pikes in Neolithic times, and even higher and bleaker sites for prehistoric axe factories have since been revealed close to the summit of Scafell Pike at three thousand feet above sea level. Extensive forest clearance began among the central mountains in the Bronze Age and, at a later time, the Romans found that they could not neglect the fell country completely when they drove a road from Brougham across the bare, corrie-scarred summit of the High Street, leaving behind a place-name for all time. Upland pastures and hard glassy rock for the making of axes were the economic incentives that drew prehistoric men to the high central fells. The wealth of the Lake District still lies in its upland sheep pastures, that must have been first exploited more than four thousand years ago.

From Mesolithic times to the Iron Age
The record of man in the Lake District is far shorter than in most parts of southern Britain. The Palaeolithic period spans the greater part of the Ice Age and its important inter-glacial epochs, but no trace of man-made implements has been found anywhere in the Lake District. This cannot mean that early man as a hunter and food-gatherer totally neglected the north-west. Because the region was a major gathering ground of glaciers in every cold period of the Ice Age, one can only assume that all traces of occupation before the last twenty thousand years have been swept away. Even the Mesolithic cultures that flourished between 10000 and 3000 B.C. are traced with only the slenderest evidence in the Lake District. Small flint blades, typical of the sparsely scattered hunting groups in the British Isles about 8000 B.C., have been picked up among the sand dunes at the mouth of the Esk and from a site on the low boulder-clay cliffs of Walney Island. Unless new discoveries of Mesolithic flints come to light, perhaps from under the blankets of peat in the high fells, one must conclude that the region was largely neglected by man until the third millennium B.C. The analysis of pollen accumulated in the muds and silts on the floors of tarns has shown that man had no effect on the natural forest cover of the region in Mesolithic times. Even the highest of the tarns subjected to this investigation, Red Tarn (2603) caught in the bleak treeless gap, at 1,800 ft between Pike of Blisco and Cold Pike, was surrounded by an unbroken forest cover in the late Mesolithic period about 5000 B.C.

The continuous history of man in the Lake District and its surrounding lowlands begins with the Neolithic settlements about 3000 B.C. These settlers began the shaping of the landscape that we see today. The earliest and most important Neolithic sites lie in the coastal lowland outside the limits of the mountains. The maze of shifting dunes that covers most of the raised beach at the north end of Walney Island has revealed the site of a flint factory where pebbles from the boulder clay cliffs were shaped into scrapers for skins and tools for carving wood and bone. The sites of hearths, shell refuse from prehistoric feasts, and fragments of late Neolithic and early Bronze-age pottery all testify to the occupation of this place that looked across the Duddon estuary to the vast dark hummock of Black Combe. There is a similar Neolithic and early Bronze Age site on a raised beach among the sand dunes at Eskmeals (0893), and again two miles further north in the complex of sand dunes at Drigg.

The coastal flint-working sites provide only one clue to the life and economy of Neolithic man in the Lake District. In fact, it is believed that they represent temporary summer encampments and that the permanent settlements lay further inland. By a stroke of good fortune one of these places is known. It was discovered almost a hundred years ago when a small tarn was drained near Beckermet in West Cumberland. As the land was cleared and ploughed up there came to light the remains of a Neolithic settlement, with hearths, several stone axes and a number of remarkably well preserved wooden objects – two fish spears, a dug-out canoe with its paddle and a beech haft that was still attached to a polished stone axe. Ehenside Tarn also yielded an abundance of Neolithic pottery and a stone quern for grinding corn which suggests that cereals were grown there. Although the site was discovered in the 1870s, it still yields fresh facts about the Neolithic period through a re-examination of its material by techniques that were undreamt of only a few years ago. Recently the radio-carbon technique of dating archaeological finds has been applied to the wooden objects from the site and has revealed a date of between 3314 and 2714 B.C. Ehenside Tarn presents a tantalizing glimpse of the life and economy of the lowland fringe of the Lake District almost five thousand years ago. It cannot be the only settlement of Neolithic farmers who were raising stock and growing corn in this region at that time, about 3000 B.C. Only within the past three years the remains of another prehistoric settlement have come to light on the edge of an extensive moss, Storrs Moss, set in a bowl of the limestone hills between Carnforth and Silverdale. Here the remains of a house have already been uncovered – proof of a permanent settlement preserved, as at Ehenside, down the centuries in an enveloping peat-bog.*

The most fascinating clues to the human geography of the Lake District in Neolithic and early Bronze Age times are provided by the pale grey-green stone axes found at several places in the surrounding lowlands. Two such axes were discovered at Ehenside tarn and another has turned up at the Gray Crofts stone circle near Seascale. A small collection of four axes, made of the same pale green rock, was uncovered in a crevice of a limestone outcrop on the flat-topped hill to the north of Urswick tarn – an area rich in the evidence of prehistoric

* Personal communication from Professor Frank Oldfield.

settlement. The source of these axes and many others lies in the highest and least accessible part of the Lake District's mountain core between upper Langdale and the summit of Scafell. The distinctive rock of which the axes are made has been traced to its source in an outcrop among the precipitous crags of the Langdale Pikes (2707). It is a fine-grained volcanic ash, part of the Borrowdale Volcanic Series that forms all the rough and shaggy mountains of the central Lake District. The rock was hardened and compressed in the mountain-building movements of the Palaeozoic period, and as a result sharp and durable cutting edges can be made from this material. The stone axes were roughly shaped at chipping floors on the terraces beneath the crag of Pike of Stickle and at the head of the steep scree that falls towards the windy trough of Mickleden (Map 18). The site was discovered in 1947 and a thorough exploration of these precipitous and scarcely accessible slopes has uncovered the details of the industry. The screes and the ledges of Pike of Stickle are littered with roughly-shaped axes and broken cast-offs, but no finished polished specimen has yet been found here. It is believed that the manufacturing process at Great Langdale was carried only as far as the making of 'rough-outs'. The axes were then exported from Langdale by tracks that led across the mountains to coastal settlements where the implements were finally shaped and polished, perhaps with the help of rubbing stones made from such suitable material as the gritty St Bees sandstone.

At Pike of Stickle it is believed that the chief source of material for the making of the axes lay in the tumbled masses of boulders at the head of the scree, and that the Neolithic craftsmen found little need to quarry the living rock from the face of the precipice. On the east side of the crag, at almost two thousand feet above sea-level, lies a tiny cave. It is scarcely seven feet in depth and only five feet wide at its mouth. The vertical sides of this bleak shelter and the horizontal roof, split along a bedding plane in the rock, suggest that it is a man-made feature. Though no certain proof of the age and origin of this rock shelter has yet been found, it seems most likely that it was made and used by the colony of workers on these high and inhospitable slopes above Great Langdale more than four thousand years ago.

The striking discovery of the axe factory at Pike of Stickle has been followed by the revelation of several other sites on suitable outcrops of volcanic tuff in the high mountain core of the Lake District. For instance, in 1952 'rough-outs' were picked up beneath the precipices on the south face of Harrison Stickle (2807) and still another axe factory has been located around Mart Crag (2608) on the dreary moor, flecked with the rich dark brown of peat hags, that drops northward into the head of the Langstrath. Apart from the group of factory sites around the

103

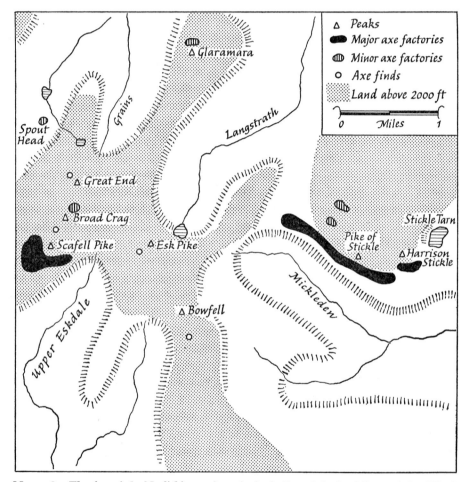

Map 18 *The sites of the Neolithic axe factories in the Langdale–Scafell area (after Plint).*

Langdale Pikes, the most spectacular discovery which was made in 1959 with the location of another cluster of Neolithic sites close to the summit of Scafell Pike (2107). Here the outcrop of a blue-grey volcanic tuff, part of the Borrowdale Series, provided another suitable axe material that was easily quarried from the screes on the higher slopes of the mountain. In the same year two more axe factories of Neolithic origin were revealed to add to the complex of workings in the highest and most inaccessible fells at the heart of the Lake District. One was discovered on Great End, the dark, precipice-bound northern tip of the Scafell range (Plate 38a); the other lies on the tumbled rocky crest of Glaramara, a place blanketed in peat with protruding crags and tiny glassy tarns.

Within the past twenty years our knowledge of the Lake District in prehistoric times has been revolutionized. Formerly it was thought that men shunned these bleak heights. One could believe that the builders of the magnificent stone circle (2923) near Keswick turned their backs on the encircling panorama of mountains. Now one knows that they and their forerunners had carefully explored and exploited the resources of the highest and most inaccessible places in the quest for the right material for the making of axes. The central parts of the Lake District can no longer be reckoned as a region that was first effectively exploited by the Viking farmers of the tenth century with their flocks of sheep grazing the high summer pastures of the fells; instead we have to cast our thoughts back over at least another three thousand years to the time when the axes from the Langdale Pikes were valued all over the British Isles. It has been estimated that a third of the Neolithic axes found in the Isle of Man have been made of rock from the Lake District. The same distinctive material appears in finds at Bournemouth and Gloucester, all implying a long-distance trade by sea and land from the manufacturing centres of the Lake District (Map 19). Again the Langdale rock appears in axes found in the Aire Gap and the Yorkshire Dales, implying an easterly traffic of the factories' products.

If the mountains of the Lake District lay at the centre of a wide-spreading Neolithic trade network, one can, alas, only speculate upon the details of its organization. Probably the axe factories worked for only a few weeks in the summer, parties of experts making their way into the mountains from the lowland settlements to prepare the 'rough-outs' for transport to the finishing sites. But this implies a network of beaten paths into the interior of the Lake District, of trade routes for the export of half-finished axes from Scafell and Great Langdale. One of the curious facts about the discovery of the Neolithic axes on the Scafell range is that the first implements were picked up on the marked tracks and clearly beaten routes that lead to the mountain summit. In fact, one specimen

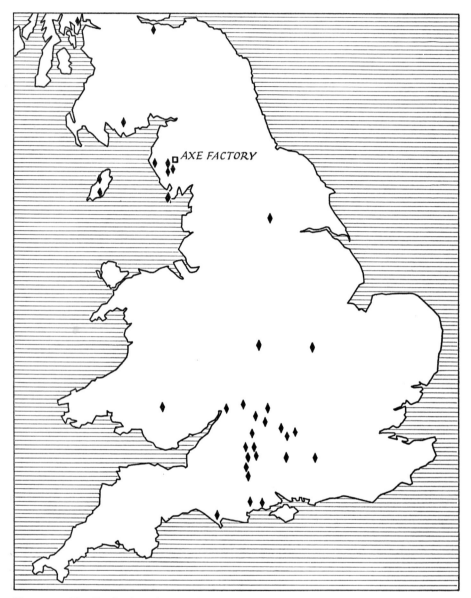

Map 19 *The distribution of axes whose source is the Great Langdale factory (after Bunch and Fell).*

was found in the centre of the path that climbs to Scafell Pike from Wastwater by Lingmell Gill, and its surfaces were scratched by the passage of countless nailed boots. Here is a hint, however faint, that the many tracks of the mountain fastness may date back to prehistoric times. The first exploiters of the hard volcanic tuffs were probably as keenly aware of the subtleties of topography – the winding routes through screes and crags – as they were of the minor differences in geology that made one place of high economic value as a source of axes and another one completely useless. It is quite possible that the present 'trunk route' of the central fells running from the head of Great Langdale by Angle Tarn (2407), Esk Hause (2308) and the Styhead Pass (2209) was already in existence four thousand years ago. The caravans of hikers that throng this airy route with its glimpses of distant mountains and valley depths are probably following in the footsteps of the axe-making specialists of the Neolithic Age who were making for Windy Gap (2110) and the descent into Ennerdale on their way to settlements and places of export in the West Cumberland plain. The distribution of stray 'rough-outs' in the country to the east of the Langdale factories suggests that export routes led in this direction across the hummocky summits of Silver Howe (3206) and Loughrigg Fell (3504) towards Ambleside and the head of Windermere. Here transport by water, down the lake, probably allowed the traffic to reach the shores of Morecambe Bay and the settlements of the Furness peninsula. Further east still, the find of a Langdale axe near Troutbeck (4102) points to a prehistoric route across Thornthwaite Crag (4309), High Street (4411) and High Raise (4413) to the Neolithic and Bronze Age settlements on the eastern fringe of the Lake District around Bampton (5118), Shap (5613) and Crosby Ravensworth among the limestone hills of east Westmorland. It seems as if the line of the road engineered by the Romans across the empty wilderness of High Street was first pioneered in the days of the Neolithic axe trade, more than two thousand years earlier.

The peoples of the Neolithic period also left their mark on the landscape in a number of stone circles. Seventeen survive in all, scattered over the Lake District and its adjoining lowlands. The most famous circle, Castlerigg, stands on what seems to be a miraculously flat piece of land in this tumbled landscape a mile to the east of Keswick (2923) (Plate 3b). Thirty-nine irregular-shaped stones are arranged in a circle of 110 ft diameter; in turn, and on a clear day, they are surrounded by one of the most breath-taking mountain panoramas that the Lake District can offer. A similar ring of standing stones, Swinside (1788), occupies a moorland bench at almost seven hundred feet above sea level beneath the dark heather-grown eastern slopes of Black Combe. Four other similar monuments lie within a mile or two of Swinside. Among the eastern fells, at Shap (5613), six granite boulders survive to locate the size of a stone circle that was partly obliterated in the making of the railway. It seems to have possessed a feature unique among the megalithic circles of northern England – a long avenue of standing stones that pointed to the north-west. Today only nine of these stones remain strewn over a distance of two miles. They suggest something of the grandeur of the monument at Shap, a grandeur that was much more evident to the traveller in Elizabeth I's reign when Camden could write of 'several huge stones standing in a row for nearly a mile'. Another monolithic circle at Mayburgh (5128), is now marked only by a grassy rampart and a single standing stone, though it is known that eight were still upright in the eighteenth century. The purpose of the great stone circles remains a complete mystery, although the remnants of hundreds still survive from Wessex to Wales and the Outer Hebrides. Victorian antiquarians connected them with religious practices and they were described as temples where fanciful rites and ceremonies connected with sun worship were carried out. In recent years a more sober study of the layout and dimensions of many of these monuments has thrown up the idea that they were all set out of fixed principles in relation to the risings and settings of sun and moon and a few bright stars at the different seasons of the year. They were, probably, the first astronomical observatories and themselves huge communal calendars that provided reminders of the great moments – the summer and winter solstices and the equinoxes – in the passage of time. Whatever the purpose of the great stone circles their sites tell us about the location of the chief centres of population in and around the Lake District about 1500 B.C. None was raised among the highest mountains, and the monuments point to the coastal plain of West Cumberland, the Eden valley and its tributary the Eamont and the widening of the Derwent plain around Keswick as the chief areas of settlement.

The great stone circles of late Neolithic times and the early Bronze Age must be distinguished in the Lake District from the many smaller rings of stones that lie half buried in the heather among the foothills of the western and eastern flanks of the region. They were constructed in the late Bronze Age, five hundred and more years later than the megalithic circles, when the burial customs of cremation were dominant all over the British Isles. One of the most important excavations of a late Bronze Age circle was made by W. G. Collingwood in 1909. It stands on Banniside Moor (2896), a bracken brown wilderness in autumn and early spring dominated by the crags of Coniston Old Man, that is rich with the remains of prehistory and neglected by tourists at every season of the year. Within the circle of low boulders Collingwood found two urns containing the ash and bone fragments from cremation burials. Banniside Circle also provided a rare glimpse into the life of the Bronze Age when it yielded a fragment of charred woollen cloth, one of the earliest proofs of textile manufacture known in the British Isles. Again, at Lacra (1480), on the miniature range of hills to the west of Millom and overlooking the sea, is a complex prehistoric site with four stone circles. Here an excavation in 1948 uncovered a burial urn similar to that from Banniside Moor, dating from the period between 1000 and 750 B.C.

The stone circles and cremation burials are only one surviving feature of the Bronze Age on the foothills of the Lake District. In addition, hundreds of cairns and tumuli on lonely sites were probably erected in the centuries about 1000 B.C. More than sixty of these cairns and barrows have been opened and investigated by antiquarians and archaeologists over the past hundred years and proved to date from the Middle and Late Bronze Age. Many more sites, rough heaps of stones in the heather, have yet failed to yield any proof of their age and origin.

The distribution pattern of the burial circles and cairns points to important changes in the human geography of the Lake District between 1000 and 500 B.C. Most of the sites are clustered on the lower fells well above the coastal plains and valleys at heights between 700 ft and 1,000 ft above sea-level. The broad dissected bench that flanks the Old Man of Coniston to the south is littered with the evidence of Bronze Age settlement. Further south the craggy hills of Woodland Fell (2689) and Subberthwaite Common (2587) are covered with hundreds of tiny, roughly heaped stone cairns which are now overgrown with heather and hard to recognize. But in this region the most impressive site lies on the gentle slopes of a boggy hollow on Heathwaite Fell (2587). Here the footings of stone huts and relics of an enclosing wall seem to indicate a permanent settlement. The same kind of prehistoric patterns on the landscape are resumed in the fells that overlook the West Cumberland plain. A long series of scarcely explored sites stretches from the scattered clusters of cairns on the fells above Bootle (1289) to Kinniside Common (0811) and the approaches to Ennerdale. At one place alone, on the bare rocky slopes around Devoke Water (1597), twelve hundred cairns have been counted within a two-mile radius of the tarn. In the same area the hut circles and walled enclosures at Barnscar point to a permanent settlement and here archaeologists have unearthed two Middle Bronze Age burial urns that help to date the occupation of these fells. Even more tantalizing is the lonely country beyond Wastwater on the western slopes of Copeland Forest, unfrequented by the Lake District tourist and, as yet, scarcely explored by the archaeologist. Here Stockdale Moor (0908) rises to almost a thousand feet above sea level out of the dark green mantle of coniferous forest plantations in the Bleng valley. It is thickly strewn with the evidence of prehistoric settlement, faint though it may seem to the superficial eye scanning the ground for the first time. Stone cairns occur by the hundred; and walled enclosures, hut circles and the evidence of former fields point to former settlements. The use of this land by farmers and mountain shepherds could range from almost any period between the later Bronze Age and the Middle Ages. Until the sites yield objects that help to date their origins and time of occupation, one can imagine Stockdale Moor inhabited in turn by Bronze Age farmers, communities of Celtic speaking Britons at the time of the Roman occupation, Viking shepherds in the tenth century, or again sheep farmers from the Cumberland plain exploiting the grazings of the higher fells during the summers of the fourteenth and fifteenth centuries. Nature soon reclaims her own; within a few decades an abandoned settlement and its fields are transformed into faint mounds and hollows in the landscape.

The inner heart of the Lake District from Buttermere to the high mountains above Ullswater is devoid of evidence of late Bronze Age settlement, but once one descends in the east to the fells at about a thousand feet extending from Shap towards Penrith the clusters of cairns and other signs of occupation return. Both to the east and west of the highland core of the Lake District there seems to have been an advance of settlement in the Middle Bronze Age, about 1000 B.C. One can only speculate upon the reasons for the taking in of fresh land, in many places beyond the thousand-foot contour, at this time. The pressure of growing population in the coastal plain possibly compelled the new clearances in the foothills. There is certainly no evidence of population disturbances and resettlement caused by the influx of waves of fresh colonists from Europe. An improvement of climate expressing itself in higher mean temperatures and a lowered average of annual rainfall possibly favoured the migration of farmers into the fells. The evidence of upland settlement in the Lake District is matched by similar abandoned prehistoric sites in other parts of Britain. For instance, the high bare western slopes of Dartmoor and Bodmin Moor are thickly strewn with cairns, walled enclosures and hut circles that have been dated to the late Bronze Age. Similarly, the moors of north-east Yorkshire were colonized at this time about 1000 B.C.

Although the prehistory of the Lake District presents so many unsolved problems, research has recently revealed the profound effects of man on the landscape of the region in the Neolithic and Bronze Ages. A systematic investigation of pollen preserved in the muds and silts deposited on the floors of mountain tarns is producing details of the Lake District's vegetation in prehistoric times. Sites at a number of tarns in the south-west have already been published and they reveal a pattern of vegetation change that points to the extensive clearance of woodland by man. All the pollen records show a closed, undisturbed forest until a time that has been dated at about 3000 B.C. The highest tarns in the investigation, Blind Tarn at 1,850 ft on the Old Man of Coniston (2696) and Red Tarn at 1,700 ft among the Langdale Fells (2603), suggest that forest grew up towards the two-thousand-foot contour. The higher summits of the Lake District must have protruded from a sea of forest that filled all the main valleys and spread on to the lower fells and heavily glaciated platforms that now stand rocky, bare and treeless. The first profound change in the natural forest cover of the region, about 3000 B.C., is marked by a sharp decline in the pollen of the elm. At Red Tarn (2603) and Blea Tarn (2904) the proportion of elm pollen falls from 20 per cent to between 2 per cent and 4 per cent. This striking change in the composition of the woodland probably marks the entry of Neolithic farmers into the north-west. It is believed that the earliest Neolithic settlers gathered elm leaves and young green shoots as fodder for their animals; so began the opening up of the virgin forest. The Elm Decline, as it is called, and the first forest clearances belong to the third millennium B.C., the period of the exploitation of the hard volcanic rocks at the axe factories on the Langdale Pikes and around the summit of Scafell. Both of the tarns in the vicinity of the Langdale axe factory – Blea Tarn (2904) and Red Tarn (2603) – show the first period of forest clearance vividly with the deposition of a band of mineral silt, the result of increased erosion on bared hillsides. It seems that stock-grazing in woodland clearings accompanied the specialized groups of workers who were employed high up on the screes beneath Pike of Stickle. Here perhaps is the first faint evidence of the practice of transhumance in the fells – the leading of sheep and cattle from lowland settlements to graze the valley heads and lower mountain slopes in the summer months.

The pollen record of the tarns shows a later and severer phase of prehistoric woodland clearance. This is particularly evident in the curves of tree pollen from Devoke Water (1597) and Seathwaite Tarn (2598). Devoke Water, as we have already noted, lies in a countryside rich with the evidence of prehistoric settlement. The melancholy rain-soaked moors around Seathwaite Tarn bear traces of prehistoric occupation, and close by, beyond the curving climbing ridge of Walna Scar, lies the high bench above Coniston Water clustered with cairns, enclosures and the sites of former fields. The pollen diagrams from both tarns show a sharp decline of all tree pollen and the intrusion of the pollen of cereals as well as of the weeds that accompany cultivation. A sudden rise occurs, too, in the pollen of heather. The work of the botanist here supports the findings of archaeology in suggesting a colonization of the upland fringe of the Lake District towards the close of the Bronze Age. In this period we reach one of the vital stages in the making of the landscape of the Lake District. As Winifred Pennington has written in her important piece of research on the south western Lake District 'early complete deforestation is shown in the tarns where the remains of upland settlement are abundant'. The peculiarly desolate scenery of the inter- mediate heights, as on the barren knobbly fells of the Eskdale granite around Devoke Water or the dun grassy slopes of Caw Fell (1210) that fall to Stockdale Moor, is most likely the result of extensive and thorough woodland clearance by prehistoric man from settlements such as Barnscar in the centuries after 1000 B.C. The rugged barren qualities of the Lake District, now so highly prized as the remnants of a natural landscape, are in fact the result of man's activities in farming, stock-rearing and the search for fuel three thousand years ago. The activities of these Bronze Age farmers seem to have impoverished the region, perhaps severely. The samples of mud from the lake floors show that accelerated soil erosion followed the woodland clearance. The character of the soils changed too; the humus-rich brown earths of the forest floor gave way to the pale leached podsols that are characteristic of most of the upland parts of the region today. Heather spread and flourished in the place of woodland on the acid podsols. Man's interference with nature, as Bronze Age settlement spread on to the lower fells, has been an important factor in the creation of the present landscape of the Lake District. The deposition of sediment in Devoke Water testifies to these important changes that took place after 3000 B.C. Mud and silt gathered on the floor of the tarn at a rate ten times that of the steady accumulation of the pre- vious five thousand years. Forest clearance in the catchment basin of this little tarn inevitably speeded up soil erosion. The deep gullies and gashed hillsides, so characteristic of the bare landscapes of the fell country, testify to the effect on the balance of nature of man's first dramatic large-scale forest clearances in the north-west about three thousand years ago.

The Iron Age and the Romans

The artefacts and archaeological features of the Iron Age are sparse in the Lake District and appeared late in time. One of the most characteristic objects of the Iron Age landscape in south Britain was the 'hill-fort', enclosed by deep ditches and ramparts of earth, stone and wood. Today their weathered relics crown hill- tops and windy spurs such as the Wrekin, the exposed escarpment of the Cots- wolds or the crest of the Lower Greensand ridge in Kent. Some Iron Age forts lie in lowland sites of no strategic value, presenting great problems of interpre-

15. Coniston Fells in the foreground give way to the country of the Langdales beyond. All are fashioned in volcanic rocks and have been heavily glaciated with sharp arete ridges and dark corrie basins, associated with typical ice-shorn topography.

16a. *Coppice wood with standards.*

16b. *Bobbin mill at Low Stott Park.*

16c. *Backbarrow Iron Works – ripe for preservation as a monument of the Industrial Revolution.*

tation if their primary purpose was one of defence in the disturbed times just before the Roman invasion. But detailed research at a few sites has recently uncovered a more lasting purpose with centuries of occupation from 300 B.C. until after the Roman withdrawal in some cases. Whatever the functions of the 'forts', they seem to have been important elements in the tribal societies of Iron Age Britain.

The only hill fort among the mountains of the Lake District is marked by a crumbling, ruinous wall that encloses the gaunt cold summit of Carrock Fell (3433), at a height of more than two thousand feet (Diag. 6). Little is known about Carrock Fell's hill-fort apart from a plane-table survey made by R. G. Collingwood on a still hot July day in 1937. He mapped the line of the broken wall and searched for signs of hut circles within the five-acre enclosure, but found nothing. Neither has anything been discovered yet that will allow a dating of this earthwork on a high and isolated Lake District summit. Only its plan, the nature of its site, and the massive masonry of the western entrance make it almost certain that the Carrock Fell enclosure belongs to the Iron Age. Collingwood believed that it was built shortly before the Roman Conquest when the Lake District passed under the control of Brigantes, a Celtic tribal federation that ruled most of northern England at that time. The site of Carrock Fell hill-fort bears a close resemblance to the ramparted summit of Ingleborough in the Pennines where there is evidence of occupation in the form of a cluster of hut circles. Collingwood saw Carrock Fell as the brief symbol of Brigantian power over the mountain country of Cumberland and Westmorland. The gashes in the rampart and the shapeless heaps of rubble among the heather where the drystone walling has collapsed represented for him the destruction wrought by the Romans upon this 'Brigantian stronghold' soon after their conquest of northern England. One wonders; time and weather, twenty centuries of north-country gales and perhaps an equally long period of grazing the high summer pastures by large flocks of sheep could have brought the Iron Age earthwork on this awesome site to its present desolate state without the help of Roman troops bent on the security of the north.

The remaining Iron Age camps of the north-west all lie outside the mountain-core of the Lake District. For instance, one site occupies the summit of the flat-topped limestone hill to the north of Urswick Tarn in Low Furness. Another camp crowns the summit of Warton Crag, a rocky limestone tableland over-looking Morecambe Bay. Farther inland, in the main valleys of the Lake District, a number of small enclosures, defended by ramparts and ditches, probably belong to the period of the late Iron Age and the Roman occupation. If they have

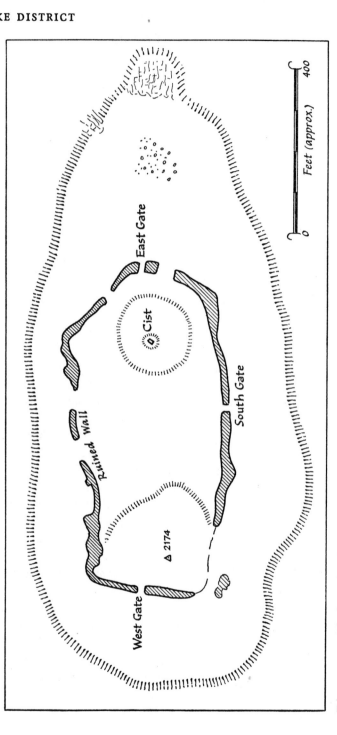

Diagram 6 *The Iron Age hill fort on Carrock Fell (after Collingwood).*

any meaning in the settlement geography of the region as assembly places, as well as defensive points, they suggest that each major valley was a separate unit. The Derwent valley contains two such sites – Castle Crag (2415), perilously placed above the Jaws of Borrowdale, and Castle How (2030) on a rocky peninsula that projects into Bassenthwaite Lake. Castle Crag has yielded some proof of its age in the form of smelted iron ore and fragments of Roman pottery. Ullswater has a similar earthwork on a steep rocky hill at the foot of the lake (4624), and in the adjoining valley of Hawes Water an encampment of the same kind occupies a remote spur at 1,200 ft above sea level (469127). Another small Iron Age earthwork overlooks the fertile Kendal basin from the southern tip of the Helm (5388). Again, at the entrance to the Vale of Troutbeck, where the ancient road comes down from the High Street, stands the rectangular-shaped enclosure on Allen Knott (4101). The little forts in the main valleys that lead to the heart of the Lake District probably point to the chief knots of settlement at the time of the Roman occupation. The exploration and uncovering of these settlements is badly needed because they could provide an important link between prehistoric and medieval times in the evolution of the Lake District's landscape.

The lower fells and valleys on the fringe of the Lake District contain abundant evidence of settlements that seem to have been abandoned for many centuries. At every site we find the same kind of features. Faint embankments, now deeply weathered and overgrown with grass and bracken, are built of upright stones with infillings of rubble. Often the embankments form enclosures that contain hut circles, the scarcely discernible outlines of the foundations of simple dwelling houses that were built of stone, turf and brushwood. The faint lines of ancient trackways can sometimes be picked out between the enclosures, and at many of these forlorn settlements one can make out the shapes of fields (Diag. 7).

One such settlement lies on the slopes of Aughertree Fell (2638) at 900 ft above sea level, where the last outposts of Cumberland's mountains fall to the Solway plain. Here, on a site that still awaits detailed exploration, three large nearly circular enclosures contain hollows that may be hut circles and are associated with a complex of tracks and fields. R. L. Bellhouse, writing about Aughertree, has said that this 'was probably a native village occupied during the Roman period'. Further south and west, at the foot of Crummock Water, we find the faint evidence of another clustered settlement with hut circles and embanked enclosures at Lanthwaite Green (1620). The western fringe of the mountains presents abundant evidence on the ground of early settlements that are now abandoned. Here we face the hard problems of dating these primitive deserted sites. A complex of enclosures, hut circles and cultivation terraces occupies the all but swallowed into nothingness over the centuries, may be faintly traced on the hills of the south-east around Kendal. At High Borrans (4300), the name of the modern hamlet refers to the 'ruins' and points to the much older occupation of the site. The upper Kent valley contains an undated site at Millrigg (4602); and the pastoral basin of Kendal, set in limestone hills, possesses the remains of a village on Heaves Fell (492870) that has yielded proof of its time of occupation. The exploration of the site, early in this century, showed two enclosures with embankments built of a double row of limestone slabs and an infilling of rock fragments. A few finds – a bronze ring and a blue glass bead – suggested that the place was inhabited in the third and fourth centuries A.D.

When the Romans entered the Lake District about the year A.D. 80, they found a Celtic-speaking population scattered through the coastal lowlands, in the Vale of Eden, and in tiny settlements that reached almost to the 1,000 ft contour in the encircling rim of fells around the high, bleak mountain core. The chief aim of the Roman occupation of north-west England was to ensure the peace and prosperity of the towns and villa estates in the south and east of the country. The Lake District stood at the very limits of the Roman Empire. Across the Solway Firth lay Scotland, never completely conquered. Westward the sea led to Ireland, a place where the Romans never set foot. The Lake District served a double purpose in the political strategy of the Romans. The coastal plain of Cumberland acted both as a springboard for invasion and the extension of Roman power and also as a defensive apron against incursions from Scotland and Ireland. Roman ports at Ravenglass (0896) and Maryport served as bases for the conquest of south-west Scotland, and the theory has been held that they were founded for the fitting out of an invasion of Ireland that never took place. The role of north-west England in the defence of the Roman Empire is best illustrated by the frontier system of Hadrian's Wall. Bowness-on-Solway stands at the western end of the continuous linear earthworks, but recent research has shown a continuation of Hadrian's defences in a chain of signal stations and forts along the coast of Cumberland almost to St Bees Head. Another element in the Roman strategy was to secure peace and cooperation from the Celtic-speaking Britons. It is believed that the road connecting the head of Windermere with the mouth of the Esk at Ravenglass was built to reach into the mountain fastness of the central Lake District.

The distribution of Roman roads and forts in and around the Lake District points clearly to their strategic intention, but they also hint at a relationship with the facts of human settlement and economy already established at the time of the Roman entry into northern England (Map 20). Most of the Roman stations and

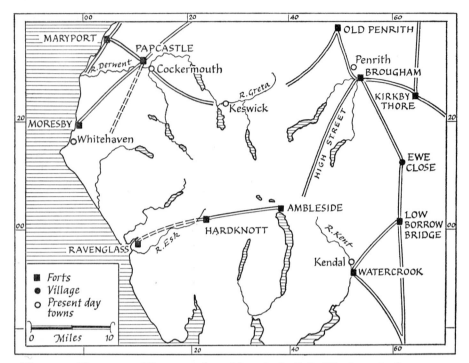

Map 20 *The system of Roman roads and forts in the Lake District and adjacent area.*

roads were probably built within half a century of Agricola's occupation of the north-west – many around A.D. 80 in the first stage of the conquest. A major centre of interest lay in the valleys of the Eden and the lower Eamont. The two main routes of entry into the north-west of England converged on the Roman fort of *Brocavum* (5328), located at the confluence of the Lowther and the Eamont. Here the Roman road through the Stainmore pass in the northern Pennines meets the route from Chester by Manchester and Ribchester and the upper Lune valley. The same district around Penrith is rich with the remains of earlier prehistoric periods, and the nearby site of the Iron Age fort on the windy lookout of Carrock Fell suggests that this region was an important unit in the tribal organization of the Brigantes before the Roman Conquest. On the south-eastern edge of the Lake District the Roman fort of *Alavne* was placed in a meander curve of the river Kent at Watercrook (5190). Again there are many hints that the conquerors were deliberately raising their standard in an established area of Celtic settlement. A little more than a mile from the Roman station

118

the relics of an Iron Age fort occupy the southern crest of the Helm (5388), a site with that most suggestive of place names – Castlesteads. Again, in west Cumberland, the fort on the steep spur of Hardknott (2101) turns its back on the wild depths at the head of Eskdale beneath Scafell and faces down the valley towards the sea and Ravenglass, a valley whose flanking upland benches are strewn with the evidence of prehistoric settlement (Diag. 8). The Roman fort

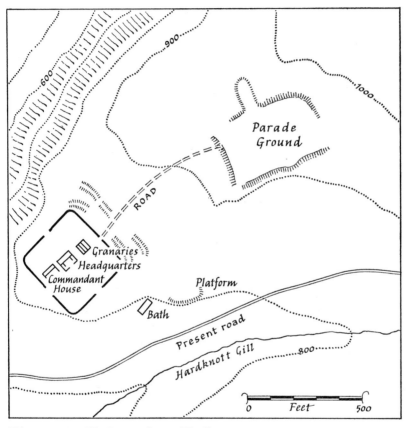

Diagram 8   *The Roman fort at Hardknott.*

and settlement at Papcastle (1031) was known as *Derventio*, a name that still lives in the river Derwent that flows beneath the Roman site. But the name Derwent is older than the Romans and comes from a Celtic source meaning 'abounding in oaks'. It must have been in existence and used by a British community before the Romans appeared in the Lake District.

Two areas of north-west England were neglected by the Romans during their three centuries of occupation – the high mountains at the heart of the Lake District and, a region of vastly different character, the Furness peninsula. Fragments of Roman pottery and stray coins have been found in both these areas, but nothing in the form of paved and surveyed roads and planned fortresses suggests that the Romans had any direct impact on the life of these regions. To the north of the Ambleside–Ravenglass road and westward of the route that climbs out of the Vale of Troutbeck across the roof of High Street there is no indication of the Roman presence until one reaches Papcastle and the hilly moraine-cluttered lowland between the northern spurs of Helvellyn and Skiddaw Forest. There, above the Trout Beck, a little tributary of the Glenderamackin River, we find the sites of two adjacent Roman camps (3827).

The Roman neglect of the Furness peninsula presents greater problems than their disdain for the mountain core of the Lake District. There were certainly British settlements on the low limestone fells at Urswick and Stainton; and the analysis of pollen preserved in the peats of Ellerside Moss, on the Leven estuary, shows that cereals were grown in the lands adjoining Morecambe Bay in Romano–British times. A Celtic-speaking population must have survived in Low Furness through the period of Roman rule without the direct presence of the armies in the peninsula or the apparatus of a military occupation. The Romans it appears, turned all their attention to the creation of a secure frontier zone northward beyond the Lake District's mountains, hence the elaborate chain of forts, signal stations, mile castles and roads that run from the Solway Firth into the Tyne Gap. For the rest, forts were planted in the main centres of population around the central core of mountains. The remotest district of all, Furness, was left alone – secure between the sands and tides of the Duddon and Leven. It has often been stated that the Roman forts at Papcastle, Hardknott and Ambleside kept watch over the rugged interior of the Lake District, a land that could be neither occupied effectively nor quelled. It seems just as likely that this was thinly-peopled country that offered little danger to the Romans and in which they showed no great interest. The Roman forts represent the political control of the already established tribal units of the north-west, units centred on the tracts of country where the valleys of the Lake District begin to open to the surrounding lowlands.

There is much evidence to suggest that the Roman forts became the centres of small urban settlements during the third century A.D. Such places, with market functions and craft industries, often took up an area larger than the fort to which they were attached and they were inhabited by retired Roman soldiers and Celtic-speaking natives. The various inscriptions collected at Brougham show that there was a civilian settlement, a small town, adjoining the fort to the east on the road that leads to Kirkby Thore, itself now proved to be an important Roman town in the Eden valley. At Ambleside a civil settlement flourished on the flat ground among the sharp little rocky knolls just to the north of the fort. But Papcastle provides the most impressive proof of the evolution of a Roman fort into a larger civil settlement. The fort of *Derventio* crowns the summit of a hill whose slopes fall gently southward to the Derwent. Its full outline was traced for the first time in the 1950s after an aerial survey by J. K. St Joseph, though the place has been an object of interest for antiquarians since the sixteenth century. Camden, writing of Papcastle in his *Britannia* in Elizabeth I's reign, refers to 'the carcase of an ancient fort whose Roman antiquity is attested by not a few monuments'. The finds of Roman objects at Papcastle suggest that a settlement stretched from the hill-top fort down to the bank of the river and that the whole site was enclosed by a rampart and a ditch. Pottery and coins from Papcastle show continuous occupation from the early years of the Roman conquest of the Lake District until the close of the fourth century. As elsewhere in the region of the northern frontier, the civil settlement seems to have grown outside the fort during the third century.

Ravenglass illustrates the same theme of a Roman fort and a Romano–British civil settlement sited in a populated lowland region. One of the finest Roman remains in the north of England stands in a pine wood some distance to the south of the rampart of *Glannaventa*, Roman Ravenglass. Antiquarians believed it was a villa, until R. G. Collingwood, in 1928, identified the building as a bath-house, sited outside the precinct of the fort as at several places along Hadrian's Wall. Walls Castle, as it is now called, is remarkable among Roman remains because the walls still stand to their full height (Plate 31b). Ravenglass boasted a civil settlement, perhaps a port-town, to the north of the fort. The Roman place-name, *Glannaventa*, throws out a dark hint about the history of this settlement. It means 'the town on the bank' and the prefix is of British origin. The suffix *venta*, meaning a place of commerce, was used by the Romans in the naming of towns in other parts of Britain. We find it in Venta Icenorum (Norwich), Venta Belgarum (Winchester) and Venta Silurum (Caerwent) – all of them capitals of British cantons. It seems most likely that a British settlement was already in existence at the mouth of the Esk when the Romans began the systematic occupation of the north-west about A.D. 80. Perhaps it was the human geography of the Cumberland plain at the time of the conquest that determined the founding of one of the most important Roman sites at this point on the coast.

The links with the Celtic past are clearly visible in the pattern of the Roman geography of the Lake District, and never more than in the road that climbs to more than 2,600 ft among the eastern fells, a road that has given its name, High Street, to the range of mountains. We have already suggested that this is a route of great antiquity along which the Langdale axes reached settlements in east Westmorland. Another clue to its age appears in an early-thirteenth-century document where the road is named as the *Brethestrete* or the 'Briton's road' – a plain hint that the upland track was not an original Roman construction but of earlier origin and a route in regular use by the British.

The Romans were not interested in the development and settlement of the Lake District and its fringes. There is, for instance, no proof that they attempted a systematic exploitation of the minerals of the region. This was a Celtic backwater in the lee of one of the most elaborately conceived frontiers of the Roman world; most of their energy in the shaping of a primitive landscape went into the making of that frontier. Over the centuries of Roman occupation the natives of the Lake District borrowed much from Roman culture and moved into settlements adjacent to their forts. The extent of this local Romanization may be sensed in the fact that a rare edible snail, said to have been brought to these islands by the Romans, may still be gathered in the fields at Papcastle.

5

The Dark Ages – from the Romans to the Vikings

The abandonment of Britain by the Romans was one of the great turning-points in the political history of these islands. In the microscope of local history the major events of the national political calendar assume less importance, and if we turn our thoughts to the slow processes by which man shaped the landscape the world of politics ceases to have any meaning. The exact date of the Roman withdrawal from the north-west is hard to determine. The absence of coins of a later date than the third quarter of the fourth century at sites along the Roman Wall led R. G. Collingwood to the view that troops were removed and Roman government was extinguished about the year 383. Others have contended that the occupation of some places continued for at least another decade. But the end of Roman rule did not destroy social life and the economy of the north-west. Instead, there are many hints that communities lived on, perhaps for several generations, in settlements attached to Roman forts. Small groups of people, deeply influenced by Roman speech and Roman ways of life, formed one thread in the human geography of the Lake District in the Dark Ages. Eric Birley points to the continuance of settlements with urban features in his account of Old Carlisle which he suspects 'survived for many a long year after the departure of the Romans as a centre of sub-Roman civilization in Cumbria'.

Apart from the settlements attached to the Roman forts, we noticed in the last chapter that the Lake District abounds in places that seem to have been inhabited from the late Iron Age onwards. Now they are deserted. Practically every valley in the Lake District yields evidence of these early settlements. A few sites have been mapped and described, as at Threlkeld (3224), Stone Carr (4128), and Millrigg (4602) above the Kentmere valley. The fact that they belong to the

Roman period and the sub-Roman decades seems to be well established, but the full length of the occupation of most deserted sites still remains a mystery. It has been suggested that the settlement at Threlkeld was actively occupied from the third to the eighth centuries A.D.

Even if so much remains to be discovered about these deserted settlements, a visit to a few of them provides a valuable exercise in the study of the Lake District's landscape history. Two such settlements, Stone Carr (4128) and Threlkeld (3224), stand in the wide corridor that extends from Penrith to Keswick. A minor Roman road runs through this countryside from Old Penrith to the site of the Roman camps north of Troutbeck station (3827). Stone Carr stands on the edge of a miniature limestone escarpment (Diag. 9). One can still pick out the grassy circular hollows with slightly raised edges that betray the foundations of huts, and a distinct sunken trackway leads into the hamlet from the west. Stone Carr persisted for a long time in the memory of the people of the district, not only as a topographical feature but also as a meeting place for sports and games. Clarke, the writer of *A Survey of the Lakes of Cumberland, Westmorland and Lancashire*, published in 1789, describes the place as 'an encampment of the Romans' and says that 'time out of mind races and other sports were held there – wrestling, leaping, tracing with dogs'. This is not the only ancient site in the Lake District to be perpetuated by the folk memory in this way, long after its real functions were extinguished. King Arthur's Round Table (5228) served a similar purpose at Eamont Bridge.

The settlement at Threlkeld (3224) occupies an even more dramatic site (Plate 3a). From a height of more than 800 ft above sea level it looks directly across the valley of the Glenderamackin to the high, dark precipices and razor-edged ridges of the southern face of Blencathra. To the west, the eye is led across the vast, treeless slopes of Skiddaw to the distant grey-blue outlines of the mountains beyond Keswick. The details of the site resemble those of Stone Carr, though now not so easily traced upon the ground. Hut circles and the foundations of old walls, made of rubble and upright stones, are almost obliterated with grass and heather. The Threlkeld settlement is divided by a high stone wall, thrown up at the enclosure of the common in the nineteenth century. The enclosure commissioners used the ancient site as a quarry and were largely responsible for its almost total obliteration from the landscape.

Today, the Threlkeld site ranks among the most instructive in the Lake District. The elementary features of the view, the mountains that lie all around, cannot be very different from the time when the settlement was inhabited more than fifteen hundred years ago. It is likely that more woodland survived along the floor of the Glenderamackin and on the lower slopes of Blencathra and Skiddaw, though this assumption is far from secure when one remembers the evidence for the prehistoric clearance of woodland in other parts of the Lake District. Apart from the site of this British village that is now almost obliterated,

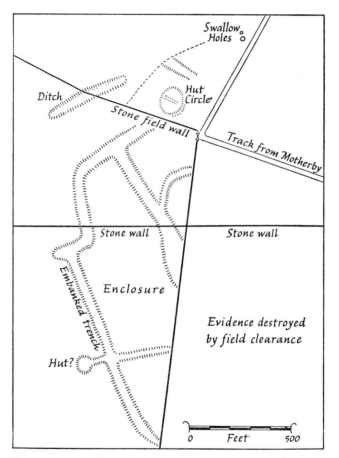

Diagram 9 *Enclosures at Stone Carr, near Motherby.*

the Celtic period has left its mark in the name of the mountain that dominates the scene. The first element of the name Blencathra is the same as the Welsh term, *blaen,* meaning 'point' or 'top'. The second part of this mountain's name has been distorted out of all recognition down the centuries so that its original

125

British form and meaning is now lost to us. Nevertheless, in the name of Blen-cathra, a mountain that is a landmark for many miles around, we find a link with the time when a Celtic-speaking community lived among the enclosures of the Threlkeld settlement. They must have referred to the overshadowing mountain by the same name. For the rest, all that this view contains has been added since. On the other side of the valley, overpowered by the massive form of Blencathra, stands the village of Threlkeld – a string of cottages and farmsteads on the Kes-wick road – and the outlying hamlet of Scales (3426). Both names are Scandi-navian by origin and probably derive from the Norse settlement of the Lake District in the tenth century. Below the farms of Threlkeld, on the gentle slopes that fall to the Glenderamackin, one can pick out clearly the walled rectangular-shaped enclosures that once formed the 'townfield' of the village – an open field whose strips were enclosed in the 1840s.

The historical relationship between the deserted Dark Age site at Threlkeld, on the south side of the valley, and the flourishing settlements at the foot of Blencathra presents a fascinating and insoluble problem. If the Celtic village represents the primary occupation of this part of the valley, the creation of Threlkeld and Scales may be considered as Norse intrusions on the uninhabited northern slopes of the Glenderamackin about A.D. 1000. Even so we are left in total darkness about the date of the abandonment of the Celtic settlement. Is it possible that Celtic and Norse-speaking communities existed side-by-side until the tenth century or later? The continuance of a British name, Blencathra, for the most important feature of the local landscape suggests that the two peoples lived there together, the Norse settlers and their descendants taking over the original name of Blencathra into their own speech. Its original sound became so much distorted that the modern philologist is unable to discern its primary form and meaning. Ultimately, the Celtic element in the population was absorbed by the later settlers and the hillside site abandoned. But this is only one hypothesis that can be constructed from the evidence presented by the landscape of Threl-keld. One striking feature of the Dark Age village, as one walks through its faint hummocks and hollows, is its unfavourable northward-facing aspect. All around the site the ground is waterlogged, even after one of the dry spells that are a feature of the late spring and early summer in the Lake District. One can only conclude that the Celtic-speaking settlers of the Glenderamackin valley chose a second-rate site for their primary settlement, if indeed this was their primary settlement. Threlkeld and Scales, south-facing and sheltered by the huge shoul-ders of Blencathra, occupy a far superior position. It seems equally likely that a British settlement once stood in this more favoured part of the valley on a site that is now completely obliterated by the farms and cottages of Threlkeld. Under this hypothesis the deserted enclosures, high on their northward-facing bench, represent a secondary settlement in the sequence of Celtic occupation. Like many of the forsaken Romano-British and Dark Age villages and hamlets of the Lake District it lies well above the level of permanent farms at the present time. The abandoned British sites may represent a wave of native settlement that colonized much of the poorer marginal land in the Lake District in the prosperous times of the late Roman period, the third and fourth centuries when towns flourished at Kirkby Thore, Brougham, Old Penrith, Papcastle and Old Carlisle. Such settlements, harsh and forbidding as many of the sites are, were probably abandoned after the fifth century, just as today we can find ruined and forgotten mountain farms that were created out of the period of high prosperity in agriculture at the beginning of the nineteenth century, to become derelict with the changes in world trade and economy after 1880. If this view of the evolution of settlement in the Glenderamackin valley is correct, the inferior north-facing slopes of the valley were probably abandoned by permanent farms before the Norse settlement took place. Threlkeld village emerged out of the mingling of Briton and Viking, and perhaps the town field goes back to a much earlier clearing of the primeval woodland in the valley floor than that accomplished by the Norsemen in the tenth century.

Celtic place names and church dedications
The roots of the Lake District's landscape history lie in the misty Celtic past of the region. The evidence of this period that reaches into the prehistoric Iron Age and looks forward for five hundred years from the Roman withdrawal to the Norse settlement is not to be found in documents, the normal sources of history. It belongs to the names of rivers, mountains, farms and villages scattered over the landscape, to holy wells and churches dedicated to the saints of the Celtic world in the centuries after the Romans, and to poems handed down the centuries to some medieval scribe by word of mouth – poems that mingle fact and fantasy in the retelling of heroic deeds that embrace all the Celtic lands from Cornwall and Brittany to the Firth of Clyde. For the whole of Cumberland only one document exists for the period before the Norman Conquest, and that is a late copy of a lost original about a grant of a fragment of land in the north-east of the county. The documentary history of the north-west only begins with the twelfth century, with the Pipe Rolls, Assize Rolls, the Pleas of Forest and the cartularies of the monasteries. In reconstructing the geography of the seven centuries between the Roman withdrawal and the creation of the great marcher lordships

by the Normans, we are concerned with the dark hints and insights contained in the landscape and the indirect evidence of place names.

We have already discussed the striking survival of a Celtic place name in Blencathra. A survey of the names of natural features, especially rivers and mountains, in Westmorland and Cumberland reveals an important Celtic element throughout the region. Many of the river and stream names are Celtic. Cocker, Derwent, Eden and Esk – to mention only a few of the important rivers of Cumberland – take us back before the penetration of the north-west by the Angles in the seventh century. The river names of Westmorland are not as strongly Celtic as those of Cumberland. They include the Kent, the Mint and probably the Winster. But of the eighteen major river names of Westmorland less than half, seven or eight, are of Celtic origin. It seems that the Anglian and Norse settlements of the southern and eastern fringes of the Lake District obliterated the Celtic past more effectively than in the north of the region.

The most striking Celtic survivals in the names of the north-west are those of the rivers, but many other elements from the British vocabulary may still be recognized in the names of topographical features. 'Glen' corresponds to the modern Welsh *glyn*, a valley; it appears in Glencoyne near Ullswater. The Welsh prefix *pen*, meaning head or summit, appears in Penruddock (4227) and Penrith. The latter place name opens up many suggestions about the evolution of the eastern flank of the Lake District in the Dark Ages. Penrith is formed from two British place-name elements – *pen*, the head or top, and *riton* which is the equivalent of the modern Welsh *rhyd* meaning a ford. As the topography lacks any outstanding feature apart from the Beacon (5231) outside the town to the east, Ekwall has suggested in his *Dictionary of English Place-names* that the element *pen* is to be understood in a political or social sense as 'the chief place' or the centre of government of the district. No documentary source exists from which one can reconstruct the political geography of the Lake District in the period after the Roman Conquest, but here in a place name that has lived down the centuries there is a hint that Penrith was the focus of an area that probably encompassed the north-eastern flank of the region from Carrock Fell, with its Iron Age fort, to the moors around Shap.

If we survey the distribution of Celtic place-name elements in the Lake District today, we find there are surprisingly few amid the mountains and deep valleys of the central core. It suggests that this area was only thinly populated before the Norse settlements of the tenth century came to make such a deep impression on the landscape. The sparsity of Celtic topographical names in the interior is supported by the distribution pattern of deserted Dark Age settlements, which are largely confined to the foothills that encircle the high central mountains. On the fringes of the Lake District two areas stand out as important tracts of British settlement. First, as we have already discussed, there are the foothills of the north-east drained by the Eamont and its tributaries. A second Celtic area lies to the north-west between the Ellen and the Derwent, where we find such names as Torpenhow (2039), Blindcrake (1434), Redmain (1333), Tallentire (1035) and Gilcrux (1138) – all containing British place-name elements.

In Westmorland Celtic elements are not as widely and richly distributed in the place names as in Cumberland. Celtic names occur most frequently in the north of the county, scattered across a band of country that reaches from the shores of Ullswater through Moor Divock (4822) and Shap into the limestone fells of the northern Pennines. For the rest the Celtic element, apart from its survival in some major river names, is negligible in southern Westmorland. However, this does not mean that the hinterland of Morecambe Bay was rejected by the British of the post-Roman period. In fact, the sites of deserted settlements such as Millrigg (4602) and High Borrans (4300) suggest the opposite. The very accessibility and attractiveness of these southward-facing hills and valleys, rich with boulder clays and good limestone pastures, means that the intensity of Anglian and Scandinavian settlement was such as to change earlier Celtic names out of all recognition or to obliterate them completely. The same theme occurs in the more westerly peninsulas of the Lake District that project into Morecambe Bay as parts of Lancashire. The district of Cartmel has only two Celtic place names, Cark and Blenket. Furness reveals the British background to its place-names in only two of its rivers, the Leven and the Crake, and the survival of the name Roose, the same as the Welsh *rhos* meaning a moor or heath. But it is most unlikely that the surviving Celtic place names present a true picture of the extent of British settlements in the two peninsulas in the post-Roman period. Not only is there the witness of several deserted settlements, but Cartmel yields a unique fragment of evidence contained in a half-sentence of a medieval history. The *History of St Cuthbert* records that the district of Cartmel was given by King Ecgfrith, who ruled Northumbria from 670 until 685, to St Cuthbert for the establishment of a monastery and he was granted 'Cartmel and all the Britons with it'. Here is proof of a British community on the southern fringe of the Lake District at the close of the seventh century.

The pattern of Celtic place-name elements surviving in the Lake District provides a clue to the distribution of population in the region between the fourth and seventh centuries A.D., from the departure of Roman troops and officials to the intrusion of the first Anglian migrants across the Pennines from the kingdom of Northumbria. Another hint of what was happening in these undocumented centuries of history in north-west England is suggested by the dedications of churches and holy wells. Cumberland alone has more than a hundred holy wells and springs dedicated to the names of saints. Many of these have no connection with the early years of the fifth century when St Ninian, founder of the monastery at Whithorn, preached Christianity in the north-west, or the later evangelizing campaign of St Kentigern in the sixth century that led to the foundation of several churches. Many of the dedications of wells and springs probably originate in the twelfth and thirteenth centuries when the Crusades stimulated the cult of pilgrimages to holy places, and the writing of the lives of St Ninian and St Kentigern had created an interest in two missionaries especially associated with the north of England. Some dedications date only from the eighteenth century when numerous antiquarians, pursuing their interests in the wake of the great national topographer Camden, littered the countryside with labels drawn from classical history and mythology, folk-lore, and the founders of the early Christian church.

Neglecting the many false trails, it is clear that St Ninian left his mark on the Penrith region. Three miles to the east of Penrith a simple grey church stands on the edge of a terrace of the Eamont in a landscape of great pastoral beauty, utterly lonely and isolated (559299) (Diag. 10). It is dedicated to St Ninian; and it seems likely that he preached at this place and founded a community of Christians there early in the fifth century. As the parish church of Brougham it acquired in late medieval times the name of Ninekirks – a name that probably preserves in its first element the memory of the founder saint. The romantic folk-lore that gathers around topographical names has suggested an alternative explanation that the church was rebuilt nine times – a most unlikely history for which there is not a scrap of evidence. Brougham Ninekirks was entirely rebuilt in 1660 by Lady Anne Clifford, Countess of Pembroke, whose anachronistic medieval tastes have left a distinct imprint on the buildings of the Appleby region. But a fragment of a moulded stone, dating from the twelfth century and now built into the east wall of the chancel, provides proof of the Norman church at this site.

St Ninian's church can only be fully appreciated if one explores the fields and woods close by, where the Eamont plunges through a shallow sandstone gorge on its way to join the Eden. Here, lost in the summer green shade of oak woods and deep with bracken, you find some shallow caves worn in the soft red rock of the undercut river cliff when the Eamont flowed at a higher level. W. Douglas

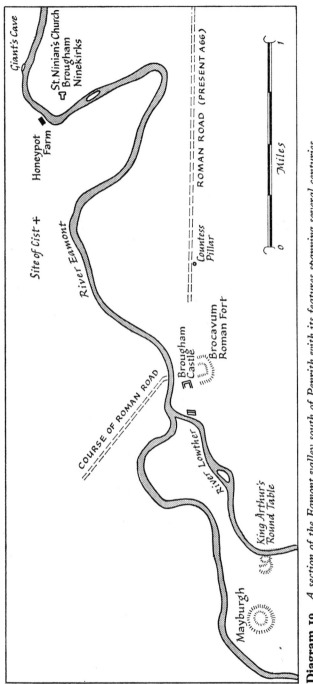

Diagram 10 *A section of the Eamont valley south of Penrith with its features spanning several centuries.*

Simpson has produced a convincing theory that the caves formed an essential element in the choice of site for the church at Brougham Ninekirks in the fifth century. The Christian church of Celtic Britain in the decades after the Roman retreat insisted upon lonely and isolated sites for the pursuit of the spiritual life. Monastic communities settled on the rocky, wind-seared islands of Atlantic Britain or chose primitive lonely places removed from the settlements which they aimed to serve. Simpson believes that St Ninian, who founded the monastery in the lonely Isle of Whithorn, chose the caves of the Eamont as a cell from which to spread the light to the inhabitants of the Penrith region. His mission to the north-west must have been guided by the distribution of population and the means of travel and communication at that time. The country around Penrith seems to have been well settled in late Romano-British times. The Roman roads focused on Brougham and the crossing of the Eamont, leading from Carlisle, Stainmore and the wild roof of High Street. At Brougham St Ninian probably found an active settlement, *Brocavum*, on the bank of the river Eamont beside the Roman fort. It also seems likely that there was an older British settlement at Penrith. Not many miles to the east and easily accessible by road was the moderate-sized Roman town at Kirkby Thore. Native farms and villages in the hill country on the eastern borders of the Lake District added to the potentialities of this region as a mission field. Close to the hermits' caves under the red sandstone cliff of the Eamont St Ninian established a preaching site, the place where the simple seventeenth-century church of Brougham Ninekirks now stands. The first church, probably a simple wooden building of which all trace is lost, served the settlement that lies beneath the green fields around Brougham's medieval castle. Here a tiny fragment of the English landscape – a mere square mile of country around Brougham – provides a slender link between the twelfth century and sub-Roman times. The faith of St Ninian helps to strengthen the faith of the historian in the continuity and settlement of the north-west through the Dark Ages.

Another Celtic saint, Patrick, inspired dedications that may date back to the period of his missionary activity at the beginning of the fifth century. There is a tradition that he was born at Bowness-on-Solway about the year 386. A study of the church dedications to Patrick and references to the saint in topographical names well illustrate the problems and pitfalls that await the local historian. Three dedications to St Patrick occur in Westmorland and Cumberland at Ousby (6234), Bampton (5218) and Preston Patrick (5585), but the most interesting attribution to the saint is Patterdale (3916), meaning St Patrick's dale, where the little chapel sheltered by dark yew trees and a holy well close by Ullswater are both associated with the name of this founder of Christianity in Celtic Britain. If the early associations of Patterdale with St Patrick could pass undisputed, they would throw some important light on the occupation of the heart of the Lake District in the fifth century. It would indicate an established community in the gloomy head of the Ullswater valley some fifteen hundred years ago. But another construction can be placed on the occurrence of this name. Patterdale first appears in the documentary record at the close of the twelfth century as *Patrichesdale*, joining the Norse element for a valley with the Old Irish personal name *Patraic*. The majority of Norse settlers who colonized the Lake District in the tenth century came from Ireland, part of a secondary settlement that took place almost a century after the primary migrations from the fjords of western Norway. The migrants who reached the Cumbrian hills had absorbed many elements of Irish speech. The Patrick who gave his name to Patterdale was probably an Irish-Norse farmer in the tenth century. To give strength to the argument there is little evidence of a Christian chapel at Patterdale before the end of the twelfth century – a period when several places of worship were founded at remote places in the deep valleys among the Lake District's mountains. When Ullswater became a focus of Victorian tourism the medieval chapel was pulled down; the present building was consecrated in 1853. Only the font, dating from about the year 1200, remains to provide any clue to the earlier chapel. It is a good rule that the font is often the oldest object in a church and a guide to the period of its foundation. Another argument may be pursued in the identification of the real Patrick at Patterdale. For centuries this settlement at the head of Ullswater – a scattering of hamlets and farmsteads a few score feet above the marshy, flood-threatened valley floor – remained a chapelry in the widespread parish of Barton (4826). It is almost certain that if St Patrick had preached here in the early years of the fifth century, baptizing at the holy well and founding a church, that Patterdale would have emerged as one of the huge medieval parishes of the Lake District. Instead, for centuries we must trace the history of Patterdale as part of St Michael's, Barton. There the fine central tower of the early Norman church still stands, bearing witness to the deeply rooted settlement of the more fertile, drier and sunnier countryside at the foot of Ullswater.

If Cumberland can lay claim to a county saint, it must be St Kentigern who preached and founded churches in the north-west about the middle of the sixth century. In Scotland he usually passes under the name of St Mungo. Jocelyn of Furness, the twelfth-century biographer of St Kentigern, tells how he fled from Glasgow to find refuge in Carlisle from pagan persecutors. There he heard of idolatry among the peoples of the Cumberland fells and set about the organization of a missionary campaign. In northern Cumberland eight ancient parish churches are dedicated to St Kentigern, four of them lying among the northern fells at Caldbeck (3239), Castle Sowerby (380362), Mungrisdale (3630) and Crosthwaite (2524), which is the mother parish of Keswick. This little group of dedications to St Kentigern probably marks the route of his mission through a district on the eastern and southern flanks of the Skiddaw massif that seems to have been a centre of British population, if we are to judge from the presence of Celtic place-name elements. But the work of St Kentigern can be best appreciated in a quiet exploration of the countryside through which he passed. There is no better place to stop and meditate upon this subject than in the churchyard at Castle Sowerby. This squat, wide-roofed church, reminiscent of Cornwall rather than northern England, lies in a most beautiful and inaccessible site a mile from one of the minor roads crossing Inglewood Forest. The parish, with its scattered farms and hamlets, extends over eight thousand acres, much of it land that was first reclaimed by settlers in Inglewood Forest after the thirteenth century. A stone's-throw away and lost in trees stands Sowerby Hall, the manor farm of this widely dispersed parish whose settlement pattern is so reminiscent of other parts of Celtic Britain. Nearby on the edge of the churchyard the holy well still flows where St Kentigern must have baptized his first converts. To the west the domed summit of Carrock Fell dominates the countryside and on its windy top the ruins of its Iron Age fort attest that this was an important area of the Celtic Lake District long before St Kentigern made his journey.

The most important of Cumberland's dedications to St Kentigern is at Great Crosthwaite (2524), the parish that contains the market-town of Keswick. The name Crosthwaite itself recalls the sixth-century journey of St Kentigern. It means 'the clearing marked by a cross'. The last part of the word contains the Scandinavian element 'thwaite', a clearing; and it must have been introduced at some time in the tenth century when the Norse colonization was taking place in the north-west. The place name describes clearly what the Scandinavian settlers found there – a clearing with a carved stone cross, a preaching site originally, standing on a clay hillock that gave a dry refuge above the marshy flood-threatened plain threaded by the Derwent.

There is not much else, apart from the slender proof contained in place names and saintly dedications, to link Great Crosthwaite with the sixth century. Jocelyn of Furness, in his *Life of St Kentigern*, written towards the close of the twelfth century, mentions a chapel at Great Crosthwaite, but the present church dates almost entirely from a rebuilding in the early years of the sixteenth century. Some fragments of an earlier church may be seen in the north wall and in the stones of the chancel arch. Another clue to the early importance of Great

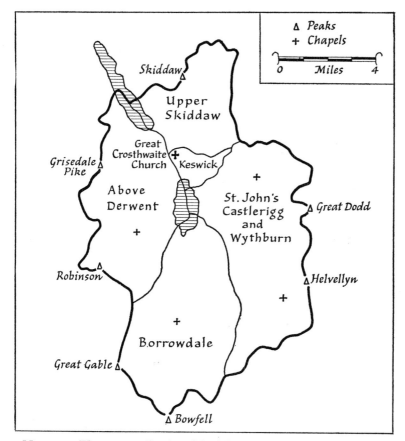

Map 21   *The great medieval parish of Crosthwaite with its later sub-division.*

Crosthwaite lies in the geography of the medieval parish. The patterns of the huge medieval parishes of the Lake District point to features of the human geography that probably predate the Norman Conquest by several centuries. Great Crosthwaite once encompassed almost 60,000 acres (Map 21). Its boundary ran from Helvellyn (3315) across the roof of mountains to Great Gable (2110) and reached westward to the grey scree-ringed plateau of Grasmoor (1720) and the scarred slate summit of Grisedale Pike (1922). The church at Great Crosthwaite and its five outlying chapels served all the northern valleys of the Lake District.

If St Kentigern planned his mission to reach some of the chief centres of population in Cumbria, it seems most likely that he found a thriving British community in the patchwork of lowland that lies between Bassenthwaite and Derwentwater. The continuity of occupation in this tiny region of the north-west stands second only in importance to the early centre of settlement in the Eden valley and around Penrith. As we have already seen, the roots of the past reach to great depths in this tract of country. The Bronze-Age stone circle on Castlerigg, ramparted enclosures of Romano-British and possibly post-Roman occupation at Peel Wyke on Bassenthwaite and Castle Crag in the Jaws of Borrowdale, and the hints of a Roman causeway lost in the muds of the delta between the lakes, all speak of the long occupation of this fragment of the Lakeland landscape.

The Lake District's landscape contains many clues to life in the region in the two and a half centuries between the withdrawal of the Romans and the settlement of the first Anglian colonists. The British communities who farmed the lowlands and foothills on the fringe of the high mountains were organized into a kingdom ruled by a line of princes. Its name, *Rheged*, is preserved in the heroic poetry of Wales that dates back to the beginning of the seventh century. The name reappears in south-west Scotland, where Dunragit, at the head of Luce Bay, means 'the fort of Rheged'. The long disused British name for the Solway Firth was Merin Rheged, and to Welshmen living in the twelfth century the name Rheged was known to belong to a district near Carlisle. All these clues point back to the British kingdom of the north-west that followed the Roman withdrawal and which in turn disintegrated under the pressure of the Anglian invasions. *Rheged* probably originated as a tribal name but at its full extent the kingdom probably stretched from south-west Scotland across the Solway Firth and the Lake District into the Yorkshire Pennines and North Lancashire. There is little doubt that the core of Rheged centred upon the Solway Firth and its hinterland of the Eden valley and the Cumberland plain.

Another clue to the reconstruction of the political geography of *Rheged* lies in the poems of the Welsh bard Taliesin. He names one of the rulers of Rheged in the sixth century, a prince called Urien who lived, perhaps among several places, at *Lluyuenyd*. It is more than likely that this dark-age place name has continued until the present day in the Westmorland river name, Lyvennet, a tributary of the Eden. The landscape itself bears out this supposition, for the grey-green limestone hills at the head of the Lyvennet are littered with the sites of deserted prehistoric settlements, the faint overgrown footings of enclosures and huts that have been plundered for building material down the centuries. One of these may well have been the home of Urien, who appears briefly and obscurely in the record of history through a saga of the Celtic world that was told and recorded in Wales.

The details of the political history of *Rheged* are lost beyond recall, but the society of that period has left its permanent impression on the landscape of the Lake District. The dispersed settlement pattern of the north-west undoubtedly has a Celtic framework. The siting of the oldest parish churches also depends upon events in the sub-Roman period. The preaching places of wandering saints or the sites of holy wells and springs, places that may well have been sacred to the pagan Celts, were often chosen for the building of churches. Today we find them lonely and devoid of settlement in places that still strike one by their inaccessibility. Brougham Ninekirks stands alone in the meadows of the Eamont. Barton (4826), a church with several early twelfth century features, occupies an isolated site at the end of a blind lane off the main road from Pooley Bridge to Penrith. One of the chief reasons for its position is probably the stream that rises just below the churchyard to join the Eamont. It was the spiritual focus of a huge parish that embraced the whole of Ullswater and its tributary valleys.

Between the seventh and the eleventh centuries Anglian and Scandinavian settlers reached the Lake District through the gaps in the Pennine Wall and Stainmore, and from the West Riding by the Aire. A silent flood of Scandinavians crossed the Irish Sea from Ireland and the Isle of Man. The place names and the settlement forms which they imprinted on the northern landscape stand out in sharpest contrast against the more ancient Celtic ground-plan.

Anglian settlers in the north-west
No contemporary account exists of the conquest of north-west England by the Angles about A.D. 600. The first documentary record of the events of this period occurs in Bede's *Historia Ecclesiastica*, written two hundred years after. Bede shows plainly that the frontiers of Northumbria extended westward across the Pennines in the reign of Aethelfrith (592–616), and says that it was accomplished by military conquest and occupation, by the removal of peoples from their established lands and the planting of colonies. 'Aethelfrith conquered more territories from the Britons than any other chieftain or king, either subduing the inhabitants and making them tributary, or driving them out and planting the English in their places.' The first phase of the Anglian settlement was probably accomplished by A.D. 625; before the end of the century Northumbria controlled the whole of the north-west peninsula. The mountain fastness of the Lake District was encircled by the tide of Anglian conquest and settlement, but it seems that the sparse British communities of the interior resisted the thrust from the east until the Anglo-Saxons were themselves threatened by the waves of Norse-Irish pirates and migrants towards the close of the ninth century.

Although no documentary sources survive for tracing out the details of the Anglian occupation of the former territories of *Rheged*, the existing map of place names and the record of those names in documents after the twelfth century yield a considerable amount of information about the events of the seventh century. The earliest Anglian place-name element in the north-west is the suffix *ham*, meaning a village, an estate or manor, a homestead. It describes a primary settlement in the Anglo-Saxon period of occupation. Even so, this element occurs only rarely among the place names of Cumberland and Westmorland. Only twelve examples survive and all of them lie outside the core of high mountains and fells, particularly in the Eden valley and on the coastal plain of north Cumberland. Other early Anglian sites may be indicated by the suffix *ceaster* or *caster*, an Old English term referring to an ancient fortification, usually of Roman date. Only two more places are added to the list. Hincaster (5184) lies in the Kendal lowland only a mile from the early Anglian site of Heversham (4983). Muncaster (1096) stands at the entrance to Eskdale and seems to refer to the Roman settlement at Ravenglass where the placid tidal reach of the Esk and Mite is screened from the Irish Sea by a mountainous ridge of sand-dunes. If this is the sum total of the earliest Anglian place names within sight of the Lake District's mountains, it suggests that the British settlements of the interior were largely unaffected by the first expansion of Northumbria. If we are to take the place-name evidence at its face value the first settlements were confined to the Eden valley, the Irthing valley in north-east Cumberland, the Solway plain, and the coastal fringe of the Kendal basin. The main approach into north-western England seems to have been through the Tyne Gap and across the fells traversed by Hadrian's Wall.

The most frequent Anglian element in the place names of north-west England is the suffix *tun*, meaning a farmstead in Old English. It was actively used in the naming of places for many centuries; consequently it is not a reliable tracer for the foundation date of a settlement. Several names ending in 'ton' point to the intrusion of the Angles in the Penrith region. Carleton (5329), for instance, a hamlet on the line of the Roman road as it climbs northward from the crossing of the Eamont, means 'the farm of the free men'. Ekwall believes that this originated as an Old English name in the early years of settlement. Stainton (4827) too probably reflects the later distortion of an Old English element, *stan*, by the Scandinavian dialect of Cumberland. Further south, in the Lowther valley, we find Helton (5122) and Bampton (5218).

The distribution of the *tun* element in the fertile lowland around Kendal provides some proof of the type of country chosen by the farmers of the seventh and eighth centuries (Map 22). This must be the choicest of the several varied minor regions on the flanks of the Lake District. The Kent winds through a lowland with scattered angular-shaped limestone hills; glacial boulder clays provide fine sites for farms and agriculture in what seems like an infinity of whaleback-shaped hills. Screened to the north by the fells that culminate in High Street and stretching southward into Morecambe Bay in blunt, hilly limestone peninsulas, the Kendal lowland enjoys a local climate that modifies many of the harsher aspects of the Lake District's weather. A dozen names with the *tun* element are scattered over the region contained by the four valleys, the Bella, Kent, Gilpin and Winster, that pour their waters into the Kent estuary. Not all of these date from the first two centuries of the Anglian settlement. For instance, Reston (4598) in the rough, grey Silurian hill country near Staveley, means 'the farm in

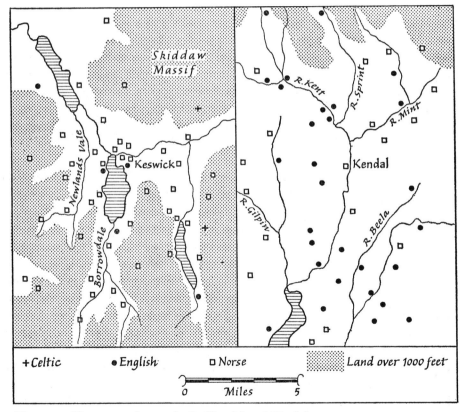

Map 22 *Place-name elements in the Keswick and Kendal areas.*

the brushwood'. The name is first recorded towards the end of the thirteenth century and it is very typical of the period of expansion after the Norman Conquest when much second-rate land was taken into cultivation for the first time. But if the place names in 'tun' provide no easy solution to the settlement history of the country around Kendal, they at least contain some clear indicators of the early intrusion of the Anglians. Helsington (4989), Stainton (5285) and Patton (5596) all seem to represent early settlements and they have additional and rare documentary support from their appearance in the record of Domesday Book. Old Hutton (5688), another name that dates back to 1086 and the Domesday Book, means 'the farmstead on the hill' – an apt description of its site on the eastern edge of the Kendal lowland. Here it is possible to make use of place names in unravelling the whole process of medieval settlement.

The name is repeated in New Hutton (5591), a little more than a mile to the north. Old Hutton, Domesday Book tells us, was in existence at the Norman Conquest, and it probably dates from the first century of the Anglians in the north-west. New Hutton does not appear in the documents until an Inquisition of 1274. The distinguishing adjective 'new' suggests that this was a daughter settlement of Old Hutton, and the nature of its origin is made even clearer when we find the phrase *in the Hay* attached to several of the medieval references to New Hutton. This was the clearing in the forest made by pioneer farmers striking out from Old Hutton to break fresh land on the edge of Hay Fell about the middle of the thirteenth century.

Another striking feature of the distribution of Anglian place names in the Kendal region is their restriction to the valley of the Kent and its eastern tributaries. Such names are notably absent from the valleys of the Winster and Gilpin. Only Newton (4082) and Helton (4284) stand out as lonely outliers from the main body of Anglian place names in the Kent valley. They suggest, even allowing for lost names and others distorted by the later Scandinavian settlers, that the frontier of Anglian settlement in the eighth century was drawn along the bold face of the limestone ridge, Underbarrow Scar (4891), that looks westward across a broken Silurian landscape of slate and flagstone hills. One is left with questions that cannot be answered with any certainty. Does this frontier represent a deliberate choice of terrain by the Anglian settlers? If so, they selected the richer limestone hills and boulder clays of the Kent valley and rejected the poorer Silurian country to the west. Or are we looking at the last relic, surviving down the centuries as a pattern of place names, of a long-lost agreement between the British and the incoming Anglian farmers about the territory that the intruder could occupy?

On the western edge of the Lake District the Anglian settlement is limited to the wider valleys among the foothills where they begin to open out to the coastal plain. Broughton, already recorded by the end of the twelfth century, suggests a core of settlement at the head of the Duddon estuary. North-west again, in the coastal lowland at the junction of the Esk and Mite, the early Anglian site at Muncaster is reinforced by two place names ending in *tun* at Irton and Santon (1100).

The distribution map of Anglian place-name elements in Cumberland and Westmorland suggests that the settlers of the seventh and eighth centuries broke little new ground. A few names occur in the central mountain core. For instance, the Old English place-name element, *mere*, appears in the names of some of the larger lakes – Grasmere, Buttermere, Thirlmere, and the now vanished Kentmere. Stockley Bridge (2310), at the head of Borrowdale among the tangle of morainic hills where the track begins to climb steeply to the Sty Head Pass, contains two Old English place-name elements in a district whose toponymy is dominantly Scandinavian. It means 'the place in the woodland clearing'. Was this a summer pasture to which the Anglian farmers from the Cumberland plain brought their animals in the summer months – a clearing in the woodland at the head of Borrowdale that served as a base for the higher mountain grazings?

The Anglian place names, however scanty, present a considerable problem in understanding the settlement history of the mountainous interior of Cumberland and Westmorland. The names may have been coined at a late date, after the Scandinavian settlements. On the other hand, if they are genuine early names they bear witness to the presence of the English in the heart of the region, in some of its most inaccessible valleys. It is possible that the Scandinavian settlement of the tenth century obliterated earlier English names among the mountains. Today we may scan the topographical map of the central Lake District in vain for the familiar Anglian *tuns*. Everywhere the eye lights on the *thwaites* and *garths*, Old Norse elements that provide a sure guide to the understanding of the demographic upheaval of the tenth century.

The Scandinavian settlements
It is hard to give an exact date for the first intrusion of the Scandinavians into north-west England. At the death of King Alfred in 899 the region was still under English control. The ravages of pirates from bases in Ireland are first reported in the *History of St Cuthbert,* an eleventh-century work that contains pieces of much older material and records historical events from the centuries before the Norman Conquest. The *History* tells how an English nobleman had fled eastward across the Pennines in the face of a pirate invasion that took place

before the year 915. For the same reasons the abbot of Heversham (4983), a monastery exposed to raiders sailing into the sandy reaches of Morecambe Bay, had made plans to remove himself to Norham-on-Tweed. In the same year pirates entering by the Solway had left Carlisle in ruins. The first impact of the Scandinavian raids must have been felt in the years about 910.

Even if the Viking pirates created political and social disorder, it is evident that in the succeeding decades groups of farmers, speaking a Scandinavian language that had absorbed some words from the Irish, settled in the Lake District. The story of this revolution in the human geography of the north-west has gone completely unrecorded. There are no documents through which we can trace the details of the settlement, but the abundance of Old Norse elements in the place names speaks of its effectiveness. Domesday Book, which includes only parts of the southern fringe of the Lake District, throws a glimmer of light on the problems of the Norse settlement. For instance, it names the owners of estates in the Kendal area at the time of the Norman Conquest. Among them we find Gilemichel, a landlord with an Irish name, who held the manor of Kendal and eight other estates. At Kirkby Lonsdale the lord of the manor held six other manors and was of Viking descent because he bore the Old Norse personal name, Torfin or Thorfinnr. The Scandinavian intruders were not only groups of free peasant farmers making their tiny clearings in the rock-strewn valleys beneath the highest summits of the Lake District, but they also acquired estates and rose to the highest places in the society of the lowland fringe.

The distribution of Scandinavian elements in the place names of the north-west reveals the outlines of the Norse settlement in the tenth century. On the eastern flank of the Lake District, where the valleys of the Lowther and Eamont converge to join the Eden, Scandinavian farmers intruded in a region previously well settled by the Anglians and occupied long before that by British, Romano-British and prehistoric peoples. A cluster of Norse place names where the Roman road descends from High Street towards the lowland of the Eamont suggests that the Scandinavian settlers followed this ancient track from the head of Windermere. It is more than likely that the High Street formed the last link of a migration route from the primary areas of Norse settlement in the west Cumberland plain along the Roman highway that climbs the Hardknott and Wrynose passes. Names that testify to the presence of Scandinavians here are Tirril (5026), 'the shieling built of fir wood', High Winder, 'the wind-swept shieling', Yanwath, 'the even wood', to mention only a few. Lowther, too, seems to be derived from an Old Norse name.

The same story of the intrusion of Norse settlers into a region long occupied by the Anglians is repeated in the valley of the Kent. The name of Kendal itself, one of the primary settlements of the district and later the centre of a huge medieval parish, shows the mark of the Norseman. Until the eighteenth century this borough was known as Kirkby Kendal, of which the first word is the Scandivian *kirku-byr*, the village with a church. Among other names that testify to Scandinavian settlers in the Kent valley we find Oxenholme (5390) with the Old Norse element *holmr*, meaning an island or water meadow, Skelsmergh (5396) or Skjaldmar's dairy farm, and, close to the landing places in the Kent estuary, Sizergh, Sigrith's shieling or dairy farm. The presence of this distinctive Norse-Irish term *erg*, a shieling or hill pasture, betrays the origins of the Scandinavian settlement of the Lake District. It is a modification of the Irish word *airghe*, a modification that was accomplished only after a half century of Scandinavian settlement in Ireland. But perhaps the most intriguing of the Norse names in the Kent valley is Natland (5289). The name means Nati's wood; the suffix *lundr* refers to the sacred grove of the pagan religions of northern Europe. Nati is the name of a giant in Norse mythology, and it is likely that Natland was a place where the Scandinavian settlers in the Kent valley built a temple in their first years to serve their pagan gods. If there is any truth in this hypothesis, it is notable that Natland lies scarcely two miles from the centre of Kendal, and between the two places we find the site of the Roman fort and settlement of *Alavna* (5190). This particular tract of Kent, where the valley narrows between the Helm, crowned by an Iron Age fort, and the ragged limestone block of Underbarrow, has remained the focus of life for the whole dale over many centuries. In prehistoric, Roman, medieval and modern Westmorland it seems to have performed the same task of organizing the life of the south-eastern fringe of the Lake District. The site of Natland and the religious functions suggested by its name hint that the Norsemen recognized this fact of the human geography of Kentdale. They must have settled within sight of one of the chief villages of their Anglian neighbours, the church town that was to become Kirkby Kendal.

The most striking achievement of the tenth century was the settlement of the mountain interior from the deep recesses around Scafell and Great Gable to the lonely beautiful valleys between Helvellyn and the High Street. In every valley the Norsemen began an important process of land clearance, not only of wood and scrub but of countless boulders that formed the harsh legacy of the Ice Age (Plate 30a). When the making of new farms and the taking-in of fresh land came to a stop is hard to determine. It is likely that the process was continued until the beginning of the thirteenth century or even later. The twelfth and thirteenth centuries saw the growth of population and prosperity in many parts of western and northern Europe. The same demographic upsurge probably reveals itself in the colonization of the inner parts of the Lake District.

If we consider the origins of settlement in Borrowdale, some of the difficulties in the understanding of this process show themselves. The place names of the valley are predominantly Scandinavian in character (Map 22). Along the main valley and its tributaries the Old Norse *thwaite* element, a clearing, occurs with almost monotonous regularity. Some of the names conjure up vividly the topography of the site or recall the scene that must have presented itself in the first years of settlement. Rosthwaite (2514) is 'the clearing marked by, or surrounding, a cairn'. Its slate and whitewashed farms sheltered by dark green yew trees are scattered along the knolls of a rocky bar that rises from the level valley floor above the Jaws of Borrowdale (Plate 1). It still gives a refuge from disastrous floods when the Derwent spills over its banks and forms a temporary lake for a few hours. Close by stands Longthwaite, 'the long clearing', marked by a single farm. Stonethwaite (2615) (Plate 4a), oppressed by the high fells and sheep pastures that tower on all sides, means the 'stone clearing' – a laconic memorial to what must have been a generation or more of painful land reclamation from a boulder spread. The upper valley, the last reach of settlement and the wettest place in England, contains Seathwaite (2312) – the clearing in the land overgrown with sedge – and Thornythwaite (2413) which means the clearing amid the thorns. Another Scandinavian element appears in the name Seatoller (2413), which means the *saetr* or summer pasture with the alder tree.

Borrowdale, like all the other valleys at the heart of the Lake District, bears the imprint of the Scandinavian settlement in every detail of its topography. For the twentieth-century traveller the sight and sound of these names form one strand in the personality of the Lake District. Unconsciously, perhaps, they provide a time element in the landscape, taking us back a thousand years to one of the most formative epochs in the history of the region. Nowhere does one become more aware of the role of place names in creating a sense of history than when one visits the newly explored and recently surveyed parts of the world. The place names of the North American Rockies are concerned with statesmen and politicians or flaunt such exaggerated topographical labels as the 'Tower of Babel'. The Norse names of the Lake District, on the other hand, speak of generations remote from our own in time and outlook who slowly tamed this wilderness.

The Scandinavian influence on the Lake District lasted much longer than the first years of the settlement from Ireland. Norse words were absorbed into the

17. *Ambleside – the original core in the background near the church, market-place on the main road and the Victorian resort in the foreground with Gilbert Scott's church in the foreground.*

18a. *Dow Crag with steeply pitching screes above Goat's Water.*

18b. *Kettle moraine at the head of Mickleden.*

19a. *Windermere – the most popular of lakes for yachting, motorboats and water-skiing.*

19b. *The stream of summer traffic on the Ambleside-Keswick road near Grasmere.*

20a. *The upper workings of Coniston copper mine.*

20b. *Elterwater slate quarry, recently re-opened.*

dialects of Cumberland and Westmorland and many of them remained until the eighteenth century as living parts of the vocabulary. Consequently, the presence of such terms as *thwaite* and *garth* in the place names of the fell country cannot be used as an unwavering proof that a settlement came into existence in the primary phase of Scandinavian colonization before the Norman Conquest. The information provided by documents throws little light on this problem because no records exist from the period of settlement. The nature of the task becomes apparent if we consider the earliest records in the documents of the names of farms and hamlets in Borrowdale. The name of the valley descends from the Old Norse words *borgar dalr*, 'the valley of the fortress' – a reference no doubt to the British earthwork on Castle Crag. It first appears in the year 1170 among the documents of St Bees Priory. The earliest evidence of Stonethwaite occurs in the Chartulary of Fountains Abbey in 1211, and Seathwaite is recorded less than a century later in 1292. Watendlath (2716), in a remote tributary above the dark cliffs of Lodore, first enters the records in the Coucher Book of Furness Abbey in the year 1209. It stems from the Old Norse, *vatns endi*, and means 'the end of the lake'. Its relative among the modern place names of Scandinavia is Vasenden, a very common place name in Norway. The records suggest that the outline of the settlement pattern of Borrowdale had been established by the thirteenth century, but the limitations of a solution of this problem solely through the use of documents becomes evident when we consider the history of Rosthwaite. The name does not enter the documentary record until Tudor times when the muniments of Cockermouth Castle contain a reference to it in 1503. A consideration of Rosthwaite's site on the rocky knolls above the meadows and pastures of middle Borrowdale and overlooked by the Iron Age fort on Castle Crag convince one that a settlement must have existed here long before the first surviving documentary record of the name. Seatoller is not written down until 1563, but it is hard to believe that the 'saeter with the alder trees', a summer grazing ground in the wide and now treeless basin that leads to the Honister Pass, was not in full use centuries before this time. The name Honister illustrates even more strikingly the gap that may occur in time between the coining of a place name and its first appearance in the documents. In the records the name goes back only to the middle of the eighteenth century, but in all probability it belongs to the earliest period of Scandinavian settlement. It means *Huni's staðir*, or Huni's place, a name that occurs on the modern map of Norway as Hunastad.

The Norse settlement of the Lake District thrust forward the frontier of colonization in the tenth century, but the process was probably not complete until the thirteenth century. This important epoch in the evolution of the land-scape of the north-west not only established the main outlines of settlement among the mountains but was accompanied by extensive forest clearance. To-day, much of the woodland of the Lake District is the legacy of plantations made within the past two centuries. For the rest, shreds of the original forest cover survive only in inaccessible places. The wide bare views that open up before the fell walker almost anywhere in the Lake District as he climbs towards the two thousand foot contour, are the result of a process that started in prehistoric times and was largely achieved by the Norse colonization. This was Words-worth's image of the untamed Lake District, of a world unsullied by man and his works. In truth, the landscape of the fells is as much the creation of man and his grazing animals as of the natural processes that shaped the architecture of mountain, corrie wall, scree and valley floor. The work of the botanists that has recovered an intelligible pattern of forest history from the tree pollen deposited in peat bogs and lake muds shows clearly the effect of the Scandinavian farmers in the north-west. At Ellerside Moss, an important site close to the eastern shore of the Leven estuary, the pollen curves reveal a steep decline in the quantity of oak pollen and a sharp rise in grasses, bracken and heather that seems to coincide with the decades of the Norse colonization. It suggests the heavy felling of oakwoods and their replacement by heather moor with scattered copses of birch. The peat bog at Ellerside probably records the extensive Norse settlement of High Furness, whose other legacy is to be found in place names such as Satterthwaite (3392), Graythwaite (3691), Finsthwaite (3687), and Haverthwaite (3383). Recent work on the pollen preserved in the muds accumulated on the floor of Blelham Tarn (3600) tells the same story. There the main decline in tree pollen appears high in the profile, and seems to coincide with the period of settlement started by the Norse farmers. The results of the full and detailed investigation of the pollen record of all the important Lake District tarns is awaited before a detailed picture of woodland evolution can be drawn, but so far the work has underlined the role of Viking farmers in the creation of the present landscape. The eternal hills only acquired their most characteristic feature, the expansive treeless vista, within the past thousand years. The Norsemen brought to a conclusion an epoch of landscape history that began almost four thousand years earlier.

Even though the details of the Viking settlement of the Lake District and its margins are hard to unravel, the political geography of the period presents similar harsh problems that can be resolved with no certainty. The power of the Anglian kingdom of Northumbria that had held sway for almost three centuries faded from the scene. The confusion of the period saw a revival of British political power, but now the centre lay to the north-west on the shores of the Clyde. The kingdom of Strathclyde reached into the Lake District, and the Cumberland plain became the focus of the smaller sub-unit of Cumbria. The record of one event survives from the early tenth century to show the new political relationships that were coming into being under the impact of the Norse invasions and settlements. In 926 some of the kings and princes of the north paid homage to the ruler of Wessex, Athelstan. The meeting took place on the banks of the river Eamont on the northern frontier of Athelstan's territories. The exact place where these princes gathered is not known. Some local historians have favoured the meadows around Brougham and Eamont Bridge where the important Roman trunk roads converged. Others believe that the assembly took place where the Dacre Beck empties into the Eamont (4726). Among those who paid homage to Athelstan were the kings of Scotland and Strathclyde and Owen who was the ruler of Cumbria. Cumbria was evolving as a new political unit in the early years of the tenth century out of the shattered territories of Northumbria. English influence in the north-west had now shifted to the distant power of Wessex. Athelstan's conference on the banks of the Eamont suggests that this river, emptying out of Ullswater, formed the frontier between Anglo-Saxon England and the block of Celtic-speaking kingdoms of north-west Britain of which Cumbria was the southernmost outlier. A political frontier that was to become the boundary between the later counties of Cumberland and Westmorland had already been established long before the Norman Conquest.

There are other pointers to the importance of the Eamont valley in the political geography of tenth-century Cumbria. W. G. Collingwood believed that the capital of Owen's kingdom was at Penrith. If this is true, one is led to speculate about the intriguing topography at the heart of the town. The parish church of St Andrew seems to lie at the centre of a large circular earthwork whose outlines are now almost totally obliterated by buildings and streets. Nevertheless the circular shape is preserved in a curving street, Bishop Yards, and a crescent of mainly Georgian houses that has been built in the ditch of the former earthwork. In the topography of the busy streets at the centre of Penrith we may be in the presence of the only surviving feature of the tenth-century capital of Cumbria, the last faint relic of an earthwork that commanded the gap between the Eamont and the Petteril and which stood only a few hundred yards from the line of the Roman road to Carlisle.

The new political relationships of the north-west in the tenth century introduce the insecurity that overshadows the history of the region until the union of the English and Scottish crowns in 1603. The Lake District and the Solway low-land became the western flank of a marchland that stretched eastward across the Tyne Gap to the basin of the Tweed and the eastern coastal plain of Scotland. In the second half of the tenth century Strathclyde disappeared from the political scene and the English contested the northern marches with a far more formid-able rival, Scotland. Frontiers fluctuated across the mountain wilderness of the Lake District and the northern Pennines in response to changes in the political balance of power. In the year 945 Cumbria was ravaged by Edmund of Wessex, probably after the intrusion of the Scots. Again, in 972 the Anglo-Saxon Chron-icle reveals a familiar theme of the Lake District's medieval history; the Scots raided as far south as the pass of Stainmore. By the close of the century Cumbria had become tributary to Scotland and the boundaries of the kingdom stretched southwards to the Rerecross, a landmark on Stainmore, and the line of the River Duddon in the south-west. Here in the Duddon valley the later county boundary between Cumberland and Lancashire is already foreshadowed by the closing years of the tenth century. Diplomacy, as well as military conquest, played its part in shaping the political geography of the Lake District before the Norman Conquest. The most important development was the shift northwards of the frontier between English and Scottish interests early in the eleventh cen-tury. The origins of the Tweed–Solway line are very obscure, but it is believed that this frontier between England and Scotland resulted from an exchange of terrritory between King Cnut and the Scot, Malcolm II, in 1032. The plain of Lothian, to the north of the Tweed, which had been settled from Northumbria in the seventh century passed to Scotland; the lands to the south of the Solway were recognized as part of England. But several centuries, interrupted at times by the bitterest warfare, were needed for the establishment without question of the frontier between England and Scotland through this northern marchland.

About the local politics of the Scandinavian settlements in the Lake District scarcely anything can be said. The place names contain a few hints that suggest an organization of government on a regional scale. Among the place names of Swindale (5113), a lonely valley with a handful of scattered farms among the Shap Fells, we find the word *Thengeheved* fossilized in the documents. The first element is probably the Old Norse word *thing*, a council; and it means 'the coun-cil place at the head of the valley'. Here perhaps is the place where the primitive open-air parliament met to discuss and manage the affairs of the community of Viking settlers in the Shap area. Ekwall, in his study of the place names of Lancashire, believed that he had found a clue to the location of the centre of a small Scandinavian kingdom in the name Coniston. It probably descends from the Old Norse *Kunungstun*, 'the king's settlement', and, as Ekwall writes, 'possibly preserves the memory of a small Scandinavian mountain kingdom'. The extent of this little state was probably coincident with the medieval territory of High Furness, a tract whose place names reveal an overwhelming number of Norse elements. But the most tantalizing clue to the political geography of the Scandinavian settlements lies in Little Langdale, at the foot of the Wrynose Pass. Immediately behind Fell Foot farm (2903) we find a flat-topped, roughly rectangular mound whose steep sides have been shaped into a short flight of grassy steps. Archaeology has revealed nothing of the age or purpose of this man-made feature. W. G. Collingwood, most eminent of the Lake District's historians, believed that it is a *thing-mount*, the meeting-place of a Viking council for Little Langdale. Certainly it occupies a strategic site beside the Roman road that might well have brought the first Norse colonists from the west across the Wrynose and Hardknott passes. To the north the low col that shelters Blea Tarn gives access to Great Langdale. We can only guess that the *thing-mount* at Fell Foot was the centre of government for both the Langdales. At least, the site today conveys a strange feeling of antiquity, a feeling that is enhanced by the solemn line of dark, gnarled yew trees planted along one side of the platform.

By the end of the eleventh century many fresh elements had been added to the sketch of prehistoric settlement in the Lake District. The medieval landscape evolved out of this older ground-plan of settlement with its British, Anglian and Norse-Irish elements. It is probably wrong to think in terms of the three great epochs of Dark Age history in the Lake District as distinct and separate from each other. The Celtic element lived on long after the Anglian invasions, prob-ably surviving as a force in the society of the north-west until the time of the Norman Conquest in the region around Penrith, between the Eden and the huge grey mass of Skiddaw Forest. The chief legacy of the Celt in the landscape is the dispersed forms of settlement, the scattered hamlets in huge parishes, and mother churches at lonely sites without any other buildings than a vicarage and a manor farm. The Anglian settlers reached the Lake District with totally different ideas of land-use and communal living. Their most distinctive contribution is the village in which the farmsteads are gathered side-by-side closely around a huge green. The Scandinavians, strongly influenced by their half century of settle-ment in Ireland before they reached the Lake District, favoured smaller units of colonization. The hamlets in the deep glaciated valleys of the mountain core or among the complex hills of High Furness were established in this major coloniza-tion of the thinly populated areas of the north-west after A.D. 900. By the close of the eleventh century the Lake District's population was composed of the

6

The medieval landscape

The important dates of regional history often bear little relationship to the major events in the chronology of the nation. Never is this idea more clearly illustrated than when we consider the Norman Conquest in the north of England. 1066 represents one of the great watersheds of our national history, but at that time it was debatable whether the Lake District would belong to Scotland or England. At the time of the Norman Conquest the armies of the Scots, under Malcolm III, overran the whole of the country from the Solway Firth to the Eamont and occupied the Vale of Eden and the western entrance to the pass of Stainmore. For a quarter of a century the frontier of Scotland lay across the dome of the Lake District. As a result, almost the whole of Cumberland and much of Westmorland lay outside the province of the Domesday Survey of 1086. Estates in the southern part of the Lake District – in Kentdale, Furness and the south-western tip of Cumberland around Millom – appear under Yorkshire in the great survey.

The political geography of the twelfth century
It was not until 1092 that the Normans, under William II, tilted the balance of power in the northern marches in favour of England. The Anglo-Saxon Chronicle relates the events of that year. 'King William marched north to Carlisle with a large army, and re-established the fortress, and built the castle, and drove out Dolfin who had previously ruled the land there, and garrisoned the castle with his men, and afterwards returned to the south, and sent thither very many English peasants with wives and stock to dwell there to till the ground.' This was not the end of the matter. The Scots regained control of the Solway region

between 1136 and 1157, and charters of the time show that their authority reached as far south as the River Esk and even beyond the Lake District to the Ribble. Under the Normans and their successors Carlisle emerged as the great royal stronghold of the north. The history of the city is punctuated with the raids and sieges of the Scots in 1173, 1174, and again in 1215; but in 1242, a further retreat of the northern power was marked by Alexander II's abandonment of all claims to lands in Cumberland and Westmorland. The next three centuries are filled with the passage southwards of Scottish armies and the cattle-stealing for-ays of moss troopers, but the political fate of the Lake District had indeed been settled by the events of the twelfth century that followed the Norman Conquest of 1092.

William II not only strengthened Norman interests in the north-west by plant-ing colonies of peasant farmers, as the Anglo-Saxon Chronicle tells us, but he organized the region under powerful barons who were responsible for the defence of the marchland. Foremost among the Norman political units was 'the land of Carlisle' focused on the inner Solway lowland and the lower Eden valley. At the beginning of the twelfth century it was granted to Ranulf de Briquessart, whose territories also included the Barony of Appleby comprising much of the upper Eden valley. To the south of Shap Fells a third great Norman lordship, the Barony of Kendal, centred on Kentdale and the country between the Lune valley and the shores of Windermere. William II gave the estates of the Kendal barony to Yvo Talboise, but on the marriage of his daughter the territories passed to her husband Ranulf de Briquessart, the marcher lord who already dominated the whole of the Lake District's northern and eastern flanks.

Ranulf de Briquessart, or le Meschin as he is also known, ruled his border baronies for a quarter of a century. In 1120, Ranulf succeeded to the Earldom of Chester and gave up his possessions in the north. The marcher baronies became the property of the Crown. The territorial reshuffle that followed at the hands of Henry II led to the creation of the counties of Cumberland and Westmorland. Two sheriffs were appointed; one to rule the northern section, *Chaerliolum* or the county of Cumberland, and the other to take charge of *Westmeringland*. Both names hark back to times before the Norman Conquest. Cumberland, the land of the Cymry (the Welsh), recalls the Celtic foundations of Lake District society. The name Westmorland means 'the district of those living west of the moors' and it may date back to the time of the Anglian settlement in the seventh century when English-speaking farmers moved through Stainmore and occupied the lowland of the Eden and Eamont westward of the bleak moorland barrier of the northern Pennines. The title Westmorland was originally applied only to the northern part of the county beyond Shap Fells. Under Ranulf de Briquessart the territory that comprised Westmorland, the Barony of Appleby as it was called, had been joined to Cumberland. The political realignments of the twelfth century placed the upper Eden valley and the hinterland of Morecambe Bay under the same sheriff and secured that the new town of Appleby, founded about the year 1110, became the capital of the county. Cumberland and Westmorland achieved their separate identities as counties by the last quarter of the twelfth century.

The most striking feature of the political geography of the Lake District is the attachment of the south-western part of the region to Lancashire, an anomaly that becomes almost repulsive to those who, mistakenly, associate that county only with the grime and desolation of Victorian industry. All the land between Windermere and the Duddon finds itself in Lancashire today because it was granted by William II in 1092 to the powerful Norman earl, Roger of Poitou. Roger's territories covered much of Lancashire, and the gift of Furness extended his properties into the Lake District. If Furness had passed into the hands of another follower of the Norman kings, it is quite likely that the south-western peninsula and its mountain hinterland in the Coniston fells would have emerged as a separate county.

If the division of the territorial spoils after William II's conquest of the Lake District deprived Furness of the chance of an individual existence, it is even more certain that the political shaping of Cumberland in the late twelfth and thirteenth centuries absorbed an embryonic county in the Barony of Copeland. The name stems from the Old Norse word *kaupaland*, meaning 'bought land'. The territory of Copeland lay to the south of the river Derwent where it pursues its course towards the sea from Bassenthwaite Lake. It included a valuable segment of the Cumberland plain and stretched into the wild fell country of Buttermere, Ennerdale and Wasdale. Whatever the origins of Copeland in pre-Norman times, this territory emerges into the light of history as a barony in the early years of the twelfth century when Ranulf de Briquessart made a grant of it to his brother William. Egremont, a Norman castle-town as important as Kendal or Appleby, was the capital of Copeland. The Barony of Copeland remained independent for almost a century, and it was only in 1178 that the sheriff of Cumberland gained authority in this region. Different political decisions, taken at the court of Henry II when the north-west was reorganized following the retreat of the Scots, could easily have established a third county, the descendant of Copeland, with its capital at Egremont.

The history of the twelfth century in the Lake District and its margins is dominated by the baronies, the political creations of the Normans, but it is almost certain that as territorial units most of them were in existence before the Norman Conquest. Ranulf de Briquessart's 'land of Carlisle' which became the core of the county of Cumberland appears before the Norman Conquest as the British kingdom of Cumbria. On the southern fringe of the Lake District Domesday Book provides clues to the relationship between estates and land-ownership before and after the Norman Conquest. The survey shows that the country on either side of the Duddon estuary belonged to the huge manor of *Hougun*. It included the greater part of Low Furness as well as estates on the narrow coastal plain of south-west Cumberland beneath Black Combe at Bootle (1088), Whicham (1382) and Kirksanton. Since the reign of King Cnut *Hougun* had belonged to the Earls of Northumbria, and Domesday Book says that just before the Conquest it was the property of Tostig. Under William I all Tostig's lands were confiscated by the Crown, and in 1092, after his successful expedition in the northern marches, William II gave the complex manor of *Hougun* to Roger of Poitou. Through the political upheavals of the eleventh century the manor of *Hougun* remains a stable element in the local scene.

The history of *Hougun* presents a fascinating regional problem. In Domesday Book *Hougun* is the capital of a huge manor containing more than thirty separate vills. At some time after the Norman Conquest, the name dropped out of active use and the very location of the place is now a matter of keen debate among local historians. Three sites are favoured – Great Urswick, a place of great antiquity in a shallow basin among the limestone hills of Low Furness, High Haume to the north of Dalton with its hill-top site and former beacon, and Millom. A few slender facts point to Millom as the head of the manor of *Hougun*. Its late-Norman church was the centre of a huge medieval parish that encompassed the whole of Duddondale and Eskdale, and it is the site of a twelfth-century castle. The name *Hougun* also provides an apt description of the isolated knoll on the inner edge of the reclaimed flats of the Duddon where the ruins of Millom's massive pele tower and heavily restored red sandstone church stand aloof from the drab streets of the Victorian iron-mining town. *Hougun* is made up of the Old Norse *haugr*, a hill or mound, combined with the Old English *eg*, meaning an island. This would be an accurate description of Old Millom a thousand years ago when the high spring tide lapped around the hillock and its settlement. Was Millom the core of an extensive pre-Conquest territorial unit that stretched from the mouth of the Leven almost to the Esk? If so, one can only guess at its origins. The Duddon estuary must have received many of the Norse-Irish immigrants from Ireland in the tenth century, settlers who were perhaps guided across the last miles of sea to their landfall by the huge dark shape of Black Combe.

Hougun was perhaps pieced together into a crude polity by the Norse settlers. On the other hand, the unity and origins of *Hougun* may lie much farther back in time, even perhaps beyond the sparse Anglian settlement of the region. The far-flung manor composed of several vills, many standing separate or interlocked with other estates, was characteristic of the organization of society in Celtic Britain. *Hougun* may be a survival into the Middle Ages of a territorial unit that was first sketched out by the Celtic-speaking British in the good lands around the Duddon estuary.

A similar history probably underlies the development of the Barony of Grey-stoke. Henry I created the Barony of Greystoke about the year 1120, but for once the overlordship of this territory was not handed to a member of the new aristocracy imported by the Norman Conquest. Greystoke was granted to Forni, a descendant of the family that held the estate before 1066. The geography of the new Norman barony suggests the former territory of a discrete manor, a structure characteristic of the Celtic west. Greystoke barony comprised the country on the eastern flanks of the Skiddaw massif and reached southward to include the hills north of Ullswater. Mungrisdale (3630), Threlkeld (3225), Dacre (4526), Water-millock (4422) and Matterdale (3923), all belonged to it. The prehistoric or Dark Age origins of this huge manor with its many scattered hamlets is suggested by the abundance of British names in the region. Greystoke itself, the chief manor and *caput* of the Norman barony, probably preserves the Old Welsh word *creic*, a hill, in its prefix. Greystoke barony invokes a territorial continuity that takes the mind back to the times of the occupation of the Iron Age fort on Carrock Fell. But if the Normans accepted and turned to their own purposes much that was already established in the landscape and society of the north-west, they were also important innovators, so that the twelfth century is marked as the beginning of a major period of expansion and development in the Lake District.

Medieval colonization and economic expansion, 1100–1350
The twelfth century was a time of economic growth and rising population in England. New towns with thriving markets and fairs came into existence, but the benefits of urban life affected only the lowland fringe of the Lake District where castles were built and market charters granted at such places as Appleby, Kendal and Egremont. In the north-west the economic advances were achieved largely through the foundation of monasteries. Although the monks chose lonely and isolated places, none sought the deep solitude of the valleys in the heart of the Lake District. Only one abbey, at Shap (5415), occupies a remote site among the mountains. All the other monasteries lay in the surrounding lowlands and

155

exploited extensive possessions among the mountains as profitable sheep farms or sources of minerals.

Ranulf de Briquessart established the first of the new monasteries in the north-west with the building of the Benedictine priory at Wetheral in the wooded sandstone gorge of the Eden on the outskirts of Carlisle. A few years later, about 1120, another Benedictine house was founded on the Cumberland coast at St Bees by Ranulf's brother, William Meschin, lord of the Barony of Copeland. About the same time Henry I established the Augustinians at Carlisle, and Furness Abbey was founded by Stephen, Count of Boulogne and the nephew of Henry I, in 1127. The site of Furness Abbey has much in common with that of Wetheral, for it lies in a sheltered gorge where green woods grow against steep cliffs of red sandstone. A few years later, in 1134, a daughter house to Furness came into existence at a secluded place in the valley of the Calder on land that had been given by Ranulph Meschin, son of the founder of St Bees.

In 1136 the Scots occupied the Lake District, and no more monasteries were endowed until their king established Holme Cultrum in 1150. Like Furness Abbey, Holme Cultrum belonged to the Cistercian order – a community famous for its role in the medieval wool trade. Furness Abbey owned compact blocks of territory, that included the greater part of High and Low Furness together with extensive sheep pastures in upper Eskdale and Borrowdale. In addition the monastery's empire stretched to the Isle of Man and many estates in Ireland and Yorkshire. Holme Cultrum's domain was much more broken and scattered. It included a compact core of territory on the Solway plain and many widely dispersed possessions in the Eden valley and the Cumberland fells. For instance, one of the many gifts to the abbey had been made by Hugh de Morville at Lazonby (5439) in the Eden valley – 'a pasture for 500 sheep, 10 oxen, 10 cows and their young for one year, one bull, two horses, four acres of arable land, and nine acres of meadow, with common pasture in all his demesene lands there'. Holme Cultrum was a daughter house to Melrose Abbey and through its associations acquired many outlying possessions in Galloway and southern Scotland.

With the return of the north-west to English rule another period of monastic foundations occupied the second half of the twelfth century. Robert de Vaux, lord of Gilsland, who had acquired the newest and most insecure of border territories in the country of Hadrian's Wall, established the Augustinian priory at Lanercost in 1166. Another Augustinian foundation appeared at Conishead, on the shore of the Leven estuary in Low Furness, and in 1190 William Marshall, Earl of Pembroke, gathered a community of Augustinians at Cartmel. The last monastery in the region, last to be founded and last to be dissolved at the Reformation, is the grey limestone ruin of the Premonstratensian order at Shap (5415). Suddenly one comes upon it in the upper valley of the Lowther, sheltered and screened from the bleak moorlands by limestone crags overhung with trees. The landscape still reveals the touch of a medieval civilization that was lost at the Reformation. The distinctive element 'grange' among the place names points to outlying sheep farms that belonged to the monastery; and faint earthen dikes that wriggle across the moors, half-buried in heather, remind us of the long forgotten works of the monks in making boundaries to show the limits of their property (5414). The location of Shap Abbey may seem bleak and inhospitable; even today the main road, roaring with traffic, and the railway seem out of place in this sea of moorland that is so often fog-bound or clogged with snow. But the enveloping moors grazed the hundreds of sheep whose fleeces provided the economic foundations of the monastery at Shap, so much so that its name was known among the cloth merchants of Italy, for a document of 1315, an Italian wool-buyer's list, names *Ciappi in Vestrebellanda* as one of the sources in the British Isles.

Although all the great monasteries but one lay outside the mountain core of the Lake District in the coastal lowland it does not mean that the interior fell beyond their sphere of interest. St Bees owned much of the land in Ennerdale, while Furness Abbey controlled for almost four hundred years territories in the Lake District that amounted almost to a kingdom. The successive abbots were scarcely distinguishable from the powerful marcher lords. Stephen's charter to Furness Abbey in 1127 shows that most of the peninsula and the fells between Windermere and lake Coniston passed into the hands of this Benedictine community that transferred itself to the Cistercians in 1147. The words of the charter, preserved in the Abbey Coucher Book or collection of documents recording in detail the affairs of the monastery, breathe the atmosphere of its period, the light and the darkness of medieval Europe. It reads:

> Considering daily the shortness of life and seeing that all the pomps of this declining age hasten to destruction and that the roses and flowers of flourishing kings, emperors and dukes and the crowns and palms of the great wither and decay and that all things in rapid course tend to dissolution and death I do therefore bestow and grant and give back to Almighty God and to St Mary of Furness and the Abbot of that place all that my forest of Furness and Walney with all privilege of hunting therein. And Dalton and all my seignorality within Furness with the men and all things pertaining to it that is to say in wood and in plain in land and in waters. . . .

The first half of the thirteenth century saw important additions among the mountains to the estates of Furness Abbey. In 1209 the monks of Furness bought the greater part of Borrowdale from Alice de Rumelli, heiress of the Barony of Allerdale. The boundaries of the property reached from the head of Derwentwater by High Scawdel (2315), the Honister Pass and Great Gable (2110) to the Sty Head Pass. The Borrowdale estate of Furness Abbey marched on the east with land owned by another great Cistercian monastery, Fountains in Yorkshire. Alice de Rumelli had given the Watendlath valley (2716), Langstrath (2610), including the hamlet of Stonethwaite (Plate 4a), and the plain between Derwentwater and Bassenthwaite to Fountains in 1195. Thus, a large segment of the central fells was used from the beginning of the thirteenth century by the two great Cistercian abbeys for the grazing of sheep and cattle. To the west, the Buttermere fells still formed part of the Forest of Copeland and much of the land was kept as a deer preserve.

Little can be gleaned from documentary sources about the relationships between the new landowners and the inhabitants of Borrowdale's scattered hamlets. Towards the end of the fourteenth century a long argument arose between Furness Abbey and Fountains over the ownership of Stonethwaite (2613). The abbot of Furness maintained that an agreement of 1211 defining the limits of the two monastic estates had been wrongly drawn up and claimed, as geography would also suggest, that this hamlet belonged with the settlements in Borrowdale. The evidence was placed before several ecclesiastical courts and showed that Stonethwaite at that time was a thriving dairy farm. The monasteries must have provided the farms of Borrowdale with a steady and expanding market for their fleeces; they were, after all, leading agents in the international wool trade. No doubt the trails by Sty Head tarn and Esk Hause that had carried the Neolithic traffic in axes from the Langdale Pikes were now followed by pack trains carrying the produce of the Borrowdale farms to the abbey storehouses and landing places on Walney Channel. Furness Abbey also left its mark on the place names of Borrowdale where Grange (2517), a hamlet nestling among a cluster of ice-smoothed rocks, indicates the chief monastic settlement in the valley – the farm from which the monks managed the day-to-day affairs of their mountain estate. The name is first recorded in the Coucher Book of Furness Abbey in 1396, where we read about 'our grange in Borrowdale' – *grangia nostra de Boroudale*. Does this mean that Grange came into existence at some time in the thirteenth or fourteenth centuries, between the date when Furness Abbey acquired the estate in Borrowdale and the first appearance of the place name in the Coucher Book? Perhaps, on the other hand, the medieval word, *Grange*, came to replace an earlier Norse or Celtic place name. This hamlet stands at an easy bridging-point of the Derwent where the river begins to meander across the marshy and frequently flooded delta at the head of the lake. It lies, too, under the shadow of Castle Crag whose hill fort was certainly used in Roman and Dark Age times. The choice of Grange for the site of Borrowdale's monastic farm suggests that the place was already the master-settlement in Furness Abbey's mountain estate (Plate 6a).

In 1242 Furness Abbey added another 14,000 acres to its mountain territory with the acquisition of upper Eskdale. This estate was the result of an exchange with David de Mulcaster who received one of the abbey's properties, Monk Foss (1185), situated at the foot of the steep western slope of Black Combe. The acquisition of the rock-strewn wilderness, held within the ring of dark peaks and crags between Scafell and Bowfell, and the abandonment of an estate on the coastal plain suggest some of the motives at work in this medieval transaction. Above all the Abbey gained a link in its Lakeland communications, a piece in the territorial jigsaw puzzle that gave a foothold on the high route across the roof of the Lake District by Esk Hause (2308). The southern edge of the Eskdale property stood astride the Hardknott Pass (2201) and the line of the Roman road that led across the Wrynose Pass towards Little Langdale and the confines of High Furness. Upper Eskdale must have represented a valuable economic gain as well for Furness Abbey because Brotherilkeld was a sheep farm of some 14,000 acres. Even today permanent settlement has advanced no further up Eskdale; Brother-ilkeld is still the last farm in the valley. The name means 'the booth of Ulfkell'. 'Booth' comes from the Old Norse word for a hut or a temporary shelter. It seems likely that Brotherilkeld represents the frontier of settlement achieved by the Norse settlers in Eskdale in the tenth century. The *booth* probably served the sheep pastures that occupied the whole of the upper valley to the ring of rocky mountain summits. When the abbot of Furness agreed to the exchange of estates in the middle of the thirteenth century he was bartering for a sheep farm that had probably been in existence for three hundred years. One wonders too whether he received with the estate the descendants of the Herdwicks that first stocked the land at some time in the tenth century.

Brotherilkeld's outlying site on the frontier of settlement was probably plainer in the Middle Ages than it is today because all the fell country was subject to the forest laws. Sheep farming conflicted with the preservation of deer, wild boars and hawks. In many places this conflict has gone unrecorded, but in upper Esk-dale one is able to sense the tensions that arose as pastures for sheep rearing were carved out among the mountains. A few facts preserved in the Furness Coucher

Book tell how a compromise was reached in 1284 between John de Hudleston, Lord of Millom, and the Abbey. The monks were given 'the liberty of enclosing the pasture of Botherhulkil and Lyncoue which adjoins the Forest of Egremont with a dyke, wall or paling as the abbot and monks should think most convenient for them; but such, nevertheless, as harts and does and their fawns could leap.' Remains of this medieval boundary that defined the sheep pasture from the wilderness are still to be found amid the bracken in that delectable piece of upper Eskdale above the blue-green pools and cold white waterfalls of Throstle Garth (2203). Again, as one crosses the narrow hump-backed packhorse bridge – a timeless piece of vernacular architecture – into the sheepfold, concealed in the little gorge by the Esk, one wonders how long the flocks from the surrounding fells have been penned at this place (Plate 28a). It is almost certain that this was the gathering place for the medieval flocks. John de Hudleston's agreement of 1284 recognized the needs of the shepherd and tried to protect those of the huntsman, but the conflict has long been settled in favour of the sheep.

The rise of sheep-rearing has left its mark on the landscape of upper Eskdale. The almost total absence of trees, except for a few wiry specimens in the inaccessible clefts along by the river, speaks of a landscape denuded by grazing animals. Place names testify to this radical deforestation. Yew Crags (2202) frown upon the farmyard of Brotherilkeld, black and menacing above the valley; a little higher the same long slope is called Yew Bank. Such names today are complete misfits. As one follows the track into upper Eskdale in the brilliant shimmering heat of the summer one could wish for the dark shade of the yew forest that once covered the screes below those crags. One stunted survivor, forlorn beside a huge rock, and a place name is all that remains of a landscape feature that was probably still there when Furness Abbey took over the management of upper Eskdale.

The role of Furness Abbey in shaping the landscape of the Lake District is most clearly visible in the territory that formed the core of the little feudal empire. In High Furness the abbey's chief possession was the manor of Hawkshead (3598), a large estate that comprised the fell country between Lake Coniston and Windermere. Until the latter half of the twelfth century Hawkshead was probably no larger and no more important than any of the other hamlets in the tiny clearings among the moors and woods of the Forest of High Furness. In fact the name Hawkshead, *Haukr's saeter*, suggests a pastoral farm that had first been cleared and settled from some more important parent community, perhaps at Coniston. Furness Abbey raised the status of Hawkshead when the monks established a grange or manor farm there. It was the centre from which they controlled the affairs of the district; and when Furness Abbey engaged in the busy

wooded plateau of the Cartmel and Furness Fells.

22a. *Troutbeck – an abandoned statesman's house.*

22b. *Middlefell Place – a statesman's farm in Great Langdale.*

23a. *Boundary of a medieval deer-park above Nab Scar, Rydal.*

23b. *The asymmetrical Helvellyn ridge with its indented eastward edge in strong contrast to the smooth slopes dropping towards Thirlmere.*

24a. *Grasmere Sports – the start of the Senior Hound Trail over ten miles of rough fell.*

24b. *The head of Langdale on the busiest track to the high central fells; in the background stands Pike of Stickle and the scree of the Neolithic axe factory.*

wool trade of western Europe as one of the largest English suppliers, so Hawkshead came to dominate the medieval economy of the Furness Fells. Hawkshead Hall (350988), a sixteenth-century farmhouse, preserves some parts of the monastic grange among its buildings.

Around Hawkshead the monks created a number of outlying farms, enclosures from the wilderness for the purpose of sheep-rearing. We can recognize them today by the distinctive place-name element *park*. This word of French origin means 'an enclosed piece of ground for pasture or arable farming', and it was introduced into England only after the Norman Conquest. Several of the *parks* of High Furness came into existence about the middle of the fourteenth century after Edward III had granted a licence to the abbey for the making of enclosures in 1338. A number of lonely sheep farms such as Lawson Park (3195) and Parkamoor (3092) were carved out of the fells that rise steeply from the east shore of Coniston Water. Farther south among the tumbled wooded hills around Colton we find Hill Park (3087) and the highly descriptive Abbot Park (3188). Similar medieval clearances have left their trace in the place names along the shore of Windermere at High Stott Park and Low Stott Park (3788).

The scattered medieval sheep farms added a fresh element to the landscape of High Furness. The hamlets of the Scandinavian settlers, distinguished by their *thwaite* names, occupied the floors of the main valleys; in contrast, the sites of the fourteenth-century granges lie high up on the slopes of the fells with easy access to the extensive rough grazings of the summits.

The manor of Hawkshead was one of the richest possessions of Furness Abbey. A survey of the monastery's resources under the last abbot, Roger Pele, in the 1530s showed that Hawkshead was worth almost three times as much as Dalton, the regional capital of Low Furness. The same rental records that the estates of the abbey produced 164 stones of wool; of this quantity almost half, 80 stones, had come from Hawkshead. The development of High Furness for specialized sheep-rearing not only brought new settlements into existence, but had a deep effect on the vegetation of the district. Grazing animals make a relentless impact on the landscape without the interference of man. Seeds and young shoots are grubbed up and eaten; over the decades the woodlands aged and lacked the replenishment of young timber. Finally they were transformed into rough pastures with here and there a gnarled and ancient tree. The analysis of pollen preserved in the peat-bogs and lake-silts of Furness has revealed a marked decline in woodland that seems to coincide with the rise of medieval sheep-farming in the region. Certainly by the seventeenth century most of High Furness had been denuded of natural forest, the price of several centuries of pastoralism.

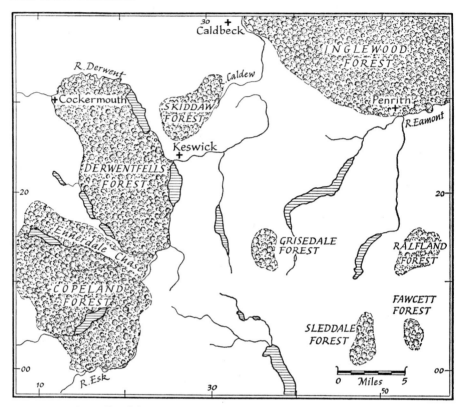

Map 23 *The medieval forests of the Lakeland fringes.*

Although the Norman Conquest led to the foundation of the great monasteries of north-west England, with all the benefits that they brought to the countryside, it also hindered the growth of settlement and the expansion of the economy when large tracts of land were placed under the Forest Laws. Mountainous and thinly populated regions were favoured areas for the creation of 'forests', and none more than Cumberland and Westmorland (Map 23). Inglewood, a royal forest, was the biggest hunting ground in England. It covered a large part of eastern Cumberland stretching from Cross Fell to the sea at Bowness-on-Solway. To the south Inglewood enveloped the whole of the Skiddaw massif, extending some forty miles from east to west and twenty-five miles from north to south. As we cross Inglewood today the landscape displays many features of late reclamation from wood and heath. The open pattern of hamlets such as Unthank (4536), whose widely-spaced farms speak of piecemeal clearance from the forest, place names

162

such as Fieldhead (4539) and Hutton End (4438), and the long straight roads that followed the large-scale enclosures of the eighteenth century – all belong to a region where the wilderness lingered late in the Middle Ages.

Apart from the vast royal forest of Inglewood, the Lake District contained many private forests. The whole of the Barony of Copeland probably lay under the Forest Laws until the early thirteenth century. Copeland Forest covered all the western fells of the Lake District between the Derwent and the Esk and reached to the coastline of the Irish Sea. Even today the name Copeland Forest still lives in the region of scree-scarred ridges and empty valleys that stretch to the north-west of Wastwater. Farther south the Forest of Millom occupied the greater part of Duddondale. The head of the lordship, Millom, lay miles away at the mouth of the Duddon estuary, but the forest continued its existence until the break-up of the estate in the eighteenth century. The private forests of the western Lake District formed one of the remotest parts of medieval England, and this is a quality that the region has not lost entirely in the middle of the twentieth century. The Duddon, from its source in the peat bogs above the Wrynose Pass to Ulpha, still is a world apart from the double-decker buses, and the endless stream of coaches, cars and chemical transporters that follow the trunk road from Grasmere to Dunmail Raise. The medieval forests of the eastern Lake District largely belonged to the Barony of Kendal and their names litter the modern map – Grisedale Forest in the deep basin beneath St Sunday Crag (3613), Thornthwaite Forest near Hawes Water that was already feeling the pressure of settlement in the late Middle Ages, Fawcett Forest (5303) and Sleddale Forest (4802) on the gentle rounded fells above Kendal.

The medieval forests of Cumberland and Westmorland displayed a considerable variety of scenery. Inglewood contained many acres of mature woodland broken by open spaces, 'lawns' whose pastures were grazed by sheep and cattle for a small fixed rent. Much of Copeland and the recesses of Grisedale Forest beneath Helvellyn were probably as bare as we see them today. Again, the forests were not totally devoid of settlement. Far from it, because in some places the forest laws were applied to some of the long settled tracts of the north-west. For instance, the royal forest of Inglewood was defined in the twelfth century and it was so called because of the large number of Anglian 'tuns' within its borders. In Edward I's reign the boundaries of Inglewood Forest were re-surveyed, and the 'perambulation' that was ratified at Lincoln in 1301 shows that it contained Castle Sowerby (3738), a huge parish of scattered settlements, and the large village of Skelton (4335) set amid its open fields, to mention only two places out of many. Again, the Forest of Millom had its long established hamlets and farms along the Duddon valley. The farmers at Ulpha (1993) and the tenements at the head of the dale – Birks (2399), Black Hall (2301) and the now deserted Gaitscale Close (2502) – all had the right to graze their stock on the common lands in the forest.

The imposition of the forest laws on the greater part of the Lake District after the Norman Conquest restricted colonization and agricultural improvement in a period of expanding population. These laws aimed at the preservation of wild life for the huntsman. In consequence it was illegal to make fresh clearances in the forests; assarting, to use the Norman term that described the conversion of waste and woodland to farmland, was forbidden. No new buildings could be erected within the bounds of the forests, and wood for burning, building and making fences could only be taken under the watchful eye of the forester. But the laws of a state that fail to express the deep unconscious forces at work in history are rarely effective or long-lasting. Colonization took place within the forests. By the end of the sixteenth century the relentless processes of change had converted the forests and 'free chaces', the hunting preserves of lords and barons, into the huge common grazing lands of the fells shared by their tenants.

The history of countless assarts, the enclosure of bits and pieces of the great game preserves, can be glimpsed in documents from the middle of the thirteenth century; but before this time we have the striking evidence of organized settlements made by the state with the aim of increasing the political security of the Normans in the northern marches. It will be remembered that the Anglo-Saxon Chronicle's account of William II's conquest of the north says that after Carlisle had been filled with troops the king 'returned to the south, and sent thither very many English peasants with wives and stock to dwell there to till the ground'. The place names of their settlements may still be recognized because they combine a *by* with a Norman personal name. Also the new settlers gathered in little nucleated villages that were composed of a formal string of farmsteads, rather openly spaced and often laid out along one side of a lane. In the settlement patterns of Cumberland they stand out from the districts of hamlets and isolated farms and also from the large Anglian villages where the farms are often closely spaced around the fringe of a wide green (Plate 14a). One cluster of late eleventh-century villages occupies the lowland around Carlisle. Another group of settlers carved fresh farms out of the woodland to the north-west of Greystoke. Here we find Johnby (4333), Ellonby (4235) and Lamonby (4135). Ellonby is named after Alein, the Breton, and Lamonby contains the Flemish personal name, Lambert. Both point to the origins of the wave of settlers who followed in the wake of William II's army, and it is likely that Alein and Lambert were soldiers who chose to take estates on the new frontier. John only became popular as a personal name in the twelfth century along with other names taken from the scriptures, so it is almost certain that Johnby belongs to this same period of settlement. One can only guess at the reasons why settlers were established on lands in the Greystoke Barony where the lordship remained in the hands of a pre-Conquest family. Was this district beneath the shadow of Carrock Fell with deep roots in the Lake District's Celtic past feared as a possible source of rebellion?

Many of the details of the slow process of taking in land from the great forests must have passed without record, but one instance from the beginning of the thirteenth century reveals the mechanics of piecemeal settlement at Mosser (1124) on the western fringe of Copeland Forest. The name means 'the shieling on the moss'. Even today the moss has not completely vanished; fragments remain in the flat-floored depression that separates Mosser from Pardshaw (0924), on the edge of a little limestone hill. The charter granted by Richard de Lucy to Adam de Mosser in 1202 shows that developments were going on about that time. The summer pasture that had been established by Norse-Irish settlers, if we derive the beginnings of Mosser from its place-name, was growing into a group of scattered farms carved out of the wooded foothills. It is likely that the process had been going on for some time and that in his agreement Richard de Lucy was accepting one of the most striking features of the landscape history of the twelfth and thirteenth centuries – the relentless colonization and improvement of waste land. The charter provided 'that the aforesaid Adam and his heirs shall till, build and assart the wood, and make sales and gifts of land between Raysthwaitbec, Pardshaw and Ulfscardbec'. It details clearly the limits of the land that was open to development on the fells between Mosser, Thackthwaite (1423) and Loweswater (1221). The charter also defined the parts where there was to be no encroachment on the wilderness – 'the aforesaid Adam and his heirs and their men dwelling on the land of Mosser, cannot and shall not till, build or take wood between *Raystuaitbec* and *Caypeltrebec* but only have pasture for their livestock; that no one else shall have it in common with them; but that if anyone else enters within the fenced bounds mentioned on this page, and my heirs will take our escape money.' This document helps us to date exactly in the first years of the thirteenth century the making of a fragment of the English landscape on the hills to the north of Loweswater. The sites of farms, the connecting lanes and field boundaries were first marked out at this time. The huntsman's preserve was defined by a fence, as Richard de Lucy's charter plainly tells us, but the farmers of Mosser were allowed to pasture their animals in the forest. This was no doubt the higher land of Mosser Fell and Darling Fell that reaches to more than a thousand feet above sea level. At Mosser we can reconstruct through the words in a medieval document the beginnings of a process of landscape development that must have happened in many parts of the Lake District, a process that separated the wilderness from the enclosed fields and farmsteads of the valley floors.

Although the indisputable evidence of the words in a medieval charter is lacking, it is possible to discern the same theme of medieval colonization through a study of the place names in Great Langdale (3006). The first settlement in the wide curving floor of upper Langdale was undoubtedly Baysbrown (3104). It is of Scandinavian origin and means 'Bruni's cowshed', containing an Old Norse personal name. As a farmstead Baysbrown may have originated in the tenth century, and its flocks of sheep probably grazed the whole of upper Langdale. After the Norman Conquest the estate belonged to the Barony of Kendal. Early in the thirteenth century it was given by William de Lancaster, baron of Kendal, to Conishead Priory. The settlement pattern of Great Langdale is very distinctive. Only two farms, Oak Howe (3005) and Side House (2906), occupy the north-facing valley slope, apart from the primary manor farm of Baysbrown. On the other hand, a string of farms within a short distance of each other lies along the congested car road along the foot of the south-facing slope. They stand on rocky knolls above the level valley-floor that was once a lake and is still subject to heavy floods. The names of these farms and their late appearance in the documentary record suggest that they were carved out of the woods and sheep pastures on the most favourable side of the valley at some time between 1200 and 1500. Harry Place (3106) is probably named after the local Harrison family. Ellers is a simple topographical name using a Lake District dialect word; it means the place of the alders. Pye Howe and Raw Head follow, and both only enter the records after 1700. Millbeck (2806) takes its name from the stream that once drove a watermill. Middlefell Place (2806) commemorates another local family, the *Mithelfels* who are named in the Lay Subsidy Rolls for 1332. These new holdings were probably carved out of Conishead Priory's estate of Baysbrown in the way that Adam de Mosser and his associates pushed forward the frontier of settlement among the fells at Loweswater. By the time of the dissolution of the monasteries in 1537 the property in Langdale was divided into two parts – the demesne, that is Baysbrown and much of the land on the southern side of the valley, went to John Atkinson of Cockermouth, while 'the tenements', the medieval farms of the northern slopes, were bought by Gawen Braithwaite.

The relentless and silent demands of the rising population of the Lake District

for agricultural land slowly converted the deer forests into the huge upland commons, the grazing grounds of sheep and cattle. By the end of the thirteenth
century landlords generally looked with favour upon these changes because
rents from the improved holdings reaped a rising money income as the frontier
of settlement pushed forward. By the fourteenth century we find that deer are
generally kept in parks, deliberately fenced and enclosed tracts of land, while
foxes, hares and rabbits were caught on the commons. About 1300, a deer park
was made by one of the lords of Millom in the Duddon valley at Ulpha. It is first
mentioned in a will of Alicia de Hudleston in 1337, which says that 'Alice holds
the manor of Millom of the said John, including a Park and another Park called
Ulpha'. A fragment of this deer park still exists in the hummocky wooded landscape below Ulpha. Frith Hall (1891) was built in the late fifteenth century as a
hunting lodge in the park which then stretched westward into the fells almost to
Devoke Water (Plate 30b). At Troutbeck a deer park of two thousand acres was
enclosed in the upper part of the valley (4206), but one of the most fascinating of
the medieval deer preserves came into existence with the fencing of the whole of
the valley of the Rydal Beck. A document, dated 3 May 1277, tells of a dispute
between Sir Roger de Lancaster, lord of the Barony of Kendal, and William de
Lyndesey. The animals of William's tenants at Ambleside had strayed into Sir
Roger's hunting preserve at Rydal (Plate 23a). A fine was imposed of a half penny
for every ox, cow, mare, pig or five sheep caught in the deer park. A higher rate of
one penny was charged for every five goats, which probably means that they
created the most damage when let loose in woodland. But the most interesting
item in this medieval dispute is that the two litigants agreed to build a fence
around the deer preserve – to define it as a park. William de Lyndesey promised
to make a fence along the spur between Rydal Beck and Scandale, from the outskirts of Ambleside to Low Pike (3707) at a height of almost 1,700 ft. Roger de
Lancaster made a similar boundary along the westerly spur that divides Rydal
Beck from Grasmere. The work was done in one summer between May and
September of 1277. We know this because the medieval court decided that 'juries
of respectable men were to fix the boundaries' and all fences were to be made
before Michaelmas 1277. As you follow the steep track today from Rydal to the
summit of Fairfield you can still see traces of this morsel of landscape history.
On the steep climb to Heron Pike, at almost two thousand feet, it is worthwhile
to take one's eyes for a moment from one of England's choicest prospects –
Grasmere far below, the silver band of Windermere in the distance and all the
high dark fells to the west – and look at the line of grey, gale-flattened stones that
winds across the hillside. That was the work of 1277. Where the track of the

167

medieval deer park's boundary passes from rock to boulder-clay and peat-bog, the fence becomes a faint overgrown embankment scarcely a foot in height with a parallel ditch.

The chief theme of landscape history in the Lake District between the twelfth and the sixteenth centuries is the decline of the deer forest at the expense of sheep-farming. The advance of settlement among the mountains is reflected in the development of the medieval parishes and the founding of chapels to serve the lonely communities of farmers. The parishes of the north-west were sketched out in the first half of the twelfth century, probably soon after the creation of the See of Carlisle in 1122. It is not known whether the Normans produced a fresh plan for the territorial organization of the church in the north-west or if they revived an older parish system that had evolved in the days of the church's missionary activity. The latter is probably the more likely. Just as the baronies of the north-west in the twelfth century seem to reflect the geography of an earlier political organization, so the parishes appear to have their roots in a pre-Norman past. The twelfth century was a time when most of the parish churches were rebuilt in stone. In Cumberland, Westmorland and the detached part of Lancashire to the north of Morecambe Bay sixty parish churches contain architectural evidence of building in the twelfth century. At twenty-one other places there is documentary proof of a church in the same period, even though no stones remain to tell the tale today because of total rebuilding at a later period. More than eighty parish churches were not created from nothing in less than a century; a rebuilding of many Saxon churches must have taken place. Again, proof is not lacking on the ground of the importance of the church in pre-Norman times. Scores of crosses or fragments of crosses, dating from the seventh to the tenth centuries, that we now find gaunt and weathered in churchyards or swept into some unused corner of the nave are evidence of places of worship long before the Norman Conquest. Cumberland, in fact, is as rich in these earliest memorials of Christianity as Cornwall. There the art was Celtic; here in the north-west the vine scrolls, geometric patterns and beasts and birds are the products of an Anglian school of artists that changed under Viking influences. Of Saxon architecture there is little evidence. Some typically narrow doorways, believed to be parts of Saxon buildings, survive in a few churches of the Vale of Eden around Appleby. The west tower at Morland – in the same rich early-settled tract between Appleby and Penrith – is the only surviving Saxon element in a church that was rebuilt in the twelfth century.

The distribution of the twelfth-century parish churches and the extent of those parishes reflects the main fact of the human geography of the region at that time –

the concentration of population on the lowlands around the Lake District and the empty nature of the mountainous core. Kendal was at the centre of one of the largest parishes in England. It included Grasmere and Windermere as well as all the eastern valleys of the Lake District, and it has now been carved up into nineteen parishes. The western valleys – Loweswater, Ennerdale, Wasdale and part of Eskdale – all turned to the mother parish at St Bees. Again, two early medieval parishes were centred on the lowland between Derwentwater and Bassenthwaite – an ancient outlier of settlement among the mountains. Crosthwaite, the place where it seems likely that St Kentigern once planted his cross in the clearing, was the centre of a parish that once stretched to Dunmail Raise. It has since been divided up into six parishes. On the east shore of Bassenthwaite Lake we find the parish church of the same name. The dedication is to St Bega, founder of the first priory at St Bees in the middle of the seventh century. The dedication suggests that there was a church at Bassenthwaite at least two centuries before the Norman Conquest. The simple Norman chancel arch bears witness to the church that was built there, close to the lake shore, in the twelfth century's great period of rebuilding. The rest of the building, Gothic in style, is a result of the drastic restoration in 1873. On the eastern fringe of the Lake District the same themes of parish geography are repeated. Barton (4826) parish contained the whole of Ullswater and its many tributaries. Its ancient parish boundary marched along the crest of Helvellyn (3415) and then south and east by Fairfield (3511) and High Street (4515). The low central tower of its substantial Norman church still stands, and inside we find the curious double chancel arch that is the result of strengthening towards the end of the thirteenth century. In the south-west Dalton, in Low Furness, and Millom at the mouth of the Duddon estuary were the centres of parishes that reached into the Furness Fells and to the head of Duddondale and upper Eskdale.

As the population of the valleys amid the Lake District's core of high mountains increased in the twelfth and thirteenth centuries the defects of the huge parishes with their distant churches made themselves felt. To avoid the rigours of the long journey to mass and the ceremonies at parish churches on the great feast days, chapels were established, serving the growing population in the mountains. The building of chapels was part of the process of land clearance and settlement and it was usually the work of the lord of the manor or the person to whom land had been granted. For instance, a chapel was built at Thornthwaite (2225), a hamlet among the woods at the foot of the Whinlatter Pass, about the year 1240, by Patrick, son of Thomas de Workington, who had a grant of freshly-cleared land from Alice de Rumelli. We have already noticed that it was she who gave so lavishly to Furness Abbey and Fountains in the Derwent valley. It seems that on a smaller scale the Romeli family were settling farmers on newly-cleared land. There is nothing in the architecture of St Mary's church at Thornthwaite to tell of a medieval chapel on this site. The present building was put up about 1760 and much remodelled on two occasions in the nineteenth century. Similarly, the little whitewashed church in Borrowdale which was completely rebuilt in 1825 stands on the site of a medieval chapel established close to the boundary of the properties of Fountains and Furness abbeys a quarter of a mile below Stonethwaite (257140). Does the siting of Borrowdale church mean that it was founded by the monks of Fountains Abbey? If Furness abbey had taken the initiative, one could expect to find the site of their chapel close by the monastic farm at Grange.

On the eastern fringe of the Lake District we can observe the same process at work in the huge parish of Barton. At the beginning of the thirteenth century a chapel was built in the wide middle section of Martindale (434184). Another medieval chapel was established to serve the neighbouring valley of Boredale (4217) where it occupied a lonely and remote site at the valley head. St Martin's chapel was rebuilt in 1633, probably with little change of plan. Its dark rubble walls form a simple rectangular plan with the nave and chancel under one roof and a little bell-cote at the western end. From the churchyard a wide prospect takes in the whole of the upper valley with its succession of isolated farms, several of them now in ruins. Beyond, at the head of Ramsgill (4315), long bare slopes rise to the crest of High Street in the last remnant of a medieval deer forest. Deer are still stalked there in the winter, but the venison goes no longer to the tables of barons or prelates, for instead the local farmers have a contract with a hotel in Huddersfield. At St Martin's chapel you can recreate in the imagination something of the atmosphere of the medieval frontier of settlement in the Lake District. The ruin of the chapel at the head of Boredale, Chapel in the Hause as it is called, serves as a reminder that highest limits of settlement among the mountains were reached before the fifteenth century.

Some of the outlying chapels evolved into parishes; others have vanished from the landscape completely. The acquisition of parish status depended upon the size of a community, and above all upon demands for a local graveyard. The distinguishing mark of the daughter chapels was the absence of a burial ground; corpses often had to be carried long hard miles across the fells to the mother church. Even today the track that climbs steeply from Hawes Water reservoir to Mardale Common still bears the name of the Old Corpse Road (4912). It led through Swindale, Tailbert (5314) and Keld (5514) to the parish church at

Shap. The arduous ritual of this journey ceased in the eighteenth century when a graveyard was made at Mardale chapel. Even more radical changes overtook this valley in 1935 with the making of the Hawes Water reservoir (Plate 10b). Mardale church is drowned in the upper reach of the reservoir and more than a hundred of the bodies that were exhumed in the little yew-shaded churchyard have been buried again at Shap. The fabric of the medieval chapel has also been dispersed. The pulpit went to Borrowdale, while the stonework of the windows was re-used by Manchester Corporation in building the octagonal intake well at Hawes Water dam. Two of the earliest chapels to be raised to parishes were Grasmere and Windermere in 1349 and 1348. The former lay sixteen miles distant from the mother church at Kendal, and it is believed that the heavy burden of the Black Death and the demand for local graveyards led to parochial status. It is also true that the shores of Windermere and the Vale of Grasmere and Rydal have ever been one of the most favoured parts of the Lake District and as attractive to settlement as the district around Keswick. We can expect that after more than two centuries of expanding settlement there were enough people here to justify the making of fresh parishes.

Many of the medieval chapels have now disappeared completely. Several vanished with the Church's internal reorganization after the Reformation, but others point to the abandonment of settlements. For instance, in the wild country of the Buttermere and Ennerdale Fells, the chapels at Lorton and Mosser have survived, but the chapel of the Blessed Mary Magdalene at Rannerdale is no longer to be found, nor is the settlement for that matter. The chapel is mentioned in a document of 1508 among the Percy muniments at Cockermouth Castle. It was one of several medieval chapels in the Vale of Lorton, daughters to the mother church at Brigham. Rannerdale's neighbour at Buttermere has survived. There the present church was built in 1841 on the site of an earlier medieval chapel. Whellan, the nineteenth-century topographer, described the chapel at Buttermere as 'the most diminutive of all in England, as it would only hold about half a dozen families'. Rannerdale chapel must have been of the same kind because it served a tiny cluster of farms on a narrow green bench where the Rannerdale Beck empties into Crummock Water. Today there is nothing at Rannerdale; only the place name with its indelible memories of Scandinavian settlers penetrating the bleak recesses of the Buttermere valley. A wood grew over the site after the desertion of the hamlet and its chapel, and now the wood itself has been cleared. The mounds of former farmsteads are covered with a sea of bluebells in May and the gaunt grey screes of Grasmoor overshadow the place. Rannerdale has not been inhabited for two centuries. It stands witness to the

171

great tide of settlement that swept the Lake District in the Middle Ages and that has since receded.

The end of an epoch of expansion
During the fourteenth and fifteenth centuries the pace of economic growth and the expansion of settlement slackened in the Lake District. The symptoms of stagnation and decline are not confined to northern England, but appeared in many parts of Europe. For instance, in England the fifteenth century was a time when villages were deserted by the hundred in an extensive depopulation of the countryside. In the uplands of central Germany fields were abandoned and the forest returned. Settlements in Norway's western fjords were deserted and it is believed that her population declined by a third in the last half of the fourteenth century. The great cycles of economic and demographic change can never be explained in simple terms. Nevertheless, the fourteenth century was overshadowed by the Black Death, and a local factor of great importance in the life of the north-west was the succession of Scots raids. The century opened with four invasions by Scottish armies. The Earl of Buchan and his troops raided Cumberland in 1296, burning Lanercost Priory. In 1314 another army of Scots passed through the Vale of Eden setting fire to Brough and Appleby. The following year saw one of the many sieges of Carlisle, and the troopers of Sir James Douglas worked their way through the Cumberland plain, devastating the priory church at St Bees, attacking the town and castle at Egremont, and doing severe damage at Calder Priory. After this raid the priory was never rebuilt on its former scale.

It is hard to assess the effects on the life and economy of the Lake District of the intermittent unsolved conflict with Scotland that dragged on until the seventeenth century. A bishop of Carlisle has left a vivid and dramatic picture of events at the beginning of the fourteenth century. He said that the Scots slew men, women and children, orphans and widows, burnt nearly all the churches, houses and buildings, drove off cattle and carried away treasures and ornaments. This account of Scottish devastations in Cumberland seems to be borne out by the valuations of church property in the diocese of Carlisle recorded in the returns of papal taxation. In 1291 the total valuation upon which the tax of one tenth was assessed came to £3,171 5s. 7½d. After the wave of destructive raids, in 1318, the assessment contracted to a seventh of the former value reaching only £480 19s. 0d. And so the story of the Scots incursions continues at intervals throughout the century. In 1322 the army of Robert Bruce plundered Holm Cultrum, desolated Cartmel Priory, and forced the abbot of Furness to buy immunity with a ransom. The year 1345 saw an army of 30,000 Scots in northern England, and four times in the 'eighties' Carlisle was besieged. The records contain an interesting royal concession of 1396 that allowed the cutting of timber for building purposes and fuel in Inglewood Forest because of the damage caused by the Scots.

Besides the disasters brought by man, the Black Death swept through the Lake District in 1348 and again in 1361 and 1362. We have seen that it probably caused the order for the consecration of parochial graveyards at Windermere and Grasmere. Again, there is some evidence of the plague's effect on population in the north-west. In a petition to the Pope, in 1363, the Bishop of Carlisle complains that 'whereas, on account of the late pestilence, there is a lack of priests in the diocese'.

The Middle Ages closed in the north-west in a mood of insecurity and gloom. It is reflected above all in the building style of the period. From the late thirteenth century onwards military architecture dominates in the region, not only in extensions to the castles at Kendal, Appleby and Brough, but also in many features of domestic building. The most striking architectural development is the pele tower, of which almost a hundred examples survive in Cumberland and Westmorland from a building period that is practically limited to the fourteenth and fifteenth centuries. They were built as refuges from sudden raids by armies and bands of cattle thieves from across the border. Thick-set and strongly constructed of stone, they rise in three storeys. The ground floor had no windows and only narrow ventilating slits; cattle could be herded there in times of danger. A spiral staircase led to the first floor with a 'hall' and fireplace. The third floor was occupied by the bower, a private quarter for the ladies. The flat roof provided a platform for defence against the attacker. Pele towers rarely stand alone, but have become the cores of more elaborate buildings. Usually a low rectangular building, the 'hall range', was added at a later date. Dacre Castle (4626) provides a rare and beautiful example of a lone standing pele tower that has not fallen into ruins (Plate 13a). Today it is a prosperous-looking manor farm with a gay garden and unusually well-preserved battlements. In the same district around Penrith, in a countryside open to the ravages of Scots armies moving between the Solway fords and Stainmore, we find Yanwath Hall (5028), where a low fourteenth-century pele tower, well preserved, has a fifteenth-century hall attached. At Greystoke Castle (4330), the site of another fourteenth-century pele tower illustrates the haphazard building history of succeeding centuries. The massive pele tower that William Lord Greystoke was given licence to crenellate in 1353 is wrapped up in a vast house built in an Elizabethan style by the Victorian architect Salvin.

The pele towers, the earliest surviving examples of domestic architecture in the north-west, are confined to the exposed borders of the Lake District where the menace of the Scots armies and cattle raiders was greatest. They are particularly numerous on the north-eastern fringe of the region from the Skiddaw massif and Ullswater to the Eden valley. Here, no doubt, the Scots threat reached its height where the armies followed the road southward into England from Carlisle. But this was also one of the richest areas of the region, a district already engaged in the lucrative cattle trade with London and the fairs of eastern England. Here the wealthier estate owners could afford to apply for 'licences to crenellate' and flaunt their place in society with the fortified type of house that had become fashionable all over England by the fifteenth century. In the secluded

Diagram 11   *Ubarrow Hall in Long Sleddale with its gaunt pele tower.*

valleys of the Lake District there was neither the need nor the capital to invest in pele towers. Only in the most easterly valleys of Kentdale and Long Sleddale do we find two isolated examples of pele towers in farm buildings. Kentmere Hall (4504) has a massive ivy-covered ruin of a fourteenth-century tower at its western end. In Long Sleddale the oldest building in the valley is the remnant of the pele tower that forms the core of Ubarrow Hall (5002) (Diag. 11) (Plate 34c). The rest of the house, now covered with a dull wash of cement, was built or rebuilt in the seventeenth century. Here the huge boulders of the ruined pele tower take us back to the earliest stage of the history of domestic building in stone in the Lake District, when the long and hardly recorded process of land clearance was far from complete. As we look at the rubble incorporated in the tower at Ubarrow we can imagine the source of this stone in some field painfully cleared from the lower slope of the valley – a wilderness once overgrown with brushwood and littered with boulders. There is nothing to tell us why the owners of the manor farms at Kentmere and Long Sleddale in the fourteenth century decided to build pele towers for themselves. Perhaps they felt exposed to the stray cattle raiders from the north following the track across the mountains from Mardale by Gatescarth (4709) and the Nan Bield (4509) passes, or did they merely follow the fashion of the times?

It is hard to calculate the effects of Scottish raids and the ravages of plague on the life and landscape of the north-west. William Rollinson in his recent book, *A History of Man in the Lake District*, has concluded that 'there is little evidence to suppose that the Lakeland valleys were raised by the Scots'. The tempo of the strenuous two centuries that followed the Norman Conquest abated amid the political confusion at the close of the Middle Ages. A crucial phase in the history of the developing landscape drew to an end with the silent, scarcely-recorded conversion of the vast medieval deer forests into pastures common to the scores of hamlets in the dales. Many details had been inscribed on the landscape since 1100 – farms and fields, chapels and deer parks – and the sixteenth century was to introduce a new stage in the social history of the region that saw the destruction of the monasteries and the rise of a class of yeomen farmers who were to build the farmhouses we see today on the sites carved out by their medieval ancestors.

7

The age of the statesmen – from the Tudors to the industrial revolution

The foundation of the Tudor dynasty in 1485 marks the conventional boundary between medieval and modern in English history. The date is practically meaningless in the regional history of the Lake District, where the Middle Ages end with the closing of the monasteries and the confiscation and sale of their extensive properties after 1536. Histories of the north of England describe the Reformation in gloomy terms as 'the northern tragedy'. Of Henry VIII it has been said, 'he found the north poor, and he robbed it of the only treasure it possessed in the wealth of the abbeys'. The social and economic upheaval that followed the destruction of the monasteries had deep effects on the life and geography of the region. By the beginning of the seventeenth century a class of yeoman farmers, known locally as 'statesmen', dominated the life of the Lake District. Trade rose in volume by Elizabeth's reign and was focused on expanding market towns such as Ulverston, Kendal, Hawkshead and Keswick.

At the outset the Lake District had entered a brief period of rising prosperity in the first quarter of the sixteenth century before the blow fell on the monasteries. The monastic houses engaged in new building programmes in the years just before the Reformation. At Carlisle, for instance, the north-west gate of the abbey precinct was built in 1528. Shap Abbey was building an imposing west tower about the same period, and this is the only impressive piece of the ruin that remains today sheltered in a constricted green haven of the Lowther valley among the stormy cloud-swept moors of the eastern fells. At Furness Abbey, too, the foundations of the great west tower were laid under Abbot Rawlinson, and it was approaching completion at the time of the dissolution in 1537.

The documents collected in the Coucher Book of Furness Abbey suggest that early in the sixteenth century important changes were afoot on the vast estates under the control of the monastery. It is not too much of an exaggeration to say that the sixteenth century introduced a major stage in the settlement of High Furness. From time to time piecemeal enclosures had probably been made from its heaths and open pastures. In 1509 and again in 1532 the abbey decided to make formal agreements with its tenants and the squatters on monastic property over the enclosure and creation of new farms. The agreements were signed at Colton (3186) and at Hawkshead Hall. They allowed the enclosure of patches of land not more than one and a half acres in extent, and the building of a farm-stead. Place names provide an important clue to the understanding of this wave of sixteenth-century settlement, because each farm had the name 'ground' attached to it. Usually it is coupled with the surname of the family that created the new farm. Atkinson Ground, Sand Ground and Hartley Ground are typical of such names. Furness alone contains thirty-six farm names ending in 'ground'; and in the south-western part of the Lake District H. S. Cowper, writer of a classic local history on Hawkshead, counted a grand total of fifty-three names. The 'grounds' that were carved out of the common pastures on the properties of Furness Abbey represent a unique fragment of the English landscape, because their origin can be dated to the first few years of the sixteenth century and they are restricted to one monastic estate.

Several 'grounds' came into being along the valley of the river Lickle (Diag. 12). Hartley Ground (2189) stands lost in a clump of trees by the river. From there a winding track climbs through five hundred feet to Pickthall Ground (2090), a farm set amidst a pocket-handkerchief collection of fields on the edge of Dunnerdale Fells. Here one can see how the site of the farm has been nibbled out of the hundreds of acres of rough grazing on the fell-top. Higher still, beneath the boggy rain-swept slopes of Caw (2394), a string of these early six-teenth-century enclosures may be traced in the names Stainton Ground (2192), Carter Ground (2292), Jackson Ground (2392) (Plate 32a) and Stephenson Ground (2393). All these farms probably came into existence about the year 1509 when the abbot made the first agreement with his tenants in the Furness Fells. It seems likely that the 'grounds' of the country between Coniston Water and Windermere came into existence in the 1530s after the signing of the agreement with the tenants of the manor of Hawkshead in 1532. Around Hawkshead we find a cluster of 'ground' names – Waterson Ground (351994), Sand Ground (3499), Sawrey Ground (3399), Keen Ground (3498), and Roger Ground (3597).

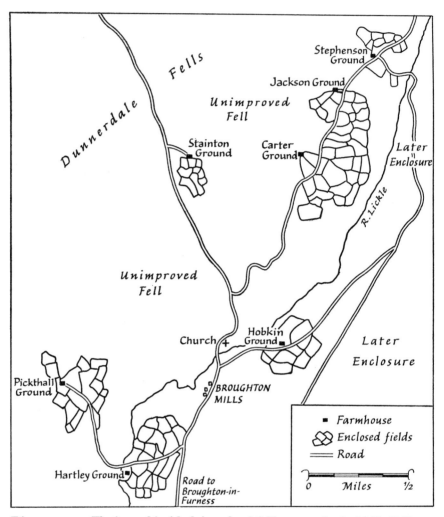

Diagram 12   *The 'grounds' with their enclosed field patterns in the Lickle Valley.*

Bank Ground (3196) and Atkinson Ground (3297) take up the same story in another tract of enclosure near Coniston.

The carving out of small farms from the edge of the waste in High Furness was only one aspect of a process that affected many other parts of the Lake District and which continued until the end of the Tudor period. If the abbots of Furness, rich and often benevolent landlords, could not resist the claims and the

178

methods of the squatter, the great earls and barons must have found it even more difficult to preserve the wilderness of the deer forest. By 1578 Copeland Forest had practically vanished as a hunting preserve. The northern section, among the hills and mountains westward of Derwentwater and Bassenthwaite, was reduced to a 'free chase' known as the Forest of Gatesgarth. The deer had been pushed back into the highest and wildest fells that form the divide between the Newlands valley and Buttermere. Around Newlands colonization was active in the late sixteenth century with the influx of German miners who were opening up the copper veins at Goldscope (228185), a name that first appears in the records in 1569 as *Gottesgab* or God's gift. Further south the limits of Copeland Forest as a hunting preserve became restricted to upper Ennerdale. Little more than a century later Gatesgarth Forest had been transformed into the commons of Buttermere and Newlands, but a writer in 1675, Edmund Sandford in *A cursory relation of all the Antiquities and Families in Cumberland*, could still say of Ennerdale 'the mountains and Forest of Innerdale, where there is red deer, and as great harts and stags as in any part of England'. The sparsity of settlement in Ennerdale is probably explained by the long history of the valley as a hunting preserve – a wild place that lives on into the twentieth century in the form of the deadly monotony of a state forest.

On the southern fringe of Copeland Forest, at Nether Wasdale, an Inquisition of 1578 reveals that piecemeal encroachment was taking place. We read that 'Henrie Patricson gent holdeth there a cottage and 36 acres of pasture improved of the lord's waste called *blen tounge* rented at 10 shillings. And also a little close or improvement adjoining to the East end thereof containing three roods, rent, 4*d*.' This Elizabethan document, the great survey of the estates of Henry Percy, earl of Northumberland, provides a glimpse of the making of the landscape of Wasdale in the sixteenth century. Small farms, not unlike the 'grounds' of High Furness, had been recently reclaimed from the wilderness. Today the pattern of settlement in Nether Wasdale bears all the marks of a haphazard process of late-medieval colonization. The only focus of settlement is at Strands (1204), a hamlet as the name implies on the bank of the Irt with a public house and a tiny parish church that was once a chapel in the vast medieval parish of St Bees. For the rest, Nether Wasdale consists of lonely farms and cottages that stretch across the hummocky bench strewn with glacial debris that reaches to the foot of the precipitous slopes of Buckbarrow (1305) and Long Crag (1506). Here are the smallholdings that were carved out of the forest and for which the lord was pleased to receive a money rent.

The Percy Survey of 1578 throws up a few dark hints of different systems of

179

land-use in the wild country around Wastwater (Plate 25). At the head of the lake lies the remote and scattered community of Wasdale Head. The Survey says that the earls of Northumberland had seventeen tenants there and that each has between three and ten acres 'of arable and meadow in Wasdale Head field'. We can still trace the outlines of this former common field, 345 acres in extent, in the pattern of little walled enclosures that fill the floor of the valley (Plate 26b). Nothing is known about the origins of the former open field at Wasdale Head. Does it date back to a community of Norse farmers occupying the tongue of stony alluvium between the two becks that empty into Wastwater in the tenth century, or is it the result of a group effort in land clearance at the very frontier of settlement in the Lake District two or three centuries later? The Percy Survey points to a different kind of settlement history in Nether Wasdale. There the record mentions forty-six tenements, and only six of these possessed strips in a common field. The rest of the farms formed compact and individual holdings with no rights in the shared field. Here we seem to have evidence of two stages of occupation. An earlier communal settlement, perhaps made at the same time as the heroic clearance of the stony acres of Wasdale Head, was followed by a later history of colonization by individual farmers in Copeland Forest. If the suggestion in the Percy Survey of the late date of these clearances is correct, we may attribute the extensive belt of dispersed settlement between the foot of Wastwater and the Bleng valley to a wave of colonization in the sixteenth century.

The most striking feature of the Tudor period in the north-west was the emergence of a rural middle class of yeomen farmers known in the Lake District as the 'statesmen'. Victorian writers about the Lake District transformed the 'statesman' into a romantic, almost heroic figure. Wordsworth probably gave birth to this legend of the 'statesman' when he idealized the life and environment of the mountains; it was an idyllic dream of his own youth and childhood rather than an objective study of rural society in the Lake District. Later writers saw the 'statesmen' through a romantic lens of history and imagined these stable yeomen families as the direct descendants of the primary Viking settlers. The truth is rather more prosaic. The statesmen emerged as a rural middle class in the late medieval period when they enjoyed the right at death to hand on their estates to their next of kin, although they themselves were tenants of a lord. This privilege that gave their tenure something of the nature of freehold was bought at the price of military service to an overlord who could call out his forces when troops and cattle raiders threatened from across the Solway. By the late sixteenth century the power of this class of yeomen farmers had strengthened immensely. They profited by the extinction of monastic overlords and they gained in wealth in a period of inflation, above all through the sale of wool, cattle and timber. It has been calculated that prices multiplied some five times between 1500 and the end of Elizabeth I's reign. While the statesmen profited from the steep rise in the price of wool, they gained also from the fixed level of their customary rents.

From late Tudor times onwards this class of holders by tenant right became freeholders. Nowhere is it possible to trace this process of social change more clearly than on the estates that belonged to Furness Abbey. In 1537 Roger Pele, the last abbot of Furness, had surrendered all the monastic properties to Henry VIII. The Liberty and Lordship of Furness, as it was now called, together with the manor of Hawkshead remained in the hands of the Crown until 1662. In Elizabeth's reign the tenants of the crown lands in Furness succeeded in defining their rights and established their independence of the control of manorial law. 'The code of the customs and bye-laws of Furness' that enshrined this regional social revolution was approved by the Crown in 1586. It gave legal recognition to the emergence of a class of yeomen farmers whose members were to contribute so much to the life of the Lake District in the next two centuries. The different 'statesmen' families, large related groups resembling clans, had each their distinct territories. The Satterthwaites centre on the hamlet from which they took their name (3392). The Turners were established around Oxen Park (3187) and the Taylors at Finsthwaite (3687). The Sandys family had long been connected with Graythwaite (3691), and after the Reformation they became powerful in both the life of Furness and the nation. For instance, Edwin Sandys rose to become Archbishop of York and obtained the letters patent for the founding of a grammar school at Hawkshead. Later, Adam Sandys secured a market charter for Hawkshead from James I.

Recent research has shown that the class of yeomen farmers in the Lake District scarcely matched the romantic picture of the 'statesman' drawn by Victorian antiquarians. For instance, by the end of the sixteenth century there was considerable mobility in this social group. Wealth gained from trade and the buying up of land gave the more energetic a pass to the ranks of the gentry and the aristocracy. The Sandys of Graythwaite climbed to the highest positions in the land. The Patricksons of Ennerdale originated as yeomen farmers and acquired a family coat-of-arms in 1592. The Fletchers emerged from statesman stock in Wasdale to achieve a baronetcy in 1640. If some succeeded in throwing off the calling of sheep farming on the fells, many other yeomen families sank without trace into the labouring classes in the course of the eighteenth century. As the yeomen farmers gained the freehold of their land and the right to dispose of it as they wished, so the stability of their society was threatened. Detailed research has shown that the stability of the statesmen, as immovable in the imaginations of Lake District antiquarians as the mountains that over-shadowed their farms, was already a myth by the beginning of the nineteenth century. The Hearth Tax Returns of 1669–72 contain twenty-five different surnames in Grasmere. G. P. Jones has shown that a century and a half later, in 1829, only six of the names remain among the farmers of the parish and of these only two belong to yeomen families. The continuity of the generations upon the land, for Wordsworth an essential element of a healthy democratic society, was already a myth at the time of his writing.

Several forces were at work in the eighteenth century to destroy the economy and society of the 'statesmen'. It is believed that a run of hard winters between 1738 and 1741, and again from 1784–7 and 1792–5, helped to ruin farmers whose livelihood depended above all upon sheep-rearing. Most of the yeomen farmers engaged in secondary trades – weaving, spinning, fulling, quarrying stone and burning lime – and many of these occupations were declining by the end of the eighteenth century. After the Napoleonic Wars and its long period of inflation many farmers found themselves in money difficulties in a decade of falling prices. Wordsworth recognized the attractions of the growing towns and the new industries for the countryman, but this was only the end of a longer revolution in the life of the statesmen that started in the seventeenth century with the freedom to sell land. The acquisitive landlord investing his wealth in the purchase of estates was a greater threat to the society of the yeomen than the manufacturer with his call for labour from the industrial towns.

The statesman's farm
The seventeenth century in the Lake District has been described with academic caution as 'a not unfavourable period for the prosperity of the yeomen'. By the end of James I's reign most of the statesmen were secure in their holdings and the century of prosperity has left its indelible mark on the landscape of the north-west in scores of farmhouses. The long low buildings with slate or stone roofs – the living quarters finished in roughcast and stark white in the summer sunshine – form one of the most characteristic features of the mountain valleys today (Plate 22b). The white rectangles of distant farmhouses against the green or red-brown fellside symbolize, perhaps more perfectly than anything else, all the processes that tamed the wilderness of the Lake District.

The pele towers of the fourteenth and fifteenth centuries form the earliest examples of domestic architecture in the north-west. But these defensive buildings, strongly constructed of stone, belonged only to the wealthiest. Quieter times and later extensions turned the pele towers into elaborate manor houses or great mansions such as Greystoke. The houses of the small farmers were built of clay and timber, perishable materials that have left no surviving examples in the landscape. One of the greatest gaps in our knowledge of the Lake District lies in the study of domestic buildings between the hut circles and earth embankments of the abandoned Dark Age villages and the solid stone-built farms of the 'statesmen' that appear after 1650. When the stone-built farmhouse under its long roof appears in the second half of the seventeenth century we are not witnessing the inception of a new and revolutionary style of vernacular architecture; rather, the traditions of many centuries are made permanent by the lavish use of stone as a building material. Lately some light has been thrown on the ancestry of the statesman farm by the discovery of the foundations of a medieval house at Millhouse in the Lune valley. Its excavator, Mr R. A. C. Lowndes, believes that the site was inhabited until the middle of the fourteenth century and he suggests that it may have been deserted as a result of the Black Death. The house stood amid a cluster of small rectangular fields and it contained two rooms, one possessing a hearth in the centre. Only the shape of the farmstead is preserved by its foundations of cobblestones and the marks of post-holes; the main structure itself was composed of perishable materials – a timber cruck-frame, thatch and walls of a thin wooden framework plastered with dried mud. Only when a site has been totally abandoned, as at Millhouse, are the details of a medieval farm-house likely to be open to archaeological investigation. Elsewhere, at countless sites in the dales of Cumberland and Westmorland, the solid stone-built states-man farms stand on the foundations of their medieval forerunners. At many places the Norse character of their names and the occurrence of those names in medieval documents, long before the great period of rebuilding in the second half of the seventeenth century, often confirm the occupation of the site in earlier centuries.

The basic element in the plan of the seventeenth-century yeoman's farm was the arrangement of the byre and store-places together with the dwelling house in a single range under one roof (Diag. 13) (Plate 22b). A passage ran through the building from front to back and opposite doors led off from it into the byre and kitchen. The passage was separated from the kitchen by a wall into which was built the only fireplace in the house. Beyond the kitchen, and separated from it by a wooden partition, lay the bower or sleeping quarters. Above the kitchen and bower there was a loft that was reached by a ladder. From the beginning of the eighteenth century some important developments begin to appear in the 'states-man plan'. The single-storeyed house gave way to a two-storey design in which the bedroom was placed upstairs and the former bower was transformed into the parlour. The staircase was built at the back of the house in a wide projecting wing under a long sloping roof that was merely a continuation of the main roof of the house. Later in the eighteenth century, particularly when internal walls had been carried up to help in bearing the load of the roof, the farmhouse underwent a radical change of interior plan. Two rooms in depth were accommodated under the single roof-span so that four bedrooms lay above the kitchen, parlour, living-room and dairy on the ground floor. Along with changes in the internal plan of the farmhouse and the raising of its elevation, the barn and byre of the statesman farm were separated from the dwelling quarters. By the end of the eighteenth century the long house had given way to the square house with the shippen and store-places arranged separately round the farmyard. We have reached the end of a long tradition in vernacular architecture in which the farmer, his family

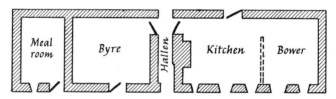

Diagram 13 *A typical early statesman's cottage which housed the family and animals under one roof.*

and his livestock have dwelt under the same roof. The Lake District's long-houses, stone-built in the second half of the seventeenth century, represent the last stage of an evolutionary history that probably reaches back into prehistoric times. One can only speculate upon the deep-seated traditions and unconscious motives that kept a man and his cattle under the same roof for so long. Nicholson, in his *History of Crosby Garrett*, suggests the power of irrational ideas over what should be the most rational of processes, the designing of a house, when he writes of the Westmorland statesmen in the seventeenth century – 'with these people it was a deeply-seated idea that the smell from cattle was healthy and an antidote against certain diseases.'

Although the wave of rebuilding began about 1650 with the reconstruction of long-houses and was resumed in full strength after 1750 with the fashionable design of the square-house, it is often very difficult to date any particular piece of domestic architecture in the Lake District. The grey and dark-blue flagstones that provide an almost universal building material in the dales do not lend themselves to embellishments and inscriptions that allow a precise dating. In many farms, particularly those of the late eighteenth century, the date of the new house is clearly marked by an inscribed and decorated stone over the main entrance. But datestones, however incontrovertible they may look, do not always yield certain proof of the year when the house was built. Sometimes inscribed slabs from an earlier structure were incorporated in the later rebuilding of a farmhouse. W. M. Williams, in his excellent study of farm buildings around Gosforth, has noted as many as three plaques with different dates built into the same wall. However, another important clue to the date of rebuilding frequently survives in the huge, oak bread cupboards that were built into the wooden partition between the kitchen and the bower. As a rule, they were elaborately carved and inscribed with the name of the farmer who had rebuilt the house and the date of the reconstruction.

Unfortunately no detailed contemporary account has come to light of the rebuilding of a Lake District farm in the period before 1800. There are many questions about which one would like to have exact answers. How long did it take? Where were the quarries from which the farmer obtained his building materials? What happened to a farmer and his family while the old house was demolished and the new one was under construction? Was the new house placed upon the foundations of its medieval predecessor? The last question opens up an interesting line of thought to which Cowper provides an answer in his *History of Hawkshead*. He believes that often the foundations of the new house were sketched out a few yards distant from the old farm. After its abandonment the medieval farmstead was sometimes converted into a barn. He claimed that barns at Sawrey Ground (3399), Field Head (3499) and Hawkshead Hill (3398) all contain stones of an older medieval house in their building and that they stand on the sites of the original farmsteads.

The statesman's farm remains one of the most characteristic features of the Lake District's landscape, although the society that created the long-houses beneath their shady yews and sycamores had been changed out of all recognition by the twentieth century. We have seen that the layout of the farmhouse, the 'statesman plan' as it has been called, was probably a medieval concept evolved out of the prehistoric long-house. The custom of applying a roughcast layer and repeated coats of whitewash to the dwelling quarters of the house with the dark naked rock exposed on the byre is probably the perpetuation of a medieval technique applied to the building styles of the seventeenth century. It has been argued that the roughcast skin gives some protection against weather, but the white-washing of the dwelling quarter probably expressed a sub-conscious wish to imitate the smooth light surfaces of the wattle and daub walls of the older medieval house. Whatever the explanation of this contrast between the external appearances of house and byre, the result of this constant motif in the simple architecture of the countryside is one of the most distinctive elements in the personality of the Lake District.

The mark of the statesman lies everywhere on the modern landscape of the Lake District. His farms, relics of the great period of rebuilding in stone, seem as common in the countryside as the repetitive surnames of the statesman families in the parish registers. The mile-long village of Troutbeck (4103) has more than a score of such buildings dating from the seventeenth and eighteenth centuries. Often their origin as sheep-farms with extensive grazings on the upland commons has been obscured by later history. Some have been degraded into cottages, parts of others have fallen into ruin and been demolished (Plate 22a), and elsewhere Victorian additions and alterations have obscured the simple outline of a seventeenth-century house. Nevertheless in many places, and especially at lonely sites towards the heads of valleys, one comes across perfect specimens of this period of building in the Lake District – the long, low roof-line drawn across a background of bracken-covered fell, the relics of a spinning gallery (Plate 12a), or a solid circular chimney stack protruding from the centre of the house. Dale Head (4316), the last farm in Martindale where the valley road finally peters out in a rocky farmyard, was rebuilt in 1666, according to the date inscribed on one of the stone piers that once supported a spinning gallery. Low Hartsop (4013), a tight cluster of blue slate farmsteads beneath the huge common pastures of Patterdale, displays several spinning galleries and panelled cupboards that date from about 1700 (Diag. 14) (Plate 12a). Most of the farms here have broken their direct links with land and now exist as neatly-kept summer residences. The grazing rights on the surrounding fells have been gathered together by the two surviving farms at Hartsop, and one of them keeps 1,300 sheep on its 1,700 acres of land. Today Hartsop is an empty husk, the shell of a hamlet that once housed a living community of statesman families. But even a century and a half ago, when Wordsworth wrote his *Guide to the Lakes,* he sensed the changes that were to overcome Hartsop: 'The opposite side has only two streams of any importance, one of which would lead up from the point where it crosses the Kirkstone-road, near the foot of Brothers-water, to the decaying hamlet of Hartsop, remarkable for its cottage architecture.' In many other places – at Nettleslack in Boredale (4218), for example – the decline of a seventeenth-century statesman's farm is absolute. The buildings stand roofless, a total ruin. Already saplings of oak and sycamore invade the kitchen and the bower, and the traveller can pick his way through the plan of the house reflecting upon that

186

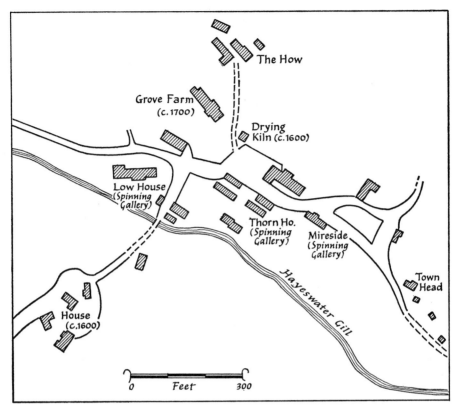

Diagram 14   *The hamlet of Low Hartsop in Patterdale.*

time two centuries ago when the society of the statesmen reached its climax and the dales and fells of the inner Lake District were as populous as they have ever been.

Open fields and commons
For centuries farming in the Lake District has been concerned with the rearing of sheep. The extensive upland commons, the rich vocabulary of the Cumbrian dialect and the relics of spinning galleries in the statesmen farms – all speak of the pastoral economy of the north-west down the centuries. Even though sheep rearing forms a continuous thread in the economic history of the Lake District, perhaps across five thousand years from the time of the first Neolithic farmers, it does not mean that the region has lacked its revolutions in farming. We are living through such a period of change at the present time. In every valley farms are

187

becoming consolidated into larger units and abandoned farmhouses that once would have fallen into ruins are now snapped up by businessmen as summer retreats. Today an air of prosperous desolation hangs over many Lake District farms. The spick-and-span colour wash and neatly trimmed gardens of former statesmen farms advertise the fact that many years have passed since sheep crowded the stockyard that now shelters the estate car and the Jaguar. The sense of desolation becomes more acute as one surveys the fellsides where many of the huge pastures, enclosed by derelict broken-down stone walls, are now deeply overrun with bracken or even invaded by the bushy woodland trees that presage return to forest. In 1844 Wordsworth wrote a sonnet and two long passionate letters to the *Morning Post* in which he expressed his fears about the damage to the society and solitude of the Lake District that would result from the building of the Windermere railway. Today, when there is talk of building a parking place for hundreds of cars at the head of the Kirkstone pass, we can measure the effects of the revolution in communications upon the economy and life of the mountains.

Not least among the changes brought about by the breakdown in the isolation of the north-west after the middle of the nineteenth century is the extinction of arable farming. Oats, barley and wheat were once grown on tiny favourable patches of land in all the valleys. Wordsworth's *Guide to the Lakes* makes frequent observations on the richness of farming in the valley floors. Where the streams that rise in the dark corries under Helvellyn empty into Ullswater at Glenridding (3817) he notices that the valley 'is adorned with fertile fields, cottages, and natural groves that agreeably unite with the transverse views of the Lake'. At another place in this valuable picture of the topography of the Lake District at the beginning of the nineteenth century Wordsworth describes how the clusters of 'statesmen-farms' shared a common patch of land that was sown with arable crops or cultivated as meadow.

> The enclosures, formed by the tenantry, are for a long time confined to the homesteads; and the arable and meadow land of the vales is possessed in common field; the several portions being marked out by stones, bushes, or trees: which portions, where the custom has survived, to this day are called *dales*, from the word *deylen* to distribute; but, while the valley was thus lying open, enclosures seem to have taken place upon the sides of the mountains; because the land there was not intermixed, and was of little comparative value.

Wordsworth writes an accurate description of the farming community among the fells as he saw it a century and a half ago. The common fields that were dwindling in his time have now vanished completely from the landscape of the Lake District, but we can still trace their sites with the help of field names, documentary records, and, in the countryside, the numerous thin rectangular enclosures, hedged by stone walls, that followed the division of the common ground among its individual farmers (Plate 11b). As you follow the rough track from Glenridding (3817) up to the dishevelled waste heaps of the abandoned mine at Greenside, you look down across the beck on to a pattern of rectangular strip-like fields on the opposite bank. They mark the site of a former common field, one of the fertile patches of arable and meadowland noted by Wordsworth. Further towards the head of the Ullswater valley, at Deepdale (3914), we find the relict pattern of an open field on the gently sloping ground (398145) between the main road and the lane that leads along the foot of the bracken-covered fell through Greenbank and Lanehead to Deepdale Hall. A Victorian survey of the Lake District, W. Whellan's *History and Topography of the Counties of Cumberland and Westmorland*, describes Deepdale as 'a grand romantic valley, mostly in a high state of cultivation'. Today the land has all passed into the hands of one farm, Greenbank. The homes of the statesmen who shared the common field at the mouth of Deepdale and enclosed it at some unknown date have ceased to be farms in the twentieth century; others have crumbled into ruins before our times.

Wordsworth's vivid impression of the methods of land-use in the hamlets around Ullswater – a scattering of open fields amidst an immensity of fell grazings – has been neglected by most of the great writers on the agrarian history of England. H. L. Gray, G. Slater and C. S. Orwin all came to the conclusion that 'only a few scattered instances' of open fields could be found in Cumberland and north-western England, and they believed that such examples of open-field farming had existed in the coastal plain rather than among the mountains. During the late 1920s this view was considerably altered when local historians, writing in the *Transactions of the Cumberland and Westmorland Antiquarian and Archaeological Society*, revealed that open fields once formed part of the landscape at several places in the very heart of the Lake District. Miss G. M. Simpson described small common fields, covering between six and fifteen acres, at Threlkeld (3225), at Mardale and now drowned by the Hawes Water reservoir (4712), in Wet Sleddale (5411) – a site more recently lost to a water storage scheme – and in Great Langdale (3006). Miss Simpson's research, based largely on the Tithe Awards of 1849, shows the open fields of the central Lake District at the point of extinction. At Threlkeld the Town field, a name that usually points to shared cultivation in earlier times, lies on the gentle ground that falls away below the village to the river Glenderamackin. Its site is still easily distinguished by a series of rectangular-shaped pastures among the patchwork of fields and enclosures at the foot of Saddleback. Threlkeld's town field covered fourteen acres and the details of the Tithe Award show that in 1849 it contained eleven strips that were farmed by five different owners. Most of the land at that time was used as meadow, though two of the strips were under arable crops. A few years later, in 1860, shared cultivation ceased at Threlkeld and the field was enclosed. Great Langdale once had two common fields, at Middlefell Place (2806) among the farms at the head of the valley, and the Mickle Ing which occupied the valley floor near Side House (2906). Six acres of the Mickle Ing were owned by Millbeck Farm (2906) and another one-and-a-quarter acres belonged to Raw Head (3006), but the most interesting feature of the distribution of ownership in this open field was that one strip belonged to Dale End (3103), a farm two miles distant on the further side of Lingmoor Fell in Little Langdale.

The open fields of the Lake District depended upon topographical features both for their location and their size. Valley floors and terraces, deltas and alluvial fans on lake shores with their gentle contours and accumulations of sediment provided the most advantageous sites for the common strips of open-field arable and meadowland (Plate 27). Coniston had an extensive system of town fields on the flat land by the lake shore to the south of the Church Beck (3096). Here the tenants of the manor of Coniston cut their rich summer crops of corn and hay, 'taking only what they could get with scythe or sickle', while the stubble, or 'winter eatage' as it was called in a Survey of 1823, was left to the manorial lord. In 1620 the town fields of Coniston became the subject of a dispute between John Fleming, lord of the manor of Coniston, and Daniel Höchstetter of Keswick, 'one of his Majesties Miners'. John Fleming and his tenants complained that the mining of copper in the mountains behind Coniston and the refining of the ore on the banks of the Church Beck had caused serious flooding, the pollution of the town fields with industrial waste, and the destruction of fish in the lake. It was said that two-thirds of the hay crop, 145 trusses in all, had been lost in 1619 from the common field at Coniston. Let us turn for a moment to the vivid and picturesque language of this seventeenth-century dispute as it has been preserved in the Rydal Hall Papers of the Fleming family. We are told that 'both meadow and cornland is decayed and wasted by reason of the stamphouse and *brayinge* of the copper ore and other rubbish at the said stamphouse and then the severinge of the same doth so muddy and corrupt the water which over-flowing the aforesaid ground leaveth such corruption upon them, there is utterly decayed and wasted of the hay and the aftergrass of the same meadow in this last year'.

190

The argument of John Fleming was strengthened by the claim that 'fishing is utterly destroyed and banished in the said beck or river only by reason of the corruption which cometh down the water from the said stamphouse'. The problems of industrial waste and its disposal reach back in time beyond the industrial revolution, and it seems that the conflict of different interests in the use of the earth's resources is not new to the twentieth century and its countless committees and commissions. The despoliation of Coniston's town field found a quick solution in the Award of 1620 that ordered the German mining engineer from Keswick 'to make Recompense, Restitution, and Payment'. Daniel Höchstetter was forced to regulate the course of the Church Beck to prevent the flooding of the meadows. As the Award said 'if there be not a new water race made it will in short time utterly decay and waste to the channel all the meadow . . .' The straightening of the course of the Church Beck below Coniston can probably be dated to this dispute between the farmers and the foreign miners that was taken to law in the winter of 1619.

The environment of the central Lake District in the deep valleys under the huge bare shoulders of the fells was hostile to arable farming and even the cultivation of good meadow grasses. Only the isolation of the region until the middle of the nineteenth century drove the farmers to make their patches of corn-land, shared by a cluster of neighbouring farmsteads, amid the extensive mountain sheep pastures. In the lowlands around the fringe of the mountain dome the conditions for crops and cattle-rearing were much more favourable. Higher sunshine figures prevail towards the coast and in the lee of the mountains, the risk of freak and devastating floods declines in the lowland fringe, and the soils of the drumlin fields and boulder clay spreads encouraged arable farming. Here one finds abundant evidence of former open-field farming in the networks of parallel stone-walled enclosures on the sites of the former common strips. G. Elliot revealed the extent of former open fields in Cumberland in a thorough piece of research published in 1959. He shows that almost every township of Cumberland once engaged in open-field farming. Out of a total of 288 townships in the county some 220 places have had open fields. The tiny patches of common field in the fell country, averaging about ten acres, fade into insignificance beside the collections of unfenced strips that once formed a variegated girdle around the green villages of the lowlands. For instance, the enclosure award for Torpenhow (2039) in 1814 provided for an area of 720 acres; and in the middle of the sixteenth century the open fields of Aspatria covered 965 acres. The farmers of north-western England divided their work between the infield, a tract of land close to the village or hamlet that was cropped every year with the help of heavy manuring, and the outfield where crops were cultivated spasmodically and the land lay fallow for periods as long as nine consecutive years. The outfield, with its shifting patches of cultivation over the years and many acres of fallow grazing, was often isolated from the huge commons and wastes by a boundary wall or bank that was known as the 'acrewall'. It is impossible to say when this system of land-use became established and it is almost as difficult to trace in detail the extinction of infield-outfield farming from the townships of the north-west. Certainly it reached its climax at the close of the Middle Ages, and the rise of the rural middle class of yeomen farmers, the statesmen, in the sixteenth century did much to hasten the extinction of collective methods of farming.

The infield-outfield system of farming, which H. L. Gray described as 'Celtic' in his book *English Field Systems*, probably originated in prehistoric times, most likely as part of the expansion of arable farming in the Romano-British Iron Age in north-west England. But there is also little doubt that this pattern of land-use was adopted by colonizers of the mountain wilderness at the heart of the Lake District at a much later date. For instance, it is unlikely that the common fields in Great Langdale were created before the late Middle Ages when most of the farms in the upper valley above Chapel Stile were founded. Similarly the large open field that formerly existed on the delta-flat at the head of Wasdale, where eighteen farmers held plots ranging from three to ten acres 'of arable and meadow', must have been carved out in the period of active colonization between the tenth and the thirteenth centuries (Plate 26b). G. Elliot, in his illuminating paper on the fields of Cumberland in the sixteenth century, has shown that open fields were in the making there as late as the middle of the Tudor period. He describes a pasture, Colt Park, that belonged to the monks of Holm Cultram Abbey which was converted into an open field of 150 acres by tenants of the surrounding hamlets after the dissolution of the monastery. Even more striking is the history of land-use at one of the outlying settlements of Holm Cultram on the shores of the Solway, Silloth Grange. There the open fields covered 546 acres when the monastic community was disbanded in 1538. The property was bought by a Robert Wheatley 'who placed tenants upon it and they built houses to the number of twenty'. But Robert Wheatley's colonists at Silloth Grange elected to continue the old methods of communal farming and by 1649 we find that the open fields had almost doubled in area with the addition of 435 fresh acres of land. It is evident that we cannot ascribe the making of the open fields of the Lake District to any one people at any particular period of time. Such a system of land-use is not a specific characteristic of some prehistoric people, the Roman Britons, the Anglians or the Viking settlers; instead it seems to represent

25. *Wastwater –*
the deepest lake
with its famous
screes. Great Gable
and Scafell
dominate the head
of the valley.

26a. *A heap of rubble in Wasdale field.*

26b. *Wasdale Head – the scattered farms of a hamlet centre on a former open field.*

the reaction of small groups of farmers to an environment in which the opportunities for growing corn and gathering good hay-crops were severely restricted. Although the recognition that open fields form part of the economy of almost every township in the north-west represents a most important change in our views of farming in the Lake District, the role of the common field must not be exaggerated. The tiny patchworks of strips were lost in the wilderness of fell and common land. For instance, the open field at Wasdale Head covered 345 acres towards the end of the sixteenth century while the common grazings of the scattered farms extended to 6,000 acres. The patches of former open field that we can still trace in the hedge patterns of the Vale of Lorton above Cockermouth were subsidiary to 12,000 acres of open grazing on the surrounding fells.

Open-field farming in the north-west reached its climax by the sixteenth century. History is almost as silent about the enclosure of the shared fields as it is about the origins of the infield-outfield system. There is no record of the disappearance of the common field at Wasdale Head, of its fossilization beneath a network of stone walls (Plate 26b). There are no documents that say anything about the rearrangement of strips to form more compact holdings in any of the valleys at the heart of the Lake District. For a few settlements on the fringe, where the open-field systems were usually more extensive, the record of enclosure is sometimes preserved in the terms of an Act of Parliament after the middle of the eighteenth century. The first recorded enclosure of this kind was for the open fields of Skelton (4335) by a Parliamentary Act of 1767. Today we can still locate the sites of the former strips in the pattern of narrow rectangular-shaped fields with their curving hedges. The woefully incomplete selection of place names printed on the modern one-inch map commemorates open-field agriculture at Skelton with the name Kirk Rigg – the patch of common arable that was once farmed by the priest. There was an enclosure award for Hutton (4326) in 1817; and the common strips at Torpenhow (2039) were rearranged and enclosed about the same time. The cultivation of the common field at Threlkeld (3225) continued, as we have noticed, until the middle of the nineteenth century. It was covered by the general act of Parliament passed in 1836 for the enclosure of the relics of open field in England, but the unfenced strips in the shared field there did not disappear until about 1860.

The seventeenth and eighteenth centuries were the great age of enclosure in the north-west, though the movement was already in progress in the Tudor period if one is to judge from the rising of small farmers, 'three hundred poor householders', in 1569 to protest about their exclusion from common grazings in the

Forest of Westward. By the end of the seventeenth century enclosures were extensive in the lush countryside around Kendal. Celia Fiennes, on her long and observant journey of the 1690s recorded in the pages of *Through England on a Side Saddle*, noted about the countryside of the Kent valley – 'inclosed lands . . . very rich good land enclosed – little round green hills flourishing with corn and grass as green and fresh . . . hedgerows round the grounds which looks very fine'. The protests and social upheaval that accompanied the Tudor enclosures and precipitated state commissions and inquiries are absent from the history of the north-west. No doubt it is a reflection of the small part played by open-field farming techniques in a region of pastoralism dependent on the boundless wilderness of the mountain grazings, but it is also a symptom of the small population.

If one of the most important developments in the landscape of the Lake District, the extinction of the open fields, was largely accomplished between 1550 and 1800 at the time of the rise of the 'statesmen', traces of the earlier ordering of life and agriculture persisted at a few places until the twentieth century. In 1929 Wilson Butler made a study of the open fields that once existed around Broughton-in-Furness (2187). One of these, Tenants Meadow, occupies the floor of the Lickle valley just to the south of Hartley Ground (214896). The Court Rolls of the manor of Broughton contain numerous references to this patch of meadowland that was shared by a number of farms, and the 'mere stones' that marked each farmer's strip of meadowland were still there when Wilson Butler made his field survey in 1928. Up to the First World War Tenants Meadow was still under communal management. For instance, on 16 January 1900 a meeting of the dale holders was held at the Blacksmiths Arms, Broughton Mills, to improve the system of management of the field. They agreed that each dale holder should keep his 'meir stones in repair' and that they were 'to stand well up out of the grass that they may be seen in cutting'. The dates for grass cutting and turning cattle on to the meadow after the hay harvest was firmly laid down, and the list of 'meadow lookers' that was drawn up for the first decade of the 1900s shows the seven farms that shared in the hay crop from the nine 'dales'. They included Hesketh Hall (2290), situated more than a mile away from Tenants Meadow up the valley, the Blacksmiths Arms (222905), Knott End (2291) and Lind End (2391) and Croglinhurst (2189). The latter farmstead adjoins Tenants Meadow, looking down on to it from a miniature rocky wooded spur. In 1900 it farmed three of the dales or strips of meadow – three times as much as any other shareholder in the common field. This arrangement suggests that at an earlier time Croglinhurst had acquired the 'dales' of other farms, properties that had failed and been wiped out in the great economic and social changes of the nineteenth century.

The history of Tenants Meadow is a striking example of the way in which the local study so often breaks the great generalizations of history. Most of the open fields of Westmorland and Cumberland disappeared without a record of their extinction before the beginning of the nineteenth century, but at this one place in the secluded Lickle valley an older system of farming still survives. Wilson Butler's paper revealed the details of the working of this piece of land in the 1920s. Today they have not changed much. Only five farms now share the land and the greatest number of 'dales' belongs to the Blacksmith's Arms at Broughton Mills, but the times of the year when the field is thrown open to the cattle of the various farms remain the same, and the mere posts, almost lost in the rank and high-grown hedgerows, still mark the plots of the different holdings. As one wanders through this irregular-shaped meadow, uncommonly large in size among the fields of the Lake District, the mind turns to the many obscure questions of its origin. For instance, the river Lickle flows along its eastern edge, contained by a low grassy embankment from which the meadow slopes gently towards a damp and winding hollow. These features suggest that at some time the river was diverted towards the margin of its broad flood plain as part of the making of Tenants Meadow. The scarcely perceptible hollow across the middle of the common field probably represents the line of the former stream bed. History tells us nothing about the origin of Tenants Meadow, but these minor features of the landscape suggest that it was shaped with an immense amount of labour out of a marshy and frequently flooded valley floor. This work, accomplished most likely at some time in the twelfth or thirteenth century, involved the diversion and embanking of the river from its former course. In still another way, the landscape throws up suggestions about which the documents are totally silent. There is no documentary evidence that Tenants Meadow was ever used for growing corn, but a walk over the ground soon reveals faint but unmistakable traces of 'ridge and furrow' suggesting that at some time the land has been ploughed and given over to arable crops.

Parks and country mansions
The seventeenth and eighteenth centuries stand out as the era of the statesman in the Lake District. He left many marks on the landscape in stone-built farmhouses, massive grey barns, and the field patterns of valley floor and fellside. In the same centuries the English aristocracy, wielding more wealth and power than the yeoman farmer, played an important role in shaping the landscape of

lowland England with the building of imposing mansions and the laying out of extensive parks. The lord and the great park, is a less important factor in the development of the Lake District. The north-west was thinly populated and too remote from the home counties and the urban society of London to attract the upper crust of the aristocracy in the eighteenth century. The scenery, too, of the central parts of the Lake District presented a most unsuitable setting for experiments whose chief object was to subject the natural landscape to the rules of art. But the softer scenery of the fringe of the Lake District contains some fine examples of the influence of the lord on the landscape, particularly at Lowther (5223) where a huge park was created across the broad spine of a limestone ridge, a medieval village destroyed and two estate villages built to serve a vast and rambling castellated house (Map 24).

The six-hundred-acre park at Lowther and the grandeur and magnificence of Robert Smirke's Gothic mansion, completed in 1811, reflect the immense wealth and power of the Lowther family in the eighteenth century. Their roots reach back to the Middle Ages when their possessions and social position placed them among the gentry of the Lake District. Lowther was then an obscure and unimportant name in no way to be compared with the Percies or the Cliffords, noble families with immense estates whose power eclipsed the influence of the crown in northern England. The Lowthers first appear in history in the twelfth century when the name is preserved in a document of Henry II's reign. In 1315 we find the first reference to the family in the countryside to the south of Penrith where they were to impress their name and influence so deeply in the eighteenth century. Hugh de Lowther is named then as the owner of a quarter of the manor of Lowther; the other lords were Adam de Coupland, Henry de Haverington, and the Prior of Watton. A century later, in 1422, Sir Robert Lowther has become the sole owner of the manor. The accumulation of estates was the secret of Lowther power and influence, and in the freer conditions for the purchase and exchange of land after 1600 the family acquired an empire in miniature on the eastern fringe of the Lake District. A Victorian topographer, P. Mannex, has clearly described the rise of the Lowthers: 'The numerous manors and estates which they now possess have been acquired at different periods, by little and little, partly by purchase and partly by other means, and being always lucky, they have raised themselves to what they are.' A few of the acquisitions point to the building of a great estate. Hackthorpe (5423) was bought in 1535. Some of the landmarks of the seventeenth century were the purchase of Rosgill (5316) and the possession of Clifton in 1646 as a result of an unredeemed mortgage to Thomas Wybergh, the former owner of the estate. Towards the end of the seven-

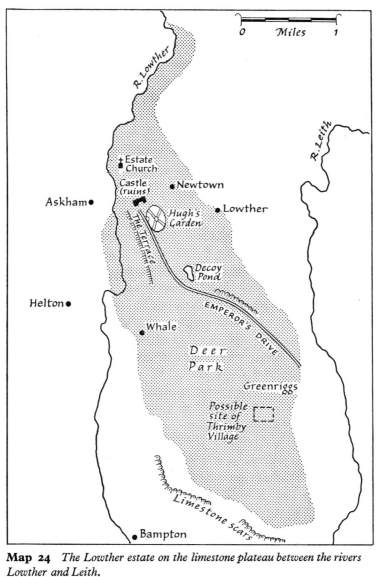

Map 24 *The Lowther estate on the limestone plateau between the rivers Lowther and Leith.*

teenth century the valuable estate of Shap, formerly the property of Shap Abbey, was bought from the Duke of Wharton, and in 1724 the Lowthers added Askham to their territorial possessions, again by purchase.

Political power accompanied the growth of the Lowther estates in the north-west. In the Tudor period we find them as sheriffs of both Westmorland and Cumberland, and in Elizabeth's reign Richard Lowther held the post of Lord Warden of the West Marches. Sir John Lowther, the second baronet, did more than any to raise the status of his family at the close of the seventeenth century. He was deeply involved in the revolution that brought William of Orange to the throne in 1688, and for his services was made vice-chamberlain to the royal household, a privy councillor, and lord-lieutenant of Westmorland. In 1696 Sir John Lowther received the titles of Baron Lowther and Viscount Lonsdale. Beside the growth of the political power and influence of the Lowthers in the seventeenth century, the family increased its economic strength with the acquisition of estates in the West Cumberland plain. The exploitation of the Cumberland coalfield and the development of the coal trade with Ireland, particularly the traffic between Whitehaven and Dublin, must have strengthened immensely the financial resources of the family. The investment of some of these resources left its mark on the landscape of the north-west in the development of the planned town and port at Whitehaven and in the shaping of the Lowther estate.

The dramatic reorganization of the Lowther estate began in 1682 under the Sir John Lowther who acquired the title of first Viscount Lonsdale. Until that time the village of Lowther stood between the church and a seventeenth-century mansion in the castle park. Sir John Lowther pulled down the village and extended his park to take in the church. Machell, the seventeenth-century antiquarian and topographer, has left a factual account of the village that disappeared. 'The ancient village of Lowther was heretofore considerable, consisting of the hall, the church, the parsonage house, and seventeen tenements, messuages, and cottages, all of which were purchased by Sir John Lowther, in the year 1682, and pulled down to enlarge his demesne, and open the prospect of his house, for they stood just in front of it.' As one explores Lowther Park today some of the features of the seventeenth-century landscape that were swept away by Sir John Lowther can still be seen faintly. The ghostly foundations of the cottages on either side of a vanished village street show as vague rectangular shapes in the wide tree-lined avenue that leads from the church (519244) to the gaunt outline of Smirke's castle. An even more striking survival from that seventeenth-century landscape is the pattern of ridge-and-furrow, evidence of the one-time open field of Lowther, that can be seen on the gentle slopes of the park below the estate village of Newtown (524243).

The landscaping of the park at Lowther in the 1680s was only the beginning of the work of a rich and ambitious family on this fragment of the Westmorland landscape. In 1683 Sir John Lowther began the building of a fresh village, Newtown (5224), to accommodate the farmers and labourers from the cottages and farmsteads of Lowther (Plate 14b). Its grey, stone houses stand singly or semi-detached inside a small rigidly laid out quadrangle of roads. The whole settlement is lost amid planted coniferous woodland that blazes with the clear pinks, reds and purple of rhododendron in the early summer. Newtown must be one of the earliest examples of an estate village in the north-west, where the ideas that guided the planned town of Whitehaven are applied to the reshaping of the mother estate at Lowther.

Sir John Lowther seems to have had in mind the creation of a model community at Newtown, one that combined rural and industrial activities, because the large block of buildings at the north end of the village, now the Lowther estates office, housed a carpet factory for a time early in the eighteenth century. Machell says that Newtown was founded primarily as an industrial settlement with the aim of manufacturing linen and carpets. He says that both occupations 'did not succeed', but 'the carpets equalled those of Persia and sold for sixty or one hundred guineas each'.

Under Sir James Lowther, holder of the estates for more than half a century from 1750 until 1802, a fresh period of development appears that has left its distinctive marks on the landscape of the park. About 1765 work started on the building of a new village half a mile to the east of Newtown on the edge of the park. The name Lowther reappeared on the map. Was this to make amends for the desolation of the previous century? The new Lowther remains incomplete to this day. It is a little grey-green hamlet overshadowed by a background of tall trees. The formally-arranged terraces of cottages look on to green lawns, and at the approach to the village a semi-circular curve of single-storeyed cottages reminds one faintly of the street patterns of Bath. In every way Lowther comes as a surprise in the scenery of the Lake District, with its urban overtones in a deeply rural setting. Building seems to have continued at the new village in the 1770s but the plan with its 'circus and square' motif, which is believed to be the work of Robert Adam, was only half finished.

The six hundred acres of Lowther Park probably represent the largest formal, man-made element in the landscapes of the Lake District. It abounds in objects that speak of the whims and taste of the successive holders of the family's titles and possessions. The parish church of St Michael has received an excessive amount of attention, so that a modern historian of architecture, Professor Niklaus Pevsner, can describe it as 'strange' and 'baffling'. Sir John Lowther seems to have rebuilt the church almost completely in 1686 at the time when he was reshaping the park and carting quantities of ready-made building stone from his property at Shap Abbey for the extension of his house. Nevertheless much of the interior is virtually that of a medieval church of the middle of the twelfth century. The high tower that gives the outside of the church a Victorian look was put up in 1856, and about the same time the curious mausoleum of the Lowther family was built in the churchyard. Although St Michael's church, standing beside the site of its deserted village, speaks so clearly of the role of the lord in shaping the landscape, it still preserves a memory of a remoter time before the land-grabbing Lowthers appeared on the scene. The porch contains three hog-back stones, coffins that date from the tenth century with their crude, archaic ornament and gabled tops that represent houses of the dead.

The other feature that dominates the park is the huge ruined outline of the castle, a lavish rebuilding of the Lowther mansion that took place in the first years of the nineteenth century. The north front with a vast prospect opening northward across the Vale of Eden looks like a medieval castle (Plate 14c). From the south the pinnacles and pointed windows were made to look like a cathedral, representing another aspect of the Gothic. The park itself abounds with the details of the Georgian landscape artist – the neatly-placed clumps of trees that were designed to improve the view, the long narrow plantations that show off the gentle contours of this limestone ridge, decoy ponds for wild duck and dense planted groves for pheasants, and all to be seen to perfection from the great drive, the Emperor's Drive, that sweeps through the heart of Lowther Park.

The landscape of the country house and its park, a landscape shaped by the principles of art, plays an insignificant role elsewhere in the Lake District. In the Penrith region Greystoke (4330) comes as a close rival to Lowther. There, too, the house was largely rebuilt about 1840 by the architect Salvin in the style of an early-seventeenth-century mansion, but the huge pele tower that William Lord Greystoke built in the fourteenth century still survives at the core of the house. Here, apart from the quiet pastoral scenery around the castle, there is little feeling of a landscape contrived by man. The land rises steeply to the north in Greystoke Forest and the impression remains of a medieval deer park, a fragment of the wilderness protected from the inroads of the squatter and the in-taker, rather than a tract of country fashioned after the ideas of the Georgian landscapers.

Various lords of the manor of Greystoke have left their own impressions on the countryside. The parish church of St Andrew is far more imposing than most Lake District churches. Its late-Perpendicular style presents a great problem about the date of the last rebuilding. Pevsner, in his volume on *Cumberland and Westmorland*, believes that the church was largely rebuilt about the middle of the seventeenth century – another example of the time-lag that affects building styles in the north-west until about 1800. The church reveals its links with the powerful line of Greystoke barons in other ways. It gained importance in the fourteenth century when William de Greystoke obtained a licence in 1358 to create a college with a master and five priests and two chaplains. Alabaster effigies on the tombs of medieval knights and commemorative brasses remind one of a society that knew more of the great world than the peasant farmers who worshipped in the dales chapels. At the time when work on the new village of Lowther was coming to a close in the eighteenth century the eleventh Duke of Norfolk decorated the countryside of Greystoke with three farmhouses that adopted the eccentricities of style fashionable in those years. At Fort Putnam (4530) a farmhouse is hidden behind battlements and turrets. Bunkers Hill (4530) has a broad six-sided tower, and at Spire House a polygonal tower is crowned with a spire. Such follies form curious objects in the landscape, the products of wealth and a taste foreign to the Lake District's simple local styles of building. They are a symptom of the gradual breakdown in the isolation of the mountainous north-west that began in the eighteenth century with the opening of turnpike routes and that was accelerated half a century later as railways penetrated the fringes of the region.

After Greystoke the fragments of parkland, of man-made landscape in a deliberate artistic sense, are small in scale and confined mainly to the circle of surrounding lowland. Hutton-in-the-Forest (4635), an old manor on the edge of Inglewood and for long held by the chief forester, probably has a complex history that has not been fully analysed. A fourteenth-century pele tower was transformed into a spacious mansion by the seventeenth-century additions of the Fletcher family, rich merchants of Cockermouth who bought the estate in 1606. Today you come across the small elegant park amid the landscape of late enclosure that makes up so much of Inglewood. Detailed research might reveal the disappearance of a small village community, perhaps early in the seventeenth century, with the making of the park. The only important estates of the southeast lowland lie in the Kent valley below Kendal. Sizergh Castle (4987) has a fourteenth-century pele tower as the focus of a fifteenth-century mansion. At Levens Hall, scarcely more than a mile away, a superb site on the banks of the

Kent just before the river reaches the mud flats and salt marshes of Morecambe Bay has been exploited. Levens Hall (4985) is the largest Elizabethan house in Cumberland and Westmorland. In many ways Levens seems far removed from the mountains of the Lake District, with its famous topiary garden designed at the beginning of the eighteenth century and a deer park through which the broad winding course of the Kent creates pastoral scenes that might belong to the quiet landscapes of southern England. Parks and country houses are almost absent from the valleys of the west, a region of great remoteness before the middle of the nineteenth century. Muncaster Castle (1096), magnificently sited above the estuary of the Esk, makes a notable exception. There Anthony Salvin built the relics of a medieval castle and pele tower into a sumptuous Victorian mansion enveloped amid plantations filled with rhododendrons and many imported conifers. Muncaster Castle and its park are romantic and Victorian in conception, rather than Georgian; they belong to the world of the tourists and guide-book writers of the nineteenth century.

We have seen that the Lake District provided an unsuitable setting for the theories of landscaping that were fashionable in the eighteenth century, but as tastes changed and wild romantic prospects of lake and mountain were sought after so the region was opened to a wave of settlement by 'off-comes' that would have been undreamt of by the deeply-rooted statesmen families a century earlier. The sites for villas were staked out along the shores of Windermere, whose chief asset was the view, and Wordsworth could deplore what his verse and letters to the Morning Post could do nothing to stop. The businessman from Manchester who complained that Wordsworth's garden at Rydal Mount would be 'a nice place if that ugly lump' of rock 'were but out of the way' was the harbinger of a new age in the region, an age that through its communications was to end the isolation of the region for ever, an age that was to present problems of destruction and conservation that are with us in an even more acute form in the middle of the twentieth century.

8

Markets and towns

Towns play only a minor role in the landscape of the Lake District. Its chief market centres – Kendal, Penrith and Keswick – all lie on the edge of the central core of mountains and serve their own tracts of lowland as well as the adjacent dales. Keswick belongs more to the Lake District than any other town of the region. Its streets lead the eye towards mountain vistas, and the bulky mass of Skiddaw seems to make its presence felt in the heart of the little market town. Ambleside, whose markets have been dead for a long time, also occupies a site enveloped on three sides by mountains (Plate 17). Like Keswick it owes its prosperity and urban expansion to the mounting tourist traffic of the past hundred years. The remaining towns of the north-west – Barrow-in-Furness, Whitehaven, Workington, Maryport and Carlisle – turn their backs on the Lake District and interest themselves in ship-building, coal-mining, and the acute problems of economic change in West Cumberland. For all these places the Lake District is something more remote – a vast prospect of distant mountains seen from church towers and other view-points on clear days, a place for week-end excursions.

Unfortunately the tourist to the Lake District usually writes off the towns as places of no interest. At least the Victorian visitors treated Ambleside and Keswick as major resorts, centres from which one valley after another could be explored for weeks on end with the pages of Murray and Baddeley to guide them through all the intricate detail and 'curiosities' of the local topography. Today the chief function of the towns as tourist centres is to act as refuges on rainy days. When low cloud and grey sheets of driving rain make the heavenly wilderness about Scafell summit and Great Gable bleak and inhospitable the tourist retreats to the tea-shops of Ambleside and Keswick. Under the pall of an August warm front and the depressed spirits of grounded mountaineers these grey-blue slate towns, harshly Victorian in their architecture, themselves look bleak and without any real interest.

The towns of the Lake District have suffered even more in the mid-twentieth century from the uncontrolled flood of traffic along the few main roads of the region. Chemical lorries, cars and tourist buses jostle their way through Ambleside's former market-place. At Keswick the same traffic stream is swollen by the burden of transport from Penrith and the trans-Pennine roads. Kendal suffers even more. Its pleasant grey streets and riverside boulevard are part of a one-way maze for the unending stream of diesel lorries over Shap Fells. The ribbons of motorway stretched across the pale green pastures to the west of Penrith have just relieved the town from years of suffocation. One can now enjoy the rich red tones of its Georgian and early Victorian architecture and the varied shapes of its several little market squares.

Although the small towns and decayed market centres of the Lake District have no buildings of outstanding interest and are sadly disfigured by the excessive traffic of the twentieth century, they still possess an atmosphere that takes one back to the time before the industrial revolution when towns fitted harmoniously into their surrounding countryside. For instance, local building stones and roofing slates were used almost without exception until the beginning of this century. Consequently each urban centre contains in its buildings the same colours and textures that make up the enveloping landscape. Penrith glows with the warm reds of its sandstone buildings and we find the same matching colours in the soils, cuttings and abandoned quarries of the countryside around. Kendal is completely different because the building stone that dominates the town in its churches and well-to-do Georgian houses, its mills and simple Victorian working-class terraces was hewn from the limestone quarries that scar the southern tip of Kendal Fell, the former common land of her burgesses. Kendal is a cool, silver-grey place, the colour of the countless walls and ragged limestone scars that form a leading element in the personality of southern Westmorland. Ambleside, Hawkshead and Coniston present still another theme in building materials. There the forbidding dark blue-greys and near-blacks of the Silurian flagstones and slates dominate the miniature urban scene and match the ragged outcrops of the same rocks in crags and stream beds, in the walls and bridges of the countryside around. The Lake District's towns and market-villages are still part of the landscape, and never more than when some viewpoint such as that gained from the graveyard of Hawkshead church opens up a distant prospect of Grasmere's mountains across the shaggy foreground of High Furness.

Markets and the founding of towns

There were no towns in the Lake District before the twelfth century, although several of the sites where towns have since flourished suggest ghostly links with the past, even though there is not a shred of evidence for a continuity of urban forms or institutions from times before the Norman Conquest. Cockermouth, for instance, was founded in the middle of the thirteenth century only a thousand yards from the extensive site of Roman Papcastle, a settlement on the gentle northern slopes of the Derwent that probably had several urban features. The link between Papcastle and Cockermouth is drawn closer when we remember that the political reorganization of the north-west after the Norman Conquest saw the building of a 'residence', no doubt a crude castle, within the enclosure of the Roman fort there by Waltheof, the first lord of Allerdale. About a hundred years later this building was demolished and the material carted away to lay the foundations of another castle strategically placed in the neck of land between the Derwent and the Cocker. At Kendal the magic of a regional location exercised its influence over many centuries to culminate in the growth of a prosperous medieval town. Scarcely a mile from the long main street of Kendal, we find the site of the Roman fort of *Alavna* that seems to have possessed a civil settlement as well. Penrith, too, throws up similar hints of an urban settlement in that part of the Eamont valley long before the emergence of a medieval market town. As at Cockermouth and Kendal we find that the new urban core, evolving after the twelfth century, lies at some distance from the site of a Roman fort, *Brocavum*, and its adjoining civil settlement.

The rise of the chief market towns of the Lake District in areas that were of primary importance in the settlement geography of the Roman occupation points to the permanent value of the basin of the middle Kent, the lower Eamont valley and the widening plain at the junction of the Derwent and Cocker. The founding of the medieval towns revived an old pattern in the human geography of the north-west.

Although markets and towns existed in many parts of England before the Norman Conquest, it is certain that these more complex features of social organization did not take root in the Lake District until the twelfth century and after. Carlisle is the only place in the north-west that displays features of urban life at an earlier date. Here there is some evidence of a walled settlement with monasteries and churches in the eighth century, but even so there is no proof that the town survived the upheavals of the period of the Viking raids. During the twelfth and thirteenth centuries hundreds of towns came into being in western Europe. It was a period of rising population and expanding trade. In England it became fashionable and profitable for earls and barons, bishops and abbots to establish markets and settle burgesses beneath the towering walls of their castles, at monastery gates or else at favoured sites on their manorial properties. But the progress from a newly established market centre with its two or three annual fairs marked by the days of saints to a fully chartered borough, governed by an elected mayor and aldermen, was often long and tortuous. Many fell by the way before the Tudor period; others had dwindled to nothing by the beginning of Victoria's reign.

The earliest record of a market charter in the Lake District belongs to Kendal (Plate 33). In 1189 Richard I gave to Gilbert fitz Roger fitz Reinfred the right to hold a Saturday market and three fairs during the course of the year in his barony of Kendal. The closing years of the twelfth century must have been filled with the promise and evidence of change at Kendal because the same fitz Reinfred, first baron of Kendal, was probably responsible for the building of a massive new circular castle on the summit of a drumlin to the east of the river. Kendal's history as a town and trading centre was one of the most successful in the north-west. By the end of Elizabeth's reign the market charter had been confirmed on three occasions, and on 28 November, 1575 the town received its charter of incorporation as a borough.

The first record of markets at Penrith does not appear until 1123 when the Close Rolls describe the establishment of a market there by Henry III. The formal legalistic phrases of the document are typical of all the medieval market charters that turned so many places into a new path of development in the twelfth and thirteenth centuries. It reads: 'the King to the sheriff of Cumberland greeting. Know that we ordain a market to be held in our manor of Penred on the Wednesday of each week; and a fair to be held in the same place each year, to continue from the eve of Pentecost till the Monday next after the Feast of the Holy Trinity.' The granting of a market charter cannot be taken as proof of the beginning of trade at any particular place. In many instances it must have been a recognition of commercial activities that were already in existence. At Penrith one suspects the existence of a settlement with some kind of market activities long before the charter of Henry III. There was certainly a church there a century earlier, because at the creation of the see of Carlisle in 1133 the living of Penrith was granted to Athelwald, the first bishop of Carlisle. But the evidence of the past at Penrith takes us beyond the Norman reorganization of the north-west, with the weather-beaten sandstone crosses and the hogback coffins in the churchyard that date from about A.D. 1000. And the name Penrith itself is of British origin, surviving the waves of settlement that preceded the Norman Conquest. Its exact meaning is far from certain, but Ekwall has suggested 'the chief place at the ford' as a likely interpretation. If Penrith was the centre of a long surviving British unit of settlement that stretched from the Eden westward into the wilderness of the Skiddaw massif, then it probably had a long history as a trading centre. When documents fail to throw any light on the origins of landscape features, we can only turn to the details of the topography itself, that is always full of obscure clues and dark hints. We have already noticed the intriguing topography of the heart of Penrith around the parish church where the elegant crescent of Bishop's terrace appears to be aligned along the ditch and rampart of some prehistoric earthwork. Immediately adjoining this feature, to the west, we find the market place. It seems possible that this same site, beneath a ramparted earthwork, acted as a trading place for the British forerunner of medieval Penrith; and the camp itself was chosen as a site for a Christian church in the centuries before the Norman Conquest.

Whatever the origins of trade at Penrith there is little doubt that Henry III's market charter gave a considerable fillip to the growth of a town. It had other advantages denied to many places. For instance, for almost two hundred years from the reign of Richard III Penrith was a royal manor. This meant that life could be lived and trade carried on without many of the irksome restrictions that abbots and earls so often imposed upon the markets and towns which they brought into being for their own personal profit and ambitions for power. The royal owners of Penrith were concerned with far greater issues than the fate of an obscure Cumberland market town. Again, Penrith was the chief centre of the Honour of Penrith – a medieval territorial unit that stretched for some miles into Inglewood Forest and the Eden valley. The inhabitants of many places could trade free of tolls at Penrith market because they were part of that medieval territory. To examine the details of the topography at the centre of the town (Plate 9), leaves no doubt about the volume of trade in Penrith. Penrith is composed of a collection of irregular-shaped open spaces strung across the line of the road that runs from the Eamont crossing towards Carlisle (Diag. 15). Astride the main road stands the Market Square where woollen yarn, butter, eggs, fruit, poultry and meat were sold. To the west the Market Square widens out into another open space still called the Corn Market. In turn the Corn Market is connected with Great Dockray, a big irregular-shaped square that was once the scene of busy cattle fairs. Eastward beyond the Market Square another large open space, Sandgate, was the centre of the stock sales that were held every other week throughout the summer. Sandgate once had the advantage of a fresh water supply that flowed across it in an open conduit. William Strickland, who founded the castle at Penrith in the 1390s as a defence against Scots raids, organized the cutting of this channel between the Petteril and the Eamont to bring a constant flow of fresh water to the centre of the town. Great Dockray and

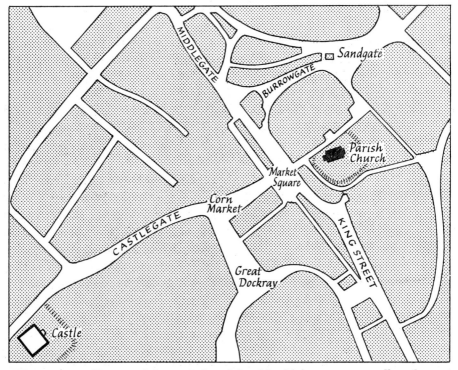

Diagram 15 *Features of the town plan of Penrith with its numerous small market places.*

Sandgate, the traditional centres of Penrith's cattle markets and fairs for at least five hundred years, were the places where bull-baiting took place until the sport was abolished at the beginning of the nineteenth century.

Penrith's topography still suggests the town's former pre-eminence as a market centre, a function in which it rivalled Kendal until the great changes of the railway age. At Cockermouth the creation of a market town followed the building of the castle, a normal pattern of urban development in the Middle

27. Buttermere and the spine of Fleetwith Pike. In the foreground the delta flat separating Buttermere from Crummock Water with the site of a former common field.

28a. *Sheepfold and packhorse bridge at Throstle Garth on Furness Abbey's estate in Eskdale.*

28b. *Eskdale from the Hardknott Pass.*

Ages. As we have already noticed, the foundation of Cockermouth castle, probably about 1140, represents transfer of the centre of political power from Papcastle to the watersmeet between Derwent and Cocker. A vital phase of activity in the town's history began in 1221 when William de Fortibus secured a market charter from Henry III. A place for the markets was established on the east bank of the Cocker between the low hills crowned by the castle and the church (Plate 8). About the same time it seems likely that William de Fortibus either rebuilt or greatly enlarged the church of All Saints, at that time and indeed until the middle of the nineteenth century a chapel in the older parish of Brigham.

Cockermouth, one suspects, established itself as a town with considerable difficulty. From the beginning it probably felt the rivalry of the older borough of Egremont, where William de Meschin had built his castle early in the twelfth century and created the administrative focus of the Barony of Copeland. In fact, Cockermouth's market charter reveals some of the handicaps under which this new town was born. One phrase stated that the market should not be to the detriment of neighbouring markets. Also Cockermouth's trading activities were limited for a long time to the local sphere of a Monday market. The holding of fairs was not allowed until 1638 when a charter from Charles I to the Earl of Northumberland stated 'that he may keep a fair in his town of Cockermouth every Wednesday from the first week of May till Michaelmas'. The weekly horse and cattle fairs that started in the seventeenth century took place on the west bank of the Cocker along the lane that led towards Brigham. By the end of the century a new quarter of the town had come into existence centred on the long lane where the cattle dealers and horse traders gathered. The growth of Cockermouth in the seventeenth century is plainly revealed if we compare the accounts of the town in Camden's *Britannia* and Bishop Nicholson's great topography of the north-west published a century later, in 1685. Camden visited Cockermouth in 1582 and he wrote of the confluence of the Derwent and the Cocker, 'which when they meet do encompass, almost round about, Cockermouth a mercate town of good wealth, and a castle of the Earls of Northumberland. The towne is built fair enough, but standeth somewhat with the lowest between two hills; upon the one of which the Church is seated, and upon the other right over against it, a very strong castle. . . . Opposite unto this beyond the river two miles off, lieth the carcass of an ancient castle called Papcastle.' Here is a clear impression of the little town contained between the two rivers and overshadowed by the church and castle (Diag. 16). There is no hint of Main Street or any building on the low ground to the west of the Cocker where much of the land remained as common until the early nineteenth century. A hundred years later Bishop Nicholson's account of Cockermouth shows that a new quarter had been added to the town. 'The houses are built of stone, and slated mostly with blue slate; they comprise two streets, one above the river Cocker, in which is the Moot Hall, Market House, Corn Market and Shambles; and in the other below is the Beast Market.' Main Street began as the cattle market on the west side of the river; by the middle of

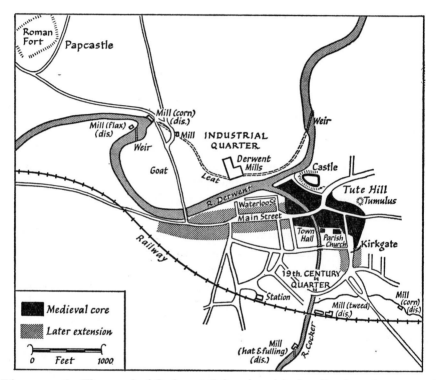

Diagram 16 *The growth of Cockermouth from its original medieval core between castle and church.*

the nineteenth century this had become the chief centre of activity in the town and life had been sapped from the original medieval urban core.

Several other places on the edge of the Lake District secured market charters when Kendal, Penrith and Cockermouth were laying the foundations of an urban life, but most of these failed to make any progress towards town status. Ravenglass perhaps displays the most interesting history of a town that might have been (Diag. 17). On 20 August 1208 King John was staying at Kendal castle and he granted to Richard de Lucy, Lord of Egremont, the right to hold a market on Saturdays at Ravenglass as well as a yearly fair on the festival of St James the Apostle. Once more we note the part played by a particular individual in shaping the economy and landscape of the Lake District, for the same Richard

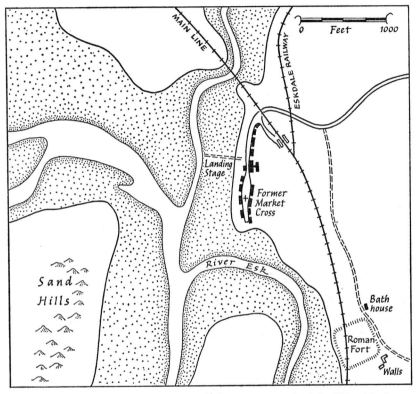

Diagram 17   *The failed town of Ravenglass at the mouth of the Esk with the Roman sites nearby.*

de Lucy was responsible for obtaining a borough charter from King John for his tenants of the manor of Egremont. One can only speculate about his motives for creating a market centre at Ravenglass. Perhaps the need for it arose from the topography of the western Lake District. The Ravenglass fairs were attended by tenants from the southern part of the Barony of Copeland in Eskdale, Miterdale and Wasdale. A list of tenants drawn up in 1754 shows that there were a hundred holdings that might send their farmers to trade at Ravenglass. Even more important were the functions of Ravenglass as a port, suggested by seventeenth- and eighteenth-century accounts of the fairs. Sandford, writing in 1675, says that St James' fair was 'a grand fair of three days long, for all sorts of cattle especially, and other commodities from Ireland, the Isle of Man and Scotland.' Richard de Lucy, when he obtained his Charter from King John, was probably determined to exploit the wider trade of the Irish Sea through the 'haven at Ravenglass', something that was denied to him by the site of Egremont.

The accounts of Ravenglass before the decay of its fairs and markets about 1800 tell us a lot about a trading system that was completely swept away in the railway age. For instance, at the opening of the three days' fair on the Feast of St James officials from the borough of Egremont, the Sergeant and Bailiffs, met the tenants of 'His Lordship' from 'the Forests of Kennyside, Netherwasdale, Eskdale, Miterdale and Wasdale-head' at Bell Hill on the outskirts of Ravenglass (0897). From there they went 'in cavalcade' to Ravenglass to proclaim the fair, and a fine sight it must have been as they approached the little market street across the sands of the Mite at low tide. Another source tells us that arrangements were made for the feeding of the horses of these people from distant places during the three days of the fair. Two strips of pasture were reserved for this purpose in the common field of Ravenglass. Among the records kept at Cockermouth Castle are some details of transactions at Ravenglass fair in the eighteenth century. They show that farmers assembled there from all over the Lake District to buy and sell; and people from such places as Wigton, Kendal, Castle Sowerby, Keswick and Blencogo, appear in the dealings.

By the end of the eighteenth century trade at Ravenglass was failing; the August fair had been reduced to one day, and an agent of the Earls of Egremont wrote to his master, 'Your lordship is always brought in debtor instead of creditor on your fair days.' In 1796 Lord Muncaster took over the control of trading at Ravenglass and obtained a new charter for two weekly markets and three fairs of one day each. By the 1880s, when Mannex published his detailed directory of Furness and West Cumberland, he could report the end of Ravenglass's long history as a market centre: 'Whatever importance formerly attached to this place as a port, it is now quite deserted. The market is little more than a name, and the fairs, which were held three times a year, have become obsolete.' Only the sports that were once the culminating festivities of the three-day August fair have survived as part of the Muncaster Flower Show. The wrestling contests and the trotting races on the foreshore have been transformed into genteel egg-and-spoon races and the sideshows and diversions of rural society in the twentieth century.

212

And the empty market street of Ravenglass remains, perched on the edge of the quiet estuary and screened from the Irish Sea by a crumpled line of sandhills.

Ravenglass failed to evolve into a town despite its advantage as a haven on the coast of Cumberland. Keswick lacked such an immense natural gift, but nevertheless developed into a successful market town, if somewhat slowly, after the first impetus of the charter acquired by Thomas de Derwentwater in 1276. Leland, the father of English topographical writing, passed through Keswick in the 1530s and dismissed it with the comment 'a poor little market town called Keswike'. By the early seventeenth century the markets at Keswick had become a focus for the life of the several mining communities in Borrowdale and the Newlands valley, and a hundred years later it had emerged as the chief trading centre of the textile industry in the northern Lake District. For the northern fells Keswick played the part that was performed by Hawkshead and Ambleside as market centres in the south. Since 1800, and the collapse of the peasant textile industry, the progress of Keswick has depended on the rise of tourism and, to a lesser extent, the founding of the pencil factory in the 1840s.

Of all the towns in the Lake District the site of Keswick would appear to be predestined by nature. It stands on the tongue of land between the River Greta and Derwentwater at the convergence of several of the great natural through-routes of Cumberland. Its general setting, with an immense panorama of mountains, placed Keswick in front of most other resorts in the growth of the Victorian tourist industry. But can we explain the site of this market town purely by the rules of geographical determinism – a blunt analytical tool at the best of times? Medieval Keswick grew up in the huge parish of Crosthwaite, and it seems surprising that the core of the town is not centred on the ancient parish church at Great Crosthwaite on the north bank of the Greta (257243). But the property of Thomas de Derwentwater who obtained the grant of a market charter for Keswick ended on the south bank of that river.

Until the last years of the thirteenth century there was nothing at Keswick, only some pastures and a dairy farm as the name implies. The real centre of the manor of Derwentwater was the hamlet of Castlerigg, on a steep hillside almost five hundred feet above the lake. A lane led down to the crossing of the Greta and part of this became the market street of Keswick. It seems that about the time when the Derwentwater family began to organize markets at Keswick a lively trading centre had already arisen outside the church at Great Crosthwaite. Great Crosthwaite's market had grown up spontaneously on Sundays, an event that is not hard to imagine in a parish that drew its worshippers from the farthest limits of all the surrounding valleys. We know about this illegal market at Great

Crosthwaite because the people of Cockermouth petitioned parliament about the matter in 1306. They claimed that 'a great concourse of people assembled every Sunday at Crosthwaite church where corn, flour, beans, peas, linen, cloth, meat, fish and other merchandise were bought and sold', and that it was 'injurious to the market at Cockermouth so that persons who farmed tolls of the king were unable to pay their rent'. History is completely silent about the fortunes of the Derwentwater family's market on the south bank of the Greta at this time, but one can only wonder whether it owed its survival to the suppression of trading at Great Crosthwaite. But for the fears of the tradesmen of Cockermouth in 1306 the town of Keswick might now be on the north side of the Greta centred upon its medieval parish church.

The advantages of geographical location and the energies of the Derwentwater family conspired in the successful creation of a market town at Keswick, but at several other places in the Lake District a deserted open space now provides almost the only clue to a long-forgotten attempt to make a market town. For instance, in 1216 William de Lancaster obtained the right to hold a market at Barton (4826), the centre of the huge medieval parish that included the whole of Ullswater and the tributary valleys from the summit of the High Street to the spine of the Helvellyn range. History has nothing more to say about Barton's market, not even about the place where it was held, though it seems most likely that the trading legalized in the thirteenth-century charter took place at Pooley Bridge (4724). By the middle of the nineteenth century the only surviving evidence of the trading centre at Pooley Bridge was a sheep and cattle fair, held on the third Monday in September, and the memory of an extinct fish market. Its former market functions are evident, too, in the little clustered settlement where the main road widens into the space of the one-time market square.

Pooley Bridge was probably overshadowed from the beginning by the growth of Penrith as a market centre. Likewise, the markets at Staveley (4798) which were chartered in 1329 grew within the ambit of the powerful and successful castle-town at Kendal. Bootle (1088), at the western foot of Black Coombe, is another extinct market town whose charter was granted to John de Hudleston in 1347. At Hesket Newmarket (3438) we find another decayed market centre whose trading activities and sheep and cattle fairs persisted until the middle of the nineteenth century. Today its spacious central green, flanked by cottages and farmhouses, reminds one of almost any of the beautiful green villages of the Eden valley; only the little eighteenth-century market cross shows that Hesket Newmarket once took the first step that in many places led to the long process of urban growth. The topography of Ireby (2338) still betrays its long history as a market centre. The built-up village street and the deserted market place with a butter cross and the Moot Hall, now converted into houses, speak of a medieval market that can be traced until the end of the eighteenth century. William de Ireby obtained the grant of a Thursday market and an annual three days' fair in 1237. Ireby was still an active market centre in Elizabeth I's reign because the traders of Cockermouth complained in 1578 that it was 'very like greatly to decay his lordship's said market at Cockermouth, and utterly impoverish the inhabitants of the said town'. At the end of the seventeenth century Ireby's trade in corn still flourished. Thomas Denton, the recorder of Carlisle and the author of the first history of Cumberland, presents a sketch of the market at Ireby in 1688. 'All sorts of grain (big and oates especially) and also salt are sold at far cheaper rates, and by larger measure, than in any market in the north; the reason is because of the great plenty of good corn that grows everywhere round the neighbourhood.' Markets before the age of the heavy waggons that rumbled along the turnpike roads after the middle of the eighteenth century must have reflected the productivity and prosperity of their immediate locality. Ireby, lying on the fringe of the rich acres of the Cumberland plain, probably attracted many a customer from the harsh mountain hinterland to the south – many who were willing to tramp a few extra miles to spurn the less competitive mart at Cockermouth.

Most of the market charters of the Lake District, indeed of the rest of England, date from the twelfth and thirteenth centuries. The last foundation in the region was the Wednesday market at Bootle (1088) for which John de Hudleston obtained the grant of a charter in 1347. The failure to create new market centres is one of the striking features of the economic history of the later Middle Ages. The great epoch of town-making in the three centuries that followed the Norman Conquest provided more than sufficient places for trade and commerce in the fourteenth and fifteenth centuries – an age of pestilence, wars and social unrest. But the rising population and growing prosperity of the Tudor period brought fresh incentives and experiments in the creation of market centres and towns. The Lake District only responded to this rising prosperity in the seventeenth century after the ascent of James I to the English throne brought a long peace to the northern border. The transformation of Hawkshead into a market town began with the granting of a charter to Adam Sandys in 1608 for the holding of a Monday market and a fair twice a year. For two centuries Hawkshead took over the role of a busy regional market centre. It emerged as the chief wool market of the Furness Fells, passing on its products to the even greater wool-trading centre and cloth town of Kendal. Even so the efforts of the Sandys family to transmute Hawkshead into something more than a simple rural settlement failed. By the end of the nineteenth century the markets and fairs were totally extinguished. As the great local topographer, H. S. Cowper, wrote in his *History of Hawkshead* in the 1890s, 'nowadays there is absolutely no market, and the fairs are merely nominal. Machinery, railways and auction marts have killed them both.' The immense changes in the economy and society of England after the middle of the nineteenth century left Hawkshead stranded, a town in embryo whose life had begun to quicken in the seventeenth century. The topography of Hawkshead today reminds us at every turn of this active period in its history. The little squares or yards with irregular connecting alleys between the cottages of whitewashed roughcast and cold blue slate give the feeling of an urban rather than a rural community. On the south side of the little Market Square, jammed in summer with day-trippers' cars, stands the Market Hall built in 1790. The open arched rooms beneath the Market Hall were once called 'the shambles' because they were occupied by five butchers who came to Hawkshead from different parts of the parish on the busy market days.

Hawkshead's market was followed by others. The Countess of Pembroke was granted a charter to set up a Wednesday market at Ambleside in 1650. The new activities brought to the place by the market charter have left their impression on the topography of the town, even though the trade directory of Westmorland, published by P. J. Mannex in 1849, reported the markets and fairs of Ambleside on the point of extinction in the middle of the nineteenth century. The earliest settlement at Ambleside grew up at the edge of Grasmere parish as a cluster of dark grey slate farmsteads and a little chapel on a spur above the precipitously wooded Stock Ghyll (Plate 17). This piece of rural Ambleside is well worth exploring today if only to escape the endless traffic on the Keswick road. The creation of the seventeenth-century market at Ambleside added a new element to the settlement on the south bank of the Stock Gyll below the chapel and the original cluster of farms. The focus of this part of the town still rests on the market place with its shops and inns that provided hospitality for the leisurely tourist in the Lake District before the age of the motor-car. The back streets around the market square have many examples of cottages built in the eighteenth century when Ambleside was a true regional trading centre, a place famous for its wool sales in the days when the galleries of Westmorland's statesmen farms hummed with the noise of the spinning wheel.

Ambleside entered the third and most important stage of its topographical history towards the close of the eighteenth century. It became a favourite tourist resort for the exploration of a wide circle of fells and valleys, with the added advantage of Windermere only a mile away to the south. Ambleside added the peculiarities of its local climate to the advantage of its position on the edge of some of the Lake District's finest scenery. The shelter of its encircling mountains and a southward-facing site add a touch of warmth and brilliance to the days of late spring and early summer. The memories of almost every fell walker in the southern Lake District must preserve impressions of clear cold days on Fairfield and Hart Crag with the last remnants of the preceding winter's snow patches swept by a north-east wind and then, in the late afternoon, the return to the shelter of Ambleside where cats bask on slate walls in the sunshine and a thermometer placed in the eye of the sun will creep up into the nineties. The Victorians – rich manufacturers from Lancashire and Yorkshire, successful authors and retired clergymen – favoured Ambleside as a place to live. William Green, author of a two-volume *Guide to the Lakes*, settled there in 1800. Harriet Martineau, who was described by one of her contemporaries as a 'brilliant and prolific genius', moved to Ambleside from London in 1835. She had written best-selling books with titles such as *Society in America, Forest and Game Law Tales*, and *Illustrations of Political Economy*. From her home at Ambleside, 'The Knoll', she was to write still another of the many popular nineteenth-century guides to the region. Another eminent Victorian, Dr Arnold Fox lived at 'How' (365049) on the bank of the Rothay to the north of Ambleside. Under the influence of tourism and the wealthy migrants who were attracted to the Lake District by its scenery and fashionable 'romantic associations' Ambleside extended in a haphazard way on to the lower slopes at the foot of Wansfell, towards Waterhead with its three-hourly service of steamers on Windermere, and especially into the rock-scarred flood-plain of the Rothay. Mannex, writing about Ambleside in his directory of 1849, noted the irregular layout of the villas in the new quarters where 'each particular house is situated upon a particular knoll'.

Today Ambleside can still be enjoyed as a small Victorian town. Its parish church, built in the early 1850s by Sir Giles Gilbert Scott, stands in the new quarter to the west of the market place. The tall broach spire strikes a discordant note in the native architecture of the Lake District but now, in the middle of the twentieth century, it seems almost appropriate in a region that was so deeply influenced by the Victorians. Several of the spacious villas are now hotels; the calf-bound libraries and the serious, bearded followers of Ruskin and Wordsworth have vanished from the scene, but Ambleside still retains an atmosphere of the last century. It has a bookshop that would be hard to match in a place with fifty times its population, and the Armitt library and museum enshrines the knowledge and the attitudes of those scores of Victorian antiquarians and local historians whose researches laid the foundations for a scientific understanding of the Lake District's history and the evolution of its landscape.

At a late date two other places on the edge of the Lake District took the first step towards urban status, the foundation of a market, but failed to pursue the long and often difficult road to the final goal. In 1687 Lord Wharton secured a charter for the holding of a Wednesday market at Shap, as well as three annual fairs. In many ways Shap seemed to be well placed for the growth of a market-town. It stands midway between Kendal and Penrith on one of the busiest trunk roads of northern England. Even before the sixteenth century Shap Abbey had acted as an important hospice for travellers on the road between Carlisle and the south. By the beginning of the nineteenth century Shap's market had become obsolete and the fairs were no longer held. It failed to encroach on the long-established spheres of influence of Kendal and Penrith. And is it not possible that the very bleakness of Shap's site in a bare, windswept saddle of the eastern fells helped to deter the traders at her markets for many weeks in the year? Today the endless traffic through Shap's mile-long street may be silenced for a few hours by a winter blizzard, but soon the long quiet that envelops our failed market towns will descend on Shap with the opening of new sections of the M6 motor-way across Westmorland's fells towards Penrith and Carlisle. Then the little market house, built in 1690 and the only topographical reminder of Lord Wharton's attempt to make a market town, will assume its true proportions beside a deserted trunk road.

Broughton-in-Furness was more successful than Shap as a market centre, Markets were already held there at the close of the seventeenth century and a hundred years later John Gilpin, the lord of the manor, gave a piece of land for the laying out of a spacious market-place. The tall dark-grey terraces of stone and roughcast around the formal square give Broughton the look of a real town, and a market day still survives there on a Thursday. But in every other sense it is a village. The streets peter out quickly amid fields and wide views of mountains and the marshes of the Duddon. It served its region well as a trade centre in the eighteenth century when ships sailed far up the estuary and the furnace at Duddon Bridge collected coppice wood from many a mountain hillside. Woollen yarn, spun in Broughton's homes and on surrounding farms, passed through its market to the manufacturers of Yorkshire, but all that traffic had disappeared before the end of the nineteenth century. By the 1880s the chief trade of Broughton market was in the secondary products of the Furness coppice woods – hoops and baskets, brush handles and the wooden shafts of farm tools. Most towns remind us in their buildings and street plans of the periods of high prosperity in their history. Broughton's time was in the years about 1800 when the new market-place was laid out. The economic forces of the Victorian epoch left Broughton stranded, turning to the shaping of the iron towns at the mouth of the estuary – Millom, a starkly simple ore-mining and smelting centre whose cycle of history is already completed, and Barrow, a boom town of the 1860s that evolved into the regional capital of Furness.

Urban growth in the nineteenth century

The powerful forces that changed the towns and cities of England in the nineteenth century lightly brushed the urban scene in the Lake District. Cockermouth and Kendal both developed small industrial quarters whose textile mills used water power far into the nineteenth century. The coming of the railways to Penrith after 1850 added a new suburb to the western edge of the town around the station.

Cockermouth's population doubled in the first half of the nineteenth century. The census of 1801 records 2,865 people there; by 1851 the figure had reached 5,775. At the same time industries became rooted in this remote market town, where one of the chief attractions was the Derwent as a source of water-power. A miniature industrial quarter developed on the south bank of the river adjoining Main Street, and an outlying suburb made up of textile mills and scattered terraces of cottages appeared within the meander curve of the Derwent. Here the factories of the mill settlement of Goat (1130) were fed by a leat half a mile long that took off from a weir above the site of Cockermouth castle (123312) (Diag. 16).

The building of warehouses and industrial premises along the bank of the Derwent to the north of Main Street is related to the enclosure of the Cockermouth commons for which an act was obtained in 1816. Up to that time the land along the river was an open piece of common known as the Sand. The act for the enclosure of the commons opened the way to speculative development. The making of Waterloo Street began the conversion of the Sand to a closely-built quarter, and the name of the new street helps to date this piece of the urban scene of Cockermouth for all time. The development of this former piece of common along the river lost to Cockermouth what could have become one of the most attractive elements in its urban landscape. The preservation of an open strip of land along the river would have presented a vista of the woods and meadows of the Derwent and the low bluff crowned by the castle. At Kendal, on the other hand, the riverside commons have been preserved as open spaces and

219

one can now walk along the left bank of the Kent with its succession of views across to the long street that formed the axis of the medieval town.

Although Cockermouth's topography evolved through three main stages from a medieval core to which was added the new market street in the seventeenth century and two small industrial quarters in the years about 1800, the general architectural impression of the town is one of the early nineteenth century. The attractive sombre grey stone buildings of the outer ward of the castle are late Georgian and early Victorian in date. The Town Hall, close by the parish church, was first built as a Methodist chapel in 1841. The façades of Main Street, neatly set off by rows of trees, epitomize the urban scene in Cumberland. Victorian banks stand out among the unremarkable roughcast, cement-washed and painted fronts of shops and houses whose buildings date largely from the early nineteenth century. The best house in Main Street dates from the middle of the eighteenth century and was the birthplace of Wordsworth. Across the river the early industrial hamlet of Goat presents as fine an example of the building style of the early decades of the industrial revolution that one could find anywhere in the north of England.

Kendal has enjoyed a longer and richer history than Cockermouth, a history that is reflected in the details of its topography at the present day. Until the end of the eighteenth century the borough was restricted to the steep slopes at the foot of Kendal Fell on the west bank of the River Kent. The original skeleton of the town's street plan can be clearly recognized in the distribution of the place-name element *gata* of Old Norse origin and meaning a 'road' or 'street'. To the north of the Market Place we find Stricklandgate; to the south the axial street is called Highgate. Stramongate that runs from the Market Place north-eastward to a bridge across the river Kent is already recorded in a document of 1365. On either side of these medieval streets that converge at the Market Place the burgesses of Kendal built their houses on long narrow plots that sloped away to the river or stretched up to the steep and rocky outcrops of limestone on the fell (Diag. 18) (Plate 33). Kendal Fell formed the common land of the borough – a place where stock could be grazed, building stone quarried, or cloth hung out to stretch and dry on the tenter grounds. To the east of the medieval town, across the river, lay the circular thirteenth-century castle crowning a steep elliptical-shaped hill of boulder clay. Kendal castle stood in a park, a partly-wooded tract of country preserved for hunting that stretched down to the bank of the Kent. Until the close of the sixteenth century two very different elements of the English landscape faced each other across the Kent. On one side was the busy wool market and cloth town that had struggled through to achieve the status of a borough in Elizabeth I's reign; on the other a ruined castle rose above a former hunting preserve. About the time when Kendal gained its borough charter the properties of Kendal Castle were 'disemparked' and the land became open to more profitable forms of development. But it was only at the beginning of the nineteenth century that the town of Kendal found the incentive to spill over on

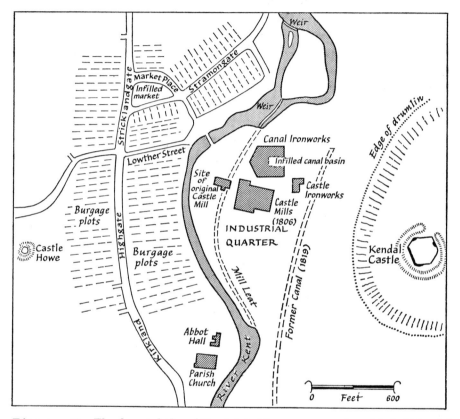

Diagram 18 *The elongated plan of Kendal sited between two castles, with the industrial quarter lying in an open bend of the River Kent.*

to the eastern bank of the river, with the opening of the Lancaster and Kendal Canal in 1819.

The canal followed closely the left bank of the river into Kendal and ended in a small dock basin beside the site of the castle's corn mill. The latter had been built across a medieval leat that drew its water from the Kent and after losing its original function had been used as a fulling mill and, later, for the carding and spinning of wool. The canal converted Kendal into a small port and gave the town easy acccess to Lancaster, Preston, and the Lancashire coalfield. A little industrial quarter grew up around its terminus and in 1822 a new industry, carpet-making, was introduced there. In 1826 Kendal gasworks was built on the canal bank. A few hundred yards upstream from the canal basin and the cluster of small factories a new quarter of the town appeared between 1820 and 1830. Several streets with terraced houses were laid out at the approach to Stramongate bridge within the decade. Although the canal added a busy little suburb to Kendal in the first half of the nineteenth century, there was no serious disturbance of the town's visual harmony. This was because building stone was drawn entirely from the traditional quarries on Kendal Fell. Grey white limestone dominates in the cottage rows, warehouses, and stumpy factory chimneys. No ministerial order could have secured a greater harmony of purpose and visual effect than this piece of early nineteenth-century *laissez faire* in industrial development. Just as the craftsmanship of the countryside, building in local stone, remained alive through the nineteenth century at Kendal, so the techniques of the industrial revolution penetrated this region late and slowly. Kendal's industries – cloth-making, marble polishing, paper, carpets and snuff manufacture – depended entirely on water power until after the middle of the nineteenth century. In fact the first steam engine in the district was not installed until 1855 at the Castle Mills. Even then steam power was meant only to supplement the energy of three water-wheels that drove a large factory employing more than three hundred workers producing railway rugs, coat-linings and tweeds.

The evolution of the industrial suburb on the east bank of the Kent was completed with the building of St George's church on a patch of waste ground close to Stramongate bridge between 1839 and 1841. The land had to be raised four feet to lift the church above the level of the Kent's floods. Its architects, the firm of Paley and Austin of Lancaster who have left their imprint on many parts of the urban scene in north-west England, drew their stone from the Kendal Fell quarries and maintained their link with the deep roots of the town's history. Today this seems to be broken. The clearance of old buildings along Highgate is resulting in half-hearted attempts to reproduce the topography of medieval Kendal in modern materials; and the tower of a post-war insurance building lacks any of the aesthetic qualities of good twentieth-century building, looking particularly out of place among the shaggy grey warehouses near the river in New Road and beside the handsome smooth-faced Georgian terraces in Lower Stramongate.

The growth of Penrith in the nineteenth century followed a different course from the evolution of either Cockermouth or Kendal. It was unable to develop the industries that depended on water power and its chief role remained as a regional market centre for one of the richest parts of the Lake District. By the end of the eighteenth century Penrith was a busy focus of stage-coach traffic. The revolutionary moment in the town's nineteenth-century history was also concerned with communications when, in 1846, the Lancaster and Carlisle Railway was opened to traffic. Before the end of the century Penrith was second only to Carlisle among the railway centres of the north-west, forming a junction between the trunk route to Scotland and cross-country lines that reached eastward across Stainmore to Tees-side and that also served the tourist traffic of Keswick and the industrial towns of the Cumberland coast to the west. The railway age created a new quarter, Castletown (5030), adjoining the station to the north-west. At the same time, in the 1850s, Penrith extended on its eastern flank up the steep lower slope of the sandstone ridge that separates the town from the Vale of Eden. Here eighty-one houses were built by a building society founded in 1850. Newlands Place, Arthur Street and Graham Street were laid out with good middle-class villas, the property of members who paid £30 for each share. The building society bought four fields for this development, and their former shapes and hedge boundaries can still be picked out in the pattern of streets. As in the nineteenth-century development of Kendal, the Victorian suburbs of Penrith, both the railway-workers' terraces and the comfortable villas of the middle class, continue with no harsh break the architectural themes of the older parts of the town. The brilliant warmth and depth of the local sandstone that we can enjoy in the fragments of the fourteenth-century castle and in the parish church of the 1720s is found also in Methodist chapels, the Salvation Army citadel, the police station and bay-windowed Boer-War villas. The only variation is provided by the favourite Cumberland technique of surfaces rendered with glossy films of paint – greys and blues, greens and white.

Revolutions in transport seem to have brought the greatest changes to Penrith. The railway age was heralded by a battle in 1845 in the streets of the town between Irish and Lancashire navvies armed with pick-axes and sticks. Now, in 1970, the navvies are back again on Shap Fell armed with the tools of the twentieth century – bulldozers, cranes and giant earth removers. A web of trunk roads enmeshes the countryside around the town, and Penrith is once more able to return to its role of a busy town on market days, freed from the blight of its unending procession of long-distance lorries.

9

Wealth from the hills

Long before the first tourists came to gaze in awe and wonder at the mountains, they had proved attractive, though in a different way, to the local inhabitants. Accustomed as they were to wrestling with thin soils and an excessively wet climate, the minerals of the mountains did offer a potential source of wealth and a chance to improve their meagre standard of living. It is true that mining seldom brought the huge profits which both the prospector and the investor of capital continually sought. It was a gamble, however, that might pay handsome dividends to those fortunate to make a lucky strike. Mining also brought in its wake benefits to people like charcoal burners, suppliers of timber for the mine galleries or those engaged in carrying ore to the smelter works. At certain times, in towns like Coniston and Keswick, there was money to be spent, especially after a rich strike. Thus, even if the balance sheet for individual mines did not show a profit, the industry brought trade and a much-needed diversity to an area which depended almost entirely on subsistence farming.

The existence of mineral veins was undoubtedly known at an early date, for on bare upper hillside slopes their different colour might stand out. This was particularly true of minerals associated with quartz, where the resulting white streaks would show up and invite the curious. It is not known whether prehistoric man actively exploited any of the metallic ores, and evidence of Roman interest is scanty and rather inconclusive. Excavations at forts like Hardknott (2101) and Papcastle (1131) have revealed bloomeries* where iron could have been made. As both these sites are close to iron ore supplies, it seems probable

* Open hearths where iron ore was smelted using charcoal.

that some sporadic mining was done during the Roman period. The main development, however, came much later in medieval times. At first it was the monks of Furness Abbey who began to make bloomery iron, often at their outlying grange sites in the heart of the Lake District. Ore was often carried some distance, as the bloomery site was usually located near a good supply of timber for charcoal-making. It is hard to imagine monks leading packhorse trains from lower Eskdale, past their grange farm of Brotherilkeld (2101), then up the valley of the Lingrove Beck (2304) and across into the headwater valleys of Borrowdale. In Langstrathdale at the junction of Greenup Gill (2712) one of their bloomeries was sited on a small island in the stream. The iron ore, in this case, probably came from the haematite deposits found on the col significantly named Ore Gap (2407).

It was copper and lead, rather than iron ore, which firmly established the reputation of the Lake District as a mining area of some standing. Copper was being won at the Goldscope mine (231183) in the Newlands valley in the early thirteenth century from a vein which ran into the hillside. The vein was nine feet thick and exceptionally rich in workable copper. It had the added attraction of a small percentage of silver and, according to some, contained minute quantities of gold. As well as the rich copper deposit there were two lead veins, one fourteen feet thick. Together these veins made Goldscope one of the richest of mines. The history of its working spans several centuries, though production was not continuous throughout. The sixteenth century saw its greatest period of prosperity. Under Elizabeth and her chief minister, Lord Burghley, a real attempt was made to exploit local resources to make the country less dependent on foreign supplies. To this end German miners were brought across under Daniel Höchstetter, after he himself had visited Keswick. To encourage production, royal patronage was granted with the setting up of The Society for the Mines Royal in 1561. Hidden subsidies, in the form of waived taxes, were given to the Society in order to promote production. The German miners were not too well received at first and for a time they lived separately on Derwent Island (2622). Gradually they came to be accepted and married into local families. The parish register of Crosthwaite Church (2524) records no fewer than 176 children of German fathers between 1565 and 1584. The population of Crosthwaite parish, including Keswick, also increased considerably from about 1,600 in 1563 to well over 2,000 by 1590.

The method of extracting the ore was both laborious and costly. Prior to the use of gunpowder, long flat pieces of iron were driven into the rock and the wedges used to shatter the ore. Only the ore vein was removed, so that some of

P

the working galleries were exceptionally narrow and extraction exceedingly slow. In spite of the richness of some of the ore veins, the cost of production was high. No less than £18,600 was spent by the Mines Royal Company between 1564 and 1568. Of this total perhaps three-quarters went in wages to the miners and the rest for fuel and the carriage of the ore. The destination of the copper from the Goldscope mine was the smelter erected at Brigham (2823) (Map 25). Here, on the banks of the River Greta, about a mile upstream from Keswick, a small industrial community grew up around the smelt house, the stamping sheds and storehouses for the ore and fuel. By 1567 there were as many as six furnaces working at Brigham. Power came from the river, the water being led off the Greta some distance upstream and carried along an artificial channel. This conduit is the only tangible remains of this once thriving industrial suburb of Keswick, as the buildings were destroyed at the time of the Civil War. Goldscope mine closed about the same time after working continuously for about eighty-five years. It was re-opened in 1690 by the Dutch, who continued to work the mine until all the accessible and worthwhile ore had been extracted. The final phase of Goldscope's long history came in 1847 when, with better techniques of mining and drainage, it was hoped to mine considerable quantities of ore. After four years only thirty-three tons had been won, and so the mine closed for copper production. Somewhat fortuitously while working the copper ore, a cross vein of lead was encountered and thereafter Goldscope entered the second phase of its history. Between 1851 and 1863 lead production varied between 300 and 480 tons a year. Goldscope lead mine closed in 1866, but opened again during the First World War and continued for some years after. Today the site of the former flourishing mine has a lonely and desolate air. Spoil heaps jut out of the hillside in the fields beyond Low Snab Farm (2218), the only remains of intermittent activity extending over almost four centuries.

Goldscope was not the only mine which supplied copper ore to the Brigham smelter. Higher up the valley the Society for the Mines Royal worked Dale Head (224155), high up on the hillside. Another mine in the Newlands valley lay at Castle Nook (228170), although in total production it could not compare with Goldscope and Dale Head. The south-west shore of Derwentwater was also an important copper-mining area in the sixteenth century. Veins which were found in the Newlands valley ran through the intervening Cat Bells ridge and out-cropped in Borrowdale. The Copper Plate mine at Ellers (248177), a quarter of a mile north-west of Grange, was opened by Höchstetter in 1566, and for a time considerable production was maintained. In digging the foundations for a nearby house in 1871 some of the original tools used by the German miners were

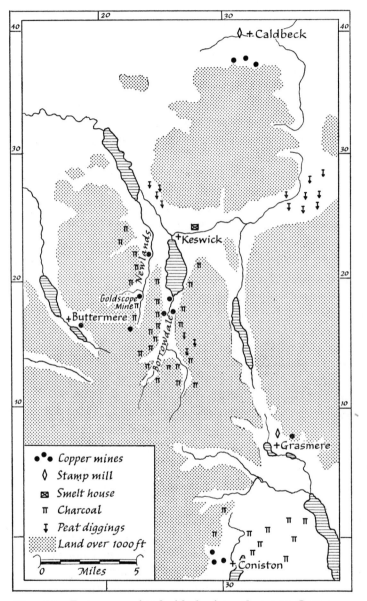

Map 25 *Features associated with the sixteenth-century German mining enterprise in the northern Lake District.*

found. The Copper Plate mine had the advantage over the others in sending its ore to the Brigham smelter, as it involved only a short journey across the lake by boat and then by packhorse to Brigham. The mines in the Newlands valley like Dale End and Goldscope had an initial packhorse haul to the lakeside at a place which became known as Copperheap Hill (253216). After passing through the smelter works at Brigham the copper had to receive the Queen's mark at the Receiving House, now the Moot Hall in the Market Place, in Keswick. This was rebuilt in 1571 by Richard Dudley of Yarnwath from the ruined courthouse. Along with the George inn, a favourite meeting-place of the miners, these two buildings form the only real links with the period when Keswick was the centre of a thriving mining industry.

The Society for the Mines Royal did not confine its activities only to the Newlands Valley–Borrowdale area. Höchstetter and his German miners also exploited the copper ores around Coniston. The size of these deposits was considerable, and it is said that when Höchstetter realized this he would have preferred to have his smelter at Coniston rather than Brigham, especially as timber for charcoal was readily available in the lower fell country. As a result the copper ores of the Coniston district were not fully exploited in Höchstetter's lifetime, and it was not until 1599 that large-scale working began. The main mine lay in Church Beck (2898), about two miles upstream from the lake edge. Although the ore was concentrated on the site, no attempt was made to smelt it. Instead it was carried in trains of packhorses to the Brigham works. By the middle of the seventeenth century production had virtually ceased, and the destruction of the Brigham smelter in 1650 was not encouraging. The main period of exploitation, and with it considerable prosperity, came later. In 1758 the Macclesfield Copper Company obtained the lease of the Coniston mines, and in the next decade almost a thousand tons of ore were raised. When the Macclesfield Company lost its important source of supply from the Parys mountain in Anglesey in 1792 steps were taken to increase production at their Coniston mines. They were successful in this for a few years but by that time all the known ore bodies had been worked and production slumped. The end of the mine was predicted and only a few men were kept on. In 1830, however, John Barratt arrived from Cornwall with other ideas. Using his knowledge of mining, he quickly stepped up production, and by 1849 his Coniston Mining Company was employing 400 men and extracting something like 250 tons of ore a month. The period between 1854 and 1864 saw the maximum output reached; thereafter production fell as the better deposits were worked out.

The main veins of the Coniston group of mines lay close to Levers Water

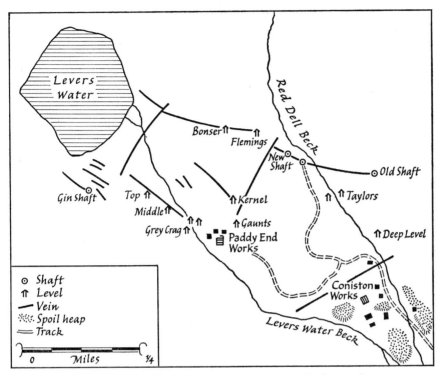

Map 26 *Coniston copper mines as they appeared in the mid nineteenth-century.*

(2799) on the valley side where the various veins outcropped. The best veins were up to two feet wide and perhaps contained 15 per cent copper. Adits* were driven into the hillside, and some of their entrances can be seen on the hillside today. Compared with the Elizabethan mines of the Newlands valley, the Coniston workings still make a considerable impression on the landscape, since their main period of activity was in the mid-nineteenth century. Also, in the present century, the original spoil heaps have been worked over again, with up to 1·5 per cent copper extracted from the waste. A walk up the valley of the Church Beck (2898) is instructive in that it is still possible to appreciate the vast scale of the working and perhaps obtain an insight into the character of the industry. Near the Youth Hostel, housed in one of the old mine buildings, are great dumps of worked-over waste spewing out into the valley. Behind are the remains of rectangular settling tanks, and the crushing plant with its rusting wheel still in

---

* Horizontal tunnels driven into a hillside during mining operations.

place, the whole an excellent industrial archaeological showpiece, even though it is less than fifty years since it last worked. Higher up the valley of Levers Water Beck (284987) there is another set of settling tanks with water still tumbling down like a gigantic artificial waterfall. Climbing still higher towards Levers Water, a natural corrie lake whose level was artificially raised, come the mine adits and tunnels driven into the hillside in search of the valuable copper ore (Map 26).

Although the principal copper mines were located around Levers Water, there were others in the Coniston area. Across the ridge top of Wetherlam, copper was also mined in the valley of the Greenburn Beck (2902). Altogether seven veins were worked and, as at Coniston, the greatest period of prosperity was between 1854 and 1861, when over a thousand tons of ore were raised. The rather isolated site, involving a seven-mile haul to the railhead at Coniston, ultimately made extraction uneconomic. A similar fate befell the Wetherlam mine (2801), with its even more remote site high up on the hillside at a height of 1,500 ft. Although 108 tons of ore were produced in 1907 this rate could not be sustained and the mine was abandoned shortly afterwards. More accessible was the mine in the Tilberthwaite valley near Dry Cove Bolton (3000), opened by the Coniston Mining Company about 1850, but here too the mine had a relatively short life.

The third area of copper mining was in the Caldbeck Fells on the northern flanks of the Skiddaw massif (Map 27). In Elizabethan times, the mines here served the Brigham smelter although they were never so important as Goldscope, in spite of the couplet which ran

> Caldbeck and Caldbeck Fells
> Are worth all England else.

One distinguishing factor about the Caldbeck ore veins is the large number of different metals found in association – copper, zinc, iron pyrites, manganese, barytes, silver all occur, sometimes within a single vein. The copper ores vary in richness from fifteen per cent to thirty-five per cent, which compares favourably with other areas. Roughtongill mine (3034) was probably the most productive and most varied in its mineral output. Lying isolated at the head of a north-running valley, it was not easy to transport the ore to Brigham, as this involved crossing the main watershed of the Skiddaw massif. Thus, when the mine was re-opened at the end of the eighteenth century a large smelting works was built alongside, but this did not last more than a few years and was later converted into miners' cottages. The period of greatest activity was between 1855 and 1877,

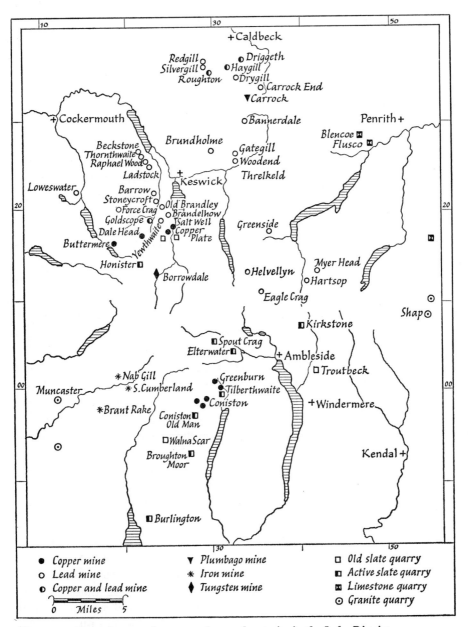

Map 27 *Sites of past and present mines and quarries in the Lake District.*

when an average of 1,500 tons was raised each year, about half the output of the Coniston mines at their peak. After the main copper veins had become exhausted, the mine was re-opened to exploit the barytes deposits, and in the present century the spoil heaps have been re-worked. Now little remains save for these, which do less than justice to this once important site. The other Caldbeck mines were much less important as producers of copper. Sites like Red Gill (294348), Driggeth (327353), Hay Gill (308361) and Dry Gill (325345) never produced more than a hundred tons of dressed copper ore a year. Many were more important for other minerals like lead and barytes.

Along with copper, lead was the most sought-after of the metallic ores in the Lake District. In appearance the lead ore possesses a livery sheen when freshly fractured, but to the miners it was also known as the 'blue ore'. It was found along with copper in the Newlands Valley and was first worked here by the Elizabethan prospectors. The largest and probably the earliest mine was Brandley, or Brandelhow (2519,) on the shore at the south-west end of Derwentwater. The lead occurs in a number of north-south veins which outcrop on the hillside of Cat Bells, but when these were exhausted the miners were forced to follow them to lower ground and ultimately to the lakeside. Here, although the lead ore was of good quality, they had to face the difficulty of water flooding the workings. Great waterwheels were erected to drain the mine, but this was largely ineffective and ultimately the workings were abandoned. In the nineteenth century, with the advent of steam pumps, the mine was re-opened and for a time the annual output of lead was about 300 tons. The ore was crushed and dressed on the site, and to supply power for this a great thirty-foot wheel was built near the edge of the lake. It excited the curiosity of the Victorian tourist, for even in 1890 water wheels were becoming rather rare. Brandelhow was one of a number of lead mines in the area. Others existed in the Newlands valley at Yewthwaite (239194) and the Barrow mine near Uzzicar Farm (234218). The latter was owned by the Keswick Mining Company between 1848 and 1868, but it was mainly leased to independent miners called 'tributers' who paid a percentage royalty on any ore raised. The great spoil banks near Uzzicar Farm date from the last phase of development round about 1883 when a gigantic sixty-foot waterwheel dominated the mine. It was in this Barrow mine that two great secret stores of lead ore were discovered, no doubt put there by the early miners as an insurance against less fortunate times. Another feature of the mine was that it ran through 'sandy veins' made up of friable quartz which at times would become so dry and unstable that they would run like an hour glass and fill some of the galleries.

Some of the mines working lead in the nineteenth century were the successors of earlier copper workings on the same site. Goldscope is a good example of this dual-purpose mine, for the site had virtually been abandoned after the rich copper ores had become exhausted. When Whelan wrote his present *History and Topography of Cumberland and Westmorland* in 1860 the mine had just been re-opened, and so his contemporary account gives a glowing picture of the recent discovery of a twenty-foot-wide vein of lead, one of the richest finds ever made in the Lake District. About fifty men were employed at the time and about 500 tons of ore were raised each year. Considerable profits were made at the outset, but as the richer lodes were exhausted it became uneconomic and was abandoned in 1864. There was considerable trouble with water in the deeper workings, which even the installation of a forty-foot wheel could not keep dry.

The valleys which bite deeply into the area around Skiddaw have also seen their share of mining activity in the past. In the Glenderaterra valley, just below the point where Roughton Gill enters (2927), lead was worked at the beginning of the nineteenth century and again for a few years from 1872 onwards. In terms of output it could never compare with the mines of the Newlands Valley. Somewhat more successful were the mines around Threlkeld on the southern slopes of Blencathra (3225). Gategill is perhaps the oldest and certainly was producing ore by the primitive 'stope and feather'* method of extraction before introduction of gunpowder for blasting. Along with Woodend mine, farther down the slope and closer to the road, production of lead and the associated zinc blende reached considerable proportions at certain periods. Between 1880 and 1900, for example, a total of over 10,000 tons of galena and 13,400 tons of zinc was produced. With a value exceeding £120,000 it brought a rapid, though short-lived, prosperity to Threlkeld. About a hundred men in the village worked in the mines and the ancillary refining sheds. What was once a small hamlet with its town fields around quickly became a typical mining village, an appearance which it retains to the present day, though it is now the roadstone quarry on the opposite side of the valley which provides employment.

On the other side of the mountains in the valleys draining northwards to the Solway Plain, the mining of lead and other metallic ores went on intermittently in the nineteenth century. The present isolated and lonely sites high up in the mountains give no indication of the time when miners from Keswick and Cald-

* A miner's term for implements used in breaking rock. The stope was a thin tapering wedge about six inches long. The feather was similar but had a round outside and a flat inside. Both were made of iron.

233

beck made the daily or perhaps weekly journey along the stony tracks across the fell tops in the hope that perhaps one day they would 'strike it rich'. Occasionally they were rewarded, for mines like Roughtongill (3034) had periods of considerable prosperity. Some veins contained no fewer than twenty-three distinct minerals, including lead, copper, zinc, manganese, iron pyrites and barytes, and each was worked at various times if the demand existed and the price was right. At first the miners concentrated on the blue galena and red copper ores, but from 1886 onwards barytes, a transparent or white mineral used in the manufacture of plate-glass and in paints, was sought. Although mining continued until quite recently all the sites are now derelict, with gaunt spoil heaps and rusting metal symbolizing the total eclipse of this phase of landscape history.

Without doubt the greatest of the lead mines was that of Greenside (3617) in the valley of the Glenridding Beck on the eastern side of the Helvellyn range. It finally closed in 1959, and therefore, not surprisingly, there are extensive remains by way of spoil heaps and mining sheds at the former mine site. Farther down the valley is a row of typical miners' cottages, brightly painted and still occupied, though the mines themselves have closed. The prosperity of the Greenside mine was based on the existence of quartz veins with strings of lead running through them. Rather surprisingly, in view of the richness of the ore, the mine was not really worked until after 1825, even though the existence of the mineral veins was known at least a century earlier. Once mining got under way, it brought considerable prosperity to the area. The population of Patterdale Parish increased from 261 in 1801 to 686 in 1851. The success of Greenside mine over a long period of time owed as much to capital spent on modern equipment as to the richness of the ore. In 1891, for example, electrical winding gear was installed in the main shaft, the first of its kind in a metalliferous mine in this country. This was followed in 1893 by the use of electric locomotives for haulage underground. On the surface there was a mixture of old and new. Great water wheels supplied some of the power needed in the washing and dressing plants, while up the hillside a mile-long flue collected any lead which escaped in the vapours from the furnace. Production of lead naturally varied from year to year but on average it was almost 1,000 tons. Between 1901 and 1911 output increased steadily to reach over 3,000 tons a year. Profits were considerable and it is therefore not surprising that the mine was the best equipped in the Lake District. Much deeper levels could be tapped and production maintained, until about ten years ago, when the last ore was brought to the surface. Now Glenridding has had to turn its back on the mine, and its people seek work in the seasonal tourist industry.

While lead and copper dominated the mining industry, other rarer minerals attracted attention from time to time. In the case of plumbago, or black lead, the mine by the side of the Seathwaite valley of upper Borrowdale established a world reputation. Although the deposit was known at least as early as the sixteenth century and the pure carbon deposit used 'as a remedy for the cholick', its real usefulness was not appreciated until much later. It was then found of great value in glazing and hardening pottery, in casting cannon balls, and as a preservative against rust. Its unique qualities and rarity led to steps being taken to preserve the deposit, and in 1752 a special Act of Parliament made it an offence to 'enter unlawfully any mines or wad-hole of wad, commonly called black lead'. This followed the attack of an organized gang the previous year when considerable quantities of the valuable mineral were carried away. In 1800 a guard-house was even erected at the entrance to the principal level. Once inside the mine a maze of tunnels followed the various strings of plumbago. One of these strings found in 1803 contained over thirty tons of plumbago, with an estimated value of £100,000. Finds of this magnitude were rare and for years the mine might produce very little. In the early part of the nineteenth century much of the material was finding its way to the pencil factories at Keswick and Braithwaite (2323). Since 1833 no worthwhile deposits have been found and the pencil works at Keswick have had to rely on imported supplies and man-made substitutes. The hillside above Seathwaite, with its spoil tips marking the old mine entrances, has now lain silent for over a hundred years. It is still possible to find small pieces of plumbago on some of the higher spoil tips. Thus Jonathan Otley's prophetic remarks, made in 1843, 'that the most prolific part of the mountain may be already explored and the principal body or trunk of the mine excavated, so that posterity must be contented with gleanings from the branches', has a true ring.

Another rare and unusual mineral found in the Lake District is wolfram (tungsten). It is a very heavy metal with a specific gravity of 19·1 – almost the same as gold. The existence of tungsten ore in an upper tributary valley of the River Caldew (3232) has been known since a prospector named Emerson first found the mineral when searching for lead a hundred years ago. At this time it had no value and it was not until its usefulness in making filaments of electric lamps and as a hardener of steel was realized that the almost forgotten deposit began to be exploited. During the 1914–18 war the wolfram of the Carrock mine proved invaluable in armament production. The mine was again opened during the 1939–45 war for the same purpose and some of the mine buildings and fresh-looking spoil heaps are very much in evidence. The road up from Mosedale has been surfaced and provides one of the few routes into this lonely fell country on the back of Blencathra.

Along with wolfram from the Carrock mine, the most recent activity in this Skiddaw–Caldbeck Fell region has centred on barytes. Until recently the Potts Ghyll mine (3136) on the north-facing slopes overlooking Caldbeck was in active production. At a height of 1,300 ft transporting the mineral proved difficult and an aerial ropeway had to be built to the road at Nether Row. Virtually nothing remains of the mine save the ubiquitous spoil heaps, concrete storage basins, gaunt towers of the former ropeway and the rusting trolley brickets lying upturned in the adjacent beck. Much the same picture applies to adjacent mines like Sandbeck (332363) and Driggeth (326353), where nature is gradually healing the scars of former mineral workings.

Slate quarrying, though perhaps lacking the glamour of the metalliferous mines, has proved a more lasting source of wealth in the economy of the Lake District. Indeed at the present time the demand for slate is increasing and the quarries are experiencing a shortage of skilled labour. Although, like the mining of copper and lead, it is a robber industry in the sense that what is taken out can never be replaced, the reserves of slate are almost limitless and so no problem is likely to arise from a lack of suitable stone. Two of the major formations of the Lake District rock sequence, the Borrowdale Volcanic Series and the Silurian Beds, both contain workable slates. On the other hand, in spite of its name, the Skiddaw Slates lack marketable slates. The colour of the slate varies in different areas depending on the character of the original rock. The pleasant soft greens are usually associated with the volcanic beds while those derived from the Silurian formations are mainly blue or a drab grey. Some of the largest quarries are found in the Kirkby Moor area (2383), where over a few square miles numerous workings occur. Slate quarrying here really began after 1771 when Lord John Cavendish purchased the manor of Kirkby Ireleth, and almost immediately there was a considerable demand from the developing industrial areas. The coastal location of the quarries helped export from small ports like Greenodd (3182). With the building of the Ulverston Canal in 1793 much of the slate exports used this outlet. By the first decade of the nineteenth century the annual production of the Kirkby quarries was about 25,000 tons. As most quarrymen earned four shillings a day, the industry brought considerable prosperity to the area. With its rich dark-blue colour and durable quality, the slate was in great demand for roofing purposes by architects all over the country, who referred to it as 'Westmorland Dark Blue', in spite of the fact that it was quarried in North Lancashire. Competition was severe in the mid-nineteenth century when the North Wales quarries were also at their peak, but even in 1900 production was over 10,000 tons a year.

The more inland quarries enjoyed a more limited prosperity, as they tended to supply only a local market initially. Even so, enterprising merchants like Thomas Rigge of Hawkshead, as early as 1818, could export the green slate from quarries around Tilberthwaite (3001) by carrying it down Lake Coniston and thence to Greenodd where 'several sloops are constantly employed in the carriage of it to almost every principal seaport town in England and Ireland where it is forwarded into the inland counties by the canals'. The siting of the quarries in the early days depended more on the quality of the slate rather than ease of export. The Honister quarries (2113), for example, lie at the head of the pass right in the mountainous heart of the Lake District and yet working has gone on continuously since 1643 (Plate 39b). The best slate lies high up on the top of the crags and it has always been a hazardous undertaking bringing it down for splitting and shaping. The early quarrymen used sledges for this purpose and made up to eight journeys a day down the rock and scree slopes with loads weighing a quarter of a ton. Writing in 1864, a visitor to the Honister quarries mentioned that a Joseph Clark from Stonethwaite brought down five tons in a single day in seventeen separate journeys. Local men like Clark were expert sledge riders for they had long carried peat from the fell tops in this way. After 1870, self-acting tramways were built to the working faces, and although these too have now been replaced their inclined tracks are still plainly visible. Today lorries make an equally hazardous journey up the crags by zig-zag roadway to bring down the slate to the splitting sheds by the roadside at the highest point of the pass. Apart from these sheds the industry here makes little impact on the scenery of the area and certainly does not form the great scars like those of the Llanberis and Penrhyn quarries of Snowdonia. Even the Elterwater quarry (3204) at the mouth of Great Langdale no longer disfigures the landscape now that conifers cover the waste heaps near the roadside.

Slate quarrying at the present time is experiencing an unprecedented boom and there are six working quarries within the National Park area (Map 27) (Plate 20b). Over 11 per cent of the total working population is now employed in the slate industry, compared with less than 10 per cent in the catering and allied trades. It is thus the largest single employer of labour within the Lake District. The revolution within the industry began about twenty years ago when the quarries began to produce slate for general building purposes as well as for roofing. Now only about 15 per cent of the finished stone is in the form of roofing slates. The remainder is largely in slabs suitable for building house walls.

Because of planning restrictions within the National Park, where new buildings are expected to harmonize with their surroundings, many contemporary houses are now built with stone. In effect there has been a return to a traditional building method, as can be seen in Coniston where the grey-green slate dominates both the old houses and new bungalows. There is also a considerable demand for the green slate outside the Lake District. Buildings like the National Library of Scotland and the Hotel Leofric in Coventry have used the slate extensively. Considerable quantities of stone are shipped abroad. One exceptionally large order worth £90,000 initially was for the Canadian Bank of Commerce in Montreal, where the slate was used for cladding the exterior walls. The slate was quarried at the Broughton Moor site (2594) and then shipped from Liverpool.

Apart from slate there is a considerable industry associated with the quarrying of granite and similar stone. Of the many quarries scattered throughout the Lake District those on Shap Fell are perhaps the most famous. The main site, where the characteristic pink granite is obtained, lies close to the A6 road as it passes over Shap near Wasdale Crag (5508). Although at one time the granite was in great demand for heavy constructional work, today there is an ever-increasing demand for crushed stone used as a road metal. All the roads in this part of Westmorland are surfaced with Shap granite, whose white mica flakes glisten in the sun after rain. Surprisingly few of the older buildings in Shap village are built of the stone, which tended to find a market much farther afield. At one time it was carried by rail but today most of the stone travels by road. Somewhat fortuitously the quarry lies close to the new motorway so that its future seems assured. The importance of good communications in developing the industry is shown by the relative failure of the Eskdale Granite quarries. These lie in the isolated south-west corner of the Lake District and the few quarries which were opened up in the granite, like those at Bridge End (1194), supplied stone mainly for local use.

Along this western fringe of the Lake District it was iron rather than stone that provided the wealth from the hills. The great haematite areas of Furness and the Cumberland coastal plain near Egremont lie outside the limits of the Ordnance Survey Tourist Sheet, but similar, though smaller, deposits occur in the foothill country both in Eskdale and on Murton Fell (0918), close to the entrance to Ennerdale. The Eskdale deposits outcrop on both sides of the valley near the village of Boot (1701). The Nab Gill mine, close to Boot village, was first opened shortly after 1870 when the Whitehaven Mining Company acquired a lease for working the deposits. An adit was driven into the hillside to reach the ore. The haematite was then carried on a three-foot gauge mineral railway to the coast at Ravenglass (0896). A branch line ran across to the south side of the valley to the Ghyll Foss mine, but after the Whitehaven Mining Company collapsed in 1877 this section was abandoned. This could well have been the fate of the main Boot–Ravenglass line after the mine ceased production in 1912, but fortuitously it was acquired in 1915 for use as a passenger railway. A new fifteen-inch track was laid from Dalegarth, near Boot, to the original terminus at Ravenglass on the main west coast line. Today it functions as a narrow gauge railway mainly carrying tourists during the summer season, although it operates a service throughout the year and has a place in British Rail London–Midland timetable.

The Murton and Kelton Fells iron mines (0918) had a very similar history. The rich haematite veins occur within the Silurian rocks of the foothill country at a height of over 800 ft. Their exploitation followed the building of a mineral railway from Rowrah in 1877 during a period of considerable expansion in the iron industry of West Cumberland. The Kelton mine had a relatively brief period of glory, for although more than a million tons of ore were mined most of it was obtained between 1877 and 1883. The whole enterprise collapsed shortly afterwards and the rich green fell country was allowed to settle once more into its former state of solitude. Only spoil heaps, old bridges and overgrown railway cuttings serve as a reminder of its brief period of intense industrial activity.

The fortunes of the iron mines of West Cumberland are inextricably linked with the iron and steel industry which had grown up on the coalfield at places like Workington and Distington in the nineteenth century. Coal had been obtained for centuries where it outcropped near the surface. Later mines tapped the deeper seams of the concealed coalfield, part of which falls within the north-west corner of the Lake District Tourist map along the valley of the River Ellen. Development here did not take place until the building of the Maryport to Carlisle railway in 1840. The Crosby Pit (0938) was sunk in 1854 close to the railway. A loop line ran off to the south-west to connect other collieries established at about the same time. The late arrival of coal mining in this area on the very doorstep of the Lake District has had little detrimental effect, for no new colliery villages were established. Miners were content to live in existing hamlets like Gilcrux (1138) or even Wigton. The collieries were usually small, and now that mining has ceased entirely they have left little that can be looked upon as really distasteful in this rural landscape. The scars which do remain are most likely the result of quarrying limestone for the iron industry at places like Plumbland (1539) and Brigham (0830). Most of them are now abandoned and today the active limestone quarries lie mainly on the east side of the Lake District at places like Flusco

239

(4629), where road metal is the main product. Although the quarries are unsightly in themselves and spread a grey dust over the surrounding countryside, they are fortunately limited to the fringes of the Lake District and outside the limits of the National Park. Problems similar to those encountered in the Peak District are therefore not likely to arise.

The Lake District can boast one unusual and unique mining project, that of diatomite in the Kentmere valley (4502). This is composed of the siliceous skeletons of plants which formerly existed in a shallow lake in the middle section of the valley. The brown black sludge is now dredged from the old lake bed and carried to the nearby processing works of Cape Insulation. Here the diatomite is extracted and packed for use in making products like soundproof boarding and heat-insulated bricks. The industry has remained small, and with the screen of trees around the drying sheds many visitors to Kentmere pass by unaware. It is only farther up the valley where the dredgers are scooping out the lake sludge that the landscape is being radically altered as man re-creates the former lake basin by his own excavation.

29. The lake just at Ballacher. Grasmoor (snow-covered) and Whiteless Pike are typical from of the Cumbrian

30a. *A fragment of the Lakeland landscape from the centuries before the medieval clearances.*

30b. *Frith Hall – on the site of a medieval hunting lodge in Ulpha Hall.*

30c. *Hardknott Forest Park at the head of the Duddon valley.*

31a. *Hut circle at prehistoric settlement on Heathwaite Fell.*

31b. *Roman bath-house at Ravenglass.*

32a. *Jackson Ground – an early sixteenth-century clearance.*

32b. *Fire-back made from sixteenth-century bloomery iron – at Carter Ground.*

10

The railway age and after

The decade between 1850 and 1860 marks something of a watershed in the history of man's contribution to the developing landscape of the Lake District. In this short span of years the gradual change which the area had been undergoing for the past century suddenly quickened in pace. Almost overnight the old order was seen to give place to the new. No single factor was wholly responsible but undoubtedly the coming of the railway, first to Windermere in 1847 and later to Coniston (1859) and Keswick (1864), opened up the area and finally broke down the characteristic isolation of the region. The railway brought in a new class of tourist, perhaps less adventurous than his eighteenth-century predecessor but one who nevertheless, by his mere presence, acted as a catalyst to the changes which were just beginning. Wordsworth was against the railway extending its tentacles into the heart of the Lake District, and by his forceful letter to the *Morning Post* on the subject probably prevented Ambleside from becoming the terminus, as the railway barons must have wished. Not everyone took the Wordsworth view that the peace and tranquillity of the Lake District would be disturbed by the hordes of excursionists from the Lancashire cotton towns disgorging themselves at Windermere station. Some, indeed, like Harriet Martineau positively welcomed the effect which the railway might have on the flagging economy of the district. Admittedly it gave her an excuse for writing yet another guide book, *The Complete Guide to the English Lakes*, published in 1855. In the opening paragraph, she immediately pinpoints the most noticeable affect of the arrival of the railway only eight years before.

> Now there is a Windermere railway station, and a Windermere post office
> and hotel – a thriving village of Windermere and a populous locality. This

implies that a great many people come to the spot; and the spot is so changed by their coming and by other circumstances that a new guide book is wanted.

Shortly after Miss Martineau's guide was published, Murray's *Handbook to the English Lakes* appeared for the first time. During the next half century, when no fewer than seven editions were brought out, a copy of Murray was to be found in the pocket of every self-respecting walker and connoisseur of scenery who wanted more than simply to 'contemplate on the sublime or become rapturous over the picturesque'. Written in a compressed style by an anonymous author – the name Murray refers to the publisher – it gave sufficient factual detail to leave a lasting impression. Murray was to become as indispensable to the Victorian traveller as West's guide had been a century earlier. Unlike Thomas West's account of the Lakes, which took the tourist to selected viewpoints or stations to admire the scenery, the Murray handbooks were for the active traveller who might wish to seek out the less frequented corners and get beneath the superficial trappings of the new tourist era. The handbooks were a product of the railway age and in their design they catered for those of the Victorian upper middle class now discovering the joys of railway travel for the first time. Each book contained a number of key routes following the main railways of the area. For the Lake District volume, especially the early edition, there was clearly the difficulty of a lack of railway routes and therefore greater emphasis had to be placed on diversionary excursions from existing railway centres. Coaches could be hired for about fifteen shillings a day, and although this rate limited the number who could take advantage of some of the routes selected by Murray it was nevertheless possible to explore isolated valleys like Long Sleddale. This is recommended for 'although the valley is not of the greatest character, it has the advantage of being thoroughly free from the intensions of art. There is nothing to mar its harmony; and while passing along the narrow lanes enclosed by thickly-lichened walls, tufted with wild flowers, the eye rests on the brilliant green of the meadows, the sparkling purity of the stream or the autumnal tints of the copses, we acknowledge it to be a genuine and lovely specimen of natural scenery.' Fortunately and rather miraculously, Murray's description of Long Sleddale a century ago still holds good.

As successive editions of Murray were published, advantage was taken of the gradual extension of the railway network. After the building of the Workington–Cockermouth and the Windermere–Oxenholme branch, both in 1847, there was a slight pause until the Furness railway skirting the edge of Morecambe Bay

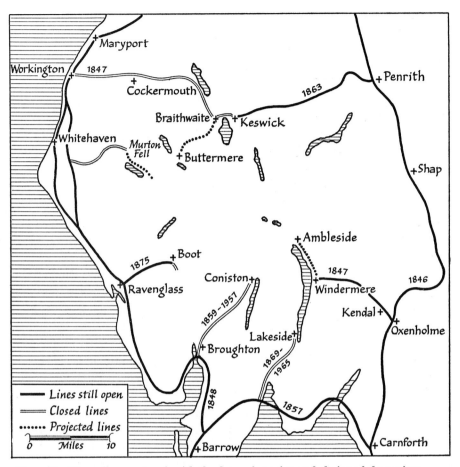

Map 28   *The railway network with the dates of opening and closing of the various branch lines.*

finally came into use in 1857 (Map 28). This line, which had to cross the heads of deeply penetrating inlets, was an engineering triumph. On no account should it be missed by the traveller, so Murray informed his readers, for it ran for at least eight miles on embankments or iron viaducts with superb views of the fluted sand flats on one side and glimpses of the Lake District mountains on the other. The completion of the Furness railway inevitably brought the relatively unknown southern Lake District within reach of the ordinary tourist and almost immediately there were proposals for branch line extensions. In 1857 the Coniston Railway Company was formed, largely to transport copper from the mines

243

above Coniston (2998), but doubtless the possibility of tourist traffic was an added attraction stressed in the prospectus to the shareholders. The Coniston line was opened in 1859 and ran for eight miles through Torver to Broughton-in-Furness (2187). Here it linked up with the Furness Railway, allowing copper ore to be taken to Piel for export. While the Coniston mines flourished, as they did between 1854 and 1875, the line was a financial success. After 1890, when mining virtually ceased, the railway had to rely mainly on the summer passenger traffic. There were fundamental difficulties in expanding tourist traffic because the station was sited high above the town, its position being dictated by the line chosen for the original mineral railway. It was also some distance from the lake and therefore railboat excursions were never as successful as on Windermere. It is true that a lake steamer, 'the Gondola', was once used for excursionists, but it is now many years since regular services have operated on Coniston Water. The railway, too, has been closed since 1957 and the station, with its superb views across the lake to the fells of High Furness, is gradually falling apart.

A hundred years ago the situation was very different for railways which could offer a unique and unchallenged mode of transport. A second penetration into the southern Lake District occurred in 1869 when a short branch line was built from the Furness railway to the southern tip of Windermere at Lakeside (3787). Here an attempt was made to build a miniature 'Parkeston Quay', as one contemporary writer put it, 'a quay where three steamers could tie up lay alongside the station'. There was also a restaurant with full orchestra playing in the summer season and a refreshment pavilion. Some idea of the expected traffic can be gauged from the fact that three long platforms, all partly under cover, were built by the railway authorities. For a time the decision to extend the railway to Windermere was justified. Excursion trains bringing parties from both the cotton towns of Lancashire and the thriving new town of Barrow were a regular feature of the summer traffic. After leaving the train the parties were taken for a sail up the lake, with tea at Ambleside. Another popular excursion in the early years of the century began at Blackpool and continued with a steamer crossing of Morecambe Bay from Fleetwood to Barrow and thence by rail to Lakeside. The steamer was waiting alongside the quay to take the party on to Ambleside for tea. The excursion then continued by coach to Coniston where the party took the train back to Barrow to board the steamer for Fleetwood. The total cost of the excursion was 7s. 6d., and for a time it proved popular. But already the railway was beginning to lose money, especially in wet summers like 1907. Surprisingly the Lakeside branch hung on until a few years ago, when the last passenger trains ran. Although the steamers still run during the summer months, Lakeside has a forlorn look, with the station gradually falling into ruins and weeds beginning to submerge the rusting metals. For Lakeside, as for Coniston, the railway age lasted just on a hundred years.

One small line which has survived to the present day, though not in its original form, is that serving the lower part of Eskdale. It was originally built in 1875 with a three-foot gauge, to transport ore from the iron mines opened at Boot (1700) (pages 238–9). Although primarily built for mineral traffic the railway company began to run passenger trains almost immediately. When the iron mines were abandoned the company lost much of its revenue and finally in 1912 the line was closed. For three years the railway lay derelict but in 1915 the unexpected happened and the line was acquired by the Narrow Gauge Railways Limited. They relaid the whole track from near Boot to Ravenglass using a fifteen-inch gauge. In this form it has continued working until the present day and now the line, affectionately known as 'Ratty', provides a unique tourist attraction in this unspoiled corner of the Lake District. Although a service is run all the year, the bulk of the revenue comes from the summer months when eight trains a day make the picturesque trip along lower Eskdale skirting Muncaster Fell to join the main Barrow–Whitehaven line at Ravenglass. It seems doubtful if the line could have survived but for the foresight of someone fifty years ago who converted it into a fifteen-inch gauge with the accompanying miniature rolling stock. This undoubtedly is its attractiveness for the summer visitor. It is perhaps a commentary on present-day attitudes of doing something different that an obscure railway in one of the more isolated of the Lakeland valleys can survive at a time when the ordinary railway routes have been so severely mutilated during the last decade.

Development in the northern Lake District was on a more limited scale, being confined to a single line connecting two existing railways at Penrith and Cockermouth. Again the impetus for construction was to carry mineral traffic, although the fact that the new line would pass through Keswick was an important consideration. The iron industry of West Cumberland based on local haematite ores soon discovered that the local coal was not really suitable for making coke, and had no alternative but to seek additional supplies from West Durham, and it was for this purpose that the Cockermouth, Keswick and Penrith Railway came into being. Mineral traffic would not be in one direction, however, for a trans-Pennine rail link would enable Cumberland pig-iron to reach European markets. Construction of the single-track line began in 1862, and it was opened in 1864 for mineral traffic. Shortly afterwards passenger trains, three a day in each direction, began running and immediately proved useful in encouraging tourists to visit the less well-known northern parts of the Lake District. A large hotel was built near the station at Keswick, a monument to Victorian enterprise in capitalizing on the extra tourists which the railway would bring. The railway itself benefited from the Keswick Convention, an evangelical conference held in July each year when thousands packed into the small Cumberland town. Special trains were put on – one named 'The Budd' after the London businessman who sponsored it – from Euston to Keswick. At the beginning of the century the 'Lakes Special' from London was introduced, and there were also direct connections with Glasgow and the Lancashire and Yorkshire industrial towns. Inevitably, as elsewhere, this type of traffic has virtually ceased and today the line, open only between Penrith and Keswick for passenger traffic, has a local diesel service. Even during the height of the summer season there are no through trains – yet another sign of changing social habits of those visiting the Lake District.

The history of railway development in the latter half of the nineteenth century is full of abortive schemes, frustrated hopes and concerted opposition to many proposals. Although Wordsworth led the way with his condemnation of the Kendal–Windermere line in 1844, others were later to take up the fight against further railway expansion. Prominent amongst these was John Ruskin. Like Wordsworth he expressed concern at the possible social consequences of bringing large numbers of people to the Lake District. In a preface to Somervell's *Protest against the extension of railways in the Lake District*, published in 1877, he wrote of 'the certainty of the deterioration of the moral character in the inhabitants of every district penetrated by a railway', and, in relation to the incoming tourist: 'I don't want to let them see Helvellyn while they are drunk.' When Somervell wrote his pamphlet there were many schemes of railway expansion in the gestation stage. In 1884 a proposed railway along Ennerdale was defeated in the House of Commons by a small majority, largely through the arguments of James Bryce, who pleaded for the preservation of 'the unspoilt and wild scenery'. Whether Bryce would have approved of the Forestry Commission taking over Ennerdale some forty years later is not easy to say. A few years later Bryce was largely instrumental in having the Ambleside Railway Bill rejected, although by this time the railway companies were themselves beginning to have doubts as to whether a short extension was a viable proposition in view of the engineering work involved in carrying the line well above the shores of Windermere. Another conservationist who attacked the threatened railway extensions was Canon Rawnsley, Vicar of Crosthwaite, and later a leading figure in the formation of the National Trust. When it was proposed to run a branch railway leaving the Keswick–Cockermouth line at Braithwaite (2323) and then running across to Buttermere, he wrote:

> Are the proprietors who work the slate quarry up in Honister to be allowed to damage irretrievably the health, rest and pleasure ground of the whole of their fellow countrymen who come here for needed quiet and rest? Let the slate trains once roar along the western side of Derwentwater, and Keswick as a resort of weary men in search of rest will cease to be.

Not everyone, of course, with the interests of the Lake District at heart could see the seeds of destruction being sown by railway development. To many the growth of rail communication offered the possibilities of economic advancement for both agriculture and traditional industries of the area. Harriet Martineau, for example, could write that 'the best, as well as the last and greatest change in the Lake District is that which is arising from the introduction of the railroad. In a generation or two, the dairy farms may yield wool that Yorkshire and Lancashire, and perhaps other countries may compete for. The cheese may find a market and the butter may be in request.' Some of this had already come to pass, for in 1860, at Mardale Green (4712), now submerged beneath the waters of Haweswater, 3,000 pounds of butter were being sent each week by rail to Manchester, presumably from Shap station.

Miss Martineau also took a very different view of the social consequences following the opening of railways. In her guide she wrote that 'the residents may find that their minds will have become more stirred and enlarged by intercourse with strangers who have, from circumstance, more vivacity of faculty and a wider knowledge'. There is no doubt that, in the minds of the guide book writers, the local inhabitants of the Lake District were still living in the peasant era. Thus the first edition of Murray's guide contained the following description under the general heading of 'Social Aspects':

> The simple, but somewhat rough, manners of the Westmorland and Cumberland peasantry, have not undergone any material change from their increased intercourse with the world; and education has hitherto had but little effect in refining their tastes, elevating their character and improving their morals.

Uncomplimentary and perhaps exaggerated though these comments might be, they did at least symbolize, to the outsider at least, that this was still an isolated and backward area, as yet insulated from the changes resulting from the nineteenth-century industrial upsurge.

The farmhouses are generally very ancient and the interior economy has been but little changed with time. They are generally built of stone with very thick walls, and are either thatched or covered with coarse blue slate. The floor of slate is kept scrupulously clean and is ornamented by scroll-work done with red and yellow ochre or chalk, according to the taste of the inmates. The great oaken beams are generally polished and bright brass and mahogany often decorate the kitchen. The furniture generally consists of a long oaken table with a bench on each side where the whole family, master, children and servants, take their meals together. At the side of the fireplace is the 'sconce', a sort of fixed bench, under which one night's elden, or fuel, is deposited each evening. The clothing of the family was formerly made from wool spun from the native fleece, and of linen made from the flax which was grown almost on every farm; the hemp ridge in fields still bears its name. Clogs and wooden-soled shoes, well adapted to a mountainous and rainy country, continue in common use.

Although change was in the offing, this mid-nineteenth-century view of a simple life held good for those parts of the Lake District which had up to then been unaffected by tourism.

By the end of the century this could no longer be said except perhaps for one or two of the more remote western valleys. Apart from an ever-increasing contact which the railways had brought in their wake, there was also a revival of mining and other industrial activity. The renewed interest in the copper and lead mines, which had known only sporadic working since the seventeenth century, coincided with improved techniques of mining and drainage which allowed deeper veins to be tapped. The draining of the mines was done initially by power from huge water wheels. At the Coniston copper mines there were no fewer than a dozen such wheels operating in the 1860s. Output at this time reached three hundred tons a week, and some nine hundred men and boys were employed in the various phases of the mining operation. New miners' cottages were built at Coniston by the side of the track which led up Church Beck to the site of the mines. They are still standing, though it is many years since they were occupied by miners. As in the earlier period of working during Elizabeth's reign the prosperity was short-lived and the output of copper at Coniston declined considerably after 1874. By 1890 the main mine workings were closed, although a few attempts have been made subsequently to find more copper and there has been some re-working of the spoil heaps (pages 228–30). The same story of renewed interest in mining, followed by a limited period of prosperity and then total decline, characterizes the Goldscope mine (2318) in the Newlands valley.

After lying dormant for well over a hundred years, this famous Elizabethan copper mine was re-opened in 1847 by a private company, who invested considerable capital in dressing machinery and roasting furnaces. Little copper was found and up to 1850 only 32 cwts were raised. The mine continued to lose money during the next two years and was on the point of being abandoned altogether when the chance discovery of a rich vein of lead changed the picture completely. The mine now began to make considerable profits, and continued to do so until 1864, when difficulties in draining the deeper workings – in spite of the erection of a forty-foot water wheel – became insurmountable and the mine was abandoned. Victorian capital and enterprise could overcome many difficulties, but as yet technological progress had not advanced sufficiently to solve every problem. Thus the second phase of mining prosperity at Goldscope petered out in just over a decade.

Across in the eastern part of the Lake District close to Ullswater the Greenside lead mine (3617) in the Glenridding valley had a much longer period of activity and only finally closed down in 1959. At the height of its prosperity at the turn of the century, water wheels, steam turbines and electrical plant supplied power for mining, crushing and dressing the lead ore (Map 29). Not everyone approved of this incursion of mining into an area which in the nineteenth century had become the preserve of the connoisseur of Lake District scenery but it did bring a much needed if limited phase of prosperity to the Patterdale area. Profits were considerable not only from lead but also from the silver associated with it. Even by 1876 it was estimated that the Greenside mines had already raised ores worth more than one million pounds sterling. When it is considered that even as late as 1911 the mine was still producing 3,000 tons of ore a year, Greenside can lay claim to have been the most profitable of all the Lake District mines. It is therefore perhaps surprising that no attempt was made to improve its transport facilities. The ore had to be carried by cart to the railway at Troutbeck or Penrith. If a direct rail connection had been suggested it would doubtless have met concerted opposition. By 1890, however, the railway companies themselves had lost interest in expansion, save where it would bring immediate and continued profits.

One of the more interesting facets of Lake District history during the late nineteenth century was the way in which water power still played an important role in the industrial life of certain areas. Sufficient survives in the way of buildings, old leats and mill races to make it possible to piece together and build up a full picture of this phase of economic activity. Water power had long been an important factor in determining the sites of the textile, gunpowder, and bobbin

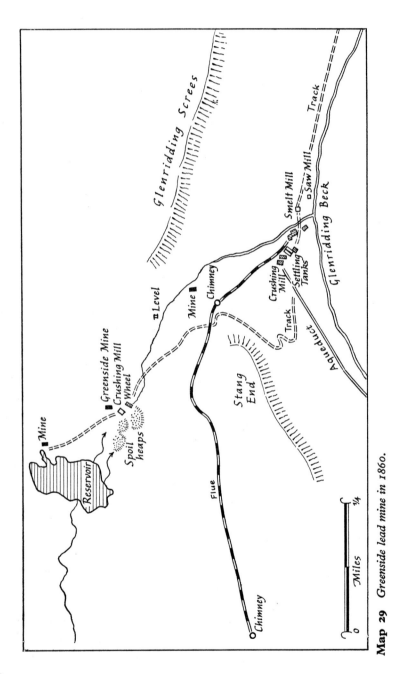

Map 29 *Greenside lead mine in 1860.*

mills amongst others. The Lake District rivers and streams, though short, were plenteously supplied with water from heavy precipitation. Though temporary short spells of dry weather might lead to difficulties over water supply and necessitate building mill ponds, every large stream had a succession of mills along its length, using the water over and over again. The rapid fall of the stream bed also meant that large water wheels could be built. At Caldbeck bobbin mill (3239), located in the limestone gorge known as The Howk, a water wheel forty-two feet in diameter was built, and claimed to be the largest in the kingdom.

One particularly favoured area in the water power revolution was that of the drainage basin of the Kent around Kendal (Map 30). Because of its relatively short course of just over twenty-five miles in which it drops a thousand feet, the Kent is reputed to be the swiftest river in the country. The volume of flow is also considerable for such a short river as its upper drainage basin receives the full effects of the rain-bearing south-westerly winds. There is, however, a marked variation in flow from time to time, and it was in order to regulate this that the Kentmere reservoir (4408) was originally built for the benefit of the mill owners. In the period between 1750 to 1850, prior to the railway incursion into this area, there were no fewer than ninety mills. After 1850 the number decreased especially as steam power began to take over in the Kendal region. Many mill owners seemed reluctant to change over from their proven water wheels, and so the impact of a new form of power was less in this region than elsewhere. The railways, too, had only a minimal effect, and although it is true that some of the mills near the Kendal–Windermere line like Burneside (5095) had rail sidings, the more isolated mills did not necessarily close down. They were sustained by a long-standing tradition of the use of water power for industrial purposes which reached its peak in this area during the first half of the nineteenth century. At that time the valley of the Kent and its tributaries was more important than the Birmingham area in terms of the number of industrial mills and the horse power they generated. In Kentdale there was one industrial mill to every 315 people, compared with a ratio of 1:1,380 in Birmingham. Rather surprisingly, therefore, this quiet corner of Westmorland had a more industrialized society than the heart of the Midlands during the first part of the nineteenth century. After 1850 this was, of course, to change quite dramatically as the full effects of steam power began to take hold on the heavy industry of the Birmingham area. Lacking local coal and iron resources, this transformation did not take place in the Kendal area and the pattern of industrial economy continued much as before. Although today none of the mills is solely dependent on water power, their sites are still

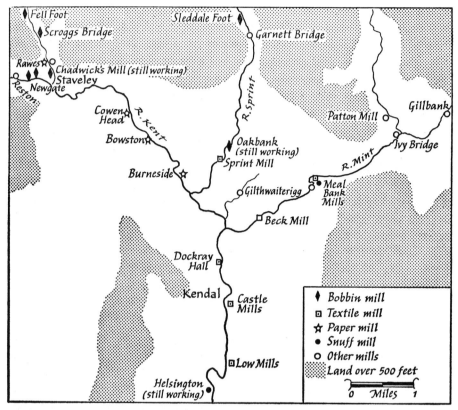

Map 30   *The mills of the Kent valley.*

used for industrial purposes, and in some cases the traditional industries have survived.

Although the history of harnessing the water power resources of the Lakeland streams and rivers goes back to the thirteenth century if not earlier, large-scale development belongs to the nineteenth century. In 1850 the mills of Kentdale were put to varying use, some grinding corn and others making woollen, linen and cotton cloth, shaping bobbins, manufacturing paper, snuff, carpets, rope and gunpowder amongst other uses. For the usage of a single mill might change over a period of time, depending on the demands for a particular product. There was also a concentration of certain types of mill in specific areas. Staveley (4798), for example, was the main centre of the bobbin industry, there being no fewer than five mills there in 1860 (Map 30). At first the local timber resources of the coppice woods were used, but as these became insufficient, up to 6,900 tons of

252

birch squares had to be imported each year from Norway. The invention of bobbin-making machinery by John Braithwaite of Ellerbeck Mill, Crook (463948) revolutionized the industry and for a time staved off competition from countries like Norway which had established their own bobbin mills. At the beginning of the century there were still twenty-five bobbin mills in the Lake District, but the industry has now almost collapsed, with the introduction of plastic substitutes (page 87–8). (Plate 35b).

Lower down the Kent from Staveley there was another concentration of mills making a single product, namely paper. Production began about 1760 when Thomas Ashburner built the Cowen Head mill (4997) (Map 30). He obviously found the enterprise profitable, for within a few years he had taken over the existing mills at Burneside (5095) and Bowston Bridge (4996) and converted them for paper-making. Water to drive the mill wheels came from the Kent by means of a leat which left the river some distance upstream. As the mills grew, especially that at Burneside, additional water was brought by pipeline from Potter Fell (5099). High quality paper and card is still produced at Burneside, while Cowen Head makes cheaper general-purpose paper, although from time to time it turns to the finer product needed for maps.

Another localized group of mills to the south of Kendal produced gunpowder (page 87). Although John Wakefield's first mill was built at Sedgwick (5087) in 1764, the family later moved their main centre of production to Gatebeck (5485) on the River Beela in 1850 to take advantage of a fifty-foot head of water. The nearness of the main railway line also proved useful to the continued prosperity of the mill, and in 1874 a horse-drawn tramway was built to connect the works with the railway sidings at Milnthorpe. If the building of gunpowder mills in this quiet countryside of South Westmorland comes as a surprise, the same can be said of another mill-based industry, that of making snuff. Again there was originally a concentration within a mile or so of Kendal. The first was established on Natland Beck (524908), a tributary of the Kent, in about 1740, and others followed in the nineteenth century in the Castle Mills and Low Mills area of Kendal. Of the seven mills which once produced snuff, only one remains working today. It lies on the west bank of the Kent opposite the Roman fort at Watercrook (513903) (Plate 35a). There are two mills at this Helsington site, with an attractive grouping of cottages around. One of the mills still has its original wheel in position, although it is now the other building which carries on the old tradition of making snuff. The whole setting of Helsington has an untidy attractiveness, perhaps worthy of preservation as a monument of industrial archaeology.

The 'industrial revolution' of the nineteenth century, centred on the Kent valley and based on water power rather than steam, saw the revival of the long-established Kendal woollen industry in a diversified form. When Whellan published his monumental *History and Topography of the counties of Cumberland and Westmorland* in 1860, almost a third of the total population of Kendal was employed in the collective woollen manufacture. The industry, famous for its 'Kendal Cottons', goes back to the fourteenth century when the manufacture of woollens was established by an Act of Parliament under the guidance of John Kempe. It was initially a cottage industry scattered throughout the hamlets of the Lake District. But with the invention of machinery to carry out the various processes of carding, preparation of dyestuffs and spinning, it became centred in places where mills provided available power. A whole variety of products was turned out, including the local 'Kendal green' cloth, carpets, horse cloths, floor cloths, trousers and hose, and 'railway rugs' which Whellan reported were in great demand. The mills located in Kendal itself were the main centres of production, though some of the ancillary processes, like fulling, were carried out farther upstream on tributaries like those of the Sprint and Mint. At Meal Bank (5495) a complete mill hamlet grew up around three mills, producing woollens, snuff and corn. Water was tapped from the River Mint some distance upstream and then carried by a leat to the mills sited within a meander loop of the river. Originally a great water wheel provided power for the main woollen mill, but later a beam engine was installed to allow production to continue when there was insufficient water to drive the huge wheel (Plate 35c).

One of the occasional delights of walking in some of the lesser-known parts of the Lake District is to come across an old mill site. Often the buildings have been altered for other uses so that their original purpose is not immediately recognizable. Only too frequently the once active mill is now simply an ivy-clad ruin rising out of a wilderness of weeds and shrubs. The mill wheel has gone and the former leat carries little or no water. And yet, a hundred years ago, these same mills were the lifeblood of the local community. In a parish like Satterthwaite (3392) in High Furness, even as late as 1905, of the thirty-two adults employed in ways other than farming, thirteen were connected with Low Force Forge mill and Middle Force Forge mill. Their trades included sawyer, wood hoop maker, joiner and wheelwright, oak basket manufacturer, bobbin turner, brush stock maker and woodcutter. Satterthwaite was typical of many of the High Furness parishes where the local coppice woodland formed the raw material for the mills.

While mills of this type might survive right down to the present day, those associated with the once flourishing woollen industry suffered a slow, lingering death, often before the end of the nineteenth century. At Millbeck (2526), nestling at the foot of the Skiddaw slopes, a whole community depended for its livelihood on the fortune of the fulling and carding mills. These were built in the early nineteenth century on the sites of older mills. For a time the mills flourished and produced blanket checks in various colours, flannel serge, kersey and carpets. Large quantities were dispatched to various places in Britain, and, perhaps more surprising, the products of the small hamlet found their way to New York, New Orleans, Quebec and Montevideo. The arrival of the railway at Keswick did not have a profound effect on the fortunes of the mill with its big export orders, for by 1865 Millbeck products were suffering intense competition from the West Riding manufacturers. With falling trade the inevitable happened and in 1886 the mills were closed and a whole community lost their livelihood. For a while the carding mill lay derelict, but in 1903 it was bought and converted into a dwelling-house, a not unusual fate for many mills. The transformation here resulted in an architectural oddity, for two 'pepperpot' towers were added to the original mill front. With the closing of the mills, the hamlet ceased to have any purpose, a fate repeated time and again in the Lake District when it had to face up to economic realities. In a few places the woollen mills lingered on into the twentieth century, especially if they produced specialized cloth. At Caldbeck, where the mill manufactured a heavy cloth for making overcoats known as Ivenson Grey, working went on much later. Today, however, even this mill by the side of Parkend Beck as it emerges from the limestone gorge of the Howk lies empty and abandoned (Plate 7b). As a similar fate overtook the bobbin mill a little distance upstream – it was never repaired after a disastrous fire – Caldbeck lost its basic industries and today can only trade on its association with John Peel. The author of this famous hunting song, John Woodcock Graves, was in fact a worker at the woollen mill for several years and the 'coat so grey' worn by John Peel was made from the local cloth.

With the closing down of mills, the decline of the mining industry and the long-continued low fortunes of hill-farming and agriculture in general, it was perhaps inevitable that the Lake District had to barter its scenic heritage with the outside world. The results might well have been completely disastrous, fears which were uppermost in the minds of Wordsworth and Ruskin, but for the setting up of conservation bodies like the National Trust. This society, dedicated to 'hold places of historic interest and natural beauty for the benefit of the nation', arose out of a meeting at Grosvenor House in London in 1894, and in the following year the association was registered as the National Trust. The honorary secretary was Canon Rawnsley, who had come in 1877 to the living of Low Wray near Ambleside and later became Vicar of Crosthwaite, near Keswick. Two other Lake District residents were members of the first executive committee, and so from the outset the area became closely associated with the ideals of the new conservation society. The first test for the National Trust came in 1900 when it successfully resisted a proposal for a tramway along the shores of Windermere from Bowness to Ambleside. Shortly afterwards it launched its first appeal for funds to buy a small area, Brandelhow Park, on the shores of Derwentwater. Thereafter purchases followed at regular intervals and mountains like Scafell were acquired in 1925 and much of Great Langdale four years later. By the latter type of acquisition the Trust became much more than the guardian of fine scenery for it now had a stake in the traditional husbandry of the Lake District. Fine country estates like Sizergh Castle (4987), sites of archaeological interest like Borrows Field, the Roman fort of Galava (3703) and the prehistoric stone circle of Castlerigg (2923), all come within its protection. Each year more and more land and buildings are acquired or given by private benefactors so that large areas of mountain top, open fell and valley land are preserved for future generations to enjoy (Map 31). Perhaps the large area within the region now administered by the National Trust offers the best answer to those who pose the question 'Whither the Lake District'.

Conditions are never static and therefore the National Trust has in recent years followed a policy of combining preservation with progress. With the region becoming an educational laboratory for people of all ages interested in exploring the many different facets which the countryside has to offer, nature walks have been laid out in collaboration with bodies like the Ambleside Field Society and the Lake District Naturalists' Trust. Two have been opened near Ambleside. One runs through Skelghyll Wood by the side of the main road opposite the Waterhead Hotel (378032). The other is at White Moss Common at Rydal by the side of the main Ambleside-Grasmere road (348065). Nature trails are now becoming an ever popular feature of the Lake District for those who wish to combine relaxation with educational pursuits. The Forestry Commission has also laid out a similar trail at Grizedale in High Furness (3394), and the Manchester Corporation Water Works, perhaps seeking a better public image after the débâcle over the Thirlmere Reservoir scheme in the last century, has two at Swirls Forest and Launch Gill Forest (3015). All this emphasizes the fact that in the last decade old ideas of conservation have been swept away to allow public access to many formerly restricted areas. The Forestry Commission in 1959 was required to take amenity into consideration in their future planning. At Grize-

33. *Kendal – lying on the dip slope of the limestone fell. In the foreground the fifteenth-century castle on a drumlin; beyond the nineteenth-century canal quarter and across the Kent the burgage plots of the medieval town.*

34a. *Barn with characteristic overhang at Swinklebank Farm, Long Sleddale.*

34b. *Limekiln at Stockdale Farm that once used the nearby Coniston Limestone.*

34c. *Ubarrow Hall – a fifteenth-century pele tower and attached hall.*

35a. *Helsingham snuff mill.*

35b. *Bobbin mill at Oakbank – storage sheds.*

35c. *Meal Bank – an industrial hamlet on the River Mint.*

36a. *Sheep-shearing at Brigsteer near the foot of the limestone escarpment.*

36b. *The wide middle section of Long Sleddale fashioned in Silurian rocks with the craggy volcanic country in the distance.*

dale, in addition to the forestry trail, they have recently established a Wild Life Centre where it is possible to study and photograph animals in their natural habitat from specially erected observation towers. All this is reminiscent of what has happened in the United States and Canada, though on a much smaller scale, and it is clearly symptomatic of the more forward-looking policy now adopted by the Commission.

Exactly half a century after the National Trust had acquired its first land in the Lake District, the whole area was declared a National Park. The area designated covers less than a thousand square miles, stretching from Caldbeck in the north to Cartmel in the south, from Gosforth in the west as far as Shap in the east. It thus includes not only the central mountainous peaks and high fells but also some of the lovely and little-known foothill country. With the creation of a National Park, one of Wordsworth's most cherished ideas, 'a sort of national property in which every man has a right and interest who has an eye to perceive and a heart to enjoy', became a reality. Without the efforts of the National Trust over the past seventy years, the National Park might have had a hollow ring. Fortunately there was much to conserve and the National Park Commission, along with other interested bodies, has done much during the last twenty years. It has not allowed the landscape to become fossilized but rather combined development with aesthetic feeling so that the best can be preserved and future demands arising from an increasing leisure can be met without altering the fundamental character of the region. During the limited period of its existence, the National Park can claim a fair measure of success, even though, in conjunction with the planning authorities, contentious problems like water extraction, improvement of roads, housing development, have all had to be faced.

When the National Park Commission was appointed, one of its stated aims was to maintain the farming pattern of the area. In the Lake District this objective has not been easy to achieve because of the conflicting demands made by recreation, forestry and water supply. There are also problems to be faced arising from multiple land use. A typical farm in the central district has three types of land. That around the farm, where crops like kale, oats, swedes and grass are grown, is known as the 'inland' and usually contains the best land. Some can be extremely fertile, especially if it consists of alluvium deposited on the valley floor. On the steep valley sides is the 'intake', that is land which has been enclosed by stone walls in the past and once formed a valuable supplement to the 'inland'. Above, on the flat plateau top, is the open fell where the farmer has grazing rights. Each type of land presents problems to the farmer. The valley bottom is particularly susceptible to waterlogging and often complete immersion during floods. Borrowdale suffers badly in this respect and in August 1966 considerable damage was done. In a single hour on the night of the 13th, over four inches of rain fell. The streams rose rapidly as water poured down the fellsides. Great boulders were carried down the main river channel above Seathwaite, and the bridge at Stockley Bridge (2311) was wrecked. In the adjacent Stonethwaite valley, the depth of flooding was over ten feet. A further storm on 2 September

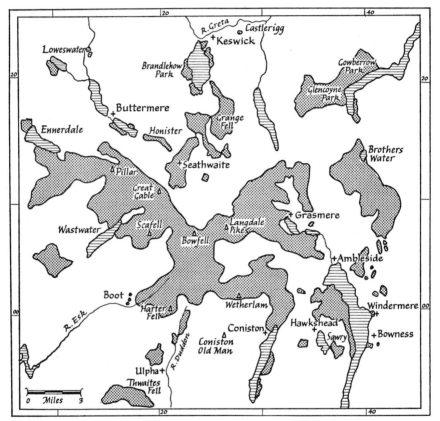

Map 31 *National Trust properties in the central part of the Lake District.*

brought more havoc, and altogether it was estimated that a quarter of a million pounds' worth of damage was done in Borrowdale alone. The valley bottom land suffers most from flood disasters of this type although the valley sides can be gullied and rilled by the storm waters rushing down from the fell top. The main problem for the farmer in the 'intake zone' is the deterioration of the pastures, with bracken spreading quickly over the enclosed land. Neglect through lack of labour and a change in the pastoral economy are contributory factors. Whereas in the past black cattle grazed these pastures and effectively kept the bracken in check by trampling and eating the young fronds, the present-day sheep are unable to do this. This pattern of change from cattle to sheep has been going on for fifty years and it is estimated that the sheep population has gone up fifty per cent during the period. The result is that, while the bracken spreads over the enclosed 'intake', the open fell above has grasslands which are completely overgrazed and are rapidly deteriorating. There is no easy solution to these problems. Each farmer holds traditional rights on the fell tops and is not even limited in the number of sheep he may graze.

Although crossbred sheep like the Swaledale and Border Leicester are found on many of the lakeland farms, the local Herdwick still survives in the higher and more isolated parts. It is hardy and nimble but nevertheless makes considerable demands on the hill farmer during the winter and lambing season. John Gilpin, on his visit to the Lake District in 1772, wrote, 'When the mountains are covered with snow, which is frequently the case, the shepherd's employment becomes then a dangerous one. It seldom happens that some part of the flock is snowed up and in preserving their lives he most often exposes his own.' Although written two hundred years ago, it still rings true today. It is not surprising therefore that fewer and fewer find the life attractive. Areas which depend mainly on farming have shown a steady decline in population during the last fifty years. Caldbeck parish, at the back of Skiddaw, is typical of many. Here, when farming and mining were flourishing in the mid-nineteenth century, the population exceeded 1,500. In 1881 it had fallen to 1,176, and by 1901 it was only 821. It hovered around this total until the outbreak of the 1939 war, partly due to the activity of the barytes mines, but since that time the population has dropped to just over 600. In areas around Keswick and Ambleside the tourist industry and people seeking retirement have, to some extent, masked this downward trend, but even here rural depopulation is apparent and is bringing many problems.

Perhaps the most pressing problem of the present time is that created by the motor car. Whereas it was relatively easy for the nineteenth-century conservationist to prevent a rash of railways covering the area, the car is less easily controlled. As the main west coast motorway is routed along the eastern side of the Lake District, it has automatically provided an easy means of access from the Midlands and Lancashire. It is only a matter of time before the northern part of the Lake District is similarly exposed – even to day-trippers – especially

259

as a new dual carriageway between Penrith and the West Cumberland industrial area is under construction. Already in 1966, when a survey was made of transport usage in the area, the dominance of the motor car was clearly discernible. Of the day visitors from home visiting the Keswick–Borrowdale area, 57 per cent came by car, 30 per cent by bus or coach and only 7 per cent by train. For day visitors entering the area from other resorts, the dominance of the motor car is even more apparent, the comparable figures being 84 per cent by car, 13 per cent by coach and only 2 per cent by train. Each year the position changes in favour of the private car to the detriment of public transport by bus or train. The railway age has virtually come to an end in the last decade and it now looks as though the coach will soon follow it to its grave, especially as the narrow roads of the more picturesque parts of the Lake District are unsuitable for the present-day monsters. The growth of motor-car traffic has posed tremendous problems for the planner. On a single Sunday in late August 1966, about 10,000 cars entered the National Park area. Certain roads bore the brunt of this traffic, in particular the Kendal–Ambleside route where, during the holiday season, 100,000 cars a week use this route. Some idea of the seasonal nature of the traffic can be obtained from comparing figures for the same route in winter, when only about 20,000 vehicles, or approximately one-fifth, use this road. Certainly this volume of traffic creates problems arising from a conflict of interests. It is now virtually impossible for the cyclist or walker to use the main roads at the peak of the holiday season. Even in valleys like Langdale and Borrowdale the problem is acute, and where possible the National Trust is building footpaths across its land parallel to the road. The inevitable outcome of the overcrowding of narrow roads is a demand by other users that certain valleys like Langdale should be made traffic free or toll roads established. Other suggestions made to cope with the problem, like one-way circuit flows over the main tourist routes, are feasible only if the resident population accept the inconvenience of access that this will inevitably cause.

For those who come to the Lake District to enjoy its solitude, it might seem at first glance that the last decade has dealt a death blow. It is still possible, however, for the climber or fell walker to practise a form of escapism. The concentration of people on the roads has left many of the fells more empty now than fifty years ago. On a summer afternoon one can leave the busy Ambleside–Grasmere road and follow the steep path up behind Nab Scar (3506), then on to Heron Pike, Greatrigg and Fairfield, and hardly meet a single walker. Looking down from the Scar, the car park by the side of Rydal Water is crowded and a steady stream of cars snakes its way along the main road. Certainly the motor age has not justified the abandonment of many of the old footpaths, so assiduously followed by the Victorian traveller with guide-book in hand. Even as a motorist it is still possible to enjoy the scenery if the by-roads on the fringe of the Lake District are sought in preference to the more usual and popular routes of the central area. As is so often the case, the choice between pleasure and frustration can be a personal one.

11

The Lake District and the arts

In the preceding chapters we have examined the physical elements in the landscape of the Lake District and the shaping of that landscape down the centuries by Man. As improving communications have opened the mountains of the north-west since the end of the eighteenth century a new relationship has developed between men and the landscape. With the coming of tourism Man has found himself an observer and interpreter of scenery, explaining and representing the lakes, mountains and valleys to his fellows. Poetry, painting and guidebooks have created a Lake District of the mind, an image that now stands between us and the reality of Nature. For the middle-class Victorians the Lake District was as much a literary idea as a geographical region. Long before the days of atmospheric colour photography Wordsworth had created some vivid impressionistic snapshots of elements in the Lake District's landscape that remain fixed in the mind. It is doubtful whether we can make a better picture with the help of all the communications technology of the twentieth century than Wordsworth's view of Grasmere on a late summer evening after a day of great heat.

> And there I sit at evening, when the steep
> Of Silver-how, and Grasmere's peaceful lake,
> And one green island, gleam between the stems
> Of the dark firs, a visionary scene

The Lake District of the poet, novelist and painter is a region as fascinating to explore as the geographical Lake District, and almost as varied. In 1794 Mrs

Radcliffe, author of a long-forgotten novel, *The Mysteries of Udolpho*, published her impressions of a tour of the Lake District. The language of the gothic horror story was transferred to her view of Borrowdale: 'Dark caverns yawn at its entrance terrific as the wildness of a maniac, and disclose a narrow strait running up between mountains of granite that are shook into almost every possible form of horror and resemble the accumulations of an earthquake splintered, shivered, piled, amassed.' If Mrs Radcliffe was able to chill the blood of readers who never got within a hundred miles of Borrowdale, the twentieth-century guide provides meticulously detailed descriptions of every footpath, rock-face and mountain gully. Of Great End, the northernmost summit of the Scafell range that looks down Borrowdale, one can read:

> There are two cairns, each centred in a rash of stones, linked by a grassy saddle of slightly lower altitude. The main cairn (trigonometrical station) is that to the south-east, although the difference in elevation between the two can be a matter of inches only. There is little interest on the actual top of the fell. . . .

The twentieth century is sparing in its vocabulary of landscape, and in the mouths of the geologist and geomorphologist it can only be described as clinical. The verbal hyperbole of the nineteenth-century tourist has now become visual with the aid of the telephoto lens and the richly exaggerated tones of colour photography. Each generation makes its own interpretation of the Lake District, but each interpretation is distorted and coloured, however faintly, by the views and feelings of its predecessors.

The literature of the Lake District
References to the Lake District are sparse in literature before the eighteenth century. The earliest allusions to the north-west occur in Welsh poems that date back to the first years of the seventh century, poems that were handed down the centuries by bards and committed to the written word in the late Middle Ages. They tell of the wars of the Britons in the north against the Anglian kingdoms on the eastern flank of the Pennines. An even more mysterious thread in the literature of northern England leads from the medieval romances back into the Celtic twilight of the centuries before the Norman Conquest. Lake District antiquarians have made many attempts to anchor the Arthurian legend in the north-west. The medieval poem, *Sir Gawayne and the Green Knight*, may well hark back over the centuries to the period after the Roman withdrawal when the

Celtic kingdom of *Rheged* flourished in the country to the south of the Solway Firth. The poem tells how Sir Gawayne, one of King Arthur's knights, accepts the challenge of the Green Knight and rides north from Camelot through North Wales, Anglesey and the Wirral to meet his opponent somewhere in the north. On Christmas Eve he comes to a castle in a deep forest.

> The comeliest that ever knight owned,
> pitched in a meadow, a park all about,
> with an ornamented pale, fortified full closely,
> that enclosed many trees more than two miles.

On New Year's morning Sir Gawayne set out for the Green Chapel, a distance of two miles, where he encountered the Green Knight in duel. Whatever the location of the poem, the writer of *Sir Gawayne and the Green Knight* provides an admirably clear sketch of a medieval park of his own period, the early fourteenth century. Nevertheless scholars have spent much energy in trying to identify the sites of the castle and the Green Chapel, even though, in the end, these may belong to the eternal archaic landscapes of the imagination. Two places in the Lake District and its borders have been identified with the Green Chapel – Castle Rock (3219), a place at the head of St John's Vale worthy of any medieval romance, and the Isis Parlis caves in the Eamont valley (559303). The castle, the Dark Age hall where Sir Gawayne was entertained over the days of Christmas, might be located either at the site of the deserted settlement of Threlkeld (3224) or else at Penrith. Both have claims to be actively occupied places in sub-Roman times and both lie in a strong core of British settlement on the flanks of the Skiddaw massif.

Even if the literature of the Middle Ages presents insoluble topographical problems, it bequeathed to the poets and novelists of the eighteenth and nineteenth centuries a great wealth of material in legends and folk tales that could be re-worked in the spirit of Victorian romanticism.

Writers not only explore the depths of their own personality but reflect the tastes and morals of the world around them. The Lake District suddenly becomes an object of literature after the middle of the eighteenth century, and the writer who above all made the region fashionable in the outside world was the poet, Thomas Gray. Before this time Celia Fiennes had made her dry comments on the eastern parts of the Lake District in *Through England on a Side Saddle*, and Daniel Defoe's *A Tour through England and Wales*, published in 1731, wrote off Westmorland as 'a country eminent only for being the wildest, most barren and frightful in England, or even in Wales itself'. Even in 1769, when tourists were beginning to discover the attractions of the Lake District, another great topographer, Thomas Pennant, condemned the fells around Shap as 'more black, dreary and melancholy than any of the Highland hills, being not only barren but destitute of every picturesque beauty'. But tastes were changing and in the same year that Pennant returned from his tour of Scotland Thomas Gray made his journey to the Lake District in the company of a friend who fell ill and was unable to go beyond Brough. Gray continued the journey and completed his tour of the Lakes in the first two weeks of October. That fortnight was probably one of the critical moments for the history of tourism in the north-west, because Gray wrote down the impressions of all that he saw for the benefit of his sick friend.

Gray's *Journal in the Lakes* provided a guide and an incentive to hundreds of eighteenth-century tourists. It also shows that a tourist industry was already present in embryo, with its recommended view-points or 'stations'. His account of the visit to Ullswater on 1 October contains so much that must have attracted many tourists to do the same and to look for the landscape features that were picked out in the *Journal*. Gray's station here was the wooded shapely hill of Dunmallet, crowned by an Iron Age or Romano-British earthwork, at the eastern end of the lake near Pooley Bridge.

> A gray autumnal day, air perfectly calm and gentle. Went to Ulzwater . . . approached Dunmallet, a fine pointed hill, covered with wood planted by old Mr Hassle before mentioned (the builder of Dalemain), who lives always at home – (think of this ye absentee landlords!) and delights in planting. Walked over a songy meadow or two, and began to mount the hill through a broad and straight green alley among the trees, and with some toil gained the summit. From hence saw the lake open directly at my feet majestic in its calmness, clear and smooth as a blue mirror, with winding shores and low points of land covered with green enclosures, white farm-houses looking out among the trees, and cattle feeding. The water is almost everywhere bordered with cultivated lands gently sloping upwards till they reach the foot of the mountains which rise very rude and awful with their broken tops upon either hand; directly in front at better than three miles' distance, Place Fell, one of the bravest among them, pushes its bold broad breast into the midst of the lake and forces it to alter its course, forming first a large bay to the left, and then bending to the right.

Gray's sharp and poetic descriptions of Lake District scenery must have done much to publicize the beauty spots and viewpoints, though his brief tour – no longer than a summer holiday in the hurried twentieth century – shows that the natives of the region were already well aware of the places to which the stranger tourists should be guided. For instance, he was led to the site of the Castlerigg stone circle above Keswick, and the Journal gives detailed instructions on how to reach the monument. He followed 'the Penrith road two miles or more' and turned 'into a cornfield to the right called Castlerigg'. There Gray described the site that met him in quiet precise language that must have conjured up the details of the scene for his sick friend, Dr Warton.

> I saw a Druid circle of large stones, one hundred and eight feet in diameter, the biggest not eight feet high, but most of them still erect: they are fifty in number, the valley of Naddle appeared in sight and the fells of St John's, particularly the summits of *Catchidecam* (called by Camden *Casticand*) and *Helvellyn*, said to be as high as *Skiddaw*, and to arise from a much higher base.

Gray was not the only poet to visit Castlerigg. Keats was there in 1818 and the place appears in *Hyperion* focused through the lens of his imagination as

> A dismal cirque
> Of Druid stones upon a forlorn moor,
> When the chill rain begins at shut of eve
> In dull November and their chancel vault
> The heaven itself, is blinded throughout night.

The season has been transposed, because Keats spent a few days in Keswick at the end of June, 1818. He walked round Derwentwater and visited Castlerigg late in the afternoon. One suspects that the day closed with the onset of a vigorous warm front and the driving rain and low ceiling of scurrying grey cloud that brings the chill of winter into the Cumbrian summer.

Gray's journey of 1769 established the pattern of Lake District tourism for several decades – Ullswater, Keswick and its lakes, the main road by Thirlmere to Grasmere and Bowness. This was the Lake District of the Victorians as it is of the five-lakes coach tour and the day-tripper at the present time. It was a long time before the tourists and those of them who put their thoughts to paper exploited fully the remoter western valleys and the different perspectives that were to be gained from the summits of the high mountains. Gray did not pass beyond Grange into the Jaws of Borrowdale where 'the crags now begin to impend terribly over your way'. The mountains at the head of the valley were not easy to reach. The first of our national poets to gain the summit of Scafell was Coleridge. He set out from Keswick on the first Sunday of August in 1802 and, armed with a long brush handle, as an *alpenstock*, and a bag on his back with writing material and food he climbed to the rock-strewn ridge of Scafell Pike by way of Sty Head pass. In the days that followed he wrote a 'Hymn before sunrise in the Vale of Chamonix':

> Has thou a charm to stay the Morning-Star
> In his steep course? So long he seems to pause
> On thy bald awful head, O sovran Blanc

It seems more likely that Scafell was the inspiration for this conventional piece of poetry. Wordsworth, a native of the Lake District and one who spent all but a few years of his long life in the region, did not see the view from the summit of Scafell until 1818, when he was forty-eight. From this excursion he produced one of those matchless pieces of prose that bring the atmosphere of the high mountains directly to the reader.

> The stillness seemed to be not of this world; we paused and kept silence to listen, and no sound could be heard. The Scafell cataracts were voiceless to us, and there was not an insect to hum in the air.

The same scene appears later in the tired poetry of his middle age:

> This is a temple built by God's own hand –
> Mountains its walls, its gorgeous roof the sky –
> Where uncontrolled the exalted soul partakes
> Her natural and high communion.
> Loses all thought of this world's pigmy pomp,
> And in the stern and distant solitude
> Feels as alone with the Invisible

With Wordsworth the worship of Nature gripped the educated middle classes and the high mountains became their sacred temples.

Wordsworth, Coleridge and Southey
By the end of the nineteenth century Wordsworth's poetry exercised an immense influence over tourists and tourism in the Lake District. Not only had the places where he lived, Dove Cottage and Rydal Mount, become objects of

excursions, but the landscape of the region itself was viewed through the poet's works. William Knight's guide-book published in 1891, *Through the Wordsworth Country – a companion to the Lake District*, typifies the attitudes of the educated tourists who explored the north-west at the end of the nineteenth century. Every topographical reference in the poems is pursued and the traveller guided to these places. For instance, *The Excursion* (Book II) describes the cottage beside Blea Tarn (2904) occupied by the 'Solitary'. Wordsworth wrote:

> When, all at once, behold!
> Beneath our feet, a little lowly vale,
> A lowly vale, and yet uplifted high
> Among the mountains; even as if the spot
> Had been from eldest time by wish of theirs
> So placed, to be shut out from all the world!
> Urn-like it was in shape, deep as an urn;
> With rocks encompassed, save that to the south
> Was one small opening, where a heath-clad ridge
> Supplied a boundary less abrupt and close:
> A quiet treeless nook, with two green fields,
> A liquid pool that glittered in the sun,
> And one bare dwelling; one abode, no more!
> It seemed the home of poverty and toil,
> Though not of want: the little fields, made green
> By husbandry of many thrifty years,
> Paid cheerful tribute to the moorland house.
> – There crows the cock, single in his domain:
> The small birds find in spring no thicket there
> To shroud them; only from neighbouring vales
> The cuckoo, straggling up to the hill tops,
> Shouteth faint tidings of some gladder place.

Knight then pursues a detailed topographical analysis of Wordsworth's description of the Blea Tarn col as seen from the summit of Lingmoor.

The 'little lowly vale' is the head of Little Langdale; 'urn-like', as seen from the top of Lingmoor; the 'one small opening' is the path into Little Langdale by Fell Foot and Busk; the 'nook' is not now 'treeless', but the fir wood, on the western side of the vale, adds to its 'quiet', and deepens the sense of seclusion; the 'liquid pool that glittered in the sun', is Blea Tarn; the 'one abode, no more', is the solitary cottage, now called Blea Tarn House; and up to this retreat among the mountains the cuckoo still comes 'from neighbouring vales'.

But Wordsworth's poetry was not only to be regarded as a complicated literary puzzle with topographical clues to be traced out on the ground like the intricate network of a maze, it was also the guide to mystical experience through a communion with Nature. As Knight says of the description of Blea Tarn in *The Excursion*, 'anyone who understands the poem, and then visits the place, will feel its unique solitude, its upland peace with "the strength of the hills" all around'.

Detailed topographical analysis of this kind is part of the bric-à-brac of Victorian tourism, little better than the interest that goes no farther than a casual visit to Dove Cottage. Today it is dead. We no longer follow in the steps of our great-grandfathers along the Duddon identifying the detailed topographical references of the sonnets. Wordsworth's relationship with the landscapes of the Lake District was far more subtle than Professor Knight's guide would allow. In his finest poetry the scenery of the Lake District provides only a key to an eternal archetypal landscape of the mind. Just as the shepherds, roadside beggars and statesmen farmers who populate the poems of Wordsworth lack so many of the attributes of common humanity, so the topography of the Lake District appears in abstract forms, an element in the mind of the poet. And yet it was the abstraction of this northern landscape in the poet's mind that helped to popularize the Lake District among the Victorians and that made this of all the parts of Britain the poet's region.

If Wordsworth's poetry creates an archetypal landscape out of the objects and forms of the Lake District, we can discover the topography and life of the region at the beginning of the nineteenth century sharply and brilliantly drawn in the prose of his sister's *Journal*. On a fine morning towards the end of April in 1802 Dorothy Wordsworth, William and Coleridge climbed the steep path from Rydal towards Nab Scar (3506) until the view was spread out southwards to Ambleside and Windermere. The *Journal*'s report of this excursion when William had to be left alone 'sitting on the stones, feasting with silence' recreates the view with an almost photographic sharpness.

> After we had lingered long, looking into the vales – Ambleside vale, with the copses, the village under the hill, and the green fields – Rydale, with a lake all alive and glittering, yet but little stirred by breezes, and our own dear Grasmere, first making a little round lake of nature's own, with never a house, never

a green field, but the copses and the bare hills enclosing it, and the river flowing out of it. Above rose the Coniston Fells, in their own shape and colour – not man's hills, but all for themselves, the sky and the clouds, and a few wild creatures.

Dorothy Wordsworth's *Journal* ranks as a classic among the literature of the Lake District not only because it records the day-to-day events in the life of the poet at Grasmere between 1800 and 1802 but also for the picture that it presents of the topography and climate of the region. The plain and delicate prose of the *Journal* has scarcely aged in its descriptions of the changing seasons and the day-to-day contrasts of the Lake District's weather. Saturday, 12 December, 1901, must have been one of those rare days that stand out in the memory of a visitor to the mountains in the winter season.

> A fine frosty morning – Snow upon the ground. . . . Helm Crag rose very bold and craggy, a Being by itself, and behind it was the large ridge of mountains, smooth as marble and snow white. All the mountains looked like solid stone, on our left, going from Grasmere, i.e. White Moss and Nab Scar. The snow hid all the grass, and all signs of vegetation, and the rocks showed themselves boldly everywhere, and seemed more stony than rock or stone. The birches on the crags beautiful, red brown and glittering. The ashes glittering spears with their upright stems. . . . We played at cards – sat up late. The moon shone upon the water below Silver-How, and above it hung, combining with Silver-How on one side, a bow-shaped moon, the curve downwards; the white fields, glittering roof of Thomas Ashburner's house, the dark yew tree, the white fields gay and beautiful. William lay with his curtains open that he might see it.

William and Dorothy Wordsworth between them created a Lake District of the mind, an eternal image of the region that places itself between the reader and the reality once he has become absorbed in their writing. Even today it is easier to believe that the road from Grasmere to Keswick 'Mounts, as you see, in mazes serpentine' to the summit of Dunmail Raise than to accept the modern straightened trunk road that hums with an endless stream of traffic.

In Wordsworth's time other poets and writers settled and worked in the Lake District, but they have added little or nothing to the regional literature – still less have their words shaped the image of the country for succeeding generations. Coleridge lived at Greta Hall on the outskirts of Keswick from 1800 to 1804. He was attracted to the north-west by the prospect of continuing his friendship and conversations with Wordsworth that had been so fruitful for the writing of poetry when they had known each other in Somerset in 1797. But he was also affected in his choice of Keswick by the stimulating qualities of the mountain and lake landscapes. Like many who have followed him to the Lakes, Coleridge felt that he would write more easily in such surroundings. In a letter to a friend he said

> The room in which I write commands six distinct landscapes – the two lakes, the vale, the river, and mountains and mists, and clouds and sunshine make endless combinations, as if heaven and earth were for ever talking to each other. Often when in a deep study I have walked to the window and remained there looking without seeing; all at once the lake of Keswick and the fantastic mountains . . . at the head of it, have entered into my mind, with a suddenness as if I had been snatched from Cheapside and placed for the first time in the spot where I stood, and that is a delightful feeling – these fits and trances of novelty received from a long known object.

But Coleridge, in the phrase of the natives, was an 'off-come'. The landscape of the region never entered his personality so that a journey to the summit of Scafell produced a poem on the Alps.

Coleridge left Keswick and the Lake District in 1804, returning only for a brief period in 1806 and again in 1807 to live with the Wordsworths at Allan Bank, Grasmere, for another three years. In 1803 the literary fame of Keswick was established when Robert Southey, Coleridge's brother-in-law, took up residence at Greta Hall. He lived there for forty years until his death in 1843. Southey's immense output of writing – reviews, histories and poems – hardly reflected the country in which he had chosen to settle, despite the daily walks around Keswick that ranged from the Newlands valley to Lodore and the woods and hamlets beneath Skiddaw. Several accounts of his upstairs study at Greta Hall with an immense panorama of lake and mountain have survived in letters and the reports of famous visitors. This same prospect appears in the *Vision of Judgment* as one of Southey's few references to the country in which he spent the greater part of his life.

> Mountain and lake and vale; the valley disrobed of its verdure;
> Derwent retaining yet from eve a glassy reflection
> Where his expanded breast, then still and smooth as a mirror,
> Under the woods reposed; the hills that, calm and majestic,
> Lifted their heads in the silent sky, from far Glaramara
> Bleacrag, and Maidenmawr, to Grizedal and westermost Withop.

271

Yet Southey was not blind to the qualities of the Lake District's landscapes, as his letters so clearly show. In writing to a friend he gave advice that is still valid for the twentieth-century tourist. 'Autumn is the best season to see the country, but spring, and even winter, is better than summer, for in settled and fine weather there are none of those goings on in heaven which at other times give these scenes such an endless variety.' In another letter he praises the beauty of the mountains in the grip of winter. 'The very snow, which you would perhaps think must monotonize the mountains, gives new varieties; it brings out their recesses and designates all their inequalities . . . and it reflects such tints of saffron, or fawn, or rose colour to the evening sun.' He climbed Skiddaw, and in a letter to his friend Danvers he wrote: 'The panorama from the summit is very grand. The summit is covered with loose stones split by the frosts, and thus gradually are they reduced to soil and washed down to the glens, so that, like old women, Skiddaw must grow shorter.' Even so, Southey's topographical writing lacks the poetry and presence of Dorothy Wordsworth's prose. One feels that the mountains in snow are seen from the comfortable book-crammed study at Greta Hall. Compare Southey's winter, an 'off-come' to Cumberland, with Dorothy Wordsworth's record of a journey, late in January, through Grisedale Hause (3411) by the ancient pack-horse trail from Ullswater to Grasmere.

> We struggled with the wind, and often rested as we went along. A hail shower met us before we reached the Tarn, and the way often was difficult over the snow; but at the Tarn the view closed in. We saw nothing but mists and snow: and at first the ice on the Tarn below us cracked and split, yet without water, a dull grey white. We lost our path, and could see the Tarn no longer. We made our way out with difficulty, guided by a heap of stones which we well remembered. We were afraid of being bewildered in the mists, till the darkness should overtake us. We were long before we knew that we were in the right track, but thanks to William's skill we knew it long before we could see our way before us. There was no footmark upon the snow of either man or beast. We saw four sheep before we had left the snow region.

Ruskin and the Lake District
Another part of the Lake District, the shores of Coniston Water, became a centre of pilgrimage in the last quarter of the nineteenth century after John Ruskin – painter, art critic, social reformer and perhaps the greatest of Victorian polymaths – made his home at Brantwood (3195) in 1871. The Lake District forms a thread through Ruskin's life. His first sight of the region was at the age of five when his parents visited Keswick. Then, in 1824, Keswick was well established

among the prosperous and educated middle class as a fashionable tourist centre. Ruskin remembered Friar's Crag as the first stimulus to the emergence of his aesthetic personality.

> This gift of taking pleasure in landscape, I assuredly possess in a greater degree than most men. . . . The first thing which I remember, as an event in life, was being taken by my nurse to the brow of Friar's Crag on Derwentwater; the intense joy, mingled with awe, that I had in looking through the mossy roots, over the crag, into the dark lake, has associated itself more or less with all twining roots of trees ever since.

Late in life Ruskin could hark back to this childhood impression of Derwentwater and say:

> The scene from Friar's Crag is one of the three or four most beautiful views in Europe. And when I first saw Keswick it was a place almost too beautiful to live in.

John Ruskin was taken to Keswick again by his parents when he was eleven. This time, in a poem written about that tour and called *Interiad*, he describes how they went to Great Crosthwaite church to get a glimpse of Robert Southey, the Poet Laureate.

> Now hurried we home, and while taking our tea
> We thought – Mr Southey at church we might see
> Next morning, the church how we wished to be reaching!
> I'm afraid 'twas as much for the poet as preaching

They found the church seats dusty and dirty, but Ruskin's precocious eleven-year-old comment was:

> Howe'er I forgave – 'deed I scarcely did know it,
> For really we were 'cheek-by-jowl' with the poet

Southey and Wordsworth did much towards creating the tourist industries of Keswick and Grasmere by their presence in those places. For the last thirty years of his life Ruskin accomplished the same for Coniston. Even today, among the faded drawings and water-colour sketches, the geological specimens and Ruskin's bill-hook for cutting coppice wood that one finds in the little museum at Coniston, there is a sense of a different intellectual atmosphere from that of Grasmere and Dove Cottage.

When Ruskin moved to Brantwood in 1871 he embarked on the long last stage of his life – thirty years of increasing isolation from the world. Coniston and its mountains provided an outward expression for two of the important concerns in Ruskin's intellectual career. In his philosophy of art, worked out through the pages of *Modern Painters* and in scores of highly successful public lectures, Ruskin placed the Gothic above all other schools. He categorized the chief characteristics of the Gothic style as Savageness, Changefulness, Naturalism and Grotesqueness. Ruskin praised mass in buildings; cathedrals were mountains shaped by man. He could write of 'the dependence of architecture on the inspiration of Nature' or 'this look of mountain brotherhood between the cathedral and the Alp'. What better place is there to consider the anatomy of a mountain landscape than Brantwood, with Coniston Old Man and its neighbouring summits standing up across the lake, the confused symmetry of corrie and arête, precipice and crag springing from the placid, horizontal foreground of the lake? In his final retreat to the Lake District Ruskin was also able to immerse himself in another aspect of the Gothic – the 'changefulness' of a mountain climate. As he wrote, 'a strong intellect will have pleasure in the solemnities of storm and twilight, and in the broken and mysterious lights that gleam among them'. The words that Ruskin chose on so many occasions to describe his ideals in painting and architecture are so often aptly applied to the environment of the Lake District – 'rigid lines, vigorous and varied masses, and daringly projecting and independent structures', or, elsewhere, 'this grey, shadowy, many-pinnacled image the Gothic spirit'.

The Lake District also represented for Ruskin an escape from the blight of the industrial revolution. He was as violently opposed to railways as Wordsworth had been. But in his old age Ruskin could survey with regret the results of this revolution in communications. 'Instead of building railways we should have built churches and houses of beauty.' The Lake District was a refuge from the polluted air and the spoliation of the industrial towns, and in its rural society a relic of the social order before the industrial age still survived. Many of the elements in Ruskin's vision of a new society were a projection of an old order of life, an order of which he could still find some remnants in the hills and valleys around Coniston. For instance, his formula for working-class housing might well be a sketch of a statesman's farm. 'I would have our ordinary dwelling houses built to last, and built to be lovely . . . with such differences as might suit and express each man's character and occupation, and partly his history.' Ruskin, like a few other fortunates of the Victorian world, was able to escape permanently to the mountains. For the rest the Lake District provided a contrast to the rapidly expanding conurbations of the late nineteenth century – a contrast that could be enjoyed for perhaps two weeks out of the year.

The Lake District in novels and children's books

Wordsworth, the Keswick poets and Ruskin have indelibly associated certain places in the Lake District with literature, but the past century and a half has seen the output of a vast quantity of writing concerned with the region. Most of it is mediocre and much of it is a by-product of the rising tourist industry. The best-selling novelists of the nineteenth century found that the Lake District made an attractive setting for their stories and their flimsy romantic plots were often derived from the legends and folk-tales of Cumbria. Five of Mrs Humphry Ward's novels are set in the region. The *Mating of Lydia* finds its locale in St John's Vale and Thirlmere, *Fenwick's Career* is a story of Langdale, and *Missing* was set around Rydal and Grasmere. Striding Edge, Helvellyn's finest arête, was guaranteed its place in literature after the accident of 1805 when Charles Gough was killed in a fall from the precipice and his dog kept watch over the dead body for three months. Wordsworth and Sir Walter Scott both wrote poems about the tragedy and what one writer has called 'the sagacity of our Cumberland collies'. Among nineteenth-century tourists Striding Edge gained an exaggerated reputation for its dangers, and it became apt material for the novelist. Miss Braddon, author of *Henry Dunbar* and *Lady Audley*, long forgotten and unread romantic novels, used the ridge for one of the scenes in *Phantom Fortune*. But this is a long way from the true regional novel, and one of her critics said that 'she might just as well have stayed at home and read it up in Baddeley'.

The absence of a regional sense, the lack of feeling for the countryside as a personality, also applies to the only reference to the Lake District in the novels of Anthony Trollope. Part of *Can You Forgive Her?*, first published in 1864–5, takes place at Vavasor Hall among the wild fells that enclose Hawes Water (Plate 10b). The house has been identified with Thornthwaite Hall (5116), but Trollope's topography is so vague, apart from references to Hawes Water and Bampton, that it seems just as likely that Vavasor Hall is no more than an object of the imagination. Certainly Thornthwaite Hall does not match the only brief descriptive reference to Vavasor Hall in Trollope's novel. Thornthwaite Hall is built around the core of a medieval pele tower, and the approach from the lane that leads to Hawes Water lies along a rough track across a field. Trollope's Vavasor Hall could be any gentlemen's seat in the home counties, for in the only topographical reference we are told that George and Kate 'walked down the carriage-road through the desolate, untended grounds to the gate'.

The Lake District has failed up to the present to produce a great regional novel. W. G. Collingwood, who was concerned with so many facets of the region's life and history as a driving force for many years in the Cumberland and Westmorland Antiquarian Society, wrote two novels, *Thorstein of the Mere* and *The Bondwoman,* that were rooted in local history. Early in the 1930s Hugh Walpole, an 'off-come' writer who had settled on the shores of Derwentwater, began the publication of his ambitious series of four novels *The Herries Chronicle.* The books centre upon Watendlath (Plate 4b) and the fells to the north of Skiddaw, and the period is the eighteenth century. Walpole was an active member of the Cumberland and Westmorland Antiquarian and Archaeological Society and he tells his complex family saga against the background of the Lake District's landscapes and in the context of its social history. The structure of statesman society is still intact, mountain farms are busily employed with spinning and weaving, the chief entertainments of the valleys are bull-baiting, cock-fighting and wrestling, and the years roll on through Christmas feasts, Easter pace-egging and the summer rush-bearing festivals. The life of late-eighteenth-century Keswick is projected into the second novel of the cycle, *Judith Paris,* with a grand firework display over Derwentwater and a tea party at Greta Hall with the Southeys. Whatever the true merits of *The Herries Chronicle,* and Walpole was probably near the mark when he described the books 'as a piece of gaily-tinted tapestry worked in English colours', it was very widely read in the years after its publication. The saga has even left its own impression on the landscape of Borrowdale, because the farm at Watendlath that was the chief focus of the novels is now labelled as 'the home of Judith Paris'. Despite the many references to the Lake District in the pages of *The Herries Chronicle,* Walpole fails to evoke the region as a personality. He failed, where Thomas Hardy and Arnold Bennett succeeded in depicting the landscapes of Dorset and the straggling industrial towns of the Potteries.

During the past half century the countryside of the Lake District has provided the inspiration and setting for quite a different kind of writing from the grand historical novel and the Victorian romance. Some notable children's books have been written in and about the region. The creatures of Beatrix Potter's gentle imagination – Peter Rabbit, Benjamin Bunny and Mrs Tittlemouse – were conjured out of the environment of Sawrey and the Furness Fells. Many of the drawings in the Peter Rabbit series are associated with Hill Top Farm and the gardens and cottages of Sawrey. The tale of *The Roly-Poly Pudding* unfolds among the cupboards and chests of a statesman's house in High Furness, and the Owl Island of *The Tale of Squirrel Nutkin* was modelled from sketches made of St Herbert's Island in Derwentwater.

Beatrix Potter was born in London in 1866, and her family had grown rich from cotton mills in Lancashire. In the rigid terminology of the natives she and her family were 'off-comes' who spent many summer holidays in rented houses in the Lake District. Only after her marriage in 1913 to an Ambleside solicitor did Beatrix Potter settle down in Sawrey, where she took up farming and developed an interest in the breeding of Herdwick sheep. During the 1920s and 1930s Beatrix Potter was able to show the depth of her feelings for her new home and the landscapes that had quickened her imagination as a writer and an artist when she used the royalties from her books to buy up farms around Hawkshead, in Little Langdale and Coniston, at Troutbeck and Buttermere which she gave to the National Trust. Beatrix Potter was concerned about the preservation of the scenery of the Lake District and the perpetuation of the life of the mountain farms. Not only did the 'off-come' do more than many of the natives for the conservation of the Lake District and its way of life, but in the pages of her *Journal*, written in a secret code between 1881 and 1897 and only lately translated, Beatrix Potter has left a succession of sketches of holidays at Windermere and Keswick before the age of the motor-car. Her writing has the directness and sharp observation of that earlier and more famous journal of Dorothy Wordsworth combined with the scientific interests of Ruskin. On a hot Monday in early September 1895 the Potter family drove to the head of Great Langdale, and their daughter recorded in the secret code of the *Journal*:

Hot, hazy day, the hottest of the summer. Drove to Dungeonghyll Hotel, two post-horses, one old stager with the hogged-mane, the other mare a chestnut, rather unpleasant up hills; a thick haze.

Noted the glaciation with much curiosity, especially the loose mound on that canny desolation, Elterwater Common. I never saw a spot more strickled with herd and ducks, many of the former garnished with knickerbockers, and the very sheep of shortest wool and every colour, like those recorded in Rob Roy!

There are some beautiful exposures of rock along the new road between Skelwith and Elterwater, a road whose newness may enrage sentimentalists but strikes me as a good thing and well done. . . . We were rather surprised at the amount of company at the Hotel, Monday, a trip day. A most marvellous family from Chicago, lavender kid-gloves, jewellery and bonnets.

The natives were working feverishly at their meadow-hay. I should say it is an unhealthy valley, and probably intermarriage. . . . After scrambling lunch, went up to the little larch-wood, deliciously cool, and a gentle sound of the stream below. It is a wonderful valley. I do not understand how a mass of ice sufficient to groove out the whole valley should condescend to leave *knobs*.

What a pity that Beatrix Potter had to spend so much of the first half of her life in London, about which the *Journal* is mainly concerned, for here is the perfect sketch of a day in Langdale at the turn of the century.

Writing for children about the Lake District ranges from the pure fantasy of a Beatrix Potter to the matter-of-fact adventure story in which every detail of the book's topography can be traced out on the ground. The 1930s saw the publication of Arthur Ransome's stories in a Lake District setting but with a fictional topography. Although *Swallows and Amazons* works out its fantasy around Wild Cat Island and Octopus Lagoon, one is left in little doubt that the landscapes are those of Windermere and High Furness. On the day when the children discover the charcoal-burners we read that:

> Captain John turned over on his haybag and looked at the barometer, which was steady. He crawled out of his tent and looked at the sky. It was without a cloud. He went up the look-out post and looked at the lake, which reflected the hills and the woods and the far-away farmhouses on the sides of the hills so closely that, as he found, if you looked at them through your own legs you could really hardly be sure which was real and which was reflection in the water.

After breakfast the crew of the *Swallow* row ashore on the eastern side of the lake and start to climb through dense woodland to a hill that provides a view 'right up the lake'. This sounds like Gummer's How (3988) that looks over the southern end of Windermere.

> They rowed south from the island down the lake, where they had been last night in the dark. It looked very different in daylight. A great wood ran up the hillside on the eastern shore of the lake. Far up it they could see smoke curling slowly above the trees, a thin trickle of smoke climbing straight up. . . . There was a far-away noise of wood-chopping.

The wood that led to the charcoal burner's clearing with its 'great mound of earth with little jets of blue wood smoke spiriting from it' was undoubtedly a piece of High Furness coppice.

> . . . The forest became much steeper. Sometimes it was a wonder how the
> little trees themselves clung on among the rocks. There were all sorts of trees.
> Here and there was a tall pine, but most of the trees were oaks and beeches
> and hazels and mountain ash.

This was the landscape of close-growing woodland that surrounded the author's home at Haverthwaite (3483).

Arthur Ransome wove his children's stories out of the elements of the Lake District's landscape. In the 1950s Marjorie Lloyd published a series of books that exploited every detail of the topography of the southern Lake District in telling the adventures of the four Browne children at Fell Farm among the crumpled hills to the south of Skelwith Bridge. They present a plain and accurate picture of the mountains at different seasons; and the work of the National Trust in the preservation of farms or the menace of tourist crowds on public holidays do not go unmentioned. In the Fell Farm books the personality of the Lake District, the region as a dominant character in the novel, is projected with much greater feeling and accuracy than in the hundreds of pages of *The Herries Chronicle*.

Guide-books

Apart from the scores of novels and the many mediocre poets, some writing in Cumbrian dialect, the Lake District has created a distinctive literary genre in the guide-books that have been written over the past two hundred years. The first important guide to the region was Thomas West's *Guide to the Lakes*, published in 1778. West's book was very important for the development of tourism. By 1812 it had passed through ten editions. The writer of the preface to the second edition of the *Guide*, after West's death in 1779, describes how it came into being.

> Having in the latter part of his life much leisure time on his hands, he
> frequently accompanied genteel parties on the Tour of the Lakes; and after
> he had formed the design of drawing up his *Guide*, besides consulting the
> most esteemed writers on the subject (as Dr Brown, Messrs Grey, Young, Pen-
> nant etc.), he took several journeys, on purpose to examine the lakes, and to
> collect such information concerning them, from the neighbouring gentlemen,
> as he thought necessary to complete the work.

In the first pages of the *Guide* Thomas West sets out with admirable clarity the reasons for making a tour of the Lake District's scenery. It makes an agreeable relaxation from anxious cares or fatiguing studies. West also foreshadows the Nature mysticism of Wordsworth and his followers.

Such as spend their lives in cities, and their time in crowds, will here meet with objects that will enlarge the mind, by contemplation, and raise it from nature to nature's first cause. Whoever takes a walk into these scenes, must return penetrated with a sense of the Creator's power in heaping mountains upon mountains, and enthroning rocks upon rocks.

West recommended the tour of the Lakes as not inferior to the grand excursion in Italy and the Alps. His route and list of viewpoints, 'stations' commanding choice prospects of lake and mountain, influenced the direction of Lake District tourism for a long time. The *Guide* suggests that the tour should begin in the east at Penrith with visits to Hawes Water and Ullswater. Then the traveller moved on to Keswick where the several 'stations' around Derwentwater include the summit of Castle Crag, from which

there is a most astonishing view of the lake and vale of Keswick, spread out to the north in the most picturesque manner. Every bend of the river is distinctly seen, from the pass of Borrowdale, till it joins the lake; the lake itself spotted with islands; the most extraordinary line of shore, varied with all the surprising accompaniments of rock and wood; the village of Grange at the foot of the crag, and the white houses of Keswick, with Crosthwaite church at the lower end of the lake; behind these, much cultivation with a beautiful mixture of villages, houses, cots, and farms, standing round the skirts of Skiddaw, which rises in the grandest manner, from a verdant base, and closes this prospect in the noblest stile of nature's true sublime. From the summit of this rock, the views are so singularly great and pleasing that they ought never to be omitted.

Station follows station along the route from Keswick to Ambleside and Bowness, and then on to Hawkshead, Coniston, and Furness Abbey to conclude the tour at Ulverston. West's route was related to the accessibility of the Lake District by the coach roads of the eighteenth century. The western valleys go unmentioned, apart from a glimpse of Buttermere from Newlands Hause. Thomas West's tourists were recommended to 'be provided with a telescope, for viewing the fronts and summits of inaccessible rocks', and 'the landscape mirror will also furnish much amusement in this tour'.

After Thomas West's *Guide* the next great landmark in the tourist literature of the Lake District was the publication of Wordsworth's *Guide to the Lakes* in 1810. It had a varied history through the first half of the nineteenth century. First it appeared as an anonymous introduction to a large volume of *Select Views in Cumberland, Westmorland and Lancashire* by the Reverend J. Wilkinson.

Wordsworth described the drawings as intolerable and said that they 'disgusted him like bad poetry'. Ten years later the *Guide* was republished under Wordsworth's own name and was coupled with the Duddon Sonnets. By the 1830s the book had established itself as an indispensable introduction to the Lake District, and one of Matthew Arnold's favourite stories was of the clergyman who asked Wordsworth 'whether he had written anything else'. In 1835 the fifth edition appeared with Wordsworth's final version of the text. The *Guide to the Lakes* appeared again and in another form in 1842 when a Kendal publisher, Hudson and Nicholson, combined it with sections on the geology and botany of the region as well as a series of itineraries. These additions to the *Guide* point to the changing tastes of the middle of the nineteenth century. In the age of Ruskin 'scenery' had become the object of scientific study; a knowledge of geology and botany and the collecting of specimens was as important as the viewing of landscape from West's appointed stations.

Wordsworth's *Guide* stands out as a classic in the literature of the Lake District. It was written by a native after forty years experience of the region, one who had developed a deep emotional attachment to the landscapes of the northwest. Wordsworth outlines the topography of each of the main valleys of the region. Here he stumbles upon the principles that were to guide the scholars who founded the great school of French regional geography in the opening decades of the twentieth century. Wordsworth foreshadows the elementary idea of the *pays*, the distinct local region on a small scale, when he writes 'every valley has its distinct and separate character'. For instance, the *Guide* sums up Wasdale as 'the deep valley of Wastdale, with its little chapel and half a dozen neat dwellings scattered upon a plain of meadow and corn-ground intersected with stone walls apparently innumerable, like a large piece of lawless patchwork'. After a discussion of the elements of the natural landscape – mountains, lakes, tarns, valleys, woods and the varieties of the Lake District climate – Wordsworth turns to Man's contribution to the scenery of the region. The pages of the *Guide* present a picture of the region at the close of the eighteenth century when communications are improving with the conversion of pack-horse trails to 'carriage roads', the patches of common field are fast disappearing, and plantations and tourism are making their first impact. Wordsworth idealizes the world of the 'statesman' where the farmhouses 'seem to have risen by an instinct of their own out of the native rock' and 'everything else, person and possession, exhibited a perfect equality, a community of shepherds and agriculturists, proprietors, for the most part, of the lands which they occupied and cultivated'. As the shores of Windermere and Derwentwater attracted tourists and settlers Wordsworth laid

281

down rules that would preserve the character of the landscape. New houses should be modelled on 'the beautiful forms of the ancient mansions of this country'. He objected to 'the craving for prospect' among the 'off-comes', to their houses that 'rise from the summits of naked hills'. Above all Wordsworth hated the planting of larch trees. He described the new plantations around Windermere with their thousands of seedlings as 'vegetable manufactories'. For Wordsworth the larch was 'an ugly tree – spiky, boughless, a graceless egotist, and a disagreeable "green" in spring, so peculiar and vivid'. The *Guide to the Lakes* is so much more than a source of information for the early-nineteenth-century tourist; it has come down to us as a valuable picture of the region at one of the most revolutionary periods in its history. Wordsworth, in its pages, was the first Englishman to lay down some of the basic principles of landscape conservation, and perhaps he sensed the problems of our own day when he wrote of the Lake District as a national property 'in which every man has a right and interest who has an eye to perceive and a heart to enjoy'.

The guide-books of the 1840s were written with a presentiment of the changes in tourism that were to follow the spread of the railway network across England. The fourth edition of *Leigh's Guide to the Lakes, Mountains and Waterfalls of Cumberland, Westmorland and Lancashire* printed in 1840 recognizes the importance of the revolution in communications for the north-west. At the beginning the book lists the inns along the coach road from London to Lancaster and 'supposes the tourist to be setting out from London to Lancaster, and afterwards visiting the ruins of Furness Abbey, as the first object of interest'. This is the world of West and 'the Lakers', of the rich and cultured tourist. But a new note is struck in the preface added to the fourth edition of the guide:

> and now that the mighty steam-engine has gained its sway, every person may be conveyed in a few hours from the metropolis to scenes of almost unrivalled sublimity and grandeur.

Six years later, Charles Mackay echoed the same theme in *The Scenery and Poetry of the English Lakes – a summer ramble*, when he wrote:

> Every year the Lakes are visited by greater numbers of tourists; and it is to be expected, *malgré* Mr Wordsworth, and his sonnets against steam, that as the Railway system is more and more developed, their numbers will still further increase.

The guide-books of the last quarter of the nineteenth century show the effects of railways on tourism. The long and arduous journey to the north-west has been eliminated and Windermere is within range of the day-tripper from the industrial towns of Lancashire. The incomparable series of handbooks published by John Murray from the 1860s onwards is characteristic of the railway age. Their itineraries are based on railway routes, and the text is always accurate, factual and scholarly. By the 1860s guide-books were making extensive use of the maps of the Ordnance Survey. As Murray's *Handbook to the Lakes*, published in 1867, says in its introduction, 'The map of the Lake District will be found to be *the most complete that has been hitherto published*. It has been constructed chiefly from the new Ordnance Survey'. But the guide-book that epitomizes the Lake District of the late Victorian period was the work of M. J. B. Baddeley, published in 1886 and illustrated with fourteen coloured maps by John Bartholomew. The high mountains come into their own in this work of immense detail. Every mountain path is described with all the dangers and attractions that await the tourist and the time that he can be expected to spend over each part of the route. For instance, the ascent of Great Gable from the Sty Head Pass is reckoned as taking between forty-five minutes and an hour. And the traveller is warned to 'Take care to keep well to the right of the crags which we have already mentioned as overlooking Wasdale. The climb is steep and continuous, but a trial of lungs rather than nerves.' Baddeley reflects the confidence of the late Victorian age when the world-map was widely splashed with imperial red. On the title page of his Lake District guide he quotes Kingsley:

> While we see God's signet
> Fresh on English ground,
> Why go gallivanting
> With the nations round?

Baddeley's is the classic guide-book to fell-walking. Its pages must have opened up the high summits to hundreds of thousands in the following decades. A wide range of literature of the high mountains has followed in its wake, from clinical descriptions of rock climbs to H. H. Symonds's classic and highly readable guide to the fells, *Walking in the Lake District*, first published in 1933.

The late Victorian period saw the appearance of several different kinds of tourist in the Lake District – the fell-walkers following the instructions of Baddeley, the rock-climbers who opened up the western valleys from lonely inns in Eskdale and at Wasdale Head, and the honeymooners who came to take over

Bowness-on-Windermere and Keswick. One guide-book of the 1890s addressed itself especially to the honeymoon couples:

> There is another section of the great middle-class who wish to get married –
> 'In the spring the young man's fancy
> Lightly turns to thoughts of love',
> and, as a not unnatural consequence, to a bridal tour. Well, what better place to spend a honeymoon in than the Lake District? The romance and poetry of the Lakes – the charming privacy and seclusion – the historical and legendary associations – all conduce to the happiness of a sensible couple; and no doubt all couples who follow these pages may be so classed.

The late nineteenth century was also the time of the marathon walks, when all the major peaks were climbed in an unbroken circuit. The limits of endurance are approached in Dr Wakefield's walk of ninety miles in 22 hours and 7 minutes on 14 August, 1905. He left Keswick at midnight and took in Robinson, Hindscarth, Honister, Great Gable, Kirk Fell, Pillar, Steeple and Yewbarrow before breakfast at Wasdale Head, and the journey continued with Scafell, Scafell Pike, Bowfell, Fairfield, Helvellyn, Blencathra and Skiddaw.

The Victorians too began the systematic exploration of the history of the Lake District with the founding of the Cumberland and Westmorland Antiquarian and Archaeological Society in 1866. The hundred volumes of its *Transactions* enshrine an immense wealth of research in the field and through documents that have transformed our knowledge of the region. Perhaps the most distinguished member of this society was Professor W. G. Collingwood. Apart from his many papers in the *Transactions* of the Antiquarian and Archaeological Society, his historical novels of the Lake District in the time of the Vikings, and his biography of Ruskin, Collingwood wrote a guide to the Lake District that deserves to rank as a classic among the literature of the region. In *The Lake Counties*, first published in 1902, Collingwood wrote of the topography and history of each of the main regions of the Lake District. It has many of the qualities of Wordsworth's *Guide to the Lakes*, where the subconscious roots of the writer's personality are deeply buried in the life and landscape of the Lake District. Collingwood's book concludes with a gazetteer that represents a masterly summary of his deep and wide-ranging knowledge of the north-west. Ruskin sought for a knowledge that was whole and all-comprehending; W. G. Collingwood, who for some years acted as Ruskin's secretary and did much to further his teaching, expresses the philosophy of his master most clearly in the structure and wide-ranging content of the *Lake Counties*.

284

The middle of the twentieth century has seen the emergence of two outstanding topographical writers on the Lake District. A. Wainwright has written a distinctive series of pocket guide-books for each segment of the mountain core. Through their pages the fell-walker can find his way into the most neglected corners of the region. Each minor peak and subsidiary ridge is explored in loving detail and expounded through brief and factual notes that are explained by detailed sketches and diagrams. Another contemporary writer who has made a permanent contribution to the topographical literature of the Lake District is A. H. Griffin, a native of Furness. He has written of the social life and folk-lore of the region and in the most vivid and personal terms of countless climbs and winter skiing excursions in the high fells, but his most original contribution has been a long series of portraits of the many different mountains. Every minor topographical feature of the central core emerges as a distinct personality in the pages of A. H. Griffin. He distinguishes the bleak plateau of Fairfield by its fierce northern precipices, whereas Kirk Fell is personified as an unusual viewpoint for the Western face of Scafell. The best of Griffin's prose contains a Wordsworthian quality in which personal experience and the observed details of the landscape become fused into a single whole.

Among contemporary writers, one alone, Norman Nicholson, has approached the Lake District and its landscapes with the single-mindedness and emotional involvement of Wordsworth. He has written several topographical books on the region as well as a study of the rise of Lake District tourism at the close of the eighteenth century. Throughout Norman Nicholson's work runs a mystical belief that the life of man and the objects of the physical landscape are inextricably joined – 'out of the rocks comes the true Lakeland life'. This theme forms a continuous thread through his several volumes of poetry. Because of an awareness that his creative roots lie in the landscapes of the north Norman Nicholson has refused to settle outside the region. Like his greatest predecessor, Nicholson finds the Lake District a land for all seasons:

> But when December mists skulk in the pikes,
> The snow holds out its bear-like paws;
> The bracken withers in the claws,
> And dead stones skid along the rotting rocks.

And, like Wordsworth, he turns to that idealized figure of the 'statesman', he who was responsible for shaping so much of the Lake District's landscape:

> He gathers boulders and cleft slate and builds
> A hut, a cairn, an intake wall;
> Hunts the wild cattle on the fell
> And drives them to his milky-pastured fields.

The visual arts and music in the Lake District

As a region the Lake District's strongest associations are with literature. No painter has yet impressed his vision of the region upon the reality of Nature in the sense that Constable created a 'Constable country' out of the landscapes of Suffolk. Music, too, has created regional associations for some parts of England that have not been achieved in the Lake District. Britten's opera, Peter Grimes, expresses the essence of the North Sea and the wide coastal landscapes of Suffolk in music. Elgar added to the personality of the valley of the Severn between Worcester and Gloucester.

Even though the Lake District has not yet provided the creative material for painting and music that it was able to give to poetry, the north-west has not been excluded from these other arts. In the eighteenth century Kendal was a centre of painters who specialized in portraits. George Romney, born near Dalton-in-Furness, was apprenticed to Christopher Steele, who had a studio in Kendal. The same town was the birthplace of another eminent portrait painter of the late eighteenth century, Daniel Gardner. Landscape painting in the Lake District begins with the age of tourism towards the end of the eighteenth century. The Gothic school of poetry and travel writing had its counterpart among the painters. One of the first sympathetic painters of mountain landscapes was Francis Towne, who painted in the Lakes in the 1780s, expressing himself in line drawings with transparent washes of water colour; and for a brief period Thomas Girtin painted around Keswick and Derwentwater. Another painter who has left a record of the landscapes of the Lake District at the beginning of the nineteenth century is Julius Caesar Ibbetson. He lived in Ambleside and later at Troutbeck from 1801 until 1805, finding a market for landscapes of Grasmere, Ullswater and Windermere in the aristocratic tourism of the period. His picture of Castle Crag, Borrowdale, may be seen in the Abbot Hall Gallery at Kendal. But the artist who penetrated the personality of the Lake District most deeply in the early nineteenth century was J. M. W. Turner. He made his first mountain studies around Coniston, and his striking picture of Buttermere and Honister Crag, a study of primeval light and darkness, is now in the Tate gallery. Constable also spent two months in the Lake District in 1806 as a guest of the Hardens at Brathay Hall. His sketches exploited the changing weather of the region and he produced a drawing of

Great Langdale that improved upon Nature with a lake at the foot of the Pikes.

Landscape painting was an adjunct to tourism in the Lake District in the nineteenth century, perhaps more than the writing of poetry and journals. The famous prospects must have been painted thousands of times over, but by the twentieth century science had come to the aid of the ordinary traveller with the growth of photography. Commercial photographers, such as the Abraham brothers, created another image of the Lake District in picture postcards of Skiddaw from Ashness bridge or feats on the notorious rock-climbs of Great Gable. By 1904, as the photographer began to take over much of the amateur's visual recording of the Lake District's landscapes, the painters, under the guidance of W. G. Collingwood, had formed the Lake Artists' Society. In the twentieth century the region has attracted artists by the very qualities of the light and colour of its environment, but also its small towns thronged with summer tourists provide a market for their works. Heaton Cooper, one among several contemporary artists, has expressed in terms intelligible to the ordinary tourist the details of the topography of every part of the Lake District at all seasons and with all the nuances of its constantly changing weather. The Lake District has become a market for art, but in the estimate of an intellectual world that has not much use for the landscape painter the region has failed to inspire work of the importance, for instance, of the group that dominated Canadian painting in the 1930s with its representations of the wild landscapes of rock and forest in the territory to the north of the Great Lakes.

Not least among the functions of the Lake District has been its role as a refuge and a retreat. Wordsworth and Ruskin escaped there from the bustle of London and the horrors of the Industrial Revolution. During the Second World War it gave shelter to one of the greatest artists of the twentieth century, Kurt Schwitters, a refugee from Nazi Germany who reached the British Isles in the summer of 1940 after a difficult escape from occupied Norway. Kurt Schwitters was one of the pioneers of abstract art and already in the Germany of the 1920s he assembled his collages, *Merzbau* as he came to call them, from the useless debris of our culture – bus and theatre tickets, postage stamps, bits of wire, corks and combs. In a barn at Elterwater and with the help of a grant from the Museum of Modern Art in New York he constructed his third Merzbau, a work that was never completed, but which may now be seen at the University of Newcastle-on-Tyne. The real genius of Schwitters passed unnoticed, except among a few close friends, in his last years at Ambleside. He was known locally as 'that crazy old man who stuck tram tickets on walls'. But to help himself to eke out a living Schwitters painted the Lake District's landscapes and sold them to passing tourists at ridiculously low prices, and some of his Langdale work has now found its way into the Tate Gallery.

The Lake District has always attracted the educated middle classes, both of Victorian England and in our own times. Apart from the transitory flood of summer tourists some of them have succeeded in making their homes in the region, especially near the shores of Windermere and at Keswick. Despite this middle-class element in the population of the Lake District, the activities and entertainments of an urban way of life have only developed slowly in the region. There are still no permanent theatres or concert halls in the chief tourist areas of the Lake District and consequently the two summer music festivals of the north-west, the Mary Wakefield Westmorland Music Festival and the Lake District Festival, are mounted under considerable difficulties – difficulties that perhaps contribute to the regional flavour of these occasions.

The Mary Wakefield Westmorland Festival is the oldest competitive music festival in the whole country. It began in 1885 when Mary Wakefield, a daughter of the family that owned and managed the Kendal Bank, organized a singing competition on the tennis court of her family home at Sedgwick, close to Kendal. Today the festival is held biennially in Kendal. Choirs, soloists and instrumentalists from the surrounding region compete for certificates and trophies, and in addition there are concerts by visiting professional orchestras in which choral works play an important part. The Hallé Orchestra and the City of Birmingham Orchestra have performed there, and since 1945 the patronage of the B.B.C. through the Northern Symphony Orchestra has been invaluable in the May music-making at Kendal.

In 1960 the first of the Lake District Festivals was successfully staged. In outlook and organization it belongs to the twentieth-century style of arts festival. Whereas the older Mary Wakefield Festival encourages local talent, the Lake District Festival aims to enrich the cultural life of the region through performances by artists of international fame. Again, the arts are given their widest meaning at the Lake District Festival, and the performances include poetry readings, lectures, revues and performances of notable films at the cinema in Windermere. This new festival of the 1960s has recognized the geography of the Lake District and its small and widely scattered centres of population in the dispersal of its events at a number of places. Churches and school halls in Kendal, Windermere, Cartmel, Grange, Ambleside and Keswick have been used. In some places the quality and associations of the buildings and their surroundings have been skilfully exploited in the festival performances. For instance, there have been concerts in Cartmel Priory, Bach's secular cantatas staged in costume

288

at Levens Hall, and readings from Wordsworth and other Lake District writers in Grasmere church.

The lack of a properly equipped theatre or a concert hall in the tourist areas of the Lake District hampers the growth of the arts in the region in the twentieth century. Plans for a large arts centre and theatre that was to be built on the lake-shore at Bowness have been abandoned after the refusal of planning permission. Since 1961 the live theatre has flourished in the region during the summer months through the pioneering activities of the Century Theatre. Their mobile theatre, stationed in a field on the outskirts of Keswick, has presented over the years several outstanding productions including *The Tempest*, *Waiting for Godot*, *A View from the Bridge*, and *Private Lives*. The season of Century Theatre now runs from June until the end of October and the twelve weeks' run at Keswick has been extended by a further month at Bowness. Of late two important developments in the cultural life of the Lake District have taken place with the establishment of permanent centres on the fringe of the region. In 1959 the Rosehill Theatre opened at Moresby near Whitehaven. Sir Nicholas Sekers, owner of the West Cumberland Silk Mills at Hensingham, first thought of the building of a centre for plays, chamber concerts and recitals in the culturally isolated region of the Cumberland coalfield. A barn in the garden of his house outside Whitehaven was rebuilt as a luxurious small theatre designed by Oliver Messel and holding an audience of a little more than two hundred. The Rosehill season runs from September until December and from February until July. It consists of about twenty concerts, four weeks of theatre and occasional lectures, jazz concerts and evenings of ballet. Its list of performers in ten seasons include some of the world's most eminent pianists and string quartets as well as productions by the Royal Shakespeare Company and the English Opera Group.

The theatre at Rosehill serves a real need in the north-west and draws its audience from distances of up to eighty miles. At Kendal another cultural need has been satisfied with the opening of the Abbot Hall Art Gallery in 1962. Here a house built in 1759 for George Wilson, and itself a fine example of Georgian domestic architecture, has been converted into a public gallery with a collection of paintings, furniture, silver, porcelain and glass and enamel work as well as the nucleus of a display of modern art. In addition Abbot Hall has organized a large number of varied exhibitions that have included twentieth-century Scottish Art, embroidery, art treasures from north-west houses and a collection of pictures illustrating Cumbrian characters, famous people of the Lake District. The first years of the Abbot Hall Gallery have not been without their public controversy. Letters in the local press have grumbled about the building up of a permanent collection of modern art; other have complained of a lack of support from the public and some have agitated for the development of a folk museum on the site. But Abbot Hall and the Rosehill Theatre have both added valuable and lively cultural contributions to the Lake District, a region whose social life has until now been largely expressed in sheep-dog trials, archaic rush-bearing festivals and the emotional outpourings of the Keswick Convention. Today we are in the midst of a revolution of taste as important as those cultural changes that came with the beginnings of tourism in the eighteenth century or again with the changes in communications of the railway age. The motorist is not only presenting grave problems for the conservation of the countryside, but he is also creating a demand for theatre and music in the resorts of the Lake District. Gone are the days when Baddeley's Guide and a mist-bound traverse of Esk Hause provided sufficient entertainment for the visitor to the Lake District; many of today's tourists prefer to keep to the valleys aided by the Good Food Guide and the prospect of Theatre-in-the-Round or an evening of quartets.

12

Exploring the Lake District

Ever since Father West first popularized, in the eighteenth century, the view-points and antiquities of the Lake District, guide-books have reflected the tastes and interests of their clientele as well as the means of travel of their different periods. The sketchpads and landscape-reflecting mirrors of leisurely eighteenth-century tourists have given way to crampons and climbing ropes on high black-buttressed crags and the fleeting impressions of lake and mountainside received through the squint-holes of cars threading nose-to-tail the main roads over Dunmail Raise and Kirkstone Pass. Wordsworth, when he wrote his long letters to the *Morning Post* in the autumn of 1844 about the projected railway to Windermere, could hardly have foreseen that the age of the motor-car would conjure into reality his own worst nightmares. 'We should have the whole of Lancashire, and no small part of Yorkshire, pouring in upon us to meet the men of Durham, and the borderers from Cumberland and Northumberland.' The opening of the north-western motorway, M6, has given easy access to the Lake District's valleys to day-trippers and week-enders from Lancashire, Merseyside and the Birmingham conurbation. This final chapter has been written with the motorist in mind. Just as the prose of Wordsworth and Ruskin could not reject the transport revolution of the nineteenth century, similarly the lover of the Lake District's landscapes in the twentieth century cannot deny the revolutionary changes that are going on around him. Perhaps he can try and use the gifts of modern transport wisely as a means of enjoying the incomparable landscapes of the north-west. The itineraries in the following pages are not meant as a complete guide to the Lake District – that task has been often performed and with much greater skill. They are presented as selected routes, by car and on foot, that reveal some of the personality of the region through the themes and topics discussed at length in the earlier chapters of this book.

KESWICK AND THE NORTHERN LAKE DISTRICT (Map 32)

Keswick has long been the chief tourist centre of the northern Lake District. Along with Bowness, Keswick was one of the first tourist resorts of the region because its setting and surroundings fulfilled so many of the demands of the traveller in search of the 'picturesque'. The Victorians counted Derwentwater 'as perhaps the most picturesque sheet of water in England' (Plate 5). The other qualities that the nineteenth-century tourist esteemed in Keswick were 'the neighbourhood of some of the highest mountains in England' and 'the good roads that diverge from it and conduct the tourist through much of the best scenery of Lakeland'. Like Bowness, Keswick was prized for its accessibility when 'the Cockermouth, Keswick, and Penrith railway' connected 'with the London and North Western system'. Most of these Victorian attributes of Keswick are still valid in the twentieth century and its ease of communications with the world beyond the Lake District will soon be enhanced with the completion of the motorway across Shap Fell.

For the modern tourist Keswick is a wet-day town, a resort of crowded cafés and gift shops that provide a refuge when the mountains at the head of Borrow-dale are buried in driving cloud and relentless rain borne on the not infrequent gales of August. As such a refuge it often seems grey and depressing when the dark slate walls glisten with streaming rain. This is a pity because in its quiet way Keswick has much to offer the traveller on sunny days, if he can find a place in the huge car-park to the west of the main street. Not only is there the late-medieval church at Crosthwaite where St Kentigern probably preached (page 135), the tall Moot Hall crushed into the Market Street when it was built in 1813, and cottage-rows of crude slate that date from Keswick's time as a busy little industrial town; it also contains some fine examples of late Victorian building. For example, the quarter to the north of the Greta around the station and Fitz Park shows Keswick as a prosperous late nineteenth-century resort; and again the curving terraces of boarding houses on the western fringe of the town have seen more earnest days when visitors to the 'Conventions' could combine evangelical Christianity with the high-mindedness that mountain scenery, Ruskin's prose and the later Wordsworth could inspire. Keswick should be enjoyed quietly as a gem of Victorian England, a gem whose streets can open up, in a properly Victorian way, the most astonishing of mountain prospects.

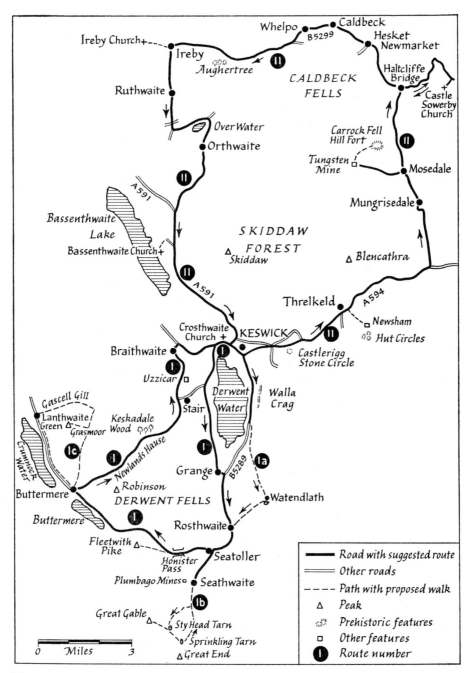

Map 32 *Routes of suggested excursions based on Keswick.*

293

(I) *A car excursion to Borrowdale and Buttermere*

Two roads lead from Keswick along the shores of Derwentwater to meet at Grange (2517) (Plate 6a), where they join to enter the Jaws of Borrowdale. The main road, on the east side of the lake, provides only occasional views, threading its way through plantation woodland and opening up at rare intervals the gentle falling outline of the Catbells on the farther side of the lake or the precipices and crags rising out of a mantle of forest around Lodore – a sight that thrilled the first professional tourists of the eighteenth century. Derwentwater is much more enjoyable from the minor road on the western side of the lake. Leave Keswick by the main exit to the north, A594. Great Crosthwaite church, the mother church of the whole of the upper Derwent and its tributaries in the Middle Ages (page 135), lies just off the road (2524). From Portinscale (2523) take the twisting lane southwards towards Grange (2517). For the first mile the route winds through plantations of the Forestry Commission on Swinside, but near Hawse End (2421) a magnificent view opens up across Newlands valley to the infrequently visited fells on the north-western edge of the Lake District. Causey Pike, with its steeply plunging eastern shoulder, smoothly contoured and grassy, sums up the scenery developed on the Skiddaw Slates. From Hawse End the lane climbs and falls gently above the western shore of Derwentwater. There are magnificent views across the lake to the ragged line of Walla Crag that marks the northern limit of the Borrowdale Volcanic Series against the Skiddaw Slates (page 26). Perhaps the most interesting viewpoint on this road occurs above the little bay on the southern edge of Brandelhow Park (252195). Peninsulas covered with conifers stretch long fingers into Derwentwater, while the waste deposited from the Brandelhow mine forms a scarred and rumpled strip that climbs the hill-slope from the bay. A dump of waste material, now overgrown with trees, stands out in the bay – a tiny man-made island (page 232). Here one can take in the whole shape of Derwentwater. The two submerged rocky ridges that run through the lake appear in their highest parts as islands at the northern end. Lord's Island protrudes from the most easterly ridge and was the site of the manor house of the Radcliffe family who founded the market town of Keswick. St Herbert's Island, on the western submerged ridge, was the sanctuary of a seventh-century hermit. A chapel was built there in 1374 at the time of a revival of his cult. Derwent Island, in the distance, was the place where the German miners, the Höckstetters, Ritselers and Steinbergers who settled at Keswick in the sixteenth century established a colony (page 228). Across the lake can be seen the volcanic outcrops of Friar's Crag and Castle Head (page 273), and in the distance the view is closed by the mountains of the Skiddaw Slate country that make up Skiddaw Forest.

The traveller should linger over the section of the route from Grange to Sea-toller (2413) through the middle part of Borrowdale, if his fellow motorists will tolerate such civilized behaviour. The huddled grey hamlet of Grange, planted on a clutch of ice-scraped *roche-moutonées* by the Derwent, marks the place where the monks of Furness Abbey built a 'grange' to administer their posses-sions in Borrowdale (page 156) (Plate 6a). After crossing the shapely slate bridge over the Derwent, the route turns into the Jaws of Borrowdale. Castle Crag, the site of an earthwork of Romano-British times (page 115), may by picked out across this wooded gorge, and to the left of the motor road a pleasant track through the woods leads past the Bowder Stone (page 49). After a mile the road suddenly opens out of the wooded gorge into the flat-floored basin of Rosthwaite, the site of a former lake that is still flooded on occasions (page 47). This section of the valley sums up so many of the themes of the heavily glaciated central Lake District with the rocky *howe* that forms the site of Rosthwaite, the hummocky moraine that lies across the valley to the south of the rock bar, the ice-marginal channel that provides an easy passage-way for a quiet, ancient track between Castle Crag and the dark precipices of Low Scawdel (248157), and the ele-mentary cross-profiles of ice-shaped valleys glimpsed in views up Stonethwaite Beck and towards the wild recesses beyond Seathwaite (pages 48, 49). Middle Borrowdale is also rich with the evidence of pioneer settlement by the Norsemen and their descendants (page 145), and a diversion to the right along the rough lane through Rosthwaite yields good examples of statesmen farms brilliant white and shaded by dark yew trees amid a patchwork of wriggling walls built of smoothed boulders gathered in the first clearance of the surrounding fields. At Seatoller (2413; page 144) the road begins a mile-long climb into the Honister Pass. The first five hundred feet of the ascent leads steeply through a shallow gorge shaded by stunted oak and birch trees to the upper lip of a huge glacial step that opens up into a wide moraine-filled basin, the gathering-ground of ice as recently as ten thousand years ago (page 55). The road climbs and winds to the summit of the pass with its youth hostel and litter of quarry-buildings, waste-heaps and abandoned tramways. Honister, often grey and bleak or dappled with patches of light beneath fast-moving skies, allows the motorist to scent the world of the high summits that for so many is the essence of the Lake District. Perhaps he may be tempted to abandon his car at this point for a couple of hours and strike off to one of the tops, above the 2,000 ft contour, that lie within an easy walking distance of the pass. Dalehead is only a mile to the north and 1,300 ft above the road (2215). Fleetwith Pike lies a mile to the west and presents an unparalleled view of the Buttermere valley (2014). To the south Grey Knotts and Brandreth, shapeless stony plateaux in themselves, feel like the roof of the world with their outlooks across to the Buttermere Fells, Pillar Rock and the wide empty spaces of upper Ennerdale (2112).

From Honister Pass the road falls steeply to the head of Buttermere. For the first third of a mile the route snakes through a wilderness littered with boulders, some of them as big as houses. Here, beneath the gloomy slate quarries high up on Fleetwith, we are presented with the kind of rock-strewn wilderness that must have been much more widespread in the Lake District before the centuries of medieval reclamation. At Gatesgarth (1914), the highest farm in the Buttermere valley and with a typical Scandinavian name, the view opens to reveal one of the classic images of the Lake District's landscape. A thin line of dark pine trees fringes a strip of grey shingle at the head of the lake; across the light-reflecting, sky-enfolding mirror of Buttermere a high line of summits from the Hay Stacks (1913) through High Crag, High Stile and Red Pike (1615) encloses a magnificent succession of corrie basins (page 67) (Plate 27).

From Buttermere with its tiny church (page 171) and scattered hamlet of colour-washed statesmen farms lost in clumps of sycamores take the right turn towards Keswick and the steep climb to Newlands Hause (1917). Backwards a fine view is opened on to the Buttermere valley with the delta flat separating the two lakes and the long band of Sourmilk Gill drawn across the shadowed mountain-side of the corrie beneath Red Pike. Two instructive views present themselves at Newlands Hause. To the left, as one enters the narrow col, the long dark-green slopes of Sail Beck lead the eye upwards to the craggy, rock-scarred summits of Wanlope and Sail. This is scenery characteristic of the Skiddaw Slates, whose flowing grassy contours contrast with the knobbly, precipice-riven landscapes of the Borrowdale Volcanics. It is a landscape without an enshrouding network of stone walls that tells of its descent in the sixteenth century from a medieval deer forest to the common pastures of farms tucked away in the Buttermere valley (page 179). The view eastward from Newlands Hause shows most of the north-eastern shoulder of Robinson (2016). The propensity of northerly-facing slopes for the accumulation of snow and ice under colder climates is shown by two corries that form deep scars in the rounded contours of the Skiddaw Slates. Below, almost in the valley floor, a morainic bar – probably a relic of the most recent glaciation of the Lake District – has been cut through by the stream that pours down from Moss Force (1917) at the head of Keskadale.

Leaving Newlands Hause the road towards Keswick first winds downwards into the glaciated trough of Keskadale Beck. From the steep hairpin bends at

37. Knobbled topography as associated with Borrowdale volcanic rocks forming Scafell. In the centre the gash of Mickledore excavated along a zone of weakened strata.

38a. *Great End across Sty Head Tarn.*

38b. *The central part of the Lake District with its ice-shorn peaks and flat-floored glaciated valleys. Langdale Pikes dominate the centre of the photograph and below their scree slopes lies the upper section of Great Langdale.*

39a. *The ice-shorn country of the Haystacks with bare rock outcrops interspersed with tarns.*

39b. *The working sheds, Honister slate quarry.*

40. *Scafell looking across Upper Eskdale from Hardknott.*

Keskadale (2119) one notices, five hundred feet higher up on the facing slope, a narrow patch of relict woodland whose ancient sessile oaks stand bent and bunched against the steep hillside (page 77). The Newlands valley, when it is compared with Borrowdale, illustrates the individuality of the landscape in each segment of the Lake District – an individuality that can be explained in the terms of the dual roles of Nature and Man in shaping the countryside. Newlands has no lake in its floor and lacks the highly romantic qualities of the Borrowdale Volcanic Series. It escaped the impact of tourism that influenced the shores of Derwentwater since the end of the eighteenth century and consequently it lacks the acres of Victorian plantations, rich with rhododendrons and exotic trees, that transformed the environment of Derwentwater. Newlands once formed part of the northern fringe of Copeland Forest (page 163). The valley was opened up to colonization at the close of the Middle Ages and was particularly affected by the search for minerals in the sixteenth century (page 226). As the road descends gradually towards Braithwaite (2323), running some hundred feet above the valley floor at the foot of the Skiddaw Slate fells, there are some excellent views to scattered white farmsteads set amid a patchwork of small fields, green and scarcely touched by the plough. The whole scene is laced with strips of woodland, flourishing along the steep and inaccessible banks of the becks. Uzzicar (2321) sums up the history of Newlands, where a typical statesman's longhouse (page 184) stands on the edge of the spoil heap of a disused copper mine (page 232). As one approaches Braithwaite and the delta plain between Derwentwater and Bassenthwaite – a plain varied by rocky knolls and the flowing shapes of drumlins – the greatest topographical landmark of Keswick, Skiddaw, cloud-shadowed and painted with larch forests, resumes its place in the landscape.

Places along the circuit of Borrowdale, Buttermere and the Newlands valley can be chosen as starting points for a more detailed exploration of the landscape on foot. Three sample itineraries are offered, each displaying some of the major variations in the scenery of the north-western Lake District.

(Ia) Follow the lane to Watendlath (2716) that leaves the Keswick–Borrowdale road at Barrow Bay (269204). This route displays well the features of a glaciated side-valley with a broken longitudinal profile (Plate 4b). In the gentler upper section above Thwaite House (2718) the sites of former tiny lakes may be discerned in the valley floor; at the lip of the Derwent's ice-truncated valley-side the Watendlath Beck plunges headlong into the gorge of Lodore. An alternative route, free from the car traffic that often destroys the enjoyment of the Watendlath lane, can be found along the path that climbs steeply from High Lodore

(262183) across the head of the gorge to rejoin the former road at Thwaite House. From Watendlath (page 276) (Plate 4b), a statesman hamlet now degraded by the impact of tourism, the bridle track should be followed south-westwards to Rosthwaite. Across Watendlath Tarn the rectangular enclosures of the strips of a former common field, once shared by the farms of the hamlet, may be seen. In the col between Watendlath and Rosthwaite a fine view of the surrounding fells opens up, a view that is much improved if one diverges across the moor to the summit of Brund Fell (264163). Southwards the wide view rises to the huge summits of the central Lake District (Plate 38b). This treeless moorland with its dark, shaggy ice-scraped crags and hollows filled with peat and tiny pools is typical of the Borrowdale Volcanic country. These are the upland sheep pastures of Borrowdale's farms, the former grazing grounds of Furness and Fountains Abbeys and of the Norse settlers before that (page 158). Descend to Rosthwaite on its rocky howe rising above a lake flat and return to Grange and the head of Derwentwater by the network of footpaths and tracks through the ice-marginal channel beneath Castle Crag (248155).

(Ib) An excursion among the highest fells of the Lake District should begin at Seathwaite (236121). Across the level and often flooded valley floor of the Derwent, Sourmilk Gill pours from its high corrie basin below the summit of Brandreth. The steep, ice-shaped slope around Sourmilk Gill is scarred with the waste heaps of mining at different levels, and dark splashes of colour against the dun hillside mark the relics of a once extensive yew forest. From Seathwaite follow the track southwards to Stockley Bridge (235109), where the path enters a cluster of mounds and hummocks that forms one of the most recent moraines of the Lake District (page 47). Take the path that diverges to the right, climbing steeply into the Styhead Pass from which Taylorgill Force plunges in a slit-like gorge over the brim of a huge ice-shaped rock-step (Plate 6b). At the junction of tracks in the col at Styhead (218095) follow the route to the right that zig-zags up the stony eastern flank of Great Gable (2110). At the summit a wide prospect opens up, particularly of the Scafell range and the lonely mountains of Ennerdale Forest; immediately below, and 2,700 feet down, we see the intricate field patterns of Wasdale Head (page 193). An attractive alternative route that can be used on the return to Seathwaite follows the track eastwards from Sty Head towards Esk Hause (page 107). Beyond Sprinkling Tarn (2209), beneath the huge frost-shattered buttresses of Great End (Plate 38a), take the path that leads northwards along the Grains valley to Stockley Bridge. To the left as one descends Grains Gill the bare slopes of Seathwaite Fell form the common grazings of the hamlet in the valley floor; to the right the rocky summit of Glaramara (2410), another centuries-old sheep pasture, is the site of one of the pre-historic axe factories (page 103).

(Ic) Buttermere is an excellent starting-point for a detailed exploration of the Skiddaw Slate country of the north-western edge of the Lake District – one of the least visited parts of the whole region. From Crag Houses (174172), two hundred yards to the north of the hamlet, take the footpath that heads up the smooth grassy shoulder of Whiteless Pike (1819) – an excellent viewpoint for the inter-lake flat at Buttermere with the high peaks of the Borrowdale Volcanic country massed in the background (Plate 27). Continue northwards for a mile along a narrow, precipice-hedged arête into the wide col between Grasmoor (1720) and Crag Hill (1920). From this col climb westward on to the billowy summit plateau of Grasmoor, a refreshing and unusual viewpoint for the mountains of the Lake District, with the bonus of a wide sweep of the Cumberland plain and the Solway Firth to the north-west. Note here the different topography of a mountain summit in the Skiddaw Slates – turf, lichens and bare patches of minutely broken rock – as compared with huge jumbled slabs and boulders that clothe the highest parts of Great Gable and Scafell in the Borrowdale Volcanics. The gentle slopes of Grasmoor's summit that fall away to a most formidable ring of precipices and giddy screes also display a series of periglacial features – stone stripes and polygons (page 64). From the top of Grasmoor return to the col and make for the head of Gasgale Gill at Coledale Hause (1821). Follow Gasgale Gill (Plate 2a) with its ruined shielings and forbidding blue-grey gorge cut through the Skiddaw Slates to Lanthwaite Green, site of a deserted settlement (1520). Return to Buttermere along the road by Crummock Water, turning aside to examine the deserted site of Rannerdale (page 171).

(II) *By car around Skiddaw Forest*

A trip from Keswick through the lanes that fringe Skiddaw Forest reveals many of the facets of the north-eastern Lake District, and ever present are the sweeping spurs and remote summits of this mountain-mass whose heart can only be reached by footpaths.

Leave Keswick by the main road for Penrith, A594. Already, before the dark slate Victorian villas have been left behind, the leisurely traveller will want to turn aside to Brigham (2824), where the wooded gorge of the Greta sheltered a sixteenth-century industrial site (page 226). A divergence from the main Penrith road, by making a right turn a few yards after the junction of the Ambleside road (A 591), leads in three-quarters of a mile to the Castlerigg stone circle, perhaps the most impressive prehistoric monument of the Lake District (page 107).

Standing amid this solemn circle of ancient stones a fine prospect of the mountains and valleys around Keswick is opened up on a clear day (Plate 3b). Above all, it is a place to take in the panorama of the southern flank of Skiddaw Forest from Latrigg, a flat-topped hill in the western foreground that once had an open field on its summit and whose lower slopes above the Greta gorge bear traces of an enormous landslip, to the V-shaped gash of the Glenderaterra Beck and on to the succession of corries gashed into the southern face of Saddleback (page 66). Return to the Penrith road by going forward from the Castlerigg stone circle along the lane that drops steeply to Naddle Beck (3024). The section of dual carriageway that leaves Threlkeld village on the left gives an excellent view of the enclosed strips of the former common field (page 190); on the other side of the road, to the right, Threlkeld quarry and, above it, the location of the deserted Dark Age settlement may be noted. The deserted site is reached by following the cart road across the river and over the railway to Newsham Farm (331247). From that point one must strike south-westwards across the moor by the upper edge of the quarry for half a mile to reach the overgrown boundaries and scarcely discernible hut circles of the first settlement at Threlkeld (page 126) (Plate 3a).

At the turning for Mungrisdale, some eight miles from Keswick, leave the main road and follow the lanes along the eastern edge of the Skiddaw massif to Hesket Newmarket (3438). The grandest object in the landscape of this section of the journey is certainly Carrock Fell, whose summit bears the best Iron Age hill-fort in the Lake District (page 113). On the approach to Mungrisdale one notices Eycott Hill, composed of lavas in the Borrowdale Volcanic Series, a little more than a mile to the east (3829; page 33). Beyond Eycott Hill the Carboniferous limestone, here largely covered in boulder clay, forms an escarpment that extends northward through Hutton Roof (3734; page 38). Mungrisdale is a pleasant, unspoilt cluster of whitewashed farms and shady sycamores against a background of blue-grey crags and soft green mountain slopes. As one approaches Mosedale (3532), the marshy, featureless divide between the Caldew and the Glenderamackin contained a former lake (page 33). From Mosedale it is possible to taste the scenery of the interior of Skiddaw Forest by following the lane on the north side of the Caldew, past Swineside Farm (3432) to the junction of rough tracks below the Carrock mine (326329), a source of tungsten (page 235). Here one can get no farther on four wheels; and lonely footpaths lead the walker on to the wild recesses below Skiddaw, or through the mountains back to Great Crosthwaite and Keswick. A footpath that snakes up the long steep northern valley slope of the Caldew from 350322 gives the easiest access to the summit of Carrock Fell, and one can muse on the motives of the builders of Iron Age hill-forts on the way up! From Mosedale to Hesket Newmarket one can diverge eastward at Low Row (3536) to discover the secluded church at Castle Sowerby (380362), one of St Kentigern's preaching sites in the sixth century (page 134). Hesket Newmarket is only one of the many pleasing surprises of the unspoilt landscapes of the Lake District's north-eastern fringe that combine the grandeur of mountains with quiet pastoralism. It is a failed market centre (page 214).

From Hesket Newmarket make for Caldbeck (3239), a village with a large untidy green, a church and holy well dedicated to St Kentigern and relics of the early stages of the Industrial Revolution (page 255) (Plate 7b). Time should be taken to follow the footpath from the village along the north bank of the beck to the Howk (3139). The route starts unobtrusively through a farmyard gate, just off the southern corner of the green, and soon enters a striking limestone gorge – green, grey, sunlit and deep with shadow – that contains the ruin of a water-powered bobbin mill that must rank high among the treasures of industrial archaeology (page 38) (Plate 7a).

Return to Caldbeck and drive westward along road B5299 through Whelpo (3039) and Parkend (3038). Just beyond Whelpo a pattern of lynchets, former cultivation terraces, may be picked out on the hillside to the right across the river. Beyond Parkend the road crosses one of the several relics of common land that still survive in Cumberland. Across the valley, near Faulds (2939), a series of rectangular enclosures betrays the presence of a former common field. As one descends towards Daleside (2638) and Ireby (2338) the faint marks of Augher-tree (264382), a deserted Iron Age settlement, can be picked out on the facing hillside to the left (page 115). Approaching Daleside farm follow the road that branches to the left into Ireby (2338), whose Moot Hall and deserted market-square commemorate a former trading centre (page 215). It is worthwhile to make a detour for one mile to the west to see Ireby's Old Church, a disused late-Norman chapel standing alone amid rank pastures and high tangled hedgebanks (224394). Return to Ireby and take the lane southwards to Ruthwaite (2336), Over Water (2535) and Orthwaite (2534). From the road near Ruthwaite there is an excellent view across the valley to Uldale, where one can pick out the rectangular pattern of enclosures that denotes the presence of a former common field; around Uldale's town field may be seen the characteristic field patterns that followed the enclosure of Cumberland's extensive commons. A magnificent view of the northern face of Skiddaw Forest opens up as one enters the ice-shaped col at 870 ft above the depression containing Over Water (2535), a tiny unfrequented lake surrounded by brown bog and scrub in a depression cluttered with smooth green hummocky drumlins.

The lane that leads through Orthwaite (2534) to the main Keswick road at High Side (235306) compounds most of the delights of a minor road on the edge of the Lake District. It snakes in and out of little wooded valleys, passes through colour-washed farms, and every now and then snapshot views of Skiddaw and its outliers, each time subtly changed in shape, are added to more distant glimpses of Bassenthwaite Lake. Return to Keswick under the high-piled larchwoods of the western flanks of Skiddaw and make a diversion to the right about a mile from High Side (at 234291) to see Bassenthwaite Old Church (227287), with an early dedication to St Bega. Its restored Victorian exterior conceals a twelfth-century chancel arch, and its site, amid pastures on the edge of a quiet bay, still suggests something of the first centuries of Christianity in the north-west.

PENRITH AND THE EASTERN LAKE DISTRICT (Map 33)

Penrith stands astride the busiest routes, both by rail and road, between England and Scotland. Fortunately the recent opening of a motorway by-pass has diverted much of the volume of poisonous heavy traffic from its streets, so that the tangle of little market-places (Plate 9), the intriguing precinct of an eighteenth-century parish church, and the warm reds of sandstones employed at several different periods of the town's building history may be enjoyed before exploring the Ullswater Fells or the lanes of Inglewood Forest (pages 162–3).

(III) *A car excursion to Ullswater*
The first stage of the journey takes one from Penrith to the foot of Ullswater at Pooley Bridge (4724) and illustrates some of the main themes of an early area of settlement on the lowland fringe of the Lake District. Leave Penrith by the A6 trunk road to the south; at Eamont Bridge (5228) follow road A592 towards Ullswater. Two Bronze Age 'henge' monuments lie within sight of this route at Eamont Bridge – King Arthur's Round Table (523283) and Mayburgh (519284). They provide pointers to the great antiquity of settlement in the Penrith area (page 108). A mile along the road at Yanwath (512278), a squat fourteenth-century pele tower, the core of the hall, represents another aspect of the Lake District's history. Tirril (5026), the place where the Roman road that comes down from the High Street loses itself in the long-settled plain of the Eamont, points in its place name to a pocket of Norse settlement among the Ullswater foothills (page 142). The near-by hamlet of Thorpe (4926), meaning an outlying farm or dependent settlement, suggests a later intrusion in the landscape. Barton (4826) typifies the softer pastoral country at the approaches to Ullswater. It is the

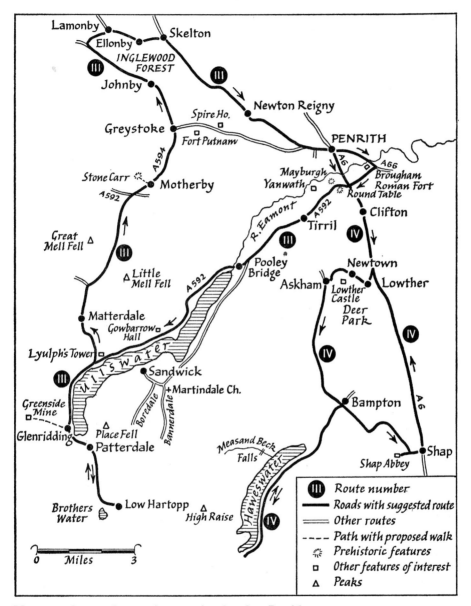

Map 33 *Suggested routes for excursions based on Penrith.*

primary parish of this part of the eastern Lake District and its former importance is suggested by the Norman church that, save for the Gleve farm, stands alone in this tract of dispersed settlement (page 169). At Pooley Bridge the road swings through a wide space that betrays an extinct market (page 214), and soon the first wide prospect of the lowest reach of Ullswater and its background of mountains is opened up (page 31). To the right above the road a shapely hill, clothed in planted coniferous woodland that Wordsworth reviled in his *Guide to the Lakes*, is crowned by a Dark Age earthwork (page 265). At this point it is worth diverting for a quarter of a mile along road B5320 to look at Soulby (4625), where the enclosed units of a former common field that was shared by the farms along its upper edge are clearly visible.

From Pooley Bridge continue by the main road along the northern shore of Ullswater as far as Hartsop (4013). For some miles to Glenridding (3816) the route passes through two medieval deer parks – Gowbarrow (4021) and Glencoyne (3818). Despite the Victorian plantations with Douglas firs and tangled masses of rhododendrons (page 50), patches of heath and rock and scattered gnarled oak trees still leave an impression of a medieval park, which is strengthened by Lyulf's Tower, a hunting lodge of 1780 in a castellated mock-medieval style (Plate 13b). The extensive views of still grey-blue lake and distant crowded mountains that appear from time to time along this road were unequalled by any other parts of the Lake District in the minds of Victorian tourists. Glenridding (3816), on the highest reach of Ullswater, reveals its past as a once-busy mining centre with terraces of dark slate cottages (Plate 13c). Here one can diverge by the lane to the right for a distance of two miles to the abandoned Greenside mine (page 249) and half-way along the lane as it climbs high above the beck one notices the outline of a former common field, below and on the other side of the valley. Patterdale (3915) stands above the delta at the head of the lake, its medieval chapel rebuilt in 1853 and its rural economy long transformed by tourism (page 133). Deepdale (3914) and Low Hartsop (4013) both illustrate the effect of recent social changes in the Lake District as farms have been bought up by outsiders with no interest in making a living from the land. The melancholy tidiness of these places can only make one thankful for the policy of the National Trust in the Lake District that has insisted upon the maintenance of its properties as active farms (pages 256). At Low Hartsop the fells thrust long steep spurs into the valley floor, green with bracken and scarred with patches of scree, and here the traveller should turn round, if he is not going on across the Kirkstone Pass to the valleys that converge on Windermere.

An alternative route back to Penrith can be made to include the southern edge of Inglewood Forest. Retrace the journey along the northern shore of Ullswater as far as the junction for Troutbeck and Keswick, A5091, by Glencoyne Park (399199). After a little more than two miles follow the lane from Matterdale End (3923) that passes beneath the eastern slopes of Great Mell Fell (page 39). This hilly basin crossed by the Aira Beck and containing the headwaters of the Dacre Beck is a region of late settlement reclaimed from deer forest after the seventeenth century. On reaching the Keswick–Penrith road, A594, side-step to the left for half a mile from Motherby (4228), a street-village of grey farms, to examine Stone Carr, a deserted late Iron Age or Dark Age site (4128; page 125). Next along the main road towards Penrith one reaches Greystoke (4430), former centre of a Norman Barony with implications of political importance in times long before the Norman Conquest. Greystoke has much to interest the traveller – a fourteenth-century pele tower built into an imposing nineteenth-century mansion, a church that presents many architectural problems and a countryside littered with the work of its improving landlords in such follies as Fort Putnam (4530), Bunkers Hill (4530) and Spire House (4631). The landscape of Greystoke, with its huge park stretching to the crest of the Carboniferous Limestone escarpment that faces the dark mass of Skiddaw Forest, is a model of the influence of the powerful landlord in the countryside, a point of contrast that Wordsworth already makes when he compares the evolution of the interior of the Lake District with its lowland fringe in his *Guide*.

From Greystoke follow the minor road through Johnby (4333), Lamonby (4035) and Ellonby (4235) to Skelton (4335). All of these except Skelton, an older and larger settlement that was set in its open fields until the eighteenth century (page 163), represent an extension of settlement early in the twelfth century when Flemings and Bretons were among others brought into the northern marches (page 164). Turn northwards through Skelton along B5305, and at the outskirts of the village take a minor road to the right that leads to Unthank and Hutton-in-the-Forest (4635). The former, a string of widely-spaced farms lying back from the road across fields, stands for a stage of colonization in Inglewood Forest later in date than that of Johnby and Ellonby (page 162). Return directly to Penrith.

An attractive variation of the Ullswater excursion may be devised by following the lane along the southern shore of the lake to Martindale and its tributary valleys. Here, as in Long Sleddale, many of the features of the Lake District that Wordsworth knew are still preserved, unaffected by the plantations and the vulgarizing wave of Victorian tourism that swept the northern shore of Ullswater. The miniature pass, Martindale Hause (4319), presents unfamiliar views on to the lake and the tiny delta plain of the Fusedale Beck at Howtown. From the plain seventeenth-century chapel dedicated to St Martin (434184) one can look up a broad flat-floored valley with scattered statesmen farms (page 186) to the deer forest beneath the massive summit of High Street. Boredale (4218) continues with variations on the same theme from the scattered farmsteads in the lush setting of Sandwick (4219) to the last enclosures against the open common at Boredalehead (4117). Ruined farms in these valleys, at Henhow (434177) for instance, tell of depopulation and the consolidation in the last half century of statesmen properties (page 186). High on the slopes above Ramsgill there is a rare survival of the original oakwoods of the Lake District whose increasing scarcity was already noticed by Wordsworth at the beginning of the last century (page 79).

(IV) *By car to Lowther and through the lanes to Shap*
A journey through the Lowther valley illustrates many themes in the development of the eastern fringe of the Lake District. Leave Penrith in an easterly direction by trunk road A66 and after two miles stop at the site of *Brocavum* (5328), a Roman fort standing on a terrace of the Eamont and containing within its grassy rampart the extensive ruin, warm and red in sandstone, of a late-thirteenth-century castle (page 132). From Brougham Castle follow B6262 past Brougham Hall, now demolished but with the little seventeenth-century chapel of St Wilfrid still standing, to trunk road A6, where one turns south through Clifton (5326), a street-village that began as an Anglian settlement on the scarp above the Lowther. Follow A6, now mercifully free of much traffic in this section with the completion of the Penrith by-pass, and turn right at the approach to Lowther Village, a pretty planned settlement of the mid-eighteenth century composed in crescents (page 199). Drive on through the Park with its screening plantations of birch and pine to Lowther Newtown (5223) (Plate 14b) a creation of the late seventeenth century that followed the desertion of the medieval village site near the church (page 198). Lowther Park is a good place to explore in detail and at leisure on foot, with its bridle roads and spinneys climbing to the crest of the limestone escarpment above the Lowther valley, and its twelfth-century church – much of which was largely reconstructed in the seventeenth and nineteenth centuries; and always there is Lowther Castle – a gaunt shell that looks more 'gothic' than when it was completed in 1811 now that the sky and shifting clouds are seen through empty casements (page 200) (Plate 14c).

Cross the Lowther gorge and climb sharply into Askham (5123) (Plate 14a), one of the finest green villages of Westmorland, with a system of former open fields that can be clearly traced in the present stone-walled enclosures. Askham is followed by Helton (5129), a linear settlement of stone farms (page 138), and on the opposite side of the valley (left) the site of the common field, formerly associated with Whale (5221), can clearly be picked out (Plate 11b). At Bampton (5118) one can make a diversion to the head of Hawes Water, a valley made desolate, but given a new kind of beauty, by Manchester's thirst for water (Plate 10b). The road along the eastern side of Hawes Water presents excellent views across to High Street, the deep corries on its eastern face, and the hanging valley of Measand Beck (4815; page 52). The upper edge of the drowned fields and enclosures at Mardale is still exposed above the western shore of the reservoir and a tributary valley to the south of the road contains the relict Naddle Forest (page 79).

Continuing from Bampton southwards towards Shap (5615) the lane climbs between grey walls and under ash trees on to the Carboniferous limestone that is heavily covered with boulder clay; an extensive view across the bare fells of the eastern Lake District opens up to the west. Within half a mile of Shap take a narrow lane to the right that drops quickly to the Lowther valley and Shap Abbey (5415), a secluded wooded place against a background of moors that has not completely lost a sense of holiness. To leave the quiet of Shap Abbey for the mile-long settlement on A6 is to make an even greater journey in time. Shap (5615) is a place of articulated lorries and diesel fumes and the noise of express trains bound for Scotland. Modern communications have opened up quarries around what must be one of the dreariest places in the north of England, granite to the south above Wasdale Beck (5508) and at Low Fell (5610), and the Carboniferous Limestone to the north (5518) (page 238). The Market Hall at Shap provides another relic of the history of this settlement that has always lived by its communications (page 218). Return to Penrith by the main road, A6.

AMBLESIDE AND THE SOUTHERN LAKE DISTRICT (Map 34)

Even in the earliest years of tourism in the Lake District a century and a half ago, when guides were hired at the rate of five shillings a day to lead travellers into the dangerous world of the high summits, the advantages of Ambleside for the exploration of the southern part of the region were soon recognized. The topography of Ambleside today records its expansion from a statesmen's hamlet into a market centre and a thriving Victorian tourist town (page 216) (Plate 17).

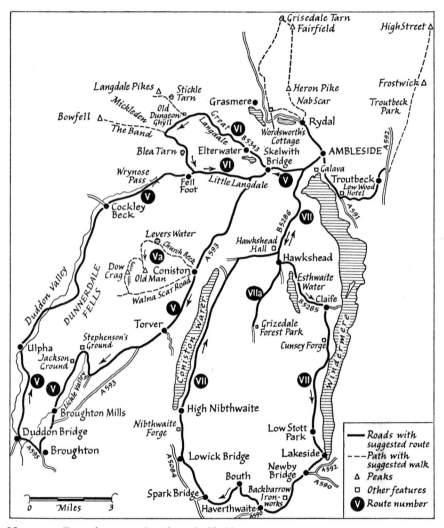

Map 34 *Excursion routes based on Ambleside as a centre.*

(V) *By car to Coniston and the Duddon Valley*

Drive out of Ambleside by road A593 following the Brathay valley as far as Skelwith Bridge (3403); to the left across the junction of the rivers Rothay and Brathay there is a brief view of the low peninsula jutting into Windermere that was the site of the Roman fort of *Galava*. The road climbs southwards from Skelwith Bridge through patches of close-growing coppice wood with occasional

308

views to the right of the Langdale Fells. At 526 ft the watershed between the drainage towards lakes Windermere and Coniston is crossed in a narrow ice-shaped corridor (327016) across the rough hummocky col of the northern Furness Fells. Approaching Coniston the dominant landscape feature is provided by the scarred and hummocky topography of the Borrowdale Volcanic Series in the massif of the Old Man (2797) and the Coniston Fells (2999), that is contrasted with the lower, milder scenery of the Silurian rocks on the eastern side of the lake (page 35).

Coniston (3097) presents the same rather grim façade of most of the larger settlements of the Lake District, an appearance that is largely the result of Victorian builders expressing the styles of their time in the intractable local slates. It is worth a little detailed exploration, with its Ruskin associations (Brantwood across the lake and a museum in the town) as well as an abandoned railway station poised high above the settlement on a line that had to gain height to reach the mines in Church Beck.

From Coniston follow the main road, A593, southwards towards Torver through patches of coppice wood that once served the iron industry of Furness (page 84). After taking the right fork in the road at Torver continue for about a mile along A593 towards Broughton, and at (271934) take the narrow lane that climbs away steeply to the right. Fine views soon open up in all directions – across the Silurian fell country of High Furness to the south and east, northwards and westward across the dissected 900–1,000 ft platform that was the scene of extensive Bronze Age settlement (page 108). As the lane falls steeply towards the Lickle valley, with its abandoned farms now absorbed in plantations of the Forestry Commission (page 88), turn sharply to the right at a scissors cross-road and follow the secluded winding lane towards Stephenson Ground (2393). This cluster of 'grounds' marks the pioneering efforts of settlers breaking new land about the beginning of the sixteenth century (page 177). The high-banked lane that winds down to the Lickle at Broughton Mills (2290) is representative of so much of the quiet, unspoilt country on the edge of the Lake District. Turn aside at Lane End (220900) to see a surviving common field in the valley floor, to the south of the road, between Hartley Ground (2189) and Croglinhurst (2189; page 194). Return to Lane End and drive on to Broughton-in-Furness, a settlement with more coherence than many in the Lake District, focused on its rectangular market-place (page 218).

Broughton is the starting-point for the exploration of the Duddon Valley. First take the main road to Duddon Bridge (1988), site of one of the most important forges of the eighteenth century (page 84). Wordsworth expressed the remote and secret qualities of the Duddon both in his poems and in the *Guide to the Lakes*; even today it has not completely lost that individuality. The lane that follows the valley on its eastern flank from Duddon Bridge gives good views across to Ulpha Park, a relict fragment of the medieval landscape (page 167). Above, to the right, footpaths lead up to Dunnerdale Fells, where cairn clusters indicate one of the many upland settlements of the late Bronze Age. Ulpha (1993) has a plain seventeenth-century dale chapel, and in the next section of the valley to Seathwaite the lower hill-slopes are clothed with tall, close-growing coppice wood. At Seathwaite (2296) the scenery of the Duddon valley changes, as a huge rock step seems to block the journey northward. The river cuts through this barrier in a narrow gash while the road winds round to the east, climbing into the higher section of the Duddon through an abandoned channel of the river (page 42). A pleasant footpath leads from Seathwaite to the mouth of the gorge (224964) and the scenery of this magnificent glacial step can be explored further by a track that climbs above the gorge on the east.

The upper part of the Duddon valley provides good views of Harter Fell Forest, where some of Wordsworth's principles for the laying out of plantations have been followed (page 90). At Cockley Beck (2401) the wild recesses of the Upper Duddon are entered and the track of the Roman road from Ravenglass to Ambleside is joined (Map 20). Gaitscale Close, a crumbling ruined farm that would have moved a Romantic poet to express himself, illustrates the retreat of the farming frontier in recent times (page 164). As the tight, sharp bends of the climb to Wrynose Pass (2702) are tackled the slopes across the moraine-filled, rock-strewn valley lead up to Red Tarn (2603), lying in a bleak, rainy col between Cold Pike and Pike of Blisco. Here, it has been shown that forests flourished some five thousand years ago (page 101). As the road drops into Little Langdale from the summit of the Wrynose Pass it diverges here and there from the Roman road, whose track can often be discerned a few yards away in the heather. Above Fell Foot farm the Brathay has etched its valley into the lip of a glacial rock step (page 56). Behind the 'statesman's' house at Fell Foot (2903) one can find a curious terraced platform that was probably a Viking 'thing' mount (page 149). Return to Skelwith Bridge and Ambleside through narrow lanes between high walls and thickets of coppiced oak, birch and hazel, a tangled and confused countryside through which the Roman road from Little Langdale to *Galava* at the head of Windermere has never been satisfactorily traced.

(Va) The landscape of the Lake District cannot be fully appreciated without visiting the higher fells and summits. One must look down on the glassy surfaces of corrie lakes as well as up to their dark semi-circles of precipice and crag. The chief features of the mountain world of the south-western Lake District may be explored in a walk of five or six hours from Coniston. Leave Coniston by the track that follows Church Beck for the Youth Hostel among the waste heaps of the abandoned mines (2898) (Plate 20a). The pretty climb through woods of birch and mountain ash rapidly changes to a landscape of grandeur and desolation. Terraces of ruined cottages and masses of waste rock from mining and quarrying operations are shadowed by the overpowering summit ridge of the Old Man to the west. From the youth hostel veer westward and climb steeply through the leats and abandoned adits of the copper mines to Levers Water (2899; page 229). Trace a way through the boulders along the western edge of Levers Water and, arriving close to its north-western corner, begin the steep thousand-foot climb to the col (271994) below Little How Crags. A wide prospect of mountains is opened up and it can be thoroughly enjoyed in an easy walk along the broad summit ridge southwards for one mile to the summit cairn of Coniston Old Man (2797; page 28).

Make the return to Coniston by Dow Crag (2698) and Walna Scar Road (2696). The northward loop along a clear track from the summit of the Old Man to Dow Crag presents a series of fine views on to Goat's Water (2697) (Plate 18a) and its vast aprons of rock scree poured down from the gullies and buttresses above (page 66). The track southwards over Dow Crag ranks among the finest walks in the Lake District, with its succession of views into the chimneys that fall to Goat's Water. Blind Tarn (2696), one of the keys to the vegetation history of the region, comes into sight (page 66). From Walna Scar turn towards Coniston. This track, rough and almost inaccessible to vehicles, gives an impression of the communications of the Lake District in the days of pack-horses that lasted until the close of the eighteenth century. The easy walk along the road across Little Arrow Moor provides a good view across the broken topography of the thousand-foot platform, a scene of dense prehistoric settlement (page 109).

(VI) *By car to the Langdales*
Within the smallest compass Langdale is able to present almost every aspect of the Lake District except that of a great lake basin, and even so there is the compensation of Elterwater, one of the most beautiful of tarns, with its deeply indented reedy margin. From Ambleside follow the Coniston road as far as Skelwith Bridge (3403). Here the road to Great Langdale branches away and climbs by the Brathay through the narrow wooded gorge that contains Skelwith Force, once the source of power for bobbin mills (page 56). Now the main occupation

at Skelwith Bridge is the dressing of slate. Above the gorge is Elterwater with a pastoral landscape of lush green drumlins, sometimes crowned with tiny spinneys, the result of extensive reclamation between 1820 and 1830. Elterwater (3204), at heart a rural hamlet, expanded into a small industrial community in the nineteenth century with the opening up of slate quarries and a gunpowder works that tapped the water power of the Langdale Beck and local supplies of charcoal (page 87). Now it is largely a tourist village.

Beyond Chapel Stile (3205), which is mainly a slate-quarrying village, we enter the wide curving floor of Great Langdale, site of a former lake, whose slopes sweep up unbroken to the summits of the Pikes. This is one of the most familiar prospects of the Lake District; it greets one again and again from every postcard rack in the region, but it can never become hackneyed. For almost three miles the road swings up and down along the northern flank of the valley, passing by a succession of statesmen farms whose history goes back five centuries and more (page 166). At the end of the motor road, near the Old Dungeon Ghyll hotel (285060), the traveller must take to the footpaths to enjoy the scenery of Langdale. A walk of two miles along the level valley floor of Mickleden leads to the huge cluster of recent moraines at the foot of Rossett Gill (263072; page 55). On the way one can look up the long scree to the site of the Neolithic axe factory beneath the crag of Pike of Stickle (page 103).

The return to Ambleside by car can be made by Blea Tarn (2904). Blea Tarn pass continues the trend of Mickleden, the highest section of Great Langdale, and both follow the line of a shatter belt in the Borrowdale Volcanic Series (page 29). The line of a fault may be seen clearly etched out in the slope of Lingmoor Fell above Bleatarn House (298046). Beyond the tarn the lane falls steeply into Little Langdale; below and to the right a huge glacial step, largely overgrown with bracken and scattered junipers, overhangs the brooks that gather together to join the Brathay. From the junction with the road from the Wrynose Pass return to Ambleside through Little Langdale.

The head of Great Langdale is the starting-off point for a wide variety of mountain walks, details of which may be found in the specialized fell guides, but two modest excursions on foot are recommended to provide a sample of the mountain world. The rocky cones of the Langdale Pikes are most easily reached by the paths that climb steeply through more than a thousand feet on either side of Millbeck (2906; Plate 38b). From the edge of Stickle tarn, a silent corrie lake beneath the stony gullies and precipitous ledges of Pavey Ark, the summit of Harrison Stickle (282073) is reached by an easy scramble across grass and scree. There one could sit for hours through a hot June day above the airy depths of

Langdale contemplating a landscape first broken by Neolithic man in his search for axe-making rock (page 103).

Bowfell (2406) reaches almost three thousand feet and provides an excellent sample of the scenery of the highest mountains in the central Lake District. It is reached in comfort from Stool End (2705) by the broad track up the spur of the Band (2605). From the col at Three Tarns (248060), with a most attractive view westward to the grey-blue profile of the Scafell range, the steepest part of the route winds up the screes below the western crags of Bowfell to the summit – a world of rock slabs and lichens typical of the highest parts of the Borrowdale Volcanic country.

(VII) *By car in High Furness*

High Furness must be one of the most distinctive minor regions of the British Isles, a region where the work of man in shaping the landscape can be most clearly traced. The landscape of Furness today is the product of monks and statesmen, eighteenth-century forgemasters, Victorian estate-owners and the modern scientific forester.

Take the Coniston road out of Ambleside, and at Clappersgate (3603), used at the end of the eighteenth century as a port for loading Langdale slate on to barges that plied down Windermere, follow the lane across the Brathay towards Hawkshead. For the first two miles the road is closed in by the boundary of Brathay Hall or else tall and close-growing birch coppice. The gentle descent into Hawkshead from Outgate (3599) is through a landscape of hummocky drumlins and scattered white-washed farms much of which was colonized at the close of the monastic era in High Furness (page 177). As one approaches Hawkshead Hall (349988), once the grange of Furness Abbey (page 161), some slate fences still survive by the road. Hawkshead, perhaps the most attractive little town in the Lake District, is worth detailed exploration, and the view from the churchyard set against the background of the smooth eastern fells sums up many of the aspects of High Furness (page 215).

The route from Hawkshead threads through the lanes on the western shore of Windermere as far as Lakeside (3787). The views are nearly all 'close-ups' – dappled light on water through trees, the silver-grey and green barriers of coppice wood, tall conifers and pocket-handkerchief patches of heath, but slow and detailed exploration uncovers much of interest. First follow road B5285 along the eastern shore of Esthwaite Water to the hamlet of Far Sawrey (3795). Esthwaite Water is a beautifully irregular lake where green drumlins and the intervening hollows make a complex pattern of peninsulas and bays. On the opposite shore is the site of Hawkshead's former common field. These are the landscapes of the young Wordsworth and the setting of Beatrix Potter's charming fantasies (page 276). Take the lane southwards from Far Sawrey to Cunsey Wood (3893); here a footpath leads to the right to the site of Cunsey Forge (376936; page 82). Continue southwards for four miles to Low Stott Park (3788) and then branch right to Lakeside (3787). With its bobbin mill that was still working in 1968 on the edge of a stream and lost in coppice wood, Low Stott Park is a rare relic of the once widespread industries of High Furness (Plate 16b). Lakeside likewise with its abandoned railway terminus, is a relic of tourism in the nineteenth century.

From Lakeside make for the trunk road, A590, at Newby Bridge (3686), and continue along the Leven valley to Haverthwaite, a place name that is only one of the many pieces of evidence for the weight of Scandinavian settlement in High Furness (page 146). On the way diverge from the busy arterial road to drive through Backbarrow (3584), an industrial hamlet with grey slate cottages and little factories from the water power era (page 85) (Plate 16c). Backbarrow iron works, perhaps the greatest name in the industrial history of Furness, crumbles into decay and cries out for preservation as one of Britain's most notable monuments of the Industrial Revolution. At Haverthwaite (3483) begin a section on minor roads and lanes that ends at the foot of Coniston Water, passing through Bouth (3385), a place that held markets until the early nineteenth century, and Spark Bridge (3084) – an early industrial site that is still active (page 87). Between Spark Bridge and High Nibthwaite (2989) the lane follows the east bank of the River Crake, with patches of coppice wood on the steep slopes above and extinct water-mill sites along the river at Lowick Bridge (2986) and Blawith (2988). On approaching the lake the lane threads its way through moraines and across a rock bar, features seen to better advantage on the main road, A5084, along the west side of the valley.

The return to Hawkshead and Ambleside should be made by continuing along the eastern side of Coniston Water, a road that presents a succession of delightful prospects of the Old Man massif across the lake. Between the head of Coniston Water and Barngates Inn (3501) a number of 'grounds', late-medieval farmsteads, lie close to the road (page 177). On rejoining B5286 return to Ambleside through Clappersgate.

(VIIa) Along this route an interesting diversion may be made from Hawkshead to Grizedale (3394), close to the head of one of the secluded interior valleys of High Furness, to follow the Nature Trail that begins at the Hall (336943).

Ambleside has a rich variety of excursions in the valleys and on the higher fells, as the leisurely Victorian tourists who occupied a centre for a month or more well realized. Today the trunk road from Windermere and on through Rydal and Grasmere is utterly ruined by its ceaseless flow of traffic, but at least it gives access to some of the finest things that the Lake District has to offer. For instance, the lane that wriggles steeply up to Troutbeck (4103) from near the Low Wood Hotel (387018) gives unusual views along almost the whole length of Windermere. Troutbeck itself, a string of hamlets that extends for more than a mile, has some fine examples of statesmen farms from the great period of re-building in stone (page 186) (Plate 22a). On from Troutbeck one can explore on foot the site of a medieval deer park and follow the trail of the Roman Road up the steep flank of Froswick (4308) to the precipice-hedged summit of High Street (4411; page 122).

The Vale of Grasmere offers an even greater variety of excursions on either side of its obnoxious trunk road. To the west, Easedale (3208) provides a route to the summits of the Langdale Pikes. To the east, starting at Rydal, an excellent mountain circuit in the scenery of the eastern fells can be made over Fairfield (3511). On the steady climb over Nab Scar to Heron Pike (3508) the traces of a medieval deer fence (page 167) are still visible on the ground (Plate 23a). Away to the right the valley of the Rydal Beck (3608) is totally devoid of settlement, a feature probably resulting from its preservation as a hunting-ground until a late date. Long gentle spurs with fine views lead up to the summit of Fairfield, where the ground drops away in a precipice to Ullswater's tangle of valleys. Return to Grasmere by the steep western spur of Fairfield, knobbly rock outcrops and much scree, to Grisedale Hause (3411) and the Old Packhorse Road – a busy trail two hundred years ago. A car parked at Rydal for the beginning of this circuit can be regained without suffering the baleful effects of other people's cars in a walk along the main road. Grasmere can be reached by a quiet lane on the west side of the Rothay across Goody Bridge (333080), and on to Rydal by the attractive old road and footpath, past Dove cottage, above the present main road along the lake.

KENDAL AND THE SOUTH-EASTERN FRINGE OF THE LAKE DISTRICT (Map 35)

The towns of Westmorland and Cumberland – small, compact and modest in their architectural features – reflect the anatomy of the landscapes in which they have evolved. Keswick and Ambleside are slate towns; Penrith has used the red sandstones of local quarries, and Kendal is almost entirely a light-grey town of

Carboniferous Limestone hewn from the quarries of the common on Kendal Fell to the west (5092). Kendal has much of interest, with the site of its Roman fort, *Alavna,* inside a meander loop of the Kent (page 118), two castles of which one crowns a drumlin and gives a magnificent prospect of the town, and a miniature industrial quarter, again in silver-grey limestone, focused on the terminal basin of the long-derelict Lancaster canal (page 221) (Plate 33).

(VIII) *By car to Windermere and the upper Kent Valley*
This journey through quiet, twisting high-banked lanes shows samples of the lower country of the Carboniferous Limestone and Silurian rocks fringing Morecambe Bay and concludes with a valley that reaches into the eastern fells. Take the minor road westward from the centre of Kendal towards Underbarrow (4692). Quarries that were the source of most of Kendal's building stone are passed on the right (5092) and soon the lane drops into a flat-floored *polje* in the Carboniferous Limestone (page 38) before climbing steeply to the summit of the escarpment of Underbarrow Scar (4892). Patches of limestone pavement occur on the summit of the escarpment, and as the road winds down its face brief glimpses appear of the Silurian landscape ahead – a landscape of confused rocky hillocks and glacial debris, bosky with rambling lanes and scattered whitewashed farms.

From the foot of Underbarrow Scar trace a route through the lanes to Bowland Bridge (4189) by way of Thorns Villa (4791), Grigghall (4691), Church Town (4491), Crosthwaite Green (4391) and High Birks (4290). This is one of the beautiful and half-forgotten tracts of the English countryside. The limestone escarpments of Underbarrow and Whitbarrow stand nobly above the crumpled complexities of the Silurian landscape. At Bowland Bridge a stiff climb with hairpin bends begins into the higher, heavily glaciated hills at the southern end of Windermere. Coppice wood gives way to plantations of conifers, and at the start of the steep descent to the lake-shore a fine view of the south-western Coniston Fells across High Furness is opened up (388876). This is one of the best places from which one can appreciate the nature of High Furness, a region of dissected and forested hills. On reaching the main road, A592, turn northwards towards Bowness. This part of the route to Windermere shows the influence of the Victorians in the making of the landscape of the Lake District even more deeply than the Keswick region. Until the last quarter of the eighteenth century this was a region of scattered farms; the chief settlement was the hamlet of Bowness gathered around its fifteenth-century church. The shores of Windermere, as Wordsworth so clearly describes in his *Guide*, were composed of pastures and

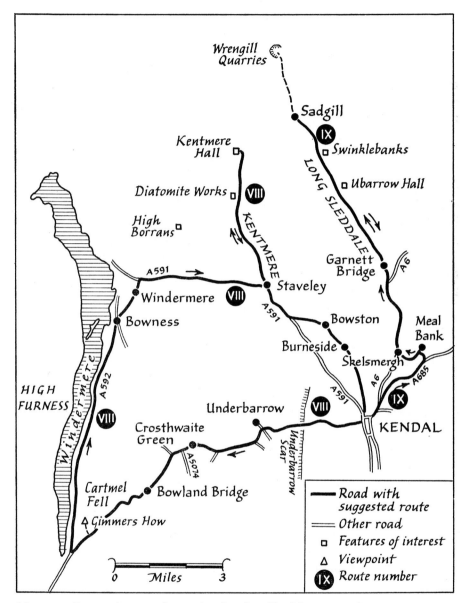

Map 35 *Routes of suggested excursions based on Kendal.*

open heath with sparsely scattered gnarled oaks and clumps of holly, the latter preserved for winter fodder and the former severely depleted through the seventeenth century with the demand for charcoal (page 82). Today, the rich woodlands that screen the road from the lake and conceal the surrounding hills are the work of improving landlords a century ago (page 81). The pinnacles and towers of the Victorian gothic and 'italianate' hotels and residences of Bowness and Windermere are the product of nineteenth-century tourism and the attractions of Windermere for the magnates of the North's industrial regions – ironmasters from Barrow-in-Furness, shipping-owners of Liverpool, and textile manufacturers of the West Riding and Manchester. The invasion of Windermere by the businessman's estate began in 1774 with the building of a cylindrical house, domed and with Ionic columns, on Belle Isle (3996). Wordsworth raged about plantations and the intrusion of alien styles of architecture into the Lake District, but Belle Isle's transformation marked the beginning of a distinctive phase in the making of the Lake District's landscape. Windermere Town (4198) expanded with the coming of the railway (page 241) in 1847, and the railway terminus and the lake port at Bowness grew together as an untidy miniature conurbation by the end of the nineteenth century.

From Windermere follow the main road A591 to Staveley (4698). A mile from Windermere a diversion can be made to the hamlet of High Borrans (4301) and its deserted Iron Age/Dark Age settlement (page 117). Staveley, a former market centre and with some good early mill sites along the rivers (page 88), is the starting-point for exploring the upper Kent valley. The Kentmere basin (4503), site of a former lake, has a ruined fourteenth-century pele tower overhung with trees at the Old Hall (4504; page 174), a deserted settlement on the eastern shoulder above the level valley floor at Millrigg (4502; page 129), and the diatomite works exploiting the sediments of the former lake (456020; page 240). At the head of the valley above Kentmere and the hamlet of Green Quarter (4604), the scenery changes dramatically as the softer Silurian country gives way to the crags and rock-scarred topography of the Borrowdale Volcanic Series. Return to Staveley and take the main road to Kendal. Cowen Head (4997) and Burneside (5095) water-mill sites can be reached down lanes to the left of the main road (page 253), and an excellent view of drumlin scenery in the Kent basin is revealed on the final descent into the town (500944).

(IX) *By car to Long Sleddale*
A short excursion from Kendal to Long Sleddale illustrates, perhaps even more beautifully than the upper Kent Valley, the scenery of the eastern fells. The first
318

section to Garnett Bridge (5299) may be used to study the landforms of glacial deposition (page 53) and the sites of several water-mills in a region that for a brief time was an important centre of the Industrial Revolution. Leave Kendal by the Appleby road, A685, and after about a mile follow the lane to the left at Spital (528944) as far as Meal Bank, a romantically attractive industrial hamlet (page 254). Retrace the route as far as Laverock Bridge (535952), and then continue on the north side of the river Mint through the hamlet of Skelsmergh (5395), amid a tumbled collection of drumlins, to join the trunk road, A6. Turn northwards in the direction of Shap and after a little more than two miles drop away steeply down a narrow lane to the left into Garnett Bridge (5299), another hamlet that was associated with industry. For the next four miles farmsteads, mainly of seventeenth-century origin (Plate 34a), follow each other along the valley, standing alone or clustered in tiny hamlets. The road meets the valley floor above the gorge that gave power to Garnett Bridge, and on the opposite flank, close to Nether House (5100), there is a pasture full of uncleared boulders and bracken that preserves an image of Long Sleddale from the days before the period of slow and painful medieval colonization. As one enters the middle part of the dale about Ubarrow Hall (5002) the course of the River Sprint has been straightened through a badly drained former lake-floor. High House (5001) has a mock pele tower, a far outpost of the Victorian gothic of Windermere, but at Ubarrow Hall the core of the statesman farm (page 174) is a genuine fifteenth-century pele (Plate 34c). This section of the valley closes with a rock bar, plastered with moraine, that provides the site for the church that was rebuilt in 1863 to replace a medieval chapel. Ubarrow Hall and the church-site suggest that this section of the valley was the core of settlement in medieval Long Sleddale.

Above the rock bar and shallow gorge the valley widens again (Plate 36b); its gentle lower slopes are extensively covered with morainic material. Whitewashed farmhouses and rubble barns follow each other in the Swinklebanks (4904). At High Swinklebank the massive byre still has the remnant of an overhanging verandah so characteristic of Lake District farms (Plate 34a). Sadgill (4805), the highest settlement in the valley, is a hamlet of three farms screened by trees. The river cuts through a narrow belt of moraine above Sadgill, and in the valley floor, behind and higher than the moraine, there are traces of a little common field once shared by the farms of the hamlet. The highest section of Long Sleddale belongs to the wilder scenery of the Borrowdale Volcanic Series (page 52). The road degenerates and winds its way up the edge of a five-hundred-foot-high rock step to the basin of Wren Gill (4708) and its abandoned slate quarries. Return by the valley road and A6 to Kendal.

ESKDALE AND THE WESTERN LAKE DISTRICT (Map 36)

The most westerly parts of the Lake District have both suffered and gained from their comparative isolation. Ennerdale, Wasdale and Eskdale were brushed only lightly by Victorian tourism. They lacked the accessibility of Keswick and Windermere and could offer none of the cultural attractions that the names of Wordsworth and Ruskin gave to the vale of Grasmere and the shores of Coniston Water. The great advantage of the western valleys is their quiet and unspoilt character and the overshadowing presence of the Lake District's wildest and most rugged mountains. Even today the most direct access to the region is along the route pioneered by the Romans across the Wrynose and Hardnott passes from Ambleside. The approaches by trunk roads are long indeed – from the south by Newby Bridge (3786) and Broughton-in-Furness (2187) or from the north by Cockermouth (1230) and Egremont. Only the building of a Morecambe Bay barrage and the construction of a motorway into the Furness peninsula would revolutionise the communications of west Cumberland.

(X) *By car in Eskdale*

The details of Eskdale can be explored with ease from centres around Ambleside, if the traveller has not chosen to make a longer stay at one of the comfortable farms or inns in the valley. Approaching from the east by the steep wriggling pitches of the Hardknott Pass a fine view of the whole of Eskdale, with the Irish Sea in the distance, opens up from the summit (Plate 28b). Its character as a valley without a lake is at once established in this prospect. An even better panorama of the whole valley may be gained by leaving the road at the summit of the pass and climbing steeply for some four hundred feet and half-an-hour's walking time to the rocky spur of Hardknott (227018) that looks down on to the Roman fort. This ranks among the finest view-points of the Lake District, an airy summit sprinkled with tiny pools and slabs of bare rock that looks into the depths of upper Eskdale and across to the semicircle of peaks from the Scafell range to Bowfell and Crinkle Crags. The bare upper valley, the property of Furness Abbey in the Middle Ages (page 159), contrasts with the scattered farms and patchwork of woods and tiny fields in lower Eskdale.

Descend the western flanks of Hardknott Pass, stopping on the way to explore the remains of the Roman fort (2101). At the foot of the hill a lane leads to the right for a quarter of a mile to Brotherilkeld (2101), a typical statesman farm (page 159). It can be made the starting point for a two-mile walk up the valley to Throstle Garth (227036). The track skirts a well-marked series of lake terraces (page 57) and passes below the aprons of rock scree below Yew Crags (page 57) to reach the simple arched packhorse bridge of slate over the Lingcove Beck (227036) – a relic of an older system of communications in the Lake District when packhorse trains used the mountain trails (Plate 28a).

Return to Brotherilkeld and follow the lane westward towards Boot (1701), the only settlement of any size in the valley. From the Woolpack Inn (1801) the road runs through a former valley of the Esk, and the river now flows to the south beyond a rocky howe in a shallow wooded gorge. It is worthwhile to step aside from the road at Boot by the narrow track that leads down to the river and the site of the little dale chapel, dedicated to St Catherine and with its nave and chancel in one. Boot is near the terminus of the light railway that serves

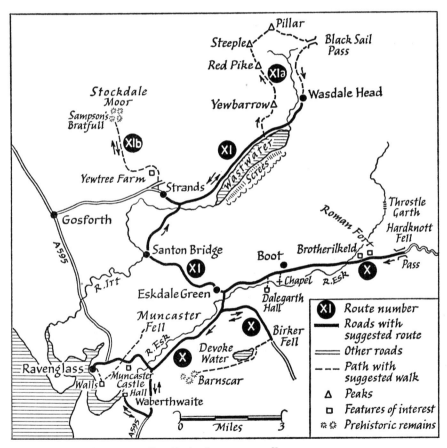

Map 36 *Car journeys and walks in the western valleys.*

Eskdale and is busy with summer tourist traffic from Ravenglass; on the hillside above Dalegarth station are the scars of the iron-ore working that was one of the main reasons for the construction of the railway. A quarter of a mile beyond the railway terminus and its parking ground a lane leads across the Esk, to the left, to Dalegarth Hall (1600), a sixteenth-century farmhouse with magnificent round chimneys and the oldest domestic building in the valley. Below Boot and on towards Eskdale Green the main road passes through the scenery of the Eskdale granite (page 36).

At the approach to Eskdale Green (149998) a road leads southwards to Ulpha (1993) which gives the motorist a chance to taste the scenery of the fells that enclose Eskdale. From Birker Fell (1797), at more than eight hundred feet, there is a magnificent view northwards to Scafell and, nearer at hand, the heavily glaciated 'moon landscape' of the Borrowdale Volcanic Series around Harter Fell. Here, too, at Birkerthwaite (1798) and High Ground we find the upper limit of medieval colonization – farms that are now decayed and ruined in the twentieth century. At the cross-road on Birker Fell (171977) it is worthwhile, if time allows, to leave the road and walk south-westwards to Devoke Water and on to the prehistoric settlement of Barnscar (1396). Return towards Eskdale Green and take the minor road to the left a third of a mile below Field Head (1599).

Lower Eskdale is best explored by the lane that follows the south bank of the valley linking a number of farms, Linbeck (1498), Knott End (1397) and Cropple How (1297). The landscape now takes on an unspoilt pastoral quality that is one of the least appreciated aspects of the Lake District's landscape but which can be enjoyed in all its border regions. After reaching the main road that joins Whitehaven to Millom (A595; grid ref. 1196) drive south for almost a mile and a half and then diverge to the right along the narrow lane to Hall Waberthwaite (1095). Here, beside the wide curving tidal estuary of the Esk, a low white church and a manor farm mark the centre of one of the primary parishes of Cumberland (page 169). Times have changed and the traffic that once used the ford at this point to enter Ravenglass has long since been diverted to the road bridge upstream or the seaward railway viaduct. The fragments of a carved cross in the churchyard speak of Christianity here before the Norman Conquest. From the seclusion of Hall Waberthwaite retrace the route to the main road and drive northwards through Muncaster (page 202) to the port and former market town of Ravenglass (0896). This is the urban equivalent of Hall Waberthwaite, a place bereft of its former life – an empty market street that ends abruptly with a view across the sheltered creek to the tumbled line of sand-dunes that separate this former Roman port from the Irish Sea. Ravenglass should not be visited without seeing Walls (088958 – in its modest way one of the most impressive Roman buildings in the North of England (Plate 31b). Ravenglass, in turn, can be made the centre for a walk that leads through Muncaster Park, past Walls, to the summit of Muncaster Fell (1198), with its fine panorama towards the mountains at the head of Wasdale.

(XI) *By car to Wasdale*

Wasdale, the most austere of the Lake District's valleys and, apart from Ennerdale, the least accessible, may be taken in as an extension of the tour of Eskdale. Diverge from the previous route at Eskdale Green (1499) and follow the main road north-westward across the Mite (132003) and on to Santon Bridge (1101), a hamlet and former industrial site on the Irt. Turn right before crossing the river and follow the road towards Wasdale through a complex topography of huge roches moutonnées and scattered morainic deposits (page 59). After a mile and a half and the crossing of the Irt turn left into Strands (1204), the hamlet of Lower Wasdale with a simple rectangular-shaped dale chapel. A quarter of a mile beyond Strands take the right turn (121045) to join the lane from Gosforth that leads into Wasdale.

The half-dozen miles to Wasdale Head reveal a magnificent succession of prospects of lake and mountain. For the first section, until the lane runs down to the edge of the lake, there are excellent views to the right across the low hummocky platform that was the scene of late-medieval colonization in the wilderness of Copeland Forest (page 163). At Wasdale Head (1808) is the overpowering presence of mountains, perhaps more than anywhere else in the Lake District that is accessible by car. It is worth some exploration in detail, with its simple dale chapel, dark-shaded by trees on brilliant summer days, the traces of a former common field (page 193) (Plate 26b), and everywhere amid the tiny patches of green pasture the huge heaps of stone that speak of the painful clearance of this land eight centuries ago (page 180) (Plate 26a).

(XIa) The heads of both Eskdale and Wasdale are accessible only on foot. Fortunately there are no linking motor roads across the high central passes of the Lake District to Borrowdale and Langdale, and let us hope that this will always remain so. The full enjoyment of the Lake District has always depended upon exploration on foot and this is particularly true of Eskdale and Wasdale, from which tracks lead to Scafell Pikes and Great Gable. Wasdale, too, is on the edge of some beautiful and little frequented mountain scenery. The gnarled spine of Yewbarrow (1708) is a fine belvedere facing the highest peaks of the north-west. From there a ridge walk of increasing grandeur can culminate on Pillar (1712), with its prospect into the Forestry Commission's green desolation of Eskdale; return by Black Sail Pass (1911) and the track that follows the lower slopes of Kirk Fell to Wasdale Head.

(XIb) At a lower level and in the one-time hunting preserve of Copeland Forest we find an important area of prehistoric settlement on Stockdale Moor (0908). It is approached on foot from Strands (1204) by following the track that climbs the fellside above Yewtree Farm (1105), across Hollow Moor and Brown Edge (1006). After the crossing of the Bleng (099073) climb towards the summit of Stockdale Moor and the site at 900 ft littered with the relics of prehistory. Here one is reminded of the problems of the Lake District's settlement history with clusters of prehistoric cairns preserved within the confines of a medieval deer forest – a tract of country that was closed to settlement until the seventeenth century. Amid the faint overgrown hillocks on Stockdale Moor stands Sampson's Bratfull (0908), a burial mound ninety-six feet long and standing to a height of six feet, that has remained up to now unexplored by archaeologists but which points back to the earliest stage of settlement in the Lake District when Neolithic man was exploiting the hard rocks of Scafell and Great Langdale.

Conclusion

In the foregoing pages we have tried to identify and analyse the many different elements that together make up the landscape of the Lake District and contribute to its regional personality. The various elements of the Lake District's scenery have been shaped at moments of time that range from the earliest epochs of the geological time-scale to the present hour. The major landscape features result from the forces of Nature operating through aeons of time, but equally important is Man himself, an agent in landscape history over the past five thousand years.

The unique qualities of the Lake District as a region cannot be ascribed to any of the individual elements of its landscape. The shaggy terrain of the Borrowdale Volcanics can be matched in the mountains of Snowdonia, and the dramatic weather changes of the region are a feature that the Lake District shares with the whole of the mountainous seaboard of Western Europe. Norse place-name elements and sturdy stone-built farms with a long-house plan are found far beyond the confines of the Lake District in the Pennines and the Hebrides. So, too, the traces of former common fields that seem to be one of the distinctive elements of the Lake District's landscape form an important trait in the rural geography of much of northern Britain. The individuality of the Lake District as a region rests in the union of these disparate elements. Climb to any of the mountain summits on a clear day – Fairfield or Great Gable, Skiddaw or the Old Man of Coniston – and the individuality of the Lake District is revealed, or at least part of this complex character. The long line of the northern Pennines to the east with the bold plateau of Cross Fell and the distinctive table-top of Ingleborough reveals a region separate and distinct from the Lake District, whilst to the west glimpses of the West Cumberland plain point to a tract whose evolution has been detached from the neighbouring mountains, particularly by the forces of the Industrial

Revolution. The unit is composed of mountains that rise to a dissected summit plain at almost three thousand feet above sea-level enfolding a circle of deep, glaciated, lake-filled valleys. Ice shaped the uplands, and from the beginnings of the Bronze Age men were engaged in the long process of forest clearance that made the barren, treeless landscapes of the Lake District that we know today – for many the very essence of the region. Over all the Norse men who carved their summer farms out of this wilderness in the tenth century threw a net of Scandinavian place names, a feature that personifies the region in the minds of so many lovers of the Cumberland and Westmorland hills. Although it is possible to delineate the features of the upland Lake District in detail, to distinguish the rock-strewn spine of Scafell from the corrie-scarred ridge of Helvellyn or flat-topped Fairfield from the heathery cone of Harter Fell, the full range of variety in the region's personality can only be appreciated when one comes to explore the depths of its valleys. Here the dimension of history is superimposed upon the differences inherent in the nature of the valleys. The topography of Borrowdale owes its individuality not only to Ice Age glaciers that engaged their strength with coarse, hard volcanic rocks and finally receded leaving a succession of moraines in the valley floor, but also to the presence of a prehistoric fort on Castle Crag, the clearings of Viking farmers, and the ownership of this dale by Fountains and Furness Abbeys in the later Middle Ages. Not least the growth of tourism towards the end of the eighteenth century and the large-scale plantations around Derwentwater in the first half of the nineteenth century added further distinctive elements to the personality of the valley. Ennerdale, on the other hand, owes the chief feature of its personality to the twentieth century with the extensive plantations of conifers by the Forestry Commission. Persons too have left their marks on places in the Lake District. The Wordsworths and 'the Wordsworth industry' are one of the elements in the personality of Grasmere, just as the dour character of Ruskin seems to fit in with a Coniston whose totality includes ruined cottages and the forlorn waste-heaps of abandoned slate quarries and copper mines.

One can identify and classify the elements that together compose the individuality of the Lake District as a region, but when this task is complete there remains that other Lake District that must be different for every person, the regional synthesis that is the result of one's own experience. We each make our own Lake District. For one of the writers of this book it can be expressed as an accumulation of such personal impressions. There is the Lake District seen from afar – grey-blue mountains crowned with evening cloud from the ridge of Cross Fell, or the Buttermere Fells distant across the sea on a spring morning from the northernmost tip of the Isle of Man. In memory, too, the Lake District is inevitably an experience of weather. The August days when a lid of cloud encloses each valley and the conifers and crags of Thirlmere disappear amid curtains of grey rain contrast with those rarer memories of hazy summer heat on the Langdale Pikes with the depths of Mickleden blurred and remote, lost in sunlight. It is the extremes of the Lake District's climate that loom largest in the memory. So often the mountain summits seem grey and directionless, lost in cloud, but there are the rare occasions when the tops ride clear of a sea of fog and valley mist. On such a day from Helvellyn the western peaks take on the primitive, ice-riven shapes of the mountain landscapes of eastern Greenland or northern Norway. Again, the not infrequent spells of heavy rain, ceaseless downpours for thirty-six or forty-eight hours, produce another impression of the Lake District. Every gully and cranny above Great Langdale streams with water and the flooded fields in the level valley floor raise a passing image of its vanished lake. Again, the sudden onset of polar maritime air in spring can cover the mountain summits with snow in a night of storm, and the ring of summits in upper Eskdale take on, however fleetingly, something of the majesty of the Alps.

Deep in one's impressions and memories of the Lake District there lies an awareness of the very textures of the landscape – the tumbled masses of rough rock on Scafell Pike, the loose-running screes spilling over the tops of boots as one glides down from Dorehead into upper Wasdale, or the cold enveloping rock of Deep Ghyll that leads one up to the airy summit of Scafell. Down the centuries men have used these native textures and materials to express their own needs and purposes. In the mind the Lake District is barns of dark shapeless natural boulders dragged from stream beds and grubbed up from tiny fields in the process of land-clearance. Its little Victorian towns are gaunt, blue-grey and dark green, in wafer-like slabs of slate. This countryside draws the mind to the very beginnings of the region's history. At Threlkeld the faint grass-grown hummocks of a deserted Dark Age settlement lie beneath the sombre mass of Blencathra, while in the south-west, on Heaves Fell, you can walk in the brilliant light and long shadows of a June evening among the walls and enclosures of a Bronze Age village. Here, under a sky brilliantly coloured in the north and against a background of violet mountains, one feels the wide gap of time between the prehistoric beginnings of the Lake District and the present suddenly closed. It is in such moments that one grasps, however briefly, the meaning of the region. The facts are forgotten and the landscape and its history become a presence.

Selected glossary of place names with their derivation and meaning

Abbreviations: [OB] Old British; [ON] Old Norse; [OE] Old English; [OI] Old Irish; [ME] Middle English; [M] Medieval.

AIRA BECK [ON], gravel-bank stream.
AMBLESIDE [ON], shieling by the river sandbank.
ASHNESS BRIDGE [ON], ash headland.
ASKHAM [OE], the farm at the ash trees.
AUGHERTREE [OE], the old cottage on the boundary.

BAMPTON [OE], the farmstead made of beams or the farm near a tree.
BAND, THE. Modern English dialect, meaning a long ridge running down from a higher mountain.
BANNERDALE [ON], valley with the holly trees.
BANNISDALE [ON], the forbidding valley.
BARTON [OE], the barley farm.
BASSENTHWAITE, first recorded in 1220 as Bastunwater – the lake of *Bastun*, an Anglo-French surname.
BAYSBROWN [ON], Brúni's cowshed.
BIRKERTHWAITE [ON], the clearing in the birches.
BLEA TARN [ON], dark tarn.
BLENG, RIVER [ON], dark river.
BEELA, RIVER [ON], roaring river.
BLENCATHRA [OB], a name containing the Welsh element *blaen*, 'point or top'. The full word has defeated interpretation.
BLENCOGO [OB] and [ON], the hill-top with the cuckoos.
BLINDCRAKE [OB], the rocky summit, named after Clints Crag a mile to the north-east.

328

BOOT [ME], derived from 'bend' or 'turn', possibly indicative of a change in the direction of Eskdale.

BOOTLE [OE], building.

BOREDALE [ON], the valley with a barn.

BORROWDALE [ON], the valley of the fortress.

BOTHEL [ON], a building.

BOWDER STONE, a dialect form of 'boulder'. The name first appeared in 1751.

BOWFELL [ON], the arch-shaped mountain.

BOWNESS [OE], bull headland.

BRAITHWAITE [ON], broad clearing.

BRATHAY [ON], the broad river.

BRIGHAM [ON], the *holme* or patch of meadow by the bridge.

BROTHERILKELD [ON], Úlfkell's *booth*, or the summer farm belonging to Úlfkell.

BROUGHAM [OE], the homestead near the fortification.

BROUGHTON [OE], the settlement by the brook.

BURNESIDE [OE], Brunulf's hill.

BUTTERMERE [OE], the pool surrounded by good grazing ground.

CALDBECK [ON], cold stream.

CALDEW [ON], cold river.

CARLETON [ON] and [OE], farm of the free men or peasants.

CARROCK FELL [OB], contains the Old Welsh element as *carrecc*, rock.

CATSTYE CAM [OE], wild cat path along the ridge.

CLAIFE [ON], steep hillside with a path.

CLAPPERSGATE [ON], the road over the rough bridge.

CLIFTON [OE], the farmstead on the steep bank.

COCKER [OB], crooked stream.

COLEDALE HAUSE [ON], the pass at the head of Kalli's valley.

COLTON [OE], Cola's farm.

CONISTON [ON], the king's *tun* or settlement.

CRAKE [OB], the rocky stream.

CROGLINHURST [ON] and [OE], the clearing by the Croglin, probably the original name of the river Lickle.

CROSTHWAITE, GREAT [ON], the clearing marked by a cross.

CRUMMOCK WATER [OB], the first element is from the Old British word, *crumbaco*, crooked.

CUMBERLAND, land of the Cymry, the Welsh.

DACRE [OB], trickling stream, with the settlement named from the adjacent beck.

DALEGARTH [ON], the clearing in the valley.

DERWENT, RIVER [OB], abounding in oaks.

DERWENTWATER, takes its name from the river.

DEVOKE WATER [OB], the black one.

DODD [ME], rounded hill.

DUDDON, a difficult word of uncertain meaning. It has been interpreted as containing the Old British *dubo*, black, or else an Old English personal name, *Dudd*.

DUNGEON GHYLL, 'dungeon', a modern element referring to the fissures in the valley side.

DUNMAIL RAISE, the first element refers to Dunmail, a tenth-century king of Strathclyde. Raise is from the Old Norse, meaning a cairn.

EAMONT, RIVER [OE], literally a 'junction of streams', possibly with reference to the valley near Eamont Bridge where the Lowther and Eamont rivers run close together for about a mile.

EDEN [OB], from a word with deep linguistic roots meaning 'water'.

ELLONBY [ME], Alein's settlement, dating from colonization in the twelfth century.

ELTERWATER [ON], lake of the swan.

ESKDALE [ON], valley of the Esk. Great uncertainty exists about the meaning of *Esk*. It is either Old Norse *eski*, ash, or is derived from the British river name *Isca*.

ESTHWAITE WATER [ON], the lake by the clearing in the ash trees.

FAIRFIELD [OE], 'a pleasant stretch of open country', probably referring to the extensive level summit.

FINSTHWAITE [ON], Finn's clearing.

FRIAR'S CRAG, first recorded in West's *Guide*, 1789.

FURNESS [ON], the headland with an island.

FUSEDALE [ON], the valley with a cattle shed.

GATESGARTH [ON], the pass of the goats, probably with reference to the approach to the Honister Pass.

GILCRUX [OB], retreat by a hill.

GILPIN, RIVER, probably derived from a similar surname common in Westmorland from the thirteenth century, but there is no satisfactory interpretation of the word.

GLARAMARA [ON], the shieling at the head of the ravine.

GLENCOYNE [OB], the valley of the reeds.

GLENRIDDING [OB], bracken valley.

GOLDSCOPE, from the German *Gottesgab*, God's gift.

GOWK HILL [ON], cuckoo hill.

GRAINS GILL [ON], shieling on a tributary valley.

GRANGE, a monastic farm belonging to Furness Abbey.

GRASMERE [OE], lake with grassy shores.

GREAT END, first recorded in the sixteenth century as *Wastall great ende*; it refers to the precipitous rock buttress at the northern end of the Scafell range.

GREAT GABLE [ON], from *gafl* meaning gable which aptly describes the triangular shape of the mountain.

GREAT MELL [OB], bare hill.

GREENODD [ON], the green promontory.

GRETA, RIVER [ON], the rocky stream.

GREYSTOKE [OB] and [OE], the enclosure by the hill.

GRISEDALE [ON], valley where young pigs are reared.

HACKTHORPE [ON] and [OE], Haki's hamlet, with the ending *thorpe* pointing to a secondary or daughter settlement.

HARDKNOTT [ON], craggy hill.

HARRISON STICKLE, named after the local family of Harrison and first recorded in the sixteenth century: *sticel*, a steep slope.

HARRY PLACE, first recorded in the seventeenth century and named after the Harrison family c.f. Harrison Stickle.

HARTER FELL [ON], fell with the deer.

HARTSOP [OE], valley of the deer.

HAVERTHWAITE [ON], the clearing with the oats.

HAWES WATER [OE], Haeger's lake.

HAWKSHEAD [ON], the dairy farm of Haukr.

HAYSTACKS, a modern name given by the dalesmen to the likeness of the topography to hay-ricks.

HELM, THE [OE], the summit of a hill, usually given to a long narrow ridge.

HELSINGTON [OE], a primary name of uncertain meaning but usually interpreted as 'the farmstead of those dwelling on the pass'.

HELTON [OE], farmstead on the slope.

HELVELLYN, although an early name, the first record dates from 1577 and so exact derivation is impossible.

HESKET NEWMARKET [ON], the first element means 'the place overgrown with ash trees'.

HEVERSHAM [OE], Heahfrid's homestead.

HIGH BORRANS, the second element is from the Old English *burgaesn*, a heap of stones or burial place. The name often points to a deserted site.

HIGH SCAWDELL [ON], the bare mountain at the head of the valley.

HIGH STREET, a late name for the Roman road that runs along the ridge top above Haweswater at more than 2,000 ft. Also used for the mountain at highest point of the route.

HINCASTER [OE], the latter element suggests a Roman fortification that has remained undiscovered.

HONISTER [ON], a later recorded name that means Huni's settlement.

HOWK, THE, a great cave or grotto, a reference to the feature in the limestone gorge. The name is first recorded in 1777.

HOWTOWN [ON], the settlement near the hill.

HUTTON ROOF [OE], the settlement on the summit of a hill. The second element has been explained topographically or as a personal name, *Rolf*.

INGLEWOOD FOREST [OE], forest of the Angles.

IREBY [ON], settlement of the Irishmen.

IRT, RIVER [OB], fresh or green river.

JOHNBY [ME], the settlement of John, a twelfth-century colony.

KAILPOT CRAG, an eighteenth-century name meaning 'cabbage pot' so called from the cavity cut in solid blue rock.

KELD [ON], a spring.

KENT, RIVER [OB], an ancient name whose exact meaning is unknown.

KENDAL [ON], formerly Kirkby Kendal, the village with a church.

KELTON [ON], settlement near the spring.

KESKADALE [ON], the valley by Ketil's shieling.

KESWICK [OE], village or dairy farm where cheese is made.

LACRA [ON], the secluded place with garlic.

LAMONBY [ME] settlement of Lambert, probably a twelfth-century colony.

LANGDALE [OE] and [ON], the long valley.

LANTHWAITE [ON], the long clearing.

LATRIGG [OE], the hill with the open field.

LAXONBY [ON], the settlement of the freemen.

LEVEN, RIVER [OB], the word contains the British element meaning 'elm'.

LICKLE, RIVER [ON], a river with loops or meanders.

LODORE [ON], the low gap.

LONG SLEDDALE [ON], the long valley.

LORTON, a difficult name of uncertain meaning: possibly the first element is a Norse stream name.

LOUGHRIGG [OE], the ridge above the lake.

LOWESWATER [ON], leafy lake.

LOWTHER, RIVER [ON], a foaming river.

MARDALE [ON], the valley with a lake.

MARTINDALE, associated with the church of St Martin.

MAYBOROUGH [OE], the maiden's fort, a reference to the Bronze Age earthwork.

MICKLEDEN [OE], the large valley.

MICKLEDORE [OE], the large gap.

MINT, RIVER [OB], the noisy river.

MITE, RIVER [OB], a name that incorporates the root *meigh*, to urinate.

MOSEDALE [ON], valley with a bog.

MOSSER [ON], shieling on the moss.

MOTHERBY [ON], the mother's settlement.

MUNCASTER [OE] or [ON], a personal name joined to the Old English *caester*, a Roman fort – a reference to Ravenglass.

MUNGRISDALE [ON], the valley of the pigs. The reference to St Mungo is a later addition.

NADDLE FOREST [ON], from *Naddr*, meaning point or wedge, a reference to the ridge-like form of the topography.

NATLAND [ON], Natti's wood.

NEWLAND [ME], land newly taken into cultivation; first reference is in 1318.

OLD MAN OF CONISTON, a name first recorded in the eighteenth century. *Man* probably refers to the summit cairn.

OUSBY [ON], Úlfr's settlement.

OXENHOLME [ON], the water meadow where oxen are pastured.

PAPCASTLE [ON] and [OE], literally 'the castle of the hermit': probably refers to the use of the ruins of the Roman fort at Deventio by a hermit in the Dark Ages.

PARKAMOOR [ME], the enclosure on the moor.

PATTERDALE [OI and ON], Patrick's valley.

PENRITH [OB], the head of the ford.

PENRUDDOCK [OB], the first element *pen*, means 'head' or 'chief'. The second is a form of the word *rhyd*, meaning 'ford'.

PILLAR, an eighteenth-century name descriptive of the mountain.

PLUMBLAND [ON], grove of plum trees.

PORTINSCALE [ON], the shieling of the harlot.

PYE HOWE [ON], the hill of the magpie.

RANNERDALE [ON], the valley of the ravens with the shieling.

RAVENGLASS [OI], the element 'glass' is probably an Irish personal name and the word has been explained as 'Glas's lot or share'.

REDMAIN [OB], the ford of the stones.

RESTON [ME], the farmstead in the brushwood.

ROSGILL [ON], ravine of the horses.

ROSSETT GILL [ON], shieling of the horses.

ROSTHWAITE [ON], clearing with heaps of stones.

RYDAL [ON], valley where rye is grown.

SADDLEBACK, an eighteenth-century name given to Blencathra and descriptive of the shape of the mountain.

SADGILL [ON], ravine with the shieling.

SAINT HERBERT'S ISLAND, an island in Derwentwater that commemorates the seventh-century saint. The name itself is first recorded in the fourteenth century.

SAMPSON'S BRATFULL, a long barrow about which the legend relates that the heap of stones was carried by the devil in an apron, a brat.

SATTERTHWAITE [ON], the clearing with a shieling.

SCAFELL [ON], the bare fell.

SCALES [ON], a shepherd's summer hut.

SEATHWAITE [ON], the clearing amid the sedge.

SEATOLLER [ON], the shieling by the alder tree.

SEAT SANDAL [ON], Sandulf's shieling.

SEDGWICK [OE], Sigg's dairy farm.

SHAP [OE], heap of stones, a reference to the adjacent stone circle.

SIZERGH [ON], Sigrith's shieling or farm.

SKELTON [OE], the settlement on the bench.

SKELMERGH [ON], the dairy farm of Skjaldmar.

SKELWITH [ON], literally 'the ford near the noisy one' – a reference to the waterfall nearby.

SKIDDAW [ON] craggy hill.

SPITAL [M], refers to a hospital for lepers.

SPRINT, RIVER [ON], the bounding stream.

STAINTON [OE], the stone farmstead.

STAVELEY [OE], the wood where staves are cut.

STEEPLE, an eighteenth-century topographical name.

STICKS PASS, the pass with the guide posts.

STOCKLEY BRIDGE [OE], the clearing with the tree stumps.

STOTT PARK [ME], the enclosure for bullocks.

STRANDS [OE], shore or bank, a reference to its site by the river Irt.

STYHEAD [OE], head of the path.

SWINKLEBANK [ON] and [ME], the slope near the spring of the swine.

TALLENTIRE [OB], end of the land.

THIRLMERE [OE], the lake in a hollow.

THORPE [OE] [ON] or [ME], an outlying farm or dependent settlement.

THRELKELD [ON], the thrall's spring.

THROSTLE GARTH [ON], the enclosure of the thrush.

TILBERTHWAITE [OE] and [ON], Tilli's clearing by the fort.

TIRRIL [ON], the shieling built of fir wood.

TORPENHOW [OB] and [OE], all three elements of this word mean park or summit and are descriptive of the core of the settlement about the church.

TORVER [ON], the shieling with the peat.

TROUTBECK [OE] and [ON], the settlement supposedly takes its name from a nearby trout stream.

UBARROW [OE], hill with yew trees.

ULDALE [ON], valley of the wolves or Ulf's valley.

ULLSWATER [ON], Ulf's lake.

ULPHA [ON], wolf hill.

UNDERBARROW [OE], the land under the hill.

UNTHANK [OE], derived from the Old English word *unpanc*, 'ill-will' or 'displeasure'. Topographically this denotes a squatter settlement, i.e. land held without the consent of its owner.

UZZICAR [OE], meaning 'a patch of cultivated land near a farmhouse'.

WALLS, refers to the Roman bath-house near Ravenglass with much of its masonry still standing. The name is first recorded in 1578.

WASDALE [ON], valley of the lake.

WATENDLATH [ON], end of the lake.

WATERMILLOCK [OE] and [OB], as first recorded in the thirteenth century, it means the bare hill with rams.

WESTMORLAND [ME], the district of those living west of the moors, i.e. the Pennines.

WHALE [ON], the isolated rounded hill.

WHELPO [ON], hills of the whelps or cubs.

WHICHAM [OE], an important primary Anglian settlement meaning the 'village of Hwita's people'.

WHINFELL [ME], gorse fell.

WHINLATTER [ME], the gorse-covered slope.

WHITBARROW [OE], the white hill, an accurate description of this fine limestone escarpment.

WINDERMERE [ON] and [OE], Vinand's lake.

WINSTER [OB], the white stream.

WRYNOSE [OE], the twisted headland.

YANWATH [OE], the even or level wood.

Common elements in the place names of the Lake District:

bekkr [ON], stream, as in Beckfoot.

335

burh [OE], fortification, as in Brougham.
by [ON], farmstead, as in Soulby.
dael [OE], valley, as in Langdale.
dalr [ON], valley, as in Grisedale.
erg [ON], shieling, hill pasture as in Sizergh.
feld [OE], stretch of open country, as in Fairfield.
fjall [ON], hill, as in Birkfell.
fors [ON], waterfall, as in Force Beck.
gata [ON], road, as in Gatebeck.
gil [ON], ravine, as in Gaisgill.
haugr [ON], hill, as in Howtown.
holmr [ON], island, water-meadow, as in Greenholme.
kelda [ON], spring, as in Keldrigg.
leah [OE], wood, woodland clearing, as in Staveley.
mere [OE], pool, lake, as in Kentmere.
rydding [OE], clearing, as in Howe Ridding.
sáetre [ON], mountain pasture, shieling, as in Rossett.
sker [ON], rock, as in Scarfoot.
tún [OE], farmstead, as in Bampton.
veit [OE], clearing, as in Brackenthwaite.

The main sources used in the above are as follows:

Cumberland, edited by A. M. Armstrong, A. Mawer, F. M. Stenton, and B. Dickens, Vols. 20–22 English Place Name Society, 1950.
Westmorland, edited by A. H. Smith, Vols. 42–43 English Place Name Society, 1967.
Place Names of Lancashire, E. Ekwall, 1922.

Bibliography

CHAPTER I

CHALLINOR J., 'Jonathan Otley's Geology of the Lake District', *North-Western Naturalist*, 23 (1948–53), pp. 113–26.

HOLLINGSWORTH S. E., *et al.* 'The Geology of the Lake District – a review', *Proceedings Geologists Association*, 65 (1954), pp. 385–414.

MARR J. E., *The Geology of the Lake District*, 1916.

POSTLETHWAITE J., '*Mines and Mining in the Lake District*', 3rd edition, 1913.

SHACKLETON E. H., *Lakeland Geology*, 1966.

SIMPSON B., 'The petrology of the Eskdale Granite', *Proceedings Geologists Association*, 45 (1934), pp. 17–34.

CLIFTON-TAYLOR A., 'Building materials'. Section in *The Buildings of England, Cumberland and Westmorland*, 1967, pp. 46–50.

CHAPTER 2

CAINE T. N., 'The origin of sorted stripes in the Lake District', *Geografiska Annaler*, 45 (1963), pp. 172–9.

DIXON E. E. L., 'The retreat of the Lake District ice cap in the Ennerdale Area', *Summary Geological Progress* (1921), pp. 118–28.

GRESSWELL R. K., 'The glacial geomorphology of the south-eastern part of the Lake District', *Liverpool and Manchester Geological Journal*, 1 (1951), pp. 57–70.

GRESSWELL R. K., 'The post glacial raised beach in Furness and Lyth, north of Morecambe Bay', *Institute of British Geographers Transactions and Papers*, 25 (1958), pp. 79–103.

GRESSWELL R. K., 'The glaciology of the Coniston Basin', *Liverpool and Manchester Geological Journal*, 3 (1962), pp. 83–96.

HAY T. H., 'Physiographic notes from Lakeland', *Geographical Journal*, 100 (1942), pp. 165–73.

HAY T. H., 'Rosthwaite Moraines', *Geographical Journal*, 103 (1944), pp. 119–24.

HOLLINGWORTH S. E., 'Some solifluction phenomena in the northern Lake District', *Proceedings Geologists Association*, 45 (1934), pp. 167–88.

MANLEY G., 'The Late-Glacial climate of North-west England', *Liverpool and Manchester Geological Journal*, 2 (1959), pp. 188–215.

MILL H. R., 'A Bathymetric survey of the English Lakes', *Geographical Journal*, 6 (1895), pp. 46–72 and pp. 135–65.

OLDFIELD F., 'Late Quaternary changes in climate, vegetation and sea level in lowland Lonsdale', *Institute of British Geographers Transactions and Papers*, 28 (1960), pp. 99–117.

RAISTRICK A., 'The glaciation of Borrowdale', *Proceedings Yorkshire Geological Society*, 20 (1925), pp. 155–81.

SMITH B., 'The Glaciation of the Black Combe district', *Quarterly Journal Geological Society*, 68 (1912), pp. 402–48.

SMITH B., 'Glacier Lakes of Eskdale, Miterdale and Wasdale, Cumberland', *Quarterly Journal Geological Society*, 88 (1932), pp. 57–83.

TEMPLE P. H., 'Some aspects of cirque distribution in the west central Lake District', *Geografiska Annaler*, 47 (1965), pp. 185–93.

TROTTER F. M., *et. al.*, 'The Gosforth District', *Memoir Geological Survey*, 1936, pp. 89–113.

WALKER D., 'The post glacial period in the Langdale Fells, English Lake District', *New Phytologist*, 64 (1965), pp. 488–504.

WALKER D., 'The glaciation of Langdale Fells', *Geological Journal*, 5 (1966), pp. 208–15.

WALKER D., 'The late Quaternary history of the Cumberland Lowland', *Philosophical Transactions of the Royal Society*, B, 251 (1966), pp. 1–205.

CHAPTER 3

DEWDNEY J. C., TAYLOR S. A., and WARDHAUGH K. G., 'The Langdales: a lakeland parish'. *Occasional Papers, University of Durham* (1959), pp. 1–23.

EDLIN H. L. (Editor), *Hardknott Forest Park Guide*, 1949.

EDLIN H. L., *Trees, Woods and Man*, New Naturalist Series, 1956.

LEACH W., 'Two relict upland oak woods in Cumberland', *Journal of Ecology*, 13 (1925), pp. 289–300.

MILES R., *Forestry in the English Landscape*, 1967.

OLDFIELD F., 'Pollen analysis and man's role in the ecological history of the South-east Lake District', *Geografiska Annaler*, 45 (1963), pp. 23–40.

PEARSALL W. H., 'The botany of the Lake District', *Report of the British Association 1936*, pp. 134–8.

PEARSALL W. H., *Mountains and Moorlands*, New Naturalist Series, 1950.

PEARSALL W. H., and PENNINGTON W., 'Ecological history of the English Lake District', *Journal of Ecology*, 34 (1947), pp. 137–48.

PENNINGTON W., 'Pollen Analyses from six upland tarns in the Lake District', *Philosophical Transactions of the Royal Society*, B. 248 (1964), pp. 204-44.

PENNINGTON W., *The history of British Vegetation*, 1969.

PURROTT R. J., and HARRIS G., 'A study of vegetation in the Patterdale area of the Lake District', *Leicester Geographical Journal*, 5 (1964), pp. 13-16.

SOMERVELL J., 'Water power and industry in Westmorland', *Transactions of the Newcomen Society*, 18 (1938), pp. 235-49.

WALKER D., 'The post-glacial period in the Langdale Fells', *New Phytologist*, 64 (1966), pp. 488-500.

WALKER D., 'The late Quaternary history of the Cumberland Lowland', *Philosophical Transactions of the Royal Society*, B, 251 (1966), pp. 1-207.

WILSON P. N., 'The gunpowder mills of Westmorland and Furness', *Transactions of the Newcomen Society*, XXXVI (1963-4), pp. 47-66.

YAPP W. B., 'The high level woodlands of the English Lake District', *The North West Naturalist*, *1* (New Series) (1958-53), pp. 190-207 and pp. 370-83.

CHAPTER 4

BELLHOUSE R. L., 'The Aughertree Fell enclosures', *Transactions of the Cumberland and Westmorland Antiquary and Archaeological Society*, Vol. LXVII (NS), 1967. pp. 26-30.

BIRLEY E., 'Materials for the history of Roman Brougham'. *Transactions of the Cumberland and Westmorland Antiquary and Archaeological Society*, Vol. XXXII (NS), 1932, pp. 124-139.

BIRLEY E., 'Roman Papcastle', *Transactions of the Cumberland and Westmorland Antiquary and Archaeological Society*, Vol. LXIII (NS), 1963, pp. 96-125.

COLLINGWOOD R. G., 'Castle How; Peel Wyke',*Transactions of the Cumberland and Westmorland Antiquary and Archaeological Society*, Vol. XXIV (NS), 1924, pp. 78-87.

COLLINGWOOD R. G., 'The last years of Roman Cumberland', *Transactions of the Cumberland and Westmorland Antiquary and Archaeological Society*, Vol. XXIV (NS), 1924, pp. 247-55.

COLLINGWOOD R. G., 'An introduction to the prehistory of Cumberland, Westmorland and Lancashire north of the Sands', *Transactions of the Cumberland and Westmorland Antiquary and Archaeological Society*, Vol. XXXIII (NS), 1933, pp. 163-200.

COLLINGWOOD R. G., 'The hill fort on Carrock Fell', *Transactions of the Cumberland and Westmorland Antiquary and Archaeological Society*, Vol. XXXVIII (NS), 1938, pp. 32-41.

COLLINGWOOD W. G., 'An exploration of the circle on Banniside Moor, Coniston', *Transactions of the Cumberland and Westmorland Antiquary and Archaeological Society*. Vol. X (NS), 1910, pp. 342-53.

COWPER H. S., 'The ancient settlements, cemeteries, and earthworks of Furness', *Archaeologia*, Vol. 53 (1893), pp. 389–423.

FELL C., 'The Great Langdale stone-axe factory', *Transactions of the Cumberland and Westmorland Antiquary and Archaeological Society*, Vol. L(NS), 1951.

FELL C. I., 'Some cairns in High Furness', *Transactions of the Cumberland and Westmorland Antiquary and Archaeological Society*, Vol. LXIV (NS), 1964.

M'KENNY HUGHES T., 'On an ancient enclosure and interment on Heaves Fell', *Transactions of the Cumberland and Westmorland Antiquary and Archaeological Society*, Vol. XII (1912), pp. 397–402.

PENNINGTON W., 'Pollen analyses from the deposits of six upland tarns in the Lake District', *Philosophical Transactions of the Royal Society of London*, Series B, Vol. 248 (Biological Sciences), 1964–5, pp. 205–44.

PLINT R. G., 'Stone-axe factory sites in the Cumbrian Fells', *Transactions of the Cumberland and Westmorland Antiquary and Archaeological Society*, Vol. LXII (NS), 1962, pp. 2–26.

ROLLINSON W., *A History of Man in the Lake District* (1968).

SPENCE J. E., 'Ancient enclosures on Town Bank, Kinniside', *Transactions of the Cumberland and Westmorland Antiquary and Archaeological Society*, Vol.. XXXVIII (NS), 1938, pp. 63–70.

CHAPTER 5

ARMSTRONG A. M., MAWER A., STENTON F. M., DICKINS B., *The place-names of Cumberland*, Vol. XX, XXI, XXII (English Place-Name Society 1950–52).

BOUCH C. M. L., 'Ninekirks, Brougham', *Transactions of the Cumberland and Westmorland Antiquary and Archaeological Society*, Vol. L (NS), 1951, pp. 80–90.

CHADWICK N. K. (editor), *Studies in Early British History*, 1959.

CHADWICK N. K., *Celtic Britain*, London 1963.

COLLINGWOOD W. G., 'The angles in Furness and Cartmel', *Transactions of the Cumberland and Westmorland Antiquary and Archaeological Society*, Vol. XXIV, 1924, pp. 288–94.

COWEN J. D., 'Viking burials in Cumbria', *Transactions of the Cumberland and Westmorland Antiquary and Archaeological Society*, Vol. LXVII (NS), 1967, pp. 31–4.

DOUGLAS SIMPSON W., 'Brocavum, Ninekirks and Brougham: a study in continuity', *Transactions of the Cumberland and Westmorland Antiquary and Archaeological Society*, Vol. LVIII (NS), 1959, pp. 68–87.

FELL C., 'A Viking spearhead from Kentmere', *Transactions of the Cumberland and Westmorland Antiquary and Archaeological Society*, Vol. LVI (NS), 1957, pp. 67–9.

HAY T., 'Threlkeld Settlement', *Transactions of the Cumberland and Westmorland Antiquary and Archaeological Society*, Vol. XLIII (NS), 1943, pp. 20–24.

HAY T., 'Stone Carr', *Transactions of the Cumberland and Westmorland Antiquary and Archaeological Society*, Vol. XLIV (NS), 1945, pp. 126–33.

JACKSON K. H., *Language and History in Early Britain*, Edinburgh 1953.

MCINTIRE W. T., 'The Holy Wells of Cumberland', *Transactions of the Cumberland and Westmorland Antiquary and Archaeological Society*, Vol. XLIV (NS), 1945, pp. 1–15.

SMITH A. H., *The place-names of Westmorland* Vol. XLII (English Place-Name Society 1967).

WILSON P. A., 'On the use of the terms "Strathclyde" and "Cumbria"', *Transactions of the Cumberland and Westmorland Antiquary and Archaeological Society*, Vol. LXVI (NS), 1966, pp. 57–92.

CHAPTER 6

BOUCH C. M. L., *Prelates and people of the Lake Counties*, Kendal 1948.

COLLINGWOOD W. G., 'The medieval fence of Rydal and other linear earthworks,, *Transactions of the Cumberland and Westmorland Antiquary and Archaeological Society*, Vol. XXX (NS), 1930, pp. 1–11.

FAIR M. C., 'Notes on the History of Ulpha', *Transactions of the Cumberland and Westmorland Antiquary and Archaeological Society*, Vol. L (NS), 1951, pp. 99–104.

FARRER W. W., 'An early Mosser charter', *Transactions of the Cumberland and Westmorland Antiquary and Archaeological Society*, Vol. LI (NS), 1952, pp. 89–91.

GRAHAM T. H. B., 'Englewood', *Transactions of the Cumberland and Westmorland Antiquary and Archaeological Society*, Vol. XXXIII (NS), 1933, pp. 15–23.

HASKETT-SMITH W. P., 'Fountains Abbey and Cumberland', *Transactions of the Cumberland and Westmorland Antiquary and Archaeological Society*, Vol. XXI (NS), 1921, pp. 152–8.

LIDDELL W. H., 'The private forests of south-west Cumberland', *Transactions of the Cumberland and Westmorland Antiquary and Archaeological Society*, Vol. LXVI (NS), 1966, pp. 106–30.

MARSHALL F. H., 'Crosthwaite Church', *Transactions of the Cumberland and Westmorland Antiquary and Archaeological Society*, Vol. LXII (NS), 1962, p. 333.

PARKER F. H. M., 'The development of Inglewood', *Transactions of the Cumberland and Westmorland Antiquary and Archaeological Society*, Vol. XII (NS), 1912, pp. 1–28.

ROLLINSON W., 'The Historical Geography of settlement in Monastic Low Furness', *Barrow Naturalists' Field Club and Photographic Society Proceedings*, IX (NS), 1963, pp. 12–23.

WASHINGTON, G., 'The Border heritage, 1066–1292', *Transactions of the Cumberland and Westmorland Antiquary and Archaeological Society*, Vol. LXII (NS), 1962, pp. 101–12.

WESTMORLAND, Royal Commission on Historical Monuments, England, (1936).

CHAPTER 7

BOUCH C. M. L., *Prelates and people of the Lake Counties*, Kendal, 1948.

BOUCH C. M. L., and JONES G. P., *A short economic and social history of the Lake Counties, 1500–1830*, Manchester, 1961.

BRUNSKILL R. W., 'Lowther Village and Robert Adam', *Transactions of the Cumberland and Westmorland Antiquary and Archaeological Society*, Vol. LXIV (NS), 1964.

BUTLER W., 'Townfields of Broughton and Subberthwaite-in-Furness', *Transactions of the Cumberland and Westmorland Antiquary and Archaeological Society*, Vol. XXIX (NS), 1929, pp. 293–302.

DOUGLAS SIMPSON W., 'Yanwath Hall', *Transactions of the Cumberland and Westmorland Antiquary and Archaeological Society*, Vol. XLIV (NS), 1945, pp. 55–67.

ELLIOTT G. G., 'The enclosure of Aspatria', *Transactions of the Cumberland and Westmorland Antiquary and Archaeological Society*, Vol. LX (NS), 1960, pp. 97–108.

JONES G. P., 'The decline of the yeomanry in the Lake District', *Transactions of the Cumberland and Westmorland Antiquary and Archaeological Society*, Vol. LXII (NS), 1962, pp. 198–223.

JONES G. P., 'Some population problems relating to Cumberland and Westmorland in the 18th century', *Transactions of the Cumberland and Westmorland Antiquary and Archaeological Society*, Vol. LVIII (NS), 1959, pp. 124–39.

PORTER R. E., 'The townfields of Coniston', *Transactions of the Cumberland and Westmorland Antiquary and Archaeological Society*, Vol. XXIX (NS), 1929, pp. 273–7.

SIMPSON G. M., 'Townfields of Threlkeld, Mardale, Wetsleddale and Langdale', *Transactions of the Cumberland and Westmorland Antiquary and Archaeological Society*, Vol. XXIX (NS), 1929, pp. 269–72.

TATE W. E., 'Field systems and enclosure movements in Cumberland', *Transactions of the Cumberland and Westmorland Antiquary and Archaeological Society*, Vol. XLIII (NS), 1943, pp. 175–85.

CHAPTER 8

ARMITT M. L., 'Ambleside Town and Chapel', *Transactions of the Cumberland and Westmorland Antiquary and Archaeological Society*, Vol. VI (NS), 1906, pp. 1–101.

BOLTON J., *The parochial history of Cockermouth*, 1912.

CAINE C., 'The Fair at Ravenglass', *Transactions of the Cumberland and Westmorland Antiquary and Archaeological Society*, Vol. XXI (NS), 1921, pp. 237–52.

COLLINGWOOD W. G., 'Thirteenth-century Keswick', *Transactions of the Cumberland and Westmorland Antiquary and Archaeological Society*, Vol. XXI (NS), 1921, pp. 159–73.

COLLINGWOOD W. G., *The Lake Counties*, London, 1902.

CURWEN J. F., 'Kendal Castle', *Transactions of the Cumberland and Westmorland Antiquary and Archaeological Society*, Vol. VIII (NS), 1908, pp. 84–94.

FRASER C. M., 'The Cumberland and Westmorland Lay Subsidies for 1332', *Transactions of the Cumberland and Westmorland Antiquary and Archaeological Society*, Vol. LXVI (NS), 1966, pp. 131–58.

FURNESS W., *History of Penrith*, 1894.

HUDLESTON F., 'Penrith Castle', *Transactions of the Cumberland and Westmorland Antiquary and Archaeological Society*, Vol. XXX (NS), pp. 13–26.

MANNEX P. J., *History, Topography and Directory of Westmorland*, 1849.

NICHOLSON C., *The Annals of Kendal*, 1861.

PEVSNER N., *Cumberland and Westmorland*, The Buildings of England, Vol. 33, 1967.

SWIFT F. B. & BULMAN C. G., 'Ireby Church', *Transactions of the Cumberland and Westmorland Antiquary and Archaeological Society*, Vol. LXV (NS), 1965, pp. 222–39.

WHELLAN W., *The History and Topography of the Counties of Cumberland and Westmorland*, 1860.

CHAPTER 9

BOUCH C. M. L. and JONES G.P., *A short economic and social history of the Lake Counties 1500–1830*, 1961.

BRIDGE J. N., 'The slate quarrying industry in the Lake District', *Journal Durham University Geographical Society*, 6 (1963–4), pp. 14–20.

DAVIDSON W. F. and THOMSON N., 'Some notes on the minerals of Cumberland and Westmorland', *The North-Western Naturalist*, 23 (1948), pp. 136–54.

DEWEY H. and EASTWOOD T., 'Copper ores of the Midlands, Wales and the Lake District', *Special report of mineral resources*, 30 (1925), pp. 60–70.

JENKINS R., 'The Society for the Mines Royal and the German Colony in the Lake District', *Transactions Newcomen Society* (1939), pp. 225–34.

MARSHALL J. D., *Furness and the Industrial Revolution*, 1958.

MONKHOUSE F. J., 'Some features of the historical geography of the German mining enterprises in Elizabethan Lakeland', *Geography*, 28 (1943), pp. 107–13.

POSTLETHWAITE J., *Mines and mining in the Lake District*, 1913.

ROLLINSON W., *A history of man in the Lake District*, 1967.

SHACKLETON E. H., *Lakeland Geology*, 1966.

WARD J. C., *The geology of the northern part of the English Lake District*, 1876.

CHAPTER 10

ABRAHAMS H. M. (Editor), *Britain's National Parks*, 1955.

BULMER J. (Editor), *History, topography and directory of Furness and Cartmel*, 1905.

DAVIES W. J. K., *The Ravenglass and Eskdale Railway*, 1968.

GRADON W. MCGOWAN, *The Furness Railway*, 1946.

GRADON W. MCGOWAN, *Ratty, a history of the Ravenglass and Eskdale railway*, 1947.

GRADON W. MCGOWAN, *A history of the Cockermouth, Keswick and Penrith Railway*, 1948.

KAYE J. W., 'The Millbeck Woollen Industry', *Transactions of the Cumberland and Westmorland Antiquary and Archaeological Society*, LVII (1958), pp. 157–73.

MANSFIELD W., 'Traffic policy in the Lake District National Park', *Journal Town Planning Industry*, 54 (1966), pp. 263–70.

MARTINEAU H., *Complete Guide to the English Lakes*, 1855.

MURRAY J. (Editor), *Handbook for Westmorland, Cumberland and the Lakes*, 2nd edition, 1869.

NOOK, O. S., *Branch Lines*, 1957.

ROLLINSON W., *A history of man in the Lake District*, 1967.

HANSON-SMITH C. J., 'The National Trust and nature conservation', *Field Naturalist*, 12 (1968), pp. 1–4.

THOMPSON B. L., *The Lake District and the National Trust*, 1946.

WATTS D. G., 'Water power and the industrial revolution', *Transactions of the Cumberland and Westmorland Antiquary and Archaeological Society*, LXVII (1967), pp. 199–205.

Whither the Lake District, Rotary Club of Ambleside, 1967.

CHAPTER II

BADDELEY M. J. B., *The English Lake District*, Thorough Guide Series, London, 1886.

CLARK C., *Home at Grasmere*, London, 1960.

HEATON COOPER W., *The Lakes*, 1966.

KNIGHT W., *Through the Wordsworth Country*, 1891.

MACKAY C., *The Scenery and Poetry of the English Lakes*, 1846, London.

MOIR E., *The Discovery of Britain*, 1964.

Murray's Handbook for Westmorland, Cumberland and the Lakes, 1867.

RAWNSLEY H. D., *Literary Associations of the English Lakes* (Vols. I & II), Glasgow, 1894.

The Journal of Beatrix Potter, 1881–97, London, 1966.

WEST T., *A guide to the Lakes in Cumberland, Westmorland and Lancashire*, 1778.

WORDSWORTH W., *Guide to the Lakes* (with introduction by E. de Selincourt), 1906.

Index

z

KEY TO ENDPAPER ILLUSTRATION

1	Scafell	20	Lobstone Band
2	Scafell Pike	21	Stonethwaite
3	Pillar	22	Derwent Water
4	Looking Stead	23	Langstrath
5	Kirk Fell	24	Pavey Ark
6	Great Gable	25	Stickle Tarn
7	Red Pike	26	Crinkle Crags
8	High Stile	27	Bowfell
9	Green Gable	28	Rossett Gill
10	Allen Crag	29	The Band
11	Brandreth	30	Mickleden
12	Crummock Water	31	Wetherlam
13	Stake Pass	32	Wrynose Pass
14	Whiteless Pike	33	High Tilberthwaite
15	Grasmoor	34	Blea Tarn
16	Robinson	35	Side Pike
17	Crag Hill	36	Little Langdale Tarn
18	Pike of Stickle	37	Path to Tarn Hows
19	Dale Head